Ready-to-Use

P.E. ACTIVITIES

for Grades K-2

Joanne M. Landy · Maxwell J. Landy

PARKER PUBLISHING COMPANY
West Nyack, New York 10995

PARKER PUBLISHING COMPANY
Professional Publishing
A Division of Simon & Schuster
West Nyack, New York 10995

10 9 8 7 6 5 4 3

*In memory of my husband, Max, who devoted his
life to his family and to the promotion of a
quality lifestyle for our youth.*

Library of Congress Cataloging-in-Publication Data

Landy, Maxwell J.
    Ready-to-use P.E. activities / Maxwell J. Landy, Joanne Landy.
        p.   cm.
    Contents: bk. 1. For grades K–2 — bk. 2. For grades 3–4 — bk.
3. For Grades 5–6 — bk. 4. For grades 7–9.
    ISBN 0-13-673054-X (v. 1)
    1. Physical education for children—Curricula.   2. Physical
education for children—Planning.   I. Landy, Joanne.   II. Title.
III. Title: Ready-to-use PE activities.
GV443.L334   1992
372.86—dc20   92-21049
                                                                           CIP

ISBN 0-13-673054-x

Parker Publishing Company
Business Information Publishing Division
West Nyack, NY 10995

Simon & Schuster. A Paramount Communications Company

Printed in the United States of America

69715

About the Authors

Maxwell J. Landy, PED, New South Wales, B.S. and M.Ed., University of Oregon, Associate Professor Emeritus, University of Regina, Canada, was actively involved in the field of physical education for 39 years. For 18 of those years, Max served as a K–12 P.E. specialist and consultant in Canadian and Australian schools. For 20 years, he taught at the university level, where he developed innovative programs in physical education and health, specializing in the P.E. internship program. Max passed away on May 7, 1991.

Joanne M. Landy, B.Ed., University of Regina, has 15 years of experience as an elementary and high school P.E. specialist in the Saskatchewan school system. She also became involved as a demonstration P.E. teacher in liaison with the University of Regina, Faculty of Education pre-internship and internship programs, and presented at several workshops for elementary and secondary teachers. Joanne and her two children now reside in Perth, Western Australia.

Max and Joanne co-presented at several major P.E./Health conferences in Canada, the United States, and Australia. In 1988 they were involved in the USA National Fitness Foundation–Youth Fitness Camp in Los Angeles, spearheaded by John Cates of UCLA. Between them they combined over 50 years of Physical Education teaching knowledge and experience to produce the *Complete Physical Education Activities Program.*

Forewords

IT IS WITH EXTREME PLEASURE that I submit this foreword on behalf of Max and Joanne's wonderful contribution to improve the health and fitness of our youth.

I first met Joanne and Max in 1986 when they were selected as faculty members of a model youth fitness camp sponsored by George Allen's National Fitness Foundation.

During the camp, I had the opportunity to observe first hand the wonderful physical education materials that Joanne and Max had created. Classroom teachers, with no formal physical education training, were able to immediately involve their students in "fun" activities that emphasized all of the components of fitness. User-friendly lesson plans provided the teachers with games and activities for the progressive development of motor skills. Students, teachers, administrators, and parents soon became advocates of quality daily physical education.

I am delighted that the Landys have published their wonderful *Complete Physical Education Activities Program.*

In the United States, the level of youth fitness has continued to decline over the past several years. Physical education specialists and classroom teachers have been searching for physical education materials that will address the individual health and fitness needs of children while developing self-confidence and self-esteem. Joanne and Max have provided the materials that can put "quality" into daily physical education.

John Cates, Supervisor
Department of Physical Education
University of California, San Diego
Assistant to Arnold Schwarzenegger
Chairman, President's Council
Physical Fitness and Sports

I AM PROUD TO SAY that Max Landy was, before his unfortunate death in 1991, one of my closest personal and professional friends. I had the pleasure of working with Max at the University of Regina from 1978–1980. He was my mentor, and out of this a lasting friendship developed with both him and his wife Joanne. I came to know and appreciate both Max and Joanne as two very extraordinary physical educators. I was impressed by their dedication to the profession and, in particular, to the development of a physical education program which they believed worth working and sacrificing for. Their goal was to develop a "user friendly, activity oriented" curriculum for teachers, designed to help promote a physically active lifestyle among children and youth. Their commitment to this work has been long-term in nature, spanning more than twelve years. After Max's death, Joanne carried on to see their project come to fruition. Now it is available for all of us in their new series of books, the *Complete Physical Education Activities Program.*

To me, this series is first of all a jumping off place for the inexperienced teacher of physical education, whether a classroom teacher or a physical education specialist, who is desirous of specific ideas as to what to teach and how to go about teaching it. In this regard, an especially unique and attractive characteristic of these teaching units/books are the many delightful cartoon-like illustrations designed to clarify the correct action, organization, and/or arrangement of students. In addition, teaching instructions are written in step-by-step form and can be read directly to students. My more than twenty years of in- and pre-service work with teachers indicates that this is exactly the kind of direction they will most benefit from. Their initial teaching experiences will prove enjoyable for both themselves and their students, thus encouraging further involvement. Their students can only benefit!

Although the *Complete Physical Education Activities Program* is of most obvious help to the teacher who has not had an in-depth background in physical education, it is a time-saver even for the experienced physical education teacher. It contains a myriad of practical, ready-to-use, and easy-to-follow activity ideas. These are organized sequentially to ensure proper progressions and allow for individualized teaching. The curriculum is divided into warm-up, fitness, core, and closing activity sections. This organization permits a flexibility and facility in lesson planning which would not be possible if detailed lesson plans were provided. The teacher is able to compile complete, well-balanced lesson plans merely by selecting activities from the various sections. Thus, teachers are encouraged to be creative in their implementation efforts.

Max and Joanne have skillfully blended together traditional activity ideas with more current ones in an effort to preserve the very best that both have to offer. However, they offer more than an academic approach. They provide many new and meaningful activity ideas, including many new, fun-packed fitness activities, which have evolved from their more than fifty years of teaching physical education in Australia and Canada. Notably, their curriculum has been field-tested in Regina schools where it received high ratings from the many teachers and student-teachers who used it. Finally, it is divided into four books or teaching units, each tailored to the specific developmental needs of the students at that level. Thus, teachers need only purchase the book(s) appropriate for their grade level.

Through Max and Joanne's professional dedication and hard work, we have moved one step closer to providing quality daily physical education experiences in our schools. They have provided teaching units which will no doubt be used by a great many classroom teachers and physical education specialists who believe that physical activity is important for our children and youth. If the ultimate utility of information lies in its ability to enhance the quality of human experience, then their work represents a substantial contribution to the literature. I am honored that Joanne has asked me to write this foreword and wish her every success in this and all her future endeavors.

Dennis Caine, Ph.D.
Western Washington University

About *Ready-to-Use P.E. Activities for Grades K–2*

This practical resource is one of four books presenting a unique curriculum for elementary and middle/junior high school educators entitled *Complete Physical Education Activities Program* (CPEP). The curriculum is designed to help classroom teachers and P.E. specialists successfully prepare and teach interesting, fun-packed physical education lessons in a sequential co-educational program. It includes the following specialized teaching units, each tailored to the specific developmental needs at the particular level:

Book 1 *Ready-to-Use P.E. Activities for Grades K–2*
Book 2 *Ready-to-Use P.E. Activities for Grades 3–4*
Book 3 *Ready-to-Use P.E. Activities for Grades 5–6*
Book 4 *Ready-to-Use P.E. Activities for Grades 7–9*

The CPEP curriculum provides a comprehensive continuity program from kindergarten through grade 9, with a strong emphasis on the *fitness* component. It is based on sound education principles, research in motor learning, exercise physiology, and teaching methodology and meets the requirements as a delivery system and resource for current P.E. curricula in the United States and Canada. Its primary objectives are:

- to foster in children a love of physical activity and play
- to instill a need for physical fitness in each child
- to develop coordination, grace, and control
- to provide opportunities for increased responsibility in planning, organizing, and leadership
- to give children as wide a skill, games, and dance experience as possible
- to present opportunities for children to belong to a group in which each child is accepted
- to provide experiences which will develop initiative, self-reliance, self-worth, loyalty, honesty, kindness to others, and a love of learning
- to develop a sense of fair play and cooperation in children and the ability to work in groups, leading to increased cultural understanding
- to provide opportunities for integration of P.E. with other subject areas: language arts, math, social studies, science, health, music, and art

For your convenience, Book 1 in the curriculum is subdivided into eight sections, including: Introductory Activities, Fitness Activities, Movement Awareness, Rhythms and Dance, Play Gymnastics, Games Skills, Special Games, and Closing Activities. This organization allows you to compile complete, well-balanced lesson plans in minutes merely by selecting activities from the various sections, thus saving valuable lesson preparation time.

Each book in the curriculum also provides a special section entitled "How to Prepare Lessons Using These P.E. Activities," which explains (a) how to prepare a Yearly/Weekly P.E. Plan, (b) how to prepare a Daily P.E. Plan, and (c) how to record the activities taught. By following the lesson format described in this section, you can use and reuse the program activities in an endless number of combinations with other activities. Moreover, many of the activities contain variations and suggested modifications, thus providing valuable repetition and reinforcement and sufficient material for an entire year of daily physical education.

Other features of the "Complete Physical Education Activities Program" curriculum include the following:

Time Allocation:

Flexibility is a key feature of the program, as the format allows you to select and adapt activities that may be taught within the allotted time.

Indoor-Outdoor:

Activities have been provided for both indoor and outdoor learning stations.

Coeducational:

All of the activities in each level book are suitable for both boys and girls.

Illustrations:

Cartoon-like, stick figures supplement the activity directions throughout. All measurements, diagrams, and ground markings are written in standard and metric measurement to fit the needs of educators in the United States and Canada.

Basic Equipment:

Most of the program activities can be taught using standard equipment already available in elementary/middle schools. Some enrichment activities may require additional items such as juggling scarves, parachutes, peacock feathers, and scooters.

By presenting K–9 students with a variety of challenging, stimulating activities during each lesson throughout the year, this P.E. program will help you create enjoyable, success-oriented experiences that reach every child. Moreover, the program provides for the mainstreaming of atypical children within the context of the regular physical education lesson. Special attention has been given to (a) social interaction and the improvement of self-concepts, cooperation, and sportsmanship; (b) fitness and skill development; and (c) acquisition of basic fundamentals through conceptual learning.

Interaction of the four F's—FUN, FITNESS, and FRIENDSHIP through the FUNDAMENTALS of physical education—stimulates children to want to participate in physical activities not only during their school years, but for the rest of their lives.

Joanne Landy
Maxwell J. Landy

Contents

Section 2 FITNESS ACTIVITIES 29

Section 3 MOVEMENT AWARENESS 45

Section 6 GAMES SKILLS **149**

Section 7 SPECIAL GAMES 249

Section 8 CLOSING ACTIVITIES 281

How to Prepare Lessons Using These P.E. Activities

The following discussion gives you suggestions for using this resource to pre-pare stimulating, well-balanced physical education activities for your students. Specifically, it provides a description of the different types of activities presented in Sections 1 through 8, a sample activity illustrating the easy-to-follow organization used for all activities in the program, and directions for creating your own yearly/weekly P.E. teaching plan. Included are a filled-in sample Yearly/Weekly Plan Chart along with a reproducible blank chart, plus a Class Record Sheet to help you evaluate the progress made by each class during the year.

DESCRIPTION OF THE ACTIVITIES

Sections 1 through 8 present a wide range of activities for creating a stimulating variety of daily P.E. lessons.

▪ Warm-Up Activities (Sections 1 and 2)

Introductory Activities

The first activity of the lesson is intended to produce a state of physical and mental readiness. This Introductory Activity produces a *general warm-up*, increasing blood flow to the major muscle groups. Mentally, it helps to get children excited about participating in the activities that follow.

Fitness Activities

The Fitness Activity functions as a *specific warm-up* and, when used in combination with an introductory activity, develops overall fitness with emphasis on cardiovascular endurance and muscular strength and endurance.

▪ Core Activities (Sections 3–6)

Movement Awareness

The activities in this section help to develop the movement principles of space awareness, body awareness, effort awareness, and relationships. Themes are used to set tasks that ask "what, where, how can, and who can?" The children respond to the task or problem by exploring and experimenting at the floor level, on low apparatus, or on large apparatus, with or without equipment

Rhythms and Dance

The Rhythms and Dance activity is intended to develop creative expression, rhythmic movement, musical appreciation, and active listening skills. Muscular growth and coordination are improved; space awareness, body awareness, effort awareness, and social skills are improved in an atmosphere of fun. Through the rhythm and dance section, specific music suggestions are provided; otherwise, lively popular music is suggested.

Play Gymnastics

The Play Gymnastics activities progressively develop muscular strength and endurance, flexibility, balance, and overall coordination. The children also develop self-confidence, improved posture, and safety awareness.

Game Skills

Game Skills activities develop the abilities children need to participate in most traditional games, such as soccer, volleyball, basketball, softball, and football as well as more innovative games, such as parachute play, scooter play, and juggling. The Games Skills activities are arranged in units that you could plan to teach over a two- or three-week period.

▪ Special Games (Section 7)

Relays, low-organized games, and tabloid sports activities develop leadership, cooperation, self-esteem, creativity, and a sense of fair play. The emphasis throughout the activities in this section is on fun and teamwork, not winning or losing.

▪ Closing Activities (Section 8)

After a vigorous physical workout, the Closing Activity serves as a quiet, cool-down activity and leaves children ready to continue with classroom work.

Each activity in the program is presented in a functional, easy-to-follow format, as illustrated by the following sample:

Highlights the main objectives and concepts involved.

Provides a detailed list of all equipment needed for this segment, with some flexibility of choice.

IA–32 UNCLE SAM

FOCUS: Running and dodging

EQUIPMENT: Four cone markers; one pinnie; set of colored flags

■ Organization:

Provides teaching points, safety guidelines, and suggestions on how to organize and teach the activities.

• Mark out the play area. Clearly mark the two endlines. Choose one player to be "Uncle Sam," who stands in the center of the play area wearing the pinnie. All other players tuck a flag in their waistband so that three-fourths of it is showing and stand behind one of the endlines.

■ Description of the Activity:

1. Endline players start the game by chanting:
   "Uncle Sam, Uncle Sam,
   May we cross your ocean dam?"

2. Uncle Sam, you answer, "Yes, if you are wearing red." Players wearing red get a free pass to the other end.

3. Then on the "Go" signal from Uncle Sam, the rest of the players try to run to the opposite endline without getting your flag pulled. Tagged players become Uncle Sam's helpers.

Written as step-by-step instructions that can be read directly to the children.

4. Begin again. This time, Uncle Sam, call out another color. Keep going until all players are caught but one. This player becomes the new Uncle Sam for the next game.

■ Variation:

Vary the criteria for a free pass: girls with short hair, wearing glasses, all the boys, all the girls. . . .

Provides additional ideas to modify or extend the activities.

Preparing the Yearly/Weekly Plan

It is important that the physical education program be planned ahead of time, whether for a two-week unit, a season, or even a year. Yearly planning allows you to meet long-range objectives, to use facilities and equipment to their utmost, and to consider seasonal activities and special days.

■ Developing the Yearly/Weekly Unit Plan

To develop the yearly/weekly plan, select the activities from the suggestions listed on the Scope and Sequence Chart and the Table of Contents of each section, and then prepare a Weekly Unit Plan Chart. Refer to the Sample Yearly/Weekly Plan Chart for Core Activities (page xviii). The chart shows the school year divided into a sequence of 40 weekly units and, when completed, should give you an outline of the order in which the material will be taught. A blank sample Weekly/Yearly Plan Chart is provided for you on pages xx and xxi.

Although decisions made on the Yearly/Weekly Unit Plan Charts will provide reliable, concrete guidelines, your decisions should never be regarded as irreversible and certainly may be changed as circumstances require.

■ Developing the Daily Lesson Plan

There are five basic steps in preparing a lesson using the "Complete Physical Education Activities Program" system:

STEP 1: Decide how much time is allocated to your lesson. Each part of the lesson can vary in length according to the objectives and focus of the lesson.

STEP 2: Select an activity from the Introductory Activities section, then one or more activities from the Fitness section.

STEP 3: Decide on the Core Unit to be taught by referring to the appropriate week on the Weekly Plan Chart. Then select the appropriate activities from the core sections of Movement/Rhythms and Dance, Gymnastics, or Game Skills.

STEP 4: Select a related game from the Game Skills section or the Special Games section.

STEP 5: Select a cool-down activity from the Closing Activities to finish the lesson.

NOTE: It is not necessary that all the material in an activity be taught in one lesson. You may decide to use two or three lessons to cover all of the tasks on that particular activity.

■ Gathering the Equipment

To make a list of all of the equipment needed for each lesson, refer to the Equipment List on the top right-hand corner of each activity. Check that all of the equipment listed is indeed available for use. Prior to the lesson, designate children to bring out and arrange the equipment in the activity area.

■ Recording the Activities Taught

When all of the tasks or components in an activity have been taught, you can circle the number of the activity on a photocopy of the Class Record Sheet provided on page xxii. By referring to the Record Sheet, you will quickly be able to evaluate the class's progress throughout the year.

Grade 1   YEARLY/WEEKLY PLAN CHART

WEEK 1 Date	WEEK 6 Date	WEEK 11 Date	WEEK 16 Date	WEEK 21 Date
IA: Signals — Starting Position MA: Space Aware GS: Hoop Play C.A.	IA: Tag Type Games MA: Body Aware GS: Decking Play SG: Relays	IA: Fire hoses-group Fit: Coop Stunt Breaks MA: Direction Pathways GS: Ball Play Familiarization C.A.	IA Walk-ercise Fit: Aerobic Routines MA: Creative Movements #1 GS: Stick Play-Related Games C.A.	Fit: Workout #4 MA: Leaping, Jumping GS: Rope Play - Long Rope SG: Org. Game Relays

WEEK 2 Date	WEEK 7 Date	WEEK 12 Date	WEEK 17 Date	WEEK 22 Date
IA: Signals — Signals Game Starting Positions MA: Space Aware GS: Hoop Play C.A.	IA: Tag Type Games Fit: Workout #1 Breaks MA: Body Aware GS: Lummi Stick Play C.A.	IA: Back to Back etc Fit: 10 min work #2 MA: Non-locomotive GS: Ball Play-Rolling Fielding, Tossing, & Catching. C.A.	IA: Hoop-ercise Fit: 10 min Workout #3 MA: Creative Movements #2 GS: Stick Play C.A.	Fit: Workout #4 MA: Skipping, Sliding GS: Rope Play - Short Rope Partners SG Relays

WEEK 3 Date	WEEK 8 Date	WEEK 13 Date	WEEK 18 Date	WEEK 23 Date
IA: Signals — Alertness Games Fit: Breaks GS: Beanbag Play C.A.	IA: Hallowe'en Signals and Games Fit: 10 min Workout #1 GS: Wand/Scarf play C.A.	IA: Tag Type Games Fit: Aerobic Routines MA: Levels, Ranges GS: Ball Play-Underhand, Throwing, Bouncing, Catch-CA	IA: Tag Type Games Fit: Exercise Game Equipment Scram. MS: Traveling on Apparatus GS: Scooter Play CA	IA: Tag Games MA: Movement sequencing Gym: Animal Walks Novelty Stunts SG: Low Org. Game

WEEK 4 Date	WEEK 9 Date	WEEK 14 Date	WEEK 19 Date	WEEK 24 Date
IA: Alertness Games Fit: Partner Breaks GS: Beanbag Play MA: Locomotion SG: Relays	IA: Traffic Games Fit: 10 min. w.o. #1 MA: Lifting & Carrying GS: Station Play - manipulative equip. C.A.	IA: Tag Type Games Fit: Aerobic Routines GS: Ball Play-overhand Throwing & Related Games C.A.	IA: Hoop-ercise Fit: 10-min. workout #3 MA: Walking, Running GS: Scooter Games Parachute Play C.A.	Fit: Equipment Scramble MA: Locomotion station work Gym: Walk thru Zoo SG: Relay Games

WEEK 5 Date	WEEK 10 Date	WEEK 15 Date	WEEK 20 Date	WEEK 25 Date
IA: Alertness Games Fit: 10 min. workout GS: Decking Play MA: Locomotion GS: Decking Games	IA: Tag Type Games Fit: Partner Breaks GS: Balloon Play C.A.	IA: Christmas signals & Related Games GS: Ball Skills, Station Work, Ball Games C.A.	IA: Aerobic Circle Fit: Fitness Testing GS: Rope Play - Patterns & Stunts C.A.	Fit: Aerobic Sport MA: Body Parts Gym: Supporting & Balancing SG: Relay Games

YEARLY/WEEKLY PLAN CHART

WEEK 26 Date	WEEK 31 Date	WEEK 36 Date	WEEK Date	WEEK Date
IA: Easter Signals Fit: 10-min. Workout #3 Gym: Walking Balance, Balancing & Shapes SG: Relays	MA: Movement Seq. Locomotion, Station RD: Singing Movement Songs GS: Low Org. Games	RD: "Skip to My Lou" "Muffin Man" GS: Ball Skills – Striking and Related Games C.A.		
WEEK 27 Date	WEEK 32 Date	WEEK 37 Date	WEEK Date	WEEK Date
MA: Locomotion-Station Fit: 10 min. workout #3 Gym: Balancing Challenges Support Stunts SG: Relays	IA: Hill Dill, Wasps RD: Even Rhythms Running, Jumping, Hopping SG: Low Org. Games	Fit: Fitness Testing #3 – Fitkid Circuit – GS: Paddle Play Balloons SG: Low Org. Game		
WEEK 28 Date	WEEK 33 Date	WEEK 38 Date	WEEK Date	WEEK Date
IA: Follow Me Gym: Balancing Partner Supports On Apparatus SG: Relays	Fit: Workout #3 RD: Singing Movement Songs SG: Relays Low Org. Games C.A.	SG: Play Days, Station Work		
WEEK 29 Date	WEEK 34 Date	WEEK 39 Date	WEEK Date	WEEK Date
IA: Running Signals GS: Scooter Play Parachute Play SG: Low Org. Games C.A.	MA: Body Parts RD: Singing Movement Songs GS: Ball Skills – Kicking SG: Low Org Games	SG: Kicking Games, Batting Games		
WEEK 30 Date	WEEK 35 Date	WEEK 40 Date	WEEK Date	WEEK Date
Fit: Aerobic Circle R & D: Introduction Even Rhythms SG: Low Organized Games C.A.	IA: Running Activities Fit: Aerobic Sports Routine GS: Ball Skills – Kicking and Re- lated Kicking Games	SG: "Favorite Games Week"		

YEARLY/WEEKLY PLAN CHART

SEPTEMBER		OCTOBER		NOVEMBER		DECEMBER		JANUARY	
WEEK 1	Date	WEEK 1	Date	WEEK 1	Date	WEEK 1	Date	WEEK 1	Date
WEEK 2	Date	WEEK 2	Date	WEEK 2	Date	WEEK 2	Date	WEEK 2	Date
WEEK 3	Date	WEEK 3	Date	WEEK 3	Date	WEEK 3	Date	WEEK 3	Date
WEEK 4	Date	WEEK 4	Date	WEEK 4	Date	WEEK 4	Date	WEEK 4	Date
WEEK 5	Date	WEEK 5	Date	WEEK 5	Date	WEEK 5	Date	WEEK 5	Date

YEARLY/WEEKLY PLAN CHART

FEBRUARY		MARCH		APRIL		MAY		JUNE	
WEEK 1	Date	WEEK 1	Date	WEEK 1	Date	WEEK 1	Date	WEEK 1	Date
WEEK 2	Date	WEEK 2	Date	WEEK 2	Date	WEEK 2	Date	WEEK 2	Date
WEEK 3	Date	WEEK 3	Date	WEEK 3	Date	WEEK 3	Date	WEEK 3	Date
WEEK 4	Date	WEEK 4	Date	WEEK 4	Date	WEEK 4	Date	WEEK 4	Date
WEEK 5	Date	WEEK 5	Date	WEEK 5	Date	WEEK 5	Date	WEEK 5	Date

Book 1: Ready-to-Use P.E. Activities for Grades K–2
Class Record Sheet

Class: _____

Year: _____

Level: _____

Teacher: _____

INTRODUCTORY ACTIVITIES

1	2	3	4	5	6
7	8	9	10	11	12
13	14	15	16	17	18
19	20	21	22	23	24
25	26	27	28	29	30
31	32	33	34	35	36
37	38	39	40	41	42
43	44	45	46		

FITNESS ACTIVITIES

1	2	3	4	5	6
7	8	9	10	11	12
13	14	15	16	17	

RHYTHMS & DANCE

1	2	3	4	5	6
7	8	9	10	11	12
13	14	15	16	17	18
19	20	21	22	23	24
25	26	27	28	29	30
31	32	33	34	35	

SPECIAL GAMES

1	2	3	4	5	6
7	8	9	10	11	12
13	14	15	16	17	18
19	20	21	22	23	24
25	26	27	28	29	30
31	32	33	34	35	36
37	38	39	40	41	42
43	44	45	46		

MOVEMENT AWARENESS

1	2	3	4	5	6
7	8	9	10	11	12
13	14	15	16	17	18
19	20	21	22	23	24
25	26	27	28	29	30
31	32	33	34	35	

PLAY GYMNASTICS

1	2	3	4	5	6
7	8	9	10	11	12
13	14	15	16	17	18
19	20	21	22	23	24
25	26	27	28	29	30
31	32	33	34	35	36
37	38	39	40	41	42
43	44	45	46	47	48
49					

CLOSING ACTIVITIES

1	2	3	4	5	6
7	8	9	10	11	12
13	14	15	16	17	18
19	20	21	22	23	24
25	26	27	28	29	30

GAME SKILLS

1	2	3	4	5	6	7	8	9	10	11	12	13	14
15	16	17	18	19	20	21	22	23	24	25	26	27	28
29	30	31	32	33	34	35	36	37	38	39	40	41	42
43	44	45	46	47	48	49	50	51	52	53	54	55	56
57	58	59	60	61	62	63	64	65	66	67	68	69	70
71	72	73	74	75	76	77	78	79	80	81	82	83	84
85	86	87	88	89	90	91	92	93	94	95	96	97	98
99	100	101	102	103	104	105	106	107	108				

Section 1

Introductory Activities

The first activity of the P.E. lesson should help produce a state of physical and mental readiness in children. It provides a general warm-up, increasing blood flow to the major muscle groups, and helps spark excitement about participating in the subsequent activities.

This section offers 46 possible Introductory Activities, including:

IA-1 ORGANIZATION SIGNALS

FOCUS: Class management; formations

EQUIPMENT: None

ORGANIZATION:

- Organization Signals mobilize the class, arranging children in various formations quickly and without confusion. Used constantly and spontaneously, these Signals will improve class control. Call out each Organization Signal and use the corresponding hand signal simultaneously. As the children become familiar with the signal's action, simply use the hand signal.

DESCRIPTION OF ACTIVITY:

1. *Listening Circle:* Run quickly to sit cross-legged in a circle near and facing me. (*Hand Signal:* Point with your index finger to the floor near you while circling the other index finger overhead.)

2. *Listening Line:* Run quickly to stand side by side in a line near me. Space yourselves at arm's length and face me. (*Hand Signal:* Point with your index finger to a line near you, and then extend your arms sideways at shoulder height.)

3. *Quiet Signal:* Immediately stop what you are doing and raise one hand. Give me your full attention. (*Hand Signal:* Hold one hand overhead. Wait until all are quiet and paying attention.)

4. *Homes:* Run to a free space in the play area and sit cross-legged there, facing me. Check your spot so that you cannot touch anyone or anything. Remember your home. (*Hand Signal:* Make a roof overhead with hands. Mats or hoops could also be used as "Homes.")

5. *Endline:* Run quickly to one end of the play area and stand in a line, equally spaced apart, facing me. (*Hand Signal:* Point with index finger to one end of play area and extend arms sideways at shoulder level.)

IA-2 FORMATION SIGNALS

FOCUS: Class management

EQUIPMENT: Chart paper;
marking pen;
and masking tape

ORGANIZATION:

- Formation Signals organize players into partners, small groups, or lines. Call out each action and use accompanying hand signal simultaneously. Establish four equal teams at the beginning of the year. List the names of the players of each team on chart paper, and tape the chart to the wall. Select a leader and co-leader for each team. Change leaders and co-leaders often throughout the year so that each team member has a turn at both positions.

DESCRIPTION OF ACTIVITY:

1. *Groups:* Quickly sit in a group with the number of players I call; for example, "Groups of 2!" or "Groups of 5!" (*Hand Signal:* Hold up the same number of fingers as players in each group.)

2. *Lines:* Leaders, run with your team to the side of the play area and sit cross-legged there, facing me. Other team members, quickly find your leader and sit cross-legged in a line behind him or her. Space yourselves evenly apart. Leader, sit at the front of the line and co-leader, sit at the back. (*Hand Signal:* Extend arms in front, parallel to each other and to the floor.)

VARIATION:

Waves: Call Lines signal and use its hand action; then move to one side of the lines and have players turn to face you.

IA-3 MOVEMENT SIGNALS

FOCUS: Class management; circle formation

EQUIPMENT: Lively music; tape or record player

ORGANIZATION:

- Movement Signals quickly get players moving. Call out combinations of formations and locomotor movements such as "Activity Circle, slide clockwise!" or "Scrambled Eggs, run!" Use hand signals as well. Change locomotor movements frequently throughout the activity. Players could jog, skip, hop, slide-step, leap, gallop, or run backwards. Motivate players with lively music.

DESCRIPTION OF ACTIVITY:

1. *Scrambled Eggs:* Run helter-skelter in any direction. Remember . . . don't touch anyone as you move! (*Hand Signal:* Roll hand over hand.)

2. *Activity Circle:* Jog clockwise (or CCW) around play area in single file. Stay in your original order; don't pass anyone. (*Hand Signal:* Circle one arm overhead in a clockwise [or CCW] direction.)

VARIATIONS:

a. Use "Scrambled Eggs" signal with different directions, pathways, and levels (call "Scrambled Eggs, run sideways!" or zig-zag, high, and low), or, with different walks (call "Scrambled Eggs, crab-walk!" or lame-dog walk and bear-walk); enhance spatial awareness by calling "Scrambled Eggs, jog in a small space," ". . . jog in a smaller space," ". . . jog in an even smaller space."

b. *Switching Sides (Movement Signals Game):* Mark out play area with cone markers. Divide the class into two equal teams. Start with each team standing behind opposite endlines of play area, facing each other. Ensure that players are well spaced along the lines to avoid collisions. Adjust the running distance and the number of runs to class level. Use a variety of locomotor skills such as walking quickly, running with arms in the air, hopping, skipping, galloping, moving on all fours, etc. On signal "Switch Sides," both teams must change sides to sit cross-legged just behind the opposite line; the first team to do so earns one point. Play each game to five points.

IA-4 SIGNALS GAME

FOCUS: Alertness; listening skills   **EQUIPMENT:** None

ORGANIZATION:

- The game of Signals consists of a locomotor movement and a simultaneous verbal and hand signal. Encourage players to respond quickly by issuing a challenge such as "You owe me three jumping jacks (push-ups, or any task) if you are last!"
- Regard the "You owe me three!" challenge as good sportsmanship, not as punishment. Caution children to watch where they are going at all times.

DESCRIPTION OF ACTIVITY:

1. Run quickly. Run slowly. Skip high. Crawl low. Now clear the deck! Get off the floor as quickly as possible to stand on a bench, a chair, the climbing frame, and so on. (*Hand Signal:* Open arms overhead.)

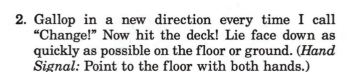

2. Gallop in a new direction every time I call "Change!" Now hit the deck! Lie face down as quickly as possible on the floor or ground. (*Hand Signal:* Point to the floor with both hands.)

3. Walk like a robot. Waddle like a duck. Crabwalk. Now corners! Run to any corner of the play area, or where any two lines cross, and sit cross-legged there. (*Hand Signal:* Cross arms overhead.)

4. Walk backwards in pairs, holding hands. Hop in pairs. Now iceberg! Stop immediately and freeze like a statue. (*Hand Signal:* Make a fist overhead.)

VARIATIONS:

a. When playing Signals indoors, use the markings on the play area floor as part of the game. For example, call "Red lines!" and stand on a red line when you want players to sit cross-legged there.

b. Challenge players to keep alert by signalling with hands only.

c. Substitute other previously taught signals such as "Scrambled Eggs!" or "Activity Circle!"

IA-5 STARTING POSITIONS

FOCUS: Class management; personal space awareness

EQUIPMENT: None

ORGANIZATION:

- Starting Positions are used to quickly organize and position the class for any activity. Teach the following positions; then have the children practice the positions by calling them out in random order and in quick succession. Stress correct body posture.

DESCRIPTION OF ACTIVITY:

1. *Long Sit:* Sit with legs outstretched and together. Lean back on hands for support.

2. *Hook Sit:* Sit with legs together, knees bent, and feet flat on the floor. Lean back on hands for support.

3. *Wide-Sit:* Sit with legs outstretched and comfortably apart. Lean back on hands for support.

4. *Cross-legged Sit:* Sit with legs crossed and arms resting on knees.

5. *All Fours:* Support your weight on hands and knees.

6. *Front Support:* Support weight on hands and toes, with face down. Hold body straight.

7. *Front-Lying:* Lie face down with legs together and arms at sides, chest level.

8. *Back-Lying:* Lie face up with legs together and arms at sides.

9. *Hook-Lying:* Lie on back with knees bent so that feet are flat on floor. Arms are relaxed at sides.

10. *Back Support:* Sit with legs outstretched and together. Lean back on hands for support, bend elbows slightly, and then raise trunk to take weight on hands and heels. Hold body straight.

11. *Squat:* Stand, and bend knees to raise heels from the floor. Place hands between knees and rest them on floor.

12. *Stand Tall:* Stand with feet comfortably apart and toes turned out slightly. Arms are at sides.

VARIATION:

As part of the Signals Game, combine Starting Position signals with Organizational signals; for example, "Scrambled Eggs, skip." "Iceberg, long sit!"

IA-6 SHAKE HANDS

FOCUS: Friendship; getting acquainted

EQUIPMENT: One hoop per player

ORGANIZATION:

• The purpose of this game is to make the children feel at ease with each other and with you and to teach them how to introduce themselves. Have children get a hoop each and find their own "home" (space on their own) and stand in the hoop. Introduce yourself and shake hands with one of the children, telling the class one thing about yourself; for example, "I really like teaching this class." Teach the children how to shake hands properly—shake firmly, but not too hard, and look into the person's eyes and smile.

DESCRIPTION OF ACTIVITY:

1. When I call "Girls shake hands," I want you to leave home, run to someone else's home, shake hands and introduce yourself by saying "My name is . . . ." Then tell one thing about yourself ("I like physical education."). When you have visited, return to your own home. Can you remember where it is? Can you remember your new friend's name?
2. Now it is the boys' turn. When you hear "Boys, shake hands," boys, leave home and run to someone else's home, shake hands, introduce yourself, and say something about yourself. Then return to your home and sit.
3. This half of the class visit the other half, then return and sit. Now the other half may visit someone else this time.
4. Now the first half visit as many "homes" as possible, greeting each other in a different way ("high ten's," "side five's," "back five's," "low ten's," "foot shake"). Go back "home" on signal.

IA-7 HUG YOUR NEIGHBOR

FOCUS: Aerobic warm-up; friendship

EQUIPMENT: None

ORGANIZATION:

• Choose one player to be IT. All other players scatter throughout the play area. Insist that IT should tag lightly on the shoulder; hugs are gentle.

DESCRIPTION OF ACTIVITY:

1. When I say "Go," IT, try to tag another player. Players, if you are tagged, you become the new IT, but you are safe while you are hugging another player.
2. When IT is not near you, you can let go and run freely in open space, but when IT comes near again, hug a new neighbor.

VARIATIONS:

a. Have players hug a neighbor and then sit down.
b. Change the game so that players are safe only when hugging in "three's."

IA-8 HERE, WHERE, THERE

FOCUS: Listening; quick reaction to directions   **EQUIPMENT:** None

ORGANIZATION:

- Arrange the players in scattered formation. Explain that you will give three directions and that they must act immediately to follow those directions. Stress that players must not touch anyone else.

DESCRIPTION OF ACTIVITY:

1. Run in general space without touching anyone. When I call "Here," I want you to run to me.

2. When I call "Where," I want you to run on the spot.

3. When I call "There" and point in one direction, I want you to all run in that direction.

VARIATIONS:

a. On signal "Where?" have children "freeze" on the spot; sit down as quickly as they can; turn around in a home space; twist in place; log roll; etc.

b. Vary the locomotor movements used: walk backwards; hop; skip; slide; gallop; jump.

IA-9 TOUCH

FOCUS: Aerobic warm-up; body awareness   **EQUIPMENT:** Small available equipment

ORGANIZATION:

- This game consists of a series of tasks performed in quick succession. Keep the activity going until a warmed-up effect is achieved. Some suggestions are given below; make up your own "touch" variations. Arrange the players in scattered formation.

DESCRIPTION OF ACTIVITY:

1. Touch the sidelines ten times by running across the play area between the two sidelines. Can you touch each sideline with a different body part each time?

2. Combine two or three of the following tasks so that you have to listen carefully. Do you think you can remember them? Touch . . . elbows to a bench; knees to a red line; chin to a wall; nose to a backline; ear to a door; back to a blue line; tummy to a circle. . . .

3. (Scatter available small equipment over the play area and call out combinations of the following tasks): Touch . . . ear to a ball; nose to a rope; elbow to a wand; hand to a teacher; knee to a mat; tummy to a deckring. . . .

IA–10 FUN WALKS

FOCUS: Warming up with rhythm walking

EQUIPMENT: Drum or music with a walking beat; record player or tape player

ORGANIZATION:

* To start, have children scatter over the play area. Encourage them to walk to the beat of your drum or in time with the music. Emphasize that they walk "tall" with tummy and seat tucked in ("suck and tuck"); arms swinging naturally; "heel-to-toe" motion with feet.

DESCRIPTION OF ACTIVITY:

1. Listen to the drum beat (or music). Can you clap your hands in time to the music? Can you walk to the beat of the music without touching anyone? Change direction on the loud beat!

2. Walk quickly; walk slowly; walk backwards; walk forwards; walk in a circle, making your circle bigger and bigger, then smaller and smaller; march in place.

3. Can you walk and swing your arms in large circles? Swing your arms the other way now, making smaller and smaller circles.

4. Show me how you can lift your knees up high as you walk! How high can you lift your knees?

5. Who can walk on his or her tippy-toes? This exercise strengthens the calf muscles. Can you show me your calf muscle? Let's all try to walk only on our heels.

6. Now walk taking giant steps; show me quick little steps.

7. Walk sideways by crossing one foot over the other as you walk.

8. Can you walk pigeon-toed (toes pointing in)? Can you waddle like a duck (toes pointing out)?

9. Walk a square; now a triangle; walk the number 8; walk the first letter of your name.

10. Can you walk like a spider? a gorilla? a penguin?

11. Invent a walk of your own!

IA-11 TRAFFIC LIGHTS

FOCUS: Listening skills; alertness

EQUIPMENT: Red, green, yellow sheets of paper

ORGANIZATION:

• Stand so that all the children can see you as you hold up the three sheets, one at a time. Explain the traffic light colors and their significance in traffic control. Change the signals frequently. Emphasize "safe" driving—look for open spaces to avoid collisions.

DESCRIPTION OF ACTIVITY:

1. Stand in your "homes." You are a car and I am the traffic lights.

2. When I flash the green paper, rev your engines, and then run around the play area without crashing into other cars.

3. When I hold up the yellow paper, run on the spot.

4. When I show the red paper, "Stop!" and freeze in a shape.

IA-12 CAR DRIVERS

FOCUS: Listening skills; alertness

EQUIPMENT: One hoop per player; suitable music; record or tape player

ORGANIZATION:

• Have players collect a hoop, find a space in the play area, and then hold the hoop horizontally around their waists.

DESCRIPTION OF ACTIVITY:

1. Start up your "car." On the signal "Go!" or when the music starts, run in general space trying not to bump into other drivers. What kind of noise does your car make?

2. Drive your cars along the "streets" (lines on the floor). When you come to an intersection, where two streets cross, give way to the car on your right.

3. When I call "Stop!" or the music stops, drive immediately to your garage (home) for a pit stop and repairs.

4. Start your engines again. This time you are a racing car driver. Race your car safely around the track in a CCW direction.

5. Uh-oh! You now have a flat tire. The air is slowly leaking out of your tires. Circle the track one more time slowly, coming to a stop in front of me, and then sit.

VARIATIONS:

a. Vary the locomotor movements: running, skipping, galloping.

b. Vary the directions: forwards, reverse, sideways.

IA-13 BACK TO BACK, FACE TO FACE_____

FOCUS: Listening; warm-up; friendliness   **EQUIPMENT:** None

ORGANIZATION:

• Have players run into a scattered formation. Explain that when the players meet their partners, they are to greet each other with a friendly greeting, such as, "Hello Jennifer"; "Hi Jason."

DESCRIPTION OF ACTIVITY:

1. When I call "Run," I want you to run in general space without touching anyone. Then, as soon as you hear me call "Back to Back," find a partner, stand back to back, and link elbows. Can you quickly sit down and stand up without using your arms?

2. Run again. This time when I call "Face to Face," find another partner, hold hands, go down into the half-squat position, and spring around each other in a complete circle.

3. Listen for the next "Back to Back" or "Face to Face" signal. Show me how quickly, but carefully, you can do the signals.

VARIATIONS:

a. Have players greet each other in different ways: Toe to Toe; Seat to Seat; Hip to Hip.

b. Call any of the positions followed by a variety of locomotor movements: hopping like a kangaroo; walking like an elephant; galloping like a horse.

IA-14 CHARLIE WANTS A HOME_____

FOCUS: Running and dodging   **EQUIPMENT:** Carpet squares or individual mats for all except one player

ORGANIZATION:

• Choose one player to be "Charlie" and have him or her stand in the center of the play area. Have each of the other players collect a carpet square and sit cross-legged on it in their homes. Ensure that carpets are well spaced apart.

DESCRIPTION OF ACTIVITY:

1. When Charlie calls "Charlie wants a home," players on the carpets try to exchange places with each other and sit on a new carpet.

2. Charlie, you must also try to get to a carpet and sit.

3. The player who cannot find a carpet to sit on becomes the new Charlie, and the game continues.

VARIATIONS:

a. Use more than one Charlie.
b. Take away carpets at any time to add to the fun.

IA-15 SIMPLE TAG GAMES

FOCUS: Establish rules; warm-up

EQUIPMENT: Several colored pinnies

ORGANIZATION:

- This activity teaches children the basic rules common to most tag games. Mark out the boundaries of the play area. Establish rules of fair play and encourage children to abide by the rules. Praise those who play fairly.

- Choose one player to be IT and have that player wear a colored pinnie.

DESCRIPTION OF ACTIVITY:

1. When I say "Go," IT will chase all the other players anywhere in the play area and try to tag you.

2. If you are tagged or run outside the play area, you become the new IT. Remember, IT, to tag lightly.

VARIATIONS:

a. There are many versions of Simple Tag that can be played merely by changing the locomotor movement. Instead of running, use some of the following tag games: Walking Tag; Skipping Tag; Hopping Tag; Galloping Tag; Sliding Tag.

b. Have more than one IT.

c. Vary the method of tagging the player. For example, each player tucks a scarf into the back of his or her shorts. IT must pull the scarf to make the tag.

d. Increase or decrease the size of the playing area.

e. Establish "safe" positions (which are given a time limit of perhaps five seconds): "Bottoms-up" (feet off floor); "Crab-Walk Position" (weight on hands and feet, with tummy facing upwards); balanced positions (such as on one leg; on one leg and one hand; knees only; bridges).

f. Have the children make up their own Simple Tag game.

VARIATION c

VARIATION e

IA-16 BIG A, LITTLE A _____

FOCUS: Aerobic warm-up

EQUIPMENT: Four traffic cones

ORGANIZATION:

• Mark out the play area with a safety zone at each end. Choose one player to be the "Cat," who stands in the middle of the playing area. Have the other players line up behind one endline.

DESCRIPTION OF ACTIVITY:

1. Stand behind the endline. When the Cat is in the middle, start singing:

"Big A"	*Stretch as high as you can.*
"Little A"	*Crouch down low.*
"Bouncing B"	*Do little hops.*
"The cat's in the cupboard"	*Tiptoe forward toward Cat.*
"But he can't catch . . . me!"	*On "me," try to run to the other end of the play area without being tagged by the cat.*

2. Those who are tagged help the Cat when the game continues. The last one tagged is the Cat for the next game.

VARIATION: For a game of shorter duration, have more than one Cat.

IA-17 FAIRY GODMOTHER TAG _____

FOCUS: Running and dodging

EQUIPMENT: One rolled newspaper (magic wand); two colored pinnies; four cone markers

ORGANIZATION:

• Define the boundaries of the play area with the cone markers. Select two players to be Catchers and one to be the Fairy Godmother (Godfather). Issue the two pinnies to the Catchers and the wand to the Fairy Godmother.

• Change the Fairy Godmother and the Catchers often to increase participation. Encourage players to move to open spaces and not to bunch.

DESCRIPTION OF ACTIVITY:

1. On the signal "Go," all players run in general space without touching anyone else.

2. The two Catchers run after the players, trying to tag as many as possible. If tagged, you must drop to the floor, lie on your back, and kick your legs and arms in the air.

3. Fairy Godmother (Godfather), move around touching tagged players with your wand. If touched by the Fairy Godmother, you are free and may rejoin the game. The Fairy Godmother cannot be tagged by the Catchers.

VARIATION: Instead of running, use other locomotor movements such as skipping, galloping, sliding.

IA-18 HALLOWEEN SIGNALS

FOCUS: *Special event:* Halloween; creative play; listening

EQUIPMENT: Ghostly music; record or tape player

ORGANIZATION:

- Explain each theme to the children, but allow them to use their own imaginations to interpret the theme. Make suggestions only when necessary. Have them create their own Halloween signal. Play ghostly music to create atmosphere.

DESCRIPTION OF ACTIVITY:

1. Listen to the signals and perform each as they are called; for example, when I call *"Witches,"* I want you all to perform to make sounds like witches (riding on your broomstick cackling to yourself). Let's try some more:
2. *Pumpkins:* Roll in a ball shape along the floor.
3. *Black Cat:* Hunch your back, spring over the floor. Make cat noises.
4. *Goblins:* Wave your hands up and down as you "float" through the air, squeaking to yourself.
5. *Ghosts:* Skip around the play area, moaning to yourself.
6. *Monster:* Make up your own monster shape and roar like a monster.

IA-19 OLD MOTHER WITCH

FOCUS: Chasing and dodging

EQUIPMENT: Six cone markers

ORGANIZATION:

- Mark out the boundaries of the play area. Choose one player to be the "Witch." All other players form a circle around him or her and hold hands.

DESCRIPTION OF ACTIVITY:

1. On the signal "Go," circle players skip CCW around the circle, teasing Old Mother Witch by singing:

   "Old Mother Witch, hi diddle, diddle
   Stands in the middle,
   With her cat and her fiddle."

2. Then Witch ask, "Whose children are you?" One of the players, answer by calling out any name you choose and the singing starts over again. But if a player answers, "Yours!", Witch, try to tag a circle player.

3. Circle players, drop your hands and run; try not to get caught by the Witch. If the Witch tags you, you become the new Witch.

VARIATION: Have circle players change direction and locomotor movement.

IA–20 FIVE NOSES

FOCUS: Aerobic endurance; listening; body awareness

EQUIPMENT: One beanbag per player; lively music; record or tape player

ORGANIZATION:

• Have the players sit in their homes. Scatter all the beanbags over the play area. Emphasize that players always watch where they are going.

DESCRIPTION OF ACTIVITY:

1. When I start the music, I want you to get up and run around the play area, looking for open spaces to run to. Try not to run on a beanbag. Watch where you are going so that you don't bump into anyone else. Can you run in time to the music?

2. Keep running until the music stops. When the music stops, I will call out a number and the name of a body part: for example, "five noses." Then run to touch your nose to five different beanbags. Make the last one you touch your home, and then sit in your home until the music starts.

3. When the music is played again, start running, but this time when the music stops listen to what I call.

4. I want you to touch a different body part to different beanbags. Suggestions: four right knees, four left knees, five left feet, five right feet, six fingers, four right elbows, three shoulders, three seats, four backs of head, four right ears, four left ears, four chins.

IA–21 GROUP SIGNALS

FOCUS: Listening; cooperation

EQUIPMENT: None

ORGANIZATION:

• Have players scatter, find a home, and then sit and listen. Throughout the game, encourage players to look for new players to form groups with each time.

DESCRIPTION OF ACTIVITY:

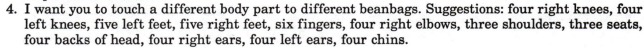

1. When I call out a "number" and then a "body part," I want you to get into groups of that number and then touch the body part to all the other members of your group; for example, "three's, touch Left Hands!"

2. This time I'm going to see which group can be the quickest: three's and touch the bottom of your right feet; four's and touch elbows; five's and touch left knees; six's and touch right pointer fingers; four's and touch backs; two's and touch ears; circles of eight, sit and touch toes.

VARIATION: Intersperse other Movement Signals throughout the game. For example, "Homes! hook-sit in groups of five!"; "Standing File! in groups of six"; "Clear the Deck! in groups of three."

IA-22 OWE ME THREE

FOCUS: Listening; alertness; spacial awareness; honesty   **EQUIPMENT:** None

ORGANIZATION:

- This activity is a powerful motivator for children to listen to directions. Explain that "owing me three" is a game and a challenge not to get caught next time. It is not a punishment. Encourage the children to do their "three's" quickly like "good sports" so that we can get on with the game. Emphasize the importance of safety. Players must not touch each other while running. Explain that you are trusting them to touch the correct number of walls. Have them count to themselves as they run. To begin, have players run to their homes and sit cross-legged facing you.

DESCRIPTION OF ACTIVITY:

1. When I call out a number one, two, three, or four, I want you to get up, run to touch that number of walls (sidelines or boundaries), and return to your homes and sit.
2. The last three players to sit each time "owe me three." This means that if you are one of the last players to sit, you have to do three of something for me as a reminder to be quicker the next time: three arm circles, three hops on one leg, three jumping jacks, three sit-ups. . . .

VARIATION: Mark out a circle (a basketball circle will do nicely) in the middle of the play area. Have the players run to touch a foot inside the circle between each wall touch.

IA-23 IN THE DOGHOUSE

FOCUS: Running and dodging   **EQUIPMENT:** Four sets of banners; several markers

ORGANIZATION:

- Mark out the doghouse areas in each corner of the play area. (See diagram.)
- Divide the class into four groups: the Green Dogs, the Yellow Dogs, the Blue Dogs, and the Red Dogs. Have each group wear the corresponding colored banners.
- Assign each group to a doghouse in each corner of the play area.

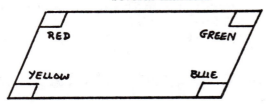

DESCRIPTION OF ACTIVITY:

1. When I call out "Green Dogs," you will chase all the other dogs. When you catch a dog, take him or her to your doghouse to stay there jogging on the spot, while you take off and try and catch more dogs.
2. Once the chase is on, players are not allowed to return to their doghouse, but may run anywhere in the play area.
3. If you have been caught, you will, of course, be good sports and go quietly and quickly to the Chaser's doghouse.
4. After one minute we will stop play and count up and record the number of dogs captured. Then I will call another group to be the chasers, and so on until all groups have had a turn. Then we will see which group has captured the most dogs.

IA-24 VEGETABLE SOUP

FOCUS: Space awareness; alertness; agility   **EQUIPMENT:** None

ORGANIZATION:

- Mark out four home bases in the corners of the play area. Divide the class into four equal groups and assign each group to a home base. Give each group the name of a vegetable; for example, Peas, Onions, Carrots, Potatoes.

DESCRIPTION OF ACTIVITY:

1. I will stand in the center of the play area and call each vegetable group into the center. When you hear the name of your group, run in and form a circle around me.
2. When I call "Soup's boiling," I want you to bounce up and down on the spot, calling "Soup's boiling!"
3. When you hear "Soup's burning!" run as quickly as you can to your home base. I will try to catch as many of you as I can. Those caught must come into my "soup bowl" with me. You will be my helpers and help me catch the others. We will continue in this way until all are caught and in my soup bowl.

VARIATIONS:

a. Allow each group to select its own vegetable name.
b. Appoint a player to make the calls and be the chaser.

IA-25 PANTHERS AND LEOPARDS

FOCUS: Alertness; agility   **EQUIPMENT:** Four cone markers; one flag per player

ORGANIZATION:

- Mark two endlines on the play area. Divide the class into two teams: the "Panthers" and the "Leopards." Have both teams stand with their backs to each other on opposite endlines. Each player has a flag tucked into the back of his or her shorts, with at least half of the flag showing.

DESCRIPTION OF ACTIVITY:

1. I will give a silent signal to one team: Panthers, creep toward the Leopards. Panthers, when you are close to the Leopards I will call "The Panthers are coming!"
2. Leopards, when you hear this, turn to give chase and try to tag the Panthers by pulling their flags before they can get back to their own line. If you tag a Panther, she or he joins your team.

VARIATIONS:

a. Use other locomotor movements: walking, skipping, hopping.
b. Vary the starting positions. Have both teams sit cross-legged with backs to each other on opposite endlines.
c. Call the game by a different name: "The Giants and the Trolls."

IA-26 MAN FROM MARS

FOCUS: Running and dodging

EQUIPMENT: Four cone markers

ORGANIZATION:

- Mark out the boundaries of the play area. Select one player to be the "Man from Mars" who stands in the middle of the play area. All other players start behind one of the endlines.

DESCRIPTION OF ACTIVITY:

1. On the signal "Go," the endline players sing:

   "Man from Mars, Man from Mars, May we chase you to the stars?"

2. The Man from Mars, you can reply by saying:

   "Yes, if you—are wearing glasses
   —have white shoes
   —are wearing red
   —have freckles
   —have a white T-shirt
   —and so on. . . ."

3. If you are called in, chase the Man from Mars and try to tag him or her. If you do tag him or her, then you become the new Man from Mars and the game starts again.

VARIATION:

For a large class, start with two Martians.

IA-27 HICKORY, DICKORY, DOCK

FOCUS: Listening; running quickly

EQUIPMENT: None

ORGANIZATION:

- Have the children form a large circle, spaced an arm's length apart facing inward, and then number off in three's. Ask them to remember their numbers.

DESCRIPTION OF ACTIVITY:

1. Start jogging on the spot and keep your feet moving during the whole game.
2. When I call "Hickory, Dickory, Dock, the mouse ran up the clock, the clock struck two!" all the two's run around the outside of the circle in a CW direction. The first one back is the winner.
3. As soon as players are back in their places, I will quickly call a new number. Listen carefully because I may call out your number!

VARIATIONS:

a. Have runners run in a CCW direction.
b. Have runners weave in and out of the circle players.
c. For large classes, form two circles.

IA-28 CHRISTMAS SIGNALS

FOCUS: *Special event:* Christmas; creative play; listening

EQUIPMENT: Christmas music; record or tape player

ORGANIZATION:

- Have players find a partner and run to stand in their home. Allow the players to interpret each theme in their own way, and you make suggestions only when necessary. Play Christmas music and create atmosphere.

DESCRIPTION OF ACTIVITY:

1. When I call out *"Reindeer,"* I want you and your partner to gallop around the play area holding hands.

2. Great reindeer! Now let's try some more:

Elves: Tiptoe lightly while making yourselves as small as you can.

Santa: Roll back and forth on your back holding your tummy, laughing, and shouting "Ho, Ho, Ho!"

Christmas Tree: Stand tall, hands outstretched overhead.

Christmas Ball: Roll up in a little ball on the floor, and roll sideways.

Candy Cane: Can you form the shape of a candy cane on the floor?

Toys: Move like a Choo Choo Train; Toy Soldier; Spinning Top; Bouncing Ball; Airplane; Rag Doll.

3. This time, can you think of something to do when I call out a Christmas name?

IA-29 RUDOLPH'S TAG GAME

FOCUS: Running and dodging; alertness

EQUIPMENT: One pinnie; cone markers

ORGANIZATION:

- Mark out the play area with the cone markers. Choose one player to be "Rudolph," who stands in the center of the play area and wears a pinnie. All other players, the "Reindeer," line up behind an endline. Give all the players a name; either "Dancer," "Dasher," "Prancer," "Vixen," "Comet," "Cupid," "Donner," or "Blitzen."

DESCRIPTION OF ACTIVITY:

1. Rudolph, call a reindeer name; for example, "Dasher." Then all the Dashers try to run to the safety of the opposite endline without being tagged by you.

2. Reindeer, when you are tagged, you become Rudolph's helper and help to tag the other reindeer.

3. Rudolph, keep calling out the names of the Reindeer until there is only one left. He or she becomes the Rudolph for the next game.

VARIATION: Start with two or more Rudolphs.

Introductory Activities / **19**

IA-30 FROZEN TAG

FOCUS: Alertness; running and dodging

EQUIPMENT: One pinnie;
four cone markers

ORGANIZATION:

• Mark out the boundaries of the play area. Choose one player to be IT and to wear the pinnie. Have all the other players scatter in general space.

DESCRIPTION OF ACTIVITY:

1. On the signal "Go," IT, try to tag as many players as you can.

2. If you are tagged by IT, you are "frozen" to the spot and must stand with your arms out and legs apart.

3. Any player can free you by crawling through your legs by the back entrance only.

VARIATIONS:

a. Start with two or more IT's.

b. Vary the shape in which the players "freeze": long, curled, wide, twisted, bridge shape.

c. Vary the method of freeing the players: leap-frog over a frozen "round" and low shape; run completely around a tall stork shape.

IA-31 SPANKER TAG

FOCUS: Running and dodging

EQUIPMENT: One rolled towel or newspaper;
four cone markers

ORGANIZATION:

• Make the "spanker" by taping a rolled towel or newspaper. Mark out the play area. Choose one player to be IT, who stands in the middle of the play area. All other players scatter.

DESCRIPTION OF ACTIVITY:

1. On the signal "Go," IT, chase the others and try to spank players on the seat with the spanker.

2. Remember, IT, you must spank lightly. After a certain time I will choose a new IT and the game will continue. The challenge is to see who will remain "unspanked" at the end of the game.

VARIATION: For more participation, have more than one IT and more spankers.

IA-32 UNCLE SAM

FOCUS: Running and dodging

EQUIPMENT: Four cone markers;
one pinnie;
set of colored flags

ORGANIZATION:

- Mark out the play area. Clearly mark the two endlines. Choose one player to be "Uncle Sam," who stands in the center of the play area wearing the pinnie. All other players tuck a flag in their waistband so that three-fourths of it is showing and stand behind one of the endlines.

DESCRIPTION OF ACTIVITY:

1. Endline players, start the game by chanting:

   "Uncle Sam, Uncle Sam, May we cross your ocean dam?"

2. Uncle Sam, you answer, "Yes, if you are wearing red." Players wearing red get a free pass to the other end.

3. Then on the "Go" signal from Uncle Sam, the rest of the players try to run to the opposite endline without getting your flag pulled. Tagged players become Uncle Sam's helpers.

4. Begin again. This time, Uncle Sam, call out another color. Keep going until all players are caught but one. This player becomes the new Uncle Sam for the next game.

VARIATION: Vary the criteria for a free pass: girls with short hair, wearing glasses, all the boys, all the girls. . . .

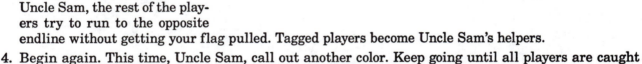

IA-33 GOLDILOCKS AND THE THREE BEARS

FOCUS: Running and dodging; alertness

EQUIPMENT: Nine cone markers

ORGANIZATION:

- Mark out the play area with a "safe" area at one end and a "bear house" at the other end. Choose three players to be "Baby Bear," "Mama Bear," and "Papa Bear," who stand inside their house. All other players stand at the other end behind their safe area.

DESCRIPTION OF ACTIVITY:

1. On the "Go" signal, players move toward the Bears' house calling, "Who's at home?" If the bears in the Bears' house answer "Baby Bear," "Mama Bear," or "Papa Bear," the players keep going and call again.

2. But if the bears answer "Goldilocks," the chase is on. If you get tagged by one of the bears, you must join them and help catch the other players.

3. Keep playing until all players have been tagged.

VARIATION: Have the bears turn their backs to the players.

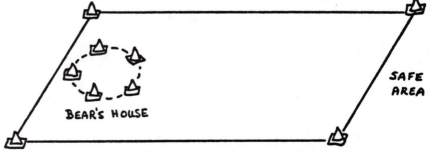

IA-34 HOUNDS AND RABBITS

FOCUS: Running and dodging; alertness

EQUIPMENT: Two pinnies;
one long rope per three players

ORGANIZATION:

• Make as many burrows as needed (knot the ends of the ropes together to make circles). Spread the burrows around the play area. Choose two players to be the "Hounds," who hold a pinnie in their hand. Divide the rest of the class, the "Rabbits," into groups of three and have each group stand in a burrow.

DESCRIPTION OF ACTIVITY:

1. On the signal "Go," Hounds, call "one, two, three"; then howl as loudly as you can.
2. Rabbits, when you hear the howl, you must run from your burrow and find another, but remember, only three to a burrow.
3. Hounds, try to tag a Rabbit as they change burrows. When you tag a Rabbit, give him or her the pinnie because he or she becomes the new Hound and you become the Rabbit.

VARIATION: Start the game with three or more Hounds.

IA-35 POUND PUPPIES

FOCUS: Running and dodging

EQUIPMENT: Ten to twelve pinnies

ORGANIZATION:

• Choose one-third of the players to be the "Dog Catchers," who each get a pinnie to wear. The other players are the "Pound Puppies" and scatter over the play area. Mark out an area to serve as the Dog Pound, or use the center circle of the basketball court.

DESCRIPTION OF ACTIVITY:

1. On the signal "Go!", Dog Catchers, try to catch as many Puppies as you can. The caught Puppies must follow you to the Dog Pound.
2. Puppies, you may run anywhere in the play area. You can also free the Puppies in the pound by running through the pound and shaking hands with them.
3. Dog Catchers, you are allowed to have only one guard on the Dog Pound.
4. When all the Puppies have been caught, a new game begins.

VARIATIONS:

a. Have the free Puppies "give ten" to the caught Puppies in the pound to free them (slap both hands together, palms to palms).
b. Allow each team a certain time limit as the Dog Catchers.

IA-36 EASTER SIGNALS

FOCUS: *Special event:* Easter; listening; space awareness

EQUIPMENT: Suitable music; tape or record player

ORGANIZATION:

- Have players find a home. Play Easter music as background music.

DESCRIPTION OF ACTIVITY:

When I call out a signal, show me how you can move about the play area:

Easter Bunny: Hop like a bunny anywhere in general space. Wiggle your tail.

Easter Eggs: Curl up into an egg shape and roll in different ways.

Easter Basket: Make a bridge using your hands and feet.

Easter Parade: March with a high knee action. Swing your arms high.

Chocolate Rabbit: As you get eaten, slowly sink to the floor.

Easter Circle: Everyone, join hands to form a big circle. Walk four steps in toward the center. On the fourth count, raise your hands up high and shout "Hi." Walk four steps back, bringing your hands down again. Repeat.

EASTER BASKET

CHOCOLATE RABBIT

EASTER PARADE

EASTER BUNNY

EASTER EGGS

VARIATION: Have the children make up their own Easter signals and teach them to the rest of the class.

IA-37 KEEP THEM MOVING

FOCUS: Running; kicking

EQUIPMENT: Any type of balls, such as soccer, utility, basketball

ORGANIZATION:

- Have the players stand in scatter formation. Scatter more balls than there are players over the play area. Explain the dangers of kicking the ball too high or too hard.

DESCRIPTION OF ACTIVITY: On the signal "Go," try to keep all the balls in motion at all times by tapping them with your feet. Keep your eyes open to spot a ball that may be slowing down; run after it and give it a kick. Do you think we can keep them all moving so that not one ball "dies" (completely stops)?

VARIATION: Call "Jogging" at any time. Players must then stop chasing the balls and jog on the spot for about eight to ten seconds. This gives the balls a chance to slow down. Then call "Go" again, but the players will have to hurry now to keep all the balls moving.

IA–38 FOLLOW ME!

FOCUS: Aerobic warm-up; listening; miming

EQUIPMENT: Music with a strong 4/4 beat; tape or record player

ORGANIZATION:

- This is a follow-the-leader activity. You may choose to start off the activity yourself, then allow one of the players to lead. Change the leader frequently so that everyone will have a chance at being a leader.
- To start, have players stand in a long line behind you.

DESCRIPTION OF ACTIVITY:

1. Follow me around the play area. Whatever I do, I want you to do also. Can you keep in time with the music?
2. Stay in line and do not pass anyone. When I clap my hands above my head, you must stop and "freeze" on the spot—don't move a muscle.
3. Use any locomotor movement, such as running, hopping, jumping, skipping, galloping, giant steps, rolling, leaping, twisting.
   — Vary the direction: forwards, backwards, sideways.
   — Vary the level: high, low, medium.
   — Use the lines on the floor to move along or over.
   — Use the equipment to go over, under, across, or around.

VARIATIONS:

a. Divide the class into two groups and do the warm-up as above.
b. Divide the class into four groups.

IA–39 RUNNING SIGNALS

FOCUS: Warm-up; running in different ways

EQUIPMENT: The same as for IA–38.

ORGANIZATION:

- Have players scatter to find a home. Play music with a strong running beat.

DESCRIPTION OF ACTIVITY:

1. On my signals, I will call out a different way of running, and then explain what I want you to do. Listen carefully:

Free running: naturally and easily with no effort.
Pigeon-toed: run with knees in and toes pointing inward.
Skeleton jogging: run as if there is a string attached to the top of your head; shuffle your feet and dangle your arms.
Knock-kneed: run with your knees touching and your feet pointing out.
Run like a wooden man: head up, body straight, arms and legs stiff.
Cross-over step: run, crossing one leg in front of the other.
Run on heels: run on heels with legs straight.
Run on toes: raise your arms overhead and make yourself tall as you move on your toes.
Run on the spot: run on the balls of your feet with knees up.

2. Repeat some or all of the above.

KNOCK-KNEED

CROSS-OVER STEP   SKELETON JOGGING

IA–40 HILL DILL

FOCUS: Running and dodging; fair play

EQUIPMENT: Four cone markers;
20–30 beanbags;
basket

ORGANIZATION:

• Mark out a safe zone at each end of the play area. If playing indoors, mark the safe zone lines three meters (ten feet) from the walls. Remove all obstacles from the play area. Place a basket of beanbags in the center of the play area. Choose one player to be IT and to stand in the middle of the play area holding a beanbag. Have all other players stand behind either of the two safe zone lines. Insist that a tag be a light touch on the arm or shoulder with the beanbag; the beanbag must not be thrown.

DESCRIPTION OF ACTIVITY:

1. When IT calls "Hill Dill come over the hill!" all players try to run across to the opposite safe zone without being tagged with the beanbag by IT.

2. If touched by IT's beanbag, collect a beanbag yourself and join IT in the middle to help tag the others.

3. The last player to be tagged becomes the new IT for the next game.

IA–41 WASPS!

FOCUS: Running and dodging; throwing

EQUIPMENT: One beanbag per player;
four cone markers;
lively music;
record or tape player

ORGANIZATION:

• Mark out the play area. Have players find a partner, and then have one partner of each pair get a "stinger" (beanbag). This partner is the "Wasp." Partners stand back to back in a free space.

DESCRIPTION OF ACTIVITY:

1. When the music starts the game, Wasp, chase your partner trying to hit him or her below the waist with the stinger.

2. If you are hit, you then pick up the stinger to become the new Wasp and chase your partner.

3. Remember to watch where you are going. Keep playing until the music stops.

VARIATIONS:

a. If the play is too vigorous, have the Wasps touch the partner with the stinger.

b. Every player is a Wasp who can sting anyone. When hit, that player must perform some exercise, such as three jumping jacks, to get back in the game. A loose beanbag on the floor may be picked up by anyone.

c. The whole class is chased by several Wasps, and when hit, those players must perform a stunt or dance step to get back in the game.

IA-42 TAIL SNATCH TAG

FOCUS: Alertness; space awareness

EQUIPMENT: One flag, banner, or jump rope per player; four cone markers

ORGANIZATION:

- Mark out the play area. Have players find a partner, scatter, and stand two giant steps apart from each other. Have one of the partners collect a "tail" (flag) and tuck it into the back of his waistband. Check that the flags are tucked loosely and are easy to snatch. Explain that players wearing flags must not touch or protect their flags.

DESCRIPTION OF ACTIVITY:

1. On the "Go!" signal, the player without the flag, chase your partner to try to snatch the tail. If you do, then you get to wear the tail and your partner chases you.

2. After a few minutes, on the signal "Change," find a new partner and begin again. (Rearrange the flags so that only one of the partners has a tail.)

VARIATIONS:

a. Use banners, strips of cloth, or folded jump ropes as flags.
b. Increase or decrease the size of the play area.

IA-43 NERF™ TAG

FOCUS: Running and dodging; accuracy throwing

EQUIPMENT: Three to four Nerf™ balls; four cone markers

ORGANIZATION:

- Mark out the boundaries of the play area. Choose three to four players to be the "Throwers." Have each get a Nerf™ ball and stand in the middle of the play area. Have the rest of the class scatter. Change Throwers frequently.

DESCRIPTION OF ACTIVITY:

1. On the signal "Go," Throwers, chase after the other players, trying to hit the players below the waist with your ball.

2. Players, if you are hit by one of the balls, form a bridge on the floor with your hands and feet. You can be freed by having one of the other players slide under your bridge.

3. A player cannot be hit while freeing another player. A ball bouncing off the floor first, then hitting a player, does not count.

VARIATIONS:

a. The ball may bounce first before hitting a player.
b. The Throwers can take a maximum of three steps before they must throw the ball.

IA-44 SHIP AHOY!

FOCUS: Listening; alertness

EQUIPMENT: None

ORGANIZATION:

- Have players imagine that the play area is a ship. You are the ship's captain and they are the crew. As the captain, give two signals: a signal to run to different parts of the ship such as the bow or the stern, and then a signal to perform a stunt of some kind. Explain and demonstrate signals before the game begins.

- At first, point in the direction players should move when they forget which part of the ship is which. When learned, mix up the signals to keep players alert.

DESCRIPTION OF ACTIVITY:

1. ***Run to the Bow!*** (Run to front end of play area.)

   Lifeboat! Form groups of three players and pretend to row to shore.

2. ***Hop to the Stern!*** (Hop to other end of play area.)

   Captain's coming! Stop and salute your captain.

3. ***Skip to Port!*** (Skip to left side of the play area as you face the bow.)

   Periscope! Lie on your back and raise one leg.

4. ***Jump to Starboard!*** (Jump to right side of play area as you face the bow.)

   Crew overboard! Grab someone's arm and hold on.

5. ***Power-walk to the bow!***

   Crow's Nest! Climb up any object.

6. ***Leap to the Stern!***

   Radar! Run with hands up and make beeping noises.

7. ***Roll to Starboard!***

   Sharks! Link a body part with another player until everyone is joined together.

VARIATIONS:

a. Have players suggest other signals.

b. Use gymnastic equipment for players to mount on such signals as "Crow's nest!", or swing from ropes on the signal "Pirates."

IA-45 WALK-ERCISE

FOCUS: Warm-up; rhythmical movement

EQUIPMENT: Music (or drum); tape or record player

ORGANIZATION:

- In this activity, children warm up by walking rhythmically or moving arms and legs in time to the music.
- To start, have children find a free space.

DESCRIPTION OF ACTIVITY:

1. When the music starts, walk briskly in general space. Listen to the music. Keep in time with the beat of the music.
2. Can you swing your right and then your left arm upward, backward and around so that you are swimming the "back crawl"?
3. Let's do the "front crawl" as you walk. Now move your arms so that you are doing the "breaststroke" as you walk.
4. Now, walk with a nice relaxed swing of your arms. Force your tummy out as you breathe in; force your tummy in as you breathe out slowly.

IA-46 HOOP-ERCISE

FOCUS: Warm-up; strength; spacial awareness

EQUIPMENT: One hoop for every player; suitable music; record or tape player

ORGANIZATION:

- Have every player get a hoop, find a home, and sit in the hoop.

DESCRIPTION OF ACTIVITY:

1. When the music starts, travel around the floor placing a foot in every hoop, and sit in your home hoop when finished.
2. Can you jump on both feet and land in five different hoops? Land in your own hoop last and sit down.
3. Who can hop on one foot only and land in four different hoops? Now change to the other foot. Can you find four more hoops to land in? Return home when finished.
4. Now, running on your hands and feet, visit five hoops and place a hand in each one.
5. On all fours again, travel sideways and place both hands in four different hoops. Now go the other way and visit four more hoops.
6. Run backward and sit down in six hoops. Curl up and lie still in the last one.

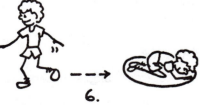

VARIATIONS:

a. Vary the number of repetitions to the fitness level of the class.
b. Repeat using different locomotor movements: skipping, sliding, walking, galloping.

Section 2

Fitness Activities

The daily Fitness Activity serves as a *specific warm-up* and, used in conjunction with an introductory activity, builds overall fitness, with emphasis on cardiovascular endurance and muscular strength and endurance.

This section presents an assortment of 17 Fitness Activities, including:

FA–1   Organizational Breaks
FA–2   Tempo Change Breaks
FA–3   Stunt Breaks
FA–4   Equipment Breaks
FA–5   Partner Breaks
FA–6   Cooperative Stunt Breaks
FA–7   10-Minute Workout 1
FA–8   10-Minute Workout 2
FA–9   10-Minute Workout 3

FA–10   10-Minute Workout 4
FA–11   10-Minute Workout 5
FA–12   Aerobic Snake
FA–13   Aerobic Circle
FA–14   Swim Routine
FA–15   The Exercise Game
FA–16   Creative Obstacle Course
FA–17   Fitkid Circuit

FA-1 ORGANIZATIONAL BREAKS

FOCUS: Class organization; fitness

EQUIPMENT: None

ORGANIZATION:

- A "break" is a short informal activity which, when introduced spontaneously into a lesson, provides relief, a change of tempo, alertness training, collection and dispersal of equipment, class organization and mobilization, challenge, and fun. It need not be related to any other part of the lesson.

- Organizational Breaks provide a transition between lesson segments and efficient mobilization of the class for the next activity. Use these breaks repeatedly throughout lessons to increase the activity of the class. For greatest effect, introduce Breaks completely without warning. Try these examples, but adapt to your own situation.

DESCRIPTION OF ACTIVITY:

1. Slide-step to touch the middle of each wall of the play area, and then fall into your teams. Go!

2. Run CCW around the play area, doing eight sit-ups in each corner; then sit cross-legged on the big circle in groups of three. Go!

3. Touch all the benches in the play area, and then fall into your teams. Go!

4. Quickly skip to one end of the play area, log roll toward the middle of the play area, jump up and sit down five times in a row, and then run to the listening circle where I am standing. Go!

5. Touch your nose to a bench; touch your elbows to a circle; touch your back to a wall; touch your knees to two different black lines; touch your ear to a door; touch your shoulder to the climbing ropes; then quickly find a partner about your size and stand one behind the other on a sideline. Go!

6. Touch a mat, a bench, a door, a climbing rope; shake my hand and long-sit at this end of the play area. Go!

7. Add your own idea!

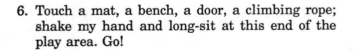

VARIATION:

Use the outdoor school environment and playground equipment with Organizational Breaks: Run around four trees, move under one object, over another, and return to my listening circle. Go!

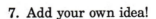

FA-2 TEMPO CHANGE BREAKS

FOCUS: Class organization; mobilization

EQUIPMENT: Indoor or outdoor play area

ORGANIZATION:

- Tempo Change Breaks provide a change of pace. Use them to get players moving quickly again after a period of inactivity, to give players a restful activity after vigorous play, or to ensure that exercising in all the fitness component areas occurs. When teaching outdoors, adapt these breaks to the playground equipment and area available. Try these examples, but adapt to your own situation.

DESCRIPTION OF ACTIVITY:

1. On signal *"Compass!"* touch one finger to the floor and run around it five times; then try to balance on one leg for five seconds.

2. On signal *"Corkscrew Stand!"* stand tall while folding your arms and crossing your feet. Now try to sit down in back-lying position. Can you stand up without unfolding your arms and legs?

3. On signal *"Touch!"* touch the four objects I name, and then sit in the listening circle. Who can be the quickest to finish? Touch a mat, a door, a circle, and a bench.

4. On signal *"Skier!"* jump from side to side over your rope twenty times.

5. On signal *"Lines!"* touch ten different lines with a different body part each time; then quickly stand at this end of the play area.

6. On signal *"Corners!"* skip to one corner of the play area; slide-step to the diagonally opposite corner; skip to the third corner; then slide-step to its diagonally opposite corner. Touch each corner with both hands. Meet in your teams when finished.

7. Add your own idea!

VARIATION:

Use any of the other Organizational Signals from the Introductory Activities.

FA-3 STUNT BREAKS

FOCUS: Class organization

EQUIPMENT: None

ORGANIZATION:

- Stunts provide excellent breaks and a change of pace. Teach players the names of these stunts and repeat them often, using one or two in your future lessons. Call out a Stunt Break immediately before changing to the next activity.

DESCRIPTION OF ACTIVITY:

Pogo Springs
Inchworm
Rockers
Log Rollers
Hoppo Bumpo
Thread the Needle
Spinning Tops
Bouncing Ball
Wicket Walk
Bucking Bronco

  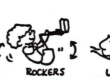 

POGO SPRINGS   INCHWORM   ROCKERS   LOG ROLLERS   WICKET WALK

HOPPO BUMPO   THREAD THE NEEDLE   SPINNING TOP   BOUNCING BALL   BUCKING BRONCO

FA-4 EQUIPMENT BREAKS

FOCUS: Class organization

EQUIPMENT: One deckring per player;
one ball per player;
one tee-ball set per pair;
one folding mat per pair;
two to four benches;
six to eight short ropes;
one whiffle ball and bat per pair

ORGANIZATION:

- Equipment Breaks provide time between parts of the lesson for equipment set-up, collection, and dispersal. The fourth break shows how to make equipment set-up a group activity. Try these examples, but adapt to your own situation.

DESCRIPTION OF ACTIVITY:

1. On signal *"Go!"* run to touch each end of the play area; then get a deckring from the basket, find a home, and toss and catch it ten times.
2. On signal *"Bounce,"* bounce your ball to each corner of the gym; touch the corner with your ball, and then drop it into the ball cart. Quickly fall into your teams.
3. Find a partner. One partner, get the tee-ball base; the other partner, collect a whiffle ball and a bat. Find a free space for you and your partner to practice batting.
4. Number off one, two, three, four.
   - All number one's jump up and down four times; then find the folding mats and lay them out in one corner of the play area.
   - All number two's collect a ball each and crab-walk while balancing the ball on your tummy to this sideline. Place all the balls on this line.
   - All number three's carry four benches to this area near me.
   - All number four's get a short rope and skip to the middle of the play area.

FA-5 PARTNER BREAKS

FOCUS: Class organization; partner work

EQUIPMENT: One ball per pair

ORGANIZATION:

• Use Partner Breaks spontaneously to generate an atmosphere of fun and challenge and to enhance listening skills. Spontaneity will come more easily if you teach players the names of the breaks and repeat them often. Use any previously taught short activity as a break, as long as the activity can be introduced quickly by name. Several suggestions follow.

DESCRIPTION OF ACTIVITY:

1. On signal *"Mirrors!"* quickly find a partner. Move around the play area copying the actions of your partner. On *"Change Mirrors!"* find a new partner and repeat the activity.

2. On signal *"Leapfrog!"* place your hands on your partner's back and jump over your partner. Repeat this action from one end of the play area to the opposite end.

3. On signal *"Walls!"* race your partner to touch with both hands the middle of each wall of the play area and return to your starting place.

4. On signal *"Saw Logs!"* face your partner, holding both hands, and place your right foot forward. Jump to change the forward foot and create a "sawing-like" action.

5. On signal *"Corners!"* link elbows with your partner and skip to each corner of the play area. At each corner, holding both hands, swing twice around. Return to sit cross-legged on the big circle.

6. On signal *"Poison Ball!"* the partner with the ball chase the other partner and try to touch him or her with the ball. If you tag your partner, he or she becomes the new chaser. Remember to watch where you are going.

7. On signal *"Quick Hands!"* quickly find a partner and face each other. One partner put your palms down; the other partner rest your hands, palms down, on your partner's. Whenever you are ready, the bottom player, try to slap the tops of your partner's hands. The top players, try to protect your hands by drawing them back. Switch, after three tries each.

8. Add your own idea!

FA-6 COOPERATIVE STUNT BREAKS

FOCUS: Class organization; partner work   **EQUIPMENT:** None

ORGANIZATION:

• In these Stunt Breaks, partners cooperate together as they work in pairs. Teach players the names of these stunts. Reinforce their learning by repeating the stunts often. Call each stunt by name quickly and without warning. The key to the success of these breaks is in the spontaneity and unpredictability of their use. Have each player find a partner and sit together in a home space.

DESCRIPTION OF ACTIVITY:

Backward Get-up

Wring the Dishrag

Tick-Tock

Teeter-Totter

Alligator Walk

Bouncing Ball

Snake Roll

Three Legs

Copy Cat

Roller Coaster

VARIATION:

Substitute any gymnastic stunt that players could do in pairs.

FA–7 10-MINUTE WORKOUT 1

FOCUS: Leg, arm and shoulder, abdominal strength; back flexibility

EQUIPMENT: Lively music; tape or record player

ORGANIZATION:

• This workout strengthens and stretches the major muscle groups. In the stretching activities, remind players to avoid bobbing or jerky movements. Have players scatter around you and stand tall in their "homes."

DESCRIPTION OF ACTIVITY:

1. *Leaping Lizards:* Run in free space and leap over as many lines as you can before I say "Freeze!" Will I catch you landing on a line? Can you leap over more than one line at a time? (Repeat this warm-up for about one minute.)

2. *Alligator Walk:* In front-lying position, take your weight on your lower arms. Show me how you can move across the play area floor from one side to the other. Remember to drag your feet behind you.

3. *Peek-a-Boo:* In hook-lying position, slowly raise just your head and shoulders off the floor to look at your feet, and then slowly lower. Can you do this ten times?

4. *Super Ball:* Bounce high, and then bounce low. Continue to bounce high and then bounce low as you move around the play area.

5. *Shoulder Shrugs:* Stand tall with feet comfortably apart. Shrug your shoulders by lifting them toward your ears as if to say, "I don't know."

6. *Dog Shake:* Shake all over like a wet dog; then "wag your tail" to show me how happy you are.

7. *Dead Bug Stretch:* In back-lying position with your arms and legs in the air, can you grab your ankles and hold for ten seconds? Repeat in front-lying position.

8. *Pencil Stretch:* In back-lying position, stretch your hands and legs away from you, keeping yourself long like a pencil. Hold this stretch for ten seconds, and then roll over onto your front and stretch again for ten seconds.

VARIATION:

In Dead Bug Stretch, have children grasp left leg with right hand and hold for ten seconds; then right leg with left hand and hold.

FOCUS: Leg, arm, and shoulder strength; lateral mobility

EQUIPMENT: Suitable music; tape or record player

ORGANIZATION:

- This workout warms, strengthens, and stretches the large muscle groups and improves lateral mobility. Have the children find a free space, stand, and face you. When performing "Belly Button Circles," remind children to keep their belly button "pushed out." In "Finger Walk," stress that they do not lean forward.
- Ask them if they can feel the stretch along the opposite side.

DESCRIPTION OF ACTIVITY:

1. **Tortoise-Hare Warm-Up:** On the signal "Tortoise," prance slowly in place by lifting just your heels, one after the other, off the floor. On the signal "Hare," move your feet up and down on the spot as quickly as possible. Can you keep in time to the music?
2. **Windmills:** Stand tall and hold your arms out sideways at shoulder height. Keeping your arms straight, circle them forward. Make bigger and bigger circles; then smaller and smaller circles.
3. **Jack-in-the-Box:** Squat down low. Pretend that you are hiding in a box. When I clap my hands, spring up, reaching as high as you can. Return to your starting position. (Repeat two more times.)
4. **Inchworm:** Stand tall. "Walk your fingers" down your legs, and then walk your hands away from your feet until you are in the front support position. Now, keeping your hands in place, walk your feet up to your hands. Then walk your hands away from your feet while your feet remain in place. Can you repeat this action keeping in time to the music?
5. **Sunflower:** Begin in back-lying position, arms at your sides and legs straight. Bring one knee to your chest, hug it for four seconds, and then return it to starting position; now hug the other knee to your chest. Show me how you can do 12 knee hugs in this way. Breathe normally as you do this.
6. **Belly Button Circles:** Standing tall, can you trace four circles with your belly button? Now trace the circles in the opposite direction. (Repeat this sequence two more times.)
7. **Noddy Heads:** Stand tall with your feet comfortably apart. Now gently nod your head as if to say "Yes." Then gently nod your head as if to say "No." (Repeat each four times.)
8. **Finger Walk:** Standing tall, slowly reach down one side of your body, "walking" your fingers down as far as possible. Slowly return to starting position, and then walk your fingers down the other side. (Repeat this stretch two more times.)

VARIATION:

Shoulder Shrugs: Children stand tall with feet comfortably apart and shrug shoulders by lifting them toward their ears as if to say "I don't know."

FA–9 10-MINUTE WORKOUT 3

FOCUS: Leg, arm and shoulder, abdominal strength; back flexibility

EQUIPMENT: Lively music; tape or record player

ORGANIZATION:

- This workout warms and strengthens the leg and abdominal muscles and stretches the muscles of the arm and shoulders and lower back.

DESCRIPTION OF ACTIVITY:

1. *Runway:* You are a Boeing 747 taking off. As you run down the runway, start to gather speed. Your wings are spread and you are flying through the air. Now begin to slow down and, at the same time, find a line on the floor to make your approach. Move along this line, gradually getting lower and slower. Stop gently in front-lying position. Repeat several times, adding "dips," "loops," "twirly-birds," and so on.

2. *Circler:* Stand tall in your "home," with your arms held high and your feet glued to the floor and spread comfortably apart. Can you trace a large circle with your hands as high and as low as you can reach? Now trace a large circle in the opposite direction. Repeat this activity one more time.

3. *Jumping Jacks:* Begin by standing tall, feet together and hands at your sides. Jump feet wide apart and, at the same time, clap hands overhead. Repeat 15 times.

4. *Side Twists:* Stand tall with your feet comfortably apart. Twist your trunk from one side to the other while your feet stay still. Let your eyes follow your hands as they swing from one side to the other. Repeat 12 times.

5. *Curl-ups:* In hook-lying position with knees up and heels on the floor and your hands resting on your upper legs, slowly curl up, sliding your hands up your legs until your wrists are just past your knees. Then slowly curl down to starting position. Take four counts to come up and four counts to come down. Repeat these curl-ups 12 times.

6. *Flutter Kicks:* In front-lying position, alternately raise and lower your legs off the floor. Remember to keep your legs straight as you kick. Can you do 20 flutter kicks?

7. *Picking Apples:* Standing tall in your "home," raise your arms overhead; then slowly reach as high as you can, first with the right hand, then with the left hand as if you were trying to pick an apple off a tree, just above your head. Repeat this eight times.

VARIATIONS:

a. *Speed-Way:* You are a Ferrari racing car. Rev up your engine by jogging on the spot; jog up to the starting line. On signal "Go!" run as fast as you can around the play area to cross the finish line. Now jog once around to the start/finish line; then again run around as quickly as you can. Cross the finish line and repeat the race one more time.

b. *Cherry Pickers:* Standing tall in your "home," pretend to pick a cherry in the tree overhead by reaching across as high as you can to the opposite side of your body, putting it in an imaginary bucket on the opposite side, and then repeating to the other side. Continue until you have "picked" 12 cherries.

FA-10 10-MINUTE WORKOUT 4

FOCUS: Leg, arm, and shoulder strength

EQUIPMENT: Popular music; tape or record player

ORGANIZATION:

- This workout warms, strengthens, and stretches the large muscle groups. Keep the "Animal Walk" distances short to avoid unnecessary fatigue. Have the players find a home and stand tall.

DESCRIPTION OF ACTIVITY:

1. **Big Steps-Little Steps:** On signal "Big Steps," walk forward with heavy, giant steps. On signal "Little Steps," move with light quick steps. On signal "Freeze!" bob up and down on the spot.
2. **Stepping Warm-up:** Run quickly in free space on your tip-toes, snapping your fingers high in the air in time to the music; now walk boldly on your heels, clapping your hands in front. Move forward with heavy, giant steps; then walk on the outside of your feet; then the inside of your feet. Continue to step out in this pattern.
3. **Lame Dog Walk:** Show me how you can walk on your hands and one foot while holding the "injured" foot off the floor. What sounds would a lame dog make?
4. **Seal Walk:** Begin in front support position with your hands turned slightly outward. Can you move forward, dragging your feet behind you and making seal-like sounds?
5. **Bear Walk:** From an all-fours position, take your weight on your hands and feet. Travel forward by moving the right hand and the right leg at the same time, then the left hand and the left leg together. Can you move backwards; sideways in this way?
6. **Emu Walk:** Keeping your legs almost straight, bend over and hold onto the front of your foot. Show me how you can walk forward in this position.
7. **Crab Walk:** From a hook-sit position, take your weight on your hands and feet without letting your seat touch the floor. Show me how you can move forward; backwards; sideways in this position.
8. **Chicken Walk:** From a squat position, put your arms between your legs and around the outside to grasp your ankles. Strut and squawk like a proud chicken.
9. **Lizard Squirm:** In front-lying position, use only your hands to slide you along the floor.
10. **Cat Stretch:** Begin in the all-fours position. Can you slowly lift your middle section upward as you take your weight on your toes and hands, stretching like a cat? Relax. Try this stretch two more times.

VARIATION:

Animal Walk Signals: When the players have learned to perform the animal walks and remember their names, give signals such as: "Chicken Walk to greet ten other players"; "Seal Walk along the black lines"; "Emu Walk from one end of the play area to the other"; "Bear Walk to one corner of the play area."

FA–11 10-MINUTE WORKOUT 5

FOCUS: Leg, arm, and shoulder strength

EQUIPMENT: Suitable music; tape or record player

ORGANIZATION:

- This workout involves working in pairs to warm, strengthen, and stretch the large muscle groups. Have players find a partner about the same size. For the first warm-up activity, one partner is "one"; the other partner is "two." Partners scatter throughout the play area.

DESCRIPTION OF ACTIVITY:

1. **Giraffes and Monkeys:** All players with the number one are the "Giraffes"; all those with the number two are the "Monkeys." Move around the play area by skipping (galloping, slide-stepping, hopping, running backward). On the signal "Giraffes!" the monkeys crawl between the Giraffes' legs; on the signal "Monkeys!" the Giraffes crawl between the Monkeys' legs. How many legs will you crawl under before I call the next signal?

2. **Bounce, Scoot, 'n Roll:** On signal "Bounce!" hold your partner's hands and together jump gently on the spot; on signal "Scoot!" run together anywhere in free space; on signal "Roll!" join hands and together roll along the floor.

3. **Partner Leapfrog:** One partner, kneel on all fours. The other partner, place your hands gently on your kneeling partner's back and leap over him or her, landing in the kneeling position yourself. Can you and your partner leapfrog from one end of the play area to the other?

4. **Twist and Touch:** Partners, stand back to back about one giant step apart. Without moving your feet, turn to the same side and touch partner's palms; turn to the other side and touch palms again. Continue this pattern for ten touches.

5. **Palm Push:** Face your partner with your arms raised straight ahead so that your palms are pressing against your partner's. Push as hard as you can against your partner's palms for ten seconds. Rest, then repeat.

6. **Foot Artist:** In hook-sit position, show me how you can lift one leg and draw a circle in the air with your pointed toes. Can you draw a circle going the opposite way? Repeat this using your other foot. Can you use your foot to spell your name? your partner's name? What else can you draw?

VARIATIONS:

a. **Tunnel Run:** One partner, stand tall with feet wide apart and one hand held palm up at waist level. The other partner, run behind and through the standing partner's legs to give him or her "five." This is one set. Change roles after every five sets.

b. **One-Hand Tug:** Have partners stand on either side of a line facing the other and grasp their right hands. Which partner can pull the other partner over to his or her side? Repeat this activity with a left hand hold. Challenge other players.

FA-12 AEROBIC SNAKE

FOCUS: Cardiovascular endurance

EQUIPMENT: Music with a strong 4/4 beat; tape or record player

ORGANIZATION:

- In this aerobic activity, children move through several different movement patterns. Vary the locomotor movements used as the "snake" moves in different patterns around the play area: walk forward, backward; gallop with one foot leading, then the other foot leading; slide-step facing one direction, then the other; skip forward; hop, alternating feet every four counts. Have children stand in a line at arm's length from each other. As you lead them at the head of the file, create various running patterns such as moving up and down the length of the play area; back and forth across the width of the area; from one diagonal corner to another; in concentric circular patterns. Emphasize staying in original order throughout the activity and moving in time to the music. Have children cool down by walking once around the play area and listening to their heartbeats. Discuss the importance of the heart needing regular activity to stay healthy.

DESCRIPTION OF ACTIVITY:

1. Clap in time to the music as we walk forward in our long aerobic snake. Let me hear the snake "hissss."
2. Jog and snap your fingers to the beat of the music. Let's pretend this is our snake "rattling."
3. Follow me around the play area as we move in different patterns. Can you keep all parts of the snake moving together?

FA-13 AEROBIC CIRCLE

FOCUS: Cardiovascular endurance

EQUIPMENT: Lively music; tape or record player

ORGANIZATION:

- During Aerobic Circle, children move continuously around a circle, alternating locomotor movements, which include walking, skipping, galloping, sliding, and hopping. Have children space themselves evenly around a large circle.
- Start and stop the warm-up with music. In the beginning, have the aerobic activity continue for one minute, and then have children jog on the spot for 20 seconds, followed by another activity session and jogging in place until three or four minutes have elapsed. Occasionally, call changes in direction, reinforcing the terms "clockwise" and "counterclockwise." As a break, use "Scrambled Eggs" signal from Organizational Signals. As children's fitness levels improve, gradually increase the duration and intensity of the movement, and increase the size of the circle. Encourage players to keep going! At the end of the warm-up, have players feel their heartbeats with one hand and tap out their pulse with their other hand.

DESCRIPTION OF ACTIVITY:

The following are movement suggestions:

—Walk, clapping hands above head; behind; in front.
—Walk on your toes; on your heels; on the inside of your feet, on the outside.
—Walk with giant steps; quick tiny steps.
—Hop, changing feet every four hops.
—Jump from side to side as you move forward.
—Walk backward, snapping fingers in time to the music.
—Leap forward with big arm swings.
—Slip forward with arm swings.
—Slide-step facing inward; facing outward.
—Gallop, changing the leading foot every eight counts.

SLIDE-STEP WITH ARM CIRCLES

FA-14 SWIM ROUTINE

FOCUS: Cardiovascular endurance; rhythm sense

EQUIPMENT: Selected music such as the Beach Boys' "Surfin' Safari"; tape or record player

ORGANIZATION:

- This routine provides a fun aerobic activity while enhancing sense of rhythm. Have children find their own home space and face you. Make sure that everyone can see you. Emphasize that children cannot touch others as they move and that they should try to move in time with the music.

DESCRIPTION OF ACTIVITY:

1. Let's pretend that our play area is the beach and we are going to go for a swim! On signal *"Beach!"* jog anywhere around the play area for 16 counts. Change directions often.

2. On signal *"Front Crawl!"* stay on the spot while lifting one arm and then the other up, forward, and around to eight slow counts, just as if you were swimming in water.

3. On signal *"Back Crawl,"* lift one arm and then the other up, back, and around for four slow counts; then repeat for eight quick counts. Now place your hands on hips, jump with feet together for two counts to the left side, then two counts to the right side. "Push" your hips out to that side each time.

4. On signal *"Beach!"* jog in free space again for 16 counts.

5. On signal *"Breast Stroke,"* stay on the spot while bringing straight arms together forward and then opening them to each side for eight slow counts.

6. Repeat the sequence in number three. Then on signal *"Beach!"* jog again in free space for 16 counts.

7. On signal *"Sidestroke!"* stay on the spot as you roll hand over hand; then extend one arm upward and at the same time the other arm downward. Repeat this action, alternating arms for eight slow counts.

8. Repeat sequence in number three; then jog in place for another eight counts while you do your own "Swim" stroke, such as the "Dog Paddle," until the music ends.

VARIATION:

Butterfly: Add this swim stroke to the routine above by having children jump forward while at the same time throwing their arms back, around, and forward for eight slow counts.

FA–15 THE EXERCISE GAME

FOCUS: Aerobic warm-up

EQUIPMENT: Lively background music; tape or record player; set of activity cards; one mat per player

ORGANIZATION:

- Prepare on 3" by 5" cards a variety of endurance, agility, strength, and flexibility tasks. Write at least two activities for every participant. Preserve the task cards by laminating them. Scatter these cards face down in the center of the play area. Ask the players to jog in place in their "homes." Choose one player to pick up a card from the center area and hand it to you; then read it aloud. On signal "Go!" players perform the challenge task on the card, and then return to their homes to jog in place. Continue in this way until you feel the players have had a sufficient warm-up.

DESCRIPTION OF ACTIVITY:

—Touch the middle of each wall or sideline. Use a different locomotor movement to get to each wall.

—Do eight Pogo Springs in each corner of the play area.

—Hop to four different mats and do eight sit-ups at each one. Slide-step along the length of the play area, facing inward, and around the width, facing outward.

—Give "ten" to ten different players.

—Touch five pieces of equipment in the play area with a different body part each time.

—Do two left elbow swing-arounds with four different people.

—"Glue" your feet to the floor and walk your hands in a circle around your feet.

—Quickly get in groups of three and together sing your favorite nursery rhyme while lunging one leg forward and stretching it, and then lunging the other leg forward to stretch it.

—Give eight different players a "Crab Walk Greeting" by touching the bottom of your foot to the bottom of another player's.

VARIATIONS:

a. To ensure that a balanced workout occurs, color-code the cards according to the fitness component areas: GREEN—Endurance; RED—Strength; BLUE—Flexibility; YELLOW—Agility. Have players select cards from each of these component areas.

b. Design an "Exercise Game" for outside, using the available space and equipment in your school area.

FA-16 CREATIVE OBSTACLE COURSE

FOCUS: Aerobic warm-up; imagination; cooperation

EQUIPMENT: Cone markers;
scooters;
balance benches;
climbing chairs;
tables and chairs;
carpet squares;
mats;
hoops;
beanbags;
music with a strong 4/4 beat;
tape or record player

ORGANIZATION:

• Divide the class into groups of five to six players. Have each group begin by sitting cross-legged in a line at one end of the play area. Discuss with the class what is an obstacle course. Issue any type of available safe equipment to the groups that they can go over, under, around, across, through, on, and off. Assign each group a set of equipment. Stress that players move safely through the course, staying in order. Use music to start and stop the activity. Have groups rotate about every two or three minutes.

DESCRIPTION OF ACTIVITY:

1. On the signal "Go!" each group collect your equipment and, working together, in front of your line, create an obstacle course that stretches to the other end of the play area. Return to your starting position when you have completed the course.

2. When you hear the music play, the leader of each group decide how your group will move through the obstacle course. You remain the leader until the music stops; then each group quickly return to sit in your starting position. Change the leader after each rotation.

3. On signal "Rotate!" each group move to the obstacle course on your right as your group faces the opposite end of the play area. The first group must march together around the play area, saying in unison: "I will never smoke! I will never smoke! . . ." until the group reaches the last obstacle course.

4. Each group continue in this way until all obstacle courses have been visited.

VARIATION:

Other ideas for creating an obstacle course include: footprints to walk on (forward, backward, sideways); handprints to creep on; climbing frame to move up, down, across, through, or hang; climbing ropes to hang or swing on; tunnels to crawl through; ladder to scamper between the rungs or to walk hands and feet on top; large tubular tires to climb through, over, or under and to jump in and out of; wands to jump over.

FA-17 FITKID CIRCUIT

FOCUS: Aerobic endurance; arm and shoulder, leg, abdominal strength; flexibility

EQUIPMENT: Activity station signs; lively music; tape or record player; cone markers; several beanbags; two to four benches

ORGANIZATION:

- Set up eight to ten "Fitkid" activity stations around the perimeter of the play area, positioning them in a circle, oval, or rectangle. Make station signs (that depict vigorous, continuous exercises) on posterboard that can be folded in half and then stand on its own. Laminate the signs to improve their durability.

- Explain how to perform each activity, emphasizing correct technique; then have a maximum of four children go to each station. Play music to begin and stop the activity. At first have children perform the activity for 20 seconds, with 10 seconds to rotate. Then gradually increase the activity time. Have children feel their heartbeats before, during, and after the circuit is completed. Discuss differences.

DESCRIPTION OF ACTIVITY:

1. **Bell Jumps:** Jump back and forth over a line.

2. **Quarter Turns:** Jump to face each wall of the play area, clapping your hands for each turn. Change direction after each full turn.

3. **Knee Push-Ups:** Begin in the all-fours position. Lean forward to take your weight on your hands. Slowly bend and straighten your arms. Keep your back flat as you lower and raise your upper body.

4. **Tummy Tightener:** Sit in long-sit position. Lean back slightly and pretend to climb a rope hand over hand. Raise feet slightly off the floor.

5. **Jumping Jacks:** Place your hands on your hips. Jump your feet apart; then together. Can you jump your feet apart and, at the same time, clap your hands overhead?

6. **Crab Walk Dance:** From hook-sit position, take your weight on your hands and feet, lifting your bottom off the floor. Now lift one hand off the floor to touch your bottom; then lift the other hand.

7. **Cone Slide:** Slide in a circle CW around a cone. Change direction after every two circles of the cone.

8. **Bench Walk:** Walk along the benches, balancing a beanbag on your head.

9. **Stretcher:** At the end of the circuit, do your favorite stretch and hold it for at least ten seconds.

VARIATIONS:

a. Have children run once around the play area before stopping at the next station.

b. Give children "Fitkid" certificates for completing the circuit and for improving their performance.

Section **3**

Movement Awareness

The Movement Awareness activities help to develop the movement principles of space awareness, body awareness, and effort awareness and relationships. These are used to set tasks that ask *What? Where? How can?* and *Who can?* The children respond to the task or problem by exploring and experimenting at the floor level, on low apparatus, or on large apparatus, with or without equipment.

This section offers 35 Movement Awareness activities, including:

MA-1 EXPLORING PERSONAL AND GENERAL SPACE

FOCUS: Space awareness; safety training

EQUIPMENT: None

ORGANIZATION:

- This section is a forerunner of the Dance, Gymnastics, and Game Skills sections and, therefore, should be taught first. The concepts, principles, and movement vocabulary can then be directly applied to these areas; in fact, to all forms of human movement.

- The four basic themes of Movement Awareness are Space Awareness, Body Awareness, Effort Awareness, and Relationships, which are integrated throughout this section. These themes are further divided into subthemes which provide a wide variety of movement experiences and are sequentially arranged. Beginning with floor tasks and progressing to manipulative equipment and apparatus, children work individually, with a partner, and in groups.

- Revise Signals, Formations, and Starting positions from Introductory Activities 1–6. To begin, train the children to move safely in general space, to identify a personal space, and to listen properly. Establish your start and stop signals and insist that on the "Freeze!" signal, they are to stop immediately—no sliding, no bumping.

DESCRIPTION OF ACTIVITY:

1. Find your own home or personal space. Check your space; can you touch anyone else or anything? If so, move to a free space. Now let's explore moving different body parts in your home space:

   — Move your feet; head; hands; elbows.

   — Can you get your feet higher than your head?

   — Can you move your hands, feet, and seat together?

2. On signal "Move!" leave your home and travel about the play area. Watch out for others. Now you are moving in general space. Freeze! Quickly return home and long-sit, facing me. Can you find your home?

3. **"Scrambled Eggs!":** Move in and out of each other in this half of the play area only. Don't touch anyone. "Freeze!" Change the way you are moving. Now travel about in half of this area. No collisions. "Freeze!" Change direction and continue. "Freeze!" Return home on three body parts.

4. Explore moving about in general space on different body parts: one foot; hands and feet; seat and feet; one knee, one foot, and one hand. "Freeze!" Now move slowly with one body part leading. "Freeze!" Travel quickly with another body part leading. (Repeat several times.)

5. Find a partner and explore moving together in personal space. Now move together in general space. "Freeze!" Quickly return home. Find another pair and join hands to form a group of four. Sit in a circle in your home space. On signal "Corners!", each group, touch the four corners of the play area with a different body part each time; then return home to sit in a circle again. Don't forget to hold hands while you move and watch out for other groups.

MA-2 IDENTIFYING BOUNDARIES

FOCUS: General space awareness; safety

EQUIPMENT: Cone markers

ORGANIZATION:

• Mark out the boundaries of the play area with cone markers. Point out the boundaries to the children: corners, sides, ends, middle, (walls, ceiling, floor if inside). Observe children to check on response to signals and their understanding of the terms "boundaries" and "diagonally opposite." Praise good listening and performance.

DESCRIPTION OF ACTIVITY:

1. Follow me as I walk around the play area. The sides and ends of the play area form the boundaries.

2. Run to touch opposite sidelines with both elbows; gallop to touch opposite endlines with one knee and one hand; slide to diagonally opposite corners and touch with any three body parts; then find a home in the play area. How quickly can you step outside of the boundaries? Jump inside the boundaries; then return to your home.

3. Now I am going to make the play area a lot smaller by moving the cone markers. Travel along the boundaries of this area. "Hit the Deck!" Let's make the play area even smaller. Move inside this area without touching anyone. "Clear the Deck!" by stepping out of bounds as quickly as you can.

4. I will number you off one, two; one, two; one, two; etc. All number one's, find a home inside the boundary area and stand still. All number two's, move in and around the standing players until I call "Freeze!" Now number one's, stand still while the number two's move in and out of you.

5. *Boundary Game:* Find a partner, scatter and stand together, holding hands, in a home space. Together, run to the boundary line that I am pointing to and touch it with four hands. Good! Run to the boundary line I am pointing to now. Touch it with your seats. Listen for the signal to stop: "Freeze!"; "Hit the Deck!"; or "Clear the Deck!" Watch where you are going at all times.

MA-3 LIFTING AND CARRYING EQUIPMENT

FOCUS: Space awareness; safety training

EQUIPMENT: One bench per group;
chairs;
hoops;
tables;
mats;
box horse;
springboard;
basket of beanbags;
cart of play balls;
cone markers;
climbing apparatus

ORGANIZATION:

- Tour the equipment room. Have the children name each piece of equipment. Show them how the equipment has been organized and stored in shelves, baskets, and carts. Explain and demonstrate how to set up the climbing apparatus and the importance of placing mats under the apparatus for safety. Form groups of five to six, each group with a Leader. Teach children how to lift, carry, arrange, and put away the equipment and apparatus safely and efficiently. Observe groups, how they lift and carry the equipment, cooperate with each other, and return the equipment. Discuss concerns. Praise good performance.

DESCRIPTION OF ACTIVITY:

1. To begin, Group 1 will demonstrate how to correctly lift and carry a bench: three children on each side of the bench, all face the same direction; bend your knees, and together lift the bench with both hands, keeping your backs straight. Walk, not run, over here, lowering the bench into place slowly. Do not drop. Make sure no toes are underneath! (The balance beam, large mats, and tables are carried in a similar way, except that one player is at each end of the equipment.)

2. Now each group lift and carry your bench to the place I point to. Set it there carefully; then straddle-sit on the bench one behind the other, facing me. Well done!

3. *Group 1,* your job is to bring out 12 hoops and scatter them around the play area.

   Group 2, place the cone markers around the boundaries of the play area, spacing them one giant step apart.

   Group 3, bring out six folding mats and place them under the climbing ropes and climbing frame.

   Group 4, bring out the basket of beanbags and cart of balls and place them in the center of the play area.

   Group 5, carry two chairs, one table, one box horse and set up an obstacle course at this end of the play area.

   Now let's observe how each group arranged the equipment. Have you any suggestions for improving the arrangement?

4. *Follow-the-Leader:* Leaders, take your group in and out, over and under, on and off, across, through and around, up and down the apparatus and use the equipment that has been set out. On signal "Change," the next team member becomes the leader. Remember to move safely at all times.

5. Now class, it is time to put all the equipment away! Each group, please return the equipment to its proper place. Remember that the balls are put into containers, not thrown in! Group 2, you will put away the climbing frame; Group 4, you will look after the climbing ropes, as well.

MA-4 DIRECTIONS, PATHWAYS, AND PATTERNS

FOCUS: Space awareness

EQUIPMENT: One drum

ORGANIZATION:

- Directions involve movement that is forward, backwards, sideways, up and down, and diagonally on different body parts, in personal and general space. To begin, have children stand in their homes, facing you. "Pathway" is the track which the body makes as it travels about in general space, on the apparatus and through the air. A "pattern" is a predictable pathway or route. On posterboard or chalkboard, draw the different pathways (zig-zagged, curved, straight, winding, and spiral) and patterns (circle, triangle, square, rectangle, figure-8, a letter, a number). Have children begin in their own homes.

DESCRIPTION OF ACTIVITY:

1. Show me how you can travel forward on different body parts: on your seat; on your tummy; on your back; on three body parts; on your hands and feet.

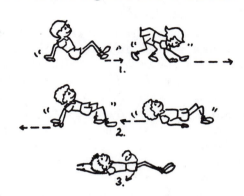

2. Now travel backwards in general space. Watch where you are going so that you don't bump into anyone! "Freeze!" Show me how you can travel backwards on different body parts: on your hands and feet, facing upward; on your back; on three body parts; on your front. Who can move slowly in a backwards direction; then quickly in a forward direction?

3. How can you travel sideways on different body parts? Show me another way. Now travel diagonally on different body parts. Can you make different body parts lead the way?

4. Make a **Directions Story.** Use any three directions you have learned. Your story should have a *Beginning*, a *Middle* part, and an *Ending*. For example: In back-lying position, roll forward; move sideways by twisting your feet; move backwards using your feet and hands.

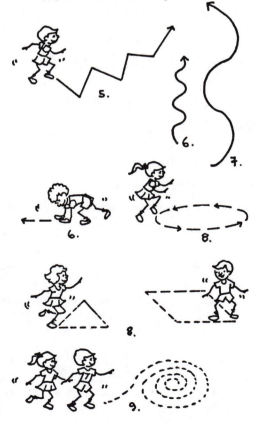

5. Now let's explore travelling in different pathways. Look at this picture of a zig-zagged pathway (sharp angled turns). Show me how you can travel around the play area in this way, then return to your home. Try not to touch anyone.

6. Now travel in a straight pathway on four body parts. "Freeze!" Change direction and travel a straight pathway of three body parts. Show me how you can travel by winding your way back home.

7. Look at this picture of a curved pathway. Show me how you can travel in this way, making small curves; then large curves. Zig-zag your way home.

8. Now let's explore travelling in different patterns. Can you travel in a circular pattern, just in your personal space? Show me how you can travel in general space in a square pattern; a triangular pattern; a figure-8 pattern; your favorite letter. Can you use different body parts as you travel in these pathways? Change directions often.

9. Follow me around the play area as we travel together in a spiral pathway. Now return to your home and travel in your own spiral pathway. Look at my pictures of the two spiral pathways. Which pathway did you travel in? How can you travel in the other direction?

10. **Pathway Story:** Choose three different pathways you have learned. Put them together to create a story, using different body parts and directions, with a beginning, a middle, and an ending. Finish in your home space.

MA-5 EXPLORING DIRECTIONS AND PATHWAYS

FOCUS: Space awareness

EQUIPMENT: Posterboard; marking pen (or chalkboard and chalk); drum (optional)

ORGANIZATION:

- Children explore various ways of combining directions and pathways they have learned. Use posterboard pictures to show examples that they can try. Provide ample opportunity for them to create their own combinations. Have children begin in their homes.

DESCRIPTION OF ACTIVITY:

1. You have learned to travel in four different directions and several different pathways. Now let's experiment with combining these. Look at the following pictures. Can you use different body parts as you move? Examples:

Directions	Pathways
backwards	zig-zag
sideways	circular
forward	spiral
backwards	winding

2. Now put together your own direction and pathway combination. Travel in this way and finish in your home.
3. Show me how you can put together any three pathways and directions and travel about the play area in this way. Now, while the girls watch, boys show us your routine; then girls, it's your turn.

MA-6 EXPLORING LEVELS

FOCUS: Space and body awareness

EQUIPMENT: None

ORGANIZATION:

- Children explore moving in personal and general space, at different levels from high, to medium, to low, in different pathways, and directions on different body parts. Have children begin in their homes.

DESCRIPTION OF ACTIVITY:

1. Show me how you can be at a high level in your personal space. Now move to a medium level; then to a low level.
2. Now let's explore taking different body parts from a high level, to a medium level, to a low level: feet; nose; elbows; hands; tummy, . . . (Reverse levels and repeat.)
3. Travel in a forward direction at a high level, in a winding pathway. "Freeze!" Move backwards at a medium level, in a circular pathway. "Freeze!" Return home by moving sideways at a low level, in a straight pathway.
4. Show me how different animals travel at a high level—giraffe, kangaroo, ostrich, eagle; at a medium level—bear, panther, frog; at a low level—snake, alligator, snail.
5. Find a partner. Show me how you can copy your partner's movements as he or she travels in general space at different levels, directions, and pathways, using different body parts. Take turns.

MA-7 EXPLORING RANGES

FOCUS: Space and body awareness

EQUIPMENT: One drum

ORGANIZATION:

- Discuss the meaning of a "Range": refers to how close one thing is to another. A range can be near to, far from; long, short; large, small; wide, narrow. Children explore using different ranges in personal and general space, noticing how their body shape also changes. Have children begin in their homes.

DESCRIPTION OF ACTIVITY:

1. In your home, make a shape with your hands and feet far away from your body; near to your body. Is your new shape small or large?
2. Can you make a shape with two body parts far away from each other and two other body parts near to each other?
3. Travel in general space. Stay far from neighbors. As soon as you come close to someone, spring away. Now move about in general space with the biggest movements you can make. Show me how you can travel with small movements. Can you change your directions and levels and find another way to do this?
4. Find a partner. One partner, try to follow the other partner, without touching. Leader, make it difficult for your partner to follow you. On my drum beat signal "Freeze!" stop immediately. Follower, are you close enough to touch your partner? If so, switch roles. (Repeat several times.)

MA-8 USING MANIPULATIVE EQUIPMENT

FOCUS: Space and body awareness; ball manipulation

EQUIPMENT: One ball per player

ORGANIZATION:

- Children learn to manipulate and control a ball in personal and general space; in different directions, pathways, levels and ranges, on different body parts. Have two children bring out a ball cart, while the others scatter and find a home. These helpers then roll a ball to each player until all have a ball.

DESCRIPTION OF ACTIVITY:

1. In your home, show me how you can hold the ball with your knees; your feet; under your chin; under your arms. How many different ways can you hold your ball high? at a medium level? low?
2. Put the ball on the floor. Can you move the ball in different directions along the floor: backwards; sideways; forward? Try moving the ball far from you; close to you; in a small area; in a large area.
3. Can you move your ball from one body part to another? Now show me how you can move the ball using different body parts.
4. Travel in different pathways while moving your ball. How can you change levels while moving your ball? Show me how you can bounce your ball from a low level to a high level.
5. With a partner, explore moving one ball between you. Can you use different body parts; different levels? How can you travel in different directions or pathways while moving the ball between you?

MA-9 TRAVELLING ON APPARATUS

FOCUS: Space and body awareness

EQUIPMENT: Mats;
benches;
hoops;
chairs;
cone markers;
box horse or tables;
climbing frame

ORGANIZATION:

• Children explore ways of travelling on the apparatus in different directions, pathways, ranges and levels, and using different body parts. Have teams collect and arrange the equipment throughout the play area. Remind players about the safety procedures for lifting and carrying the equipment. Encourage children to be creative. Praise and point out good effort. Check for changes of direction, pathways, ranges, levels, and body parts. Provide ample time for them to explore different movements, and let them observe each other. Children begin by standing near a piece of equipment.

DESCRIPTION OF ACTIVITY:

1. Can you move in different directions in general space without touching the apparatus or any person? Move in a forward direction; move backwards; move sideways to the right; move sideways to the left. On the signal "Freeze!" squat down low and stay very still. Are you in control?

2. Now show me how you can move in a different pathway to each piece of apparatus. Touch it with a different body part each time. For example, move by zig-zagging to the box horse and touching it with your elbows.

3. Show me how you can travel over, under, along, on and off, around and through the apparatus:
   — changing directions
   — changing pathways
   — changing levels
   — using different body parts

   For example, move forward on your tummy along the bench; climb a square pattern on the climbing frame; zig-zag in and out of the hoops; roll sideways in a straight pathway along a mat; wind your way backwards at a medium level through the cones; move on hands and feet over the box.

4. Can you travel on the apparatus keeping your body near to the apparatus as you go? Now try travelling keeping your body parts far from each other.

5. **Apparatus Game:** Travel on the apparatus as above. On the signal "Freeze!" make a long, wide, or rounded shape on the apparatus. Watch where you are going at all times. (Repeat several times, varying the "freezing" shape.)

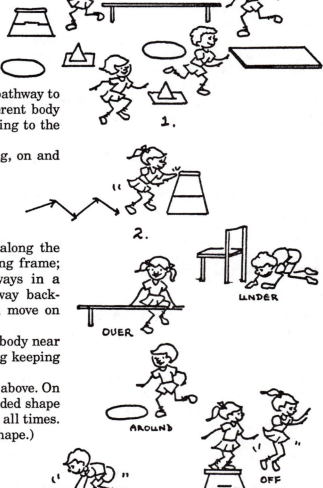

MA-10 EXPLORING WALKING MOVEMENTS

FOCUS: Space and body awareness   **EQUIPMENT:** Drum (optional)

ORGANIZATION:

- In the following activities, children explore travelling using different Locomotor Movements. In this activity, children explore Walking Movements in different directions, pathways, levels, speeds, and parts leading; and using different foot parts. Check for good walking form, listening, stopping quickly, and holding freezes.

DESCRIPTION OF ACTIVITY:

1. Walk in general space, stopping on signal (drum beat); then continue walking, changing to a different foot part: toes, heel; inside, outside; toes turned in, toes turned out; tiny steps, big steps. Watch where you are going! Now show me your best walking style: let your heel touch first; then rock to the ball and toes of your foot. Keep your head up, shoulders down, tummy tucked in, feet moving straight ahead, and arms swinging slightly.

2. Walk in different directions: forward, backwards, sideways, diagonally. Good! Now change your walking direction every time you hear one drum beat; "Freeze!" on two drum beats.

3. As you walk forward, change from a high level to a low level, low level to a high level, every time you hear the drum beat. Can you walk backwards at a low level; sideways at a high level; diagonally at a medium level?

4. Walk slowly; then gradually get faster. This is called acceleration. Walk quickly and gradually get slower until you are walking in slow motion. This is called deceleration. Walk slowly at a low level; walk quickly at a high level.

5. Let's explore walking in different pathways (zig-zag, curved; winding, straight, spiral) away from your home. "Freeze" on my drum beat on your toes! On signal "Walk!" walk in a different pathway back to your home.

6. Walk in a circle around your home; in a triangle pattern. Show me how you can walk backwards in a rectangle pattern; sideways tracing the number "8." Can you walk the first letter of your name?

7. Can you walk like a soldier marching on parade; with a limp; holding your ankles; with one stiff knee?

8. Show me how you can walk forward with your head leading. On my drum beat, "Freeze," then change direction and body part that leads. For example, walk backwards with your seat leading. Can you walk sideways with your elbow leading? (Try these again moving in different pathways.)

9. *Line Tag:* All players, including two ITs, must walk forward or backwards on the lines only. If a player is tagged on the shoulder, that player becomes the new IT and the game continues.

10. Invent your own "cool" walk!

MA-11 EXPLORING RUNNING AND DODGING MOVEMENTS

FOCUS: Space awareness; locomotion; footwork

EQUIPMENT: Several cone markers; four direction signs; one drum

ORGANIZATION:

- Children explore running in different directions, pathways, levels, and speeds, starting and stopping. They learn to run with good form: head up, eyes forward, upper body relaxed, arms swinging back and forward instead of sideways, knees lifting, contact on the balls of their feet, breathing naturally.
- Discuss the term "dodging" or darting quickly away from someone or something, and "marking" or following a player as closely as possible.
- Scatter several cones throughout one half of the play area. Make four direction signs: North, South, East, and West and tape to appropriate walls.

DESCRIPTION OF ACTIVITY:

1. Run on the balls of your feet into free space. Change direction on my drum beat. Freeze when you hear two drum beats. Show me your best style. Don't bump into anyone. Run backwards, changing direction on my drum beat. Now run and change direction on your own. Make quick, sharp changes of direction.
2. Can you run low, gradually getting taller and taller? Run changing from a high level to a low level. Show me how you can run lifting your knees high and clapping your hands. Run with your arms high in the air; behind your back; stiff at your sides; circling your arms sideways; swinging your arms at the sides. Which way feels best for you?
3. Show me how you can run in a zig-zag pathway; circular pathway; spiral pathway; figure-8; rectangular pathway. How can you run in a winding pathway in and out of the cone markers?
4. Run as lightly as possible; as heavily as possible. Run with tiny steps; with long strides.
5. Run into spaces. Stop (one drum beat) and start (two drum beats) on signal. Be sure to stop on your feet—no sliding. Run in a straight pathway back to your home. Once there, run in place.
6. Now run toward someone, stop in front of them, and then dart off in another direction. (Repeat several times.) This is called dodging. Run slowly. Show me how you can gradually speed up until you are running quickly. "Freeze!" Remember, this is called accelerating. Run quickly; then gradually slow down. This is called decelerating. Stop in your home. Now walk away from your home; then suddenly burst into a run! "Freeze!"
7. *North, South, East, West:* Point to the direction sign as I call them out. Run North; run West; run South; run Northeast; etc.
8. *Dodge and Mark:* Find a partner. One partner be the Dodger; the other partner, the Marker. On signal "Walk," Dodger, walk about in general space, moving into free spaces. Marker, follow behind as closely as you can. On signal "Freeze!" both stop immediately. Marker, take one giant step forward. If you can touch the Dodger, then trade roles; otherwise, stay as you are, waiting for the next start signal. (Use starting signals such as: walk backwards; run forward; run backwards.)

VARIATION:

Outside Signals: Run between the trees. Run uphill; run downhill. Run around the swing set; the climbing apparatus. Play "Follow the Leader." Change speeds as you move.

MA-12 EXPLORING LEAPING MOVEMENTS

FOCUS: Space awareness; flight and landings

EQUIPMENT: One hoop per team;
two short ropes per team;
one carpet square or small mat per child;
cone markers;
benches

ORGANIZATION:

• "Leaping" is the action of springing from one foot and landing on the other foot. Children learn to leap with good height by pushing off one foot and reaching up and over with the other foot and using their arms to help them. Have them practice "soft" landings—landing with toe, ball, and heel of foot while bending knees. Have children begin in a home space.

DESCRIPTION OF ACTIVITY:

1. Show me how you can run forward and leap into the air. How far can you go? How lightly can you land? Repeat in another direction. Can you leap farther this time? Leap again, but this time show me how your other foot can lead you through your leap.

2. Now show me how you can leap high for something; grab it; and land lightly with relaxed knees. Repeat. Try with your other foot leading. Explore leaping with the same arm and leg forward; with opposite arm and leg forward; with your arms swinging upward; with your arms by your sides. Which is best?

3. Pick up a carpet square and place it on the floor in your home space. Check for good spacing. Practice leaping over it. Can you leap over your square and land lightly facing the direction from which you came? Practice. Leap over ten different squares and return to your home hoop.

4. *Leap Away:* Girls, scatter, find a home and curl up, facing the floor. Boys, on signal "Leap Away!" leap over as many girls as you can. Remember to watch where you are going. "Freeze!" Boys, curl up, and girls, become the leapers.

5. Find different ways to land on your feet. Run, "fly" through the air. Land on one foot; on the other foot; on both feet; with feet close together; with feet far apart; with one foot ahead of the other. Make your landing "soft," bending at the knees, ankles, and hips, to absorb the force of your landing.

6. *Leap the Brook:* (Use floor or masking tape to mark off several brooks, which start out narrow and gradually widen. Divide the class into teams of four to six players and have each team stand in a line at the narrowest part of the brook.) Starting at the narrowest part, take turns, leaping over the brook. Explore different ways of leaping (making shapes, turning in the air) and landing softly (on one foot; other foot; both feet; feet together; feet apart). Who will leap the widest part of the brook?

7. *Leaping Lizards Relay:* (Have each team stand in a line behind a starting line and face a line of obstacles [spaced three meters or ten feet apart] in front of them. Let each team design its own course.) On the signal "Leap!" each player in turn, leap over each of the obstacles, and then return to tag the next player in your team, who repeats the task. The first team to complete the relay and sit cross-legged in a line is the winner.

MA-13 EXPLORING JUMPING AND HOPPING_____

FOCUS: Space awareness; jumping; hopping

EQUIPMENT: Mats;
hoops;
ropes;
wands;
one "footsie" per pair

"FOOTSIE"

ORGANIZATION:

- "Jumping" is the action of pushing off with both feet and landing on both feet; "hopping" is the action of springing from one foot and landing on the same foot. Children explore jumping and hopping in personal and general space in different levels, directions, and pathways, with a variety of equipment and through games. They learn to use their arms for forward motion and balance, spring off the balls of their feet, and land lightly bending at the knees, ankles, and hips to absorb the force of the landing. Use Breaks (see Section 2) in between the jumping and hopping tasks which involve body parts other than the legs.
- To make a "Footsie" or an ankle jumper, you will need one small plastic container with lid; 1–1.2-meter (four-foot) piece of rope; one large plastic bleach bottle; and one roll of masking tape. Cut out a small hole in the side of the small container. Place one end of the rope through this hole and knot it to prevent it from slipping out. Tape or glue the lid securely shut. Cut a 2.5-centimeter (one-inch) strip out of the bleach bottle to make the ankle ring. Tie the other end of the rope to it.
- To begin, have children find their homes.

DESCRIPTION OF ACTIVITY:

1. In your home, jump low; jump high; higher! Can you alternate low and high jumps? How far can you jump? How far can you jump in three jumps in a row? Jump and land with your feet sideways, apart; jump and land with your feet together again; jump and crisscross your feet sideways; jump and click your heels in the air.
2. Hop in place on your right foot four times; then hop four times on your left foot. Hop three times on each foot; two times; once. On your right foot, hop forward four times; hop backwards four times to place; hop to the right four times; hop to the left four times. Repeat on left foot.
3. Jump in different pathways: circle figure-8, favorite letter. Repeat hopping; change foot every four hops. Practice jump-turns; quarter turns; half turns; three-quarter turns; full turns. Jump in either direction.
4. Hop, holding the free foot in different positions: right hand holding right foot behind; left hand holding right foot behind; holding the free foot in front; to the side.
5. Stretch a rope along the floor. Jump back and forth over the rope from one end to the other end. Jump backwards to the start. Hop back and forth over the rope; change hopping foot to return. Stand just behind your rope. Take off and land in the following ways: from one foot to two feet; from one foot to the same foot; from one foot to the other foot; from two feet to one foot; from two feet to two feet. Repeat with a run-up.
6. *Using Equipment:* Place a hoop on the floor. Jump in and out of it in different ways. Repeat by hopping in and out of your hoop. Jump over the width of your mat. Can you jump the length of your mat? Have a partner hold a wand just off the floor. Jump over it. How high can you safely jump?
7. *Footsie:* With a partner, find a free space. Take turns jumping over the rope as you swing the ankle jumper CW; then CCW. Change to your other foot and repeat. Now, while one partner wears the footsie and keeps the rope turning, the other partner jump over it. Switch roles. Raise the ankle ring so that the rope will swing higher, and do these tasks again!
8. *Hoop Hopping:* (Divide the class into groups of four or five and have each group collect six hoops.) Arrange your hoops on the floor in any pattern that you wish. Now try hopping through your hoops in a follow-the-leader formation. Visit other groups and hop through their hoop pattern. Two groups combine your hoops to create even more interesting patterns. Explore hopping through the pattern. Visit other hoop patterns.

MA-14 HOPSCOTCH GAMES

FOCUS: Space awareness; hopping and jumping

EQUIPMENT: One beanbag per child; floor tape or chalk

ORGANIZATION:

- Use floor tape to mark out two identical hopscotch patterns from each station as shown. Divide the class into groups of four or five; assign two groups to a station and allow them to practice hopping through the pattern.
- Explain the rules of the game: take turns to play; use beanbags to toss; lose your turn if you step on a line, toss your beanbag on a line or the wrong space, change your hopping foot, or land on both feet in other than the allowed space; take your turn again when the other players in your group have had their turn. Rotate groups every ten minutes to a different hopscotch station.

DESCRIPTION OF ACTIVITY:

1. ***Basic Hopscotch:*** Toss your beanbag into the first square. Hop into the first space, pick up your beanbag, and hop out. Hop on the same foot each time. Beanbags and feet must not touch the lines. Continue your turn, throwing the beanbag into each space, following the numbered order, until you lose your turn. Remember that in spaces 4 and 5, and 7 and 8, land with both feet on the floor at the same time, one foot in each space.

2. ***Half-Moon Hopscotch:*** Toss your beanbag into the first square; then hop into this square, pick up your beanbag, and hop out. Now toss your beanbag into the second square. Hop into the first square; then into the second square; pick up your beanbag, and then hop into the first square and out. Continue in this way, up and back down. In spaces 4 and 5, and 7 and 8, land with both feet on the ground at the same time, one foot in each space. Also land with two feet in the "moon" space.

3. ***Ladder Hopscotch:*** Toss your beanbag into the first square. Hop over this square into the second square; pick up your beanbag and hop into the first square and out. Now toss your beanbag into the second square. Hop into the first square, over the second square, and into the third square. Turn around, pick up your beanbag, and hop into the second and first squares and out. Continue in this way up, then down, the ladder.

4. ***Shuffleboard Hopscotch:*** Stand on one foot and toss the beanbag into the first square. Then hop over this square into all of the other spaces: land with one foot in squares 1, 4, 7, and 10 (change hopping foot here); land with two feet in squares 2 and 3, 5 and 6, 8 and 9. Upon reaching square 2 on the return, lean forward and pick up your beanbag, hop into square 1, and out. Continue in this way.

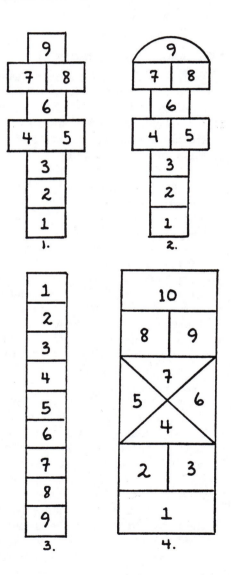

VARIATION:

If outside, use chalk on the tarmac or sidewalk surface and draw the different hopscotch games.

A–15 EXPLORING SKIPPING, GALLOPING, AND SIDE-STEPPING _____

FOCUS: Space awareness

EQUIPMENT: None

ORGANIZATION:

- "Skipping" is a series of "step-hops" performed by alternating the feet. Have children practice the alternate step-hopping in slow motion at first until they feel the rhythm easily. Point out that skipping is done on the balls of the feet with the arms swinging in opposition to the legs. Emphasize smoothness and rhythm, not distance and speed. "Galloping" is a forward movement with one foot always leading and the other foot following. Have children practice with one foot leading, then the other. "Side-Stepping" is a similar movement, except that the leading foot steps sideways, while the other foot quickly follows. The movement should be practiced in both directions so that each foot has a chance to lead as well as trail. Sliding should be a graceful, smooth, and controlled movement, done on the balls of the feet.
- Have children practice these locomotor movements, and then explore changing directions, pathways, levels, and speeds.

DESCRIPTION OF ACTIVITY:

1. Let's learn the skipping footwork. Take a step forward with one foot, followed by a small hop on that same foot: "Step, Hop." Now do the same action with the other foot: "Step, Hop." Repeat several times until the action feels smooth and rhythmical.

2. Show me how you can skip swinging your arms and lifting your knees high. Does the opposite arm and leg move at the same time? Be happy as you skip! Clap your hands; snap your fingers as you skip along. Try to side-step at a low level so that your hands touch the floor. Now side-step with your arms held out sideways at shoulder height; hands clapping overhead.

3. Skip forward in general space, in and out of your classmates, changing directions to avoid bumping into anyone. Good! Now show me how you can skip backwards. Watch where you are going! Gallop in and out of each other, with one foot leading, then the other.

4. Skip in different pathways: zig-zag; curvy; in a straight pathway; in a circle; in a figure-8 pattern. Return home and skip in place. Repeat by galloping; by side-stepping.

5. Skip lightly; heavily; skip slowly; quickly. Pretend that you are a wild horse. Gallop slowly; gallop quickly. Gallop slowly; then quickly; then slowly again. Repeat this side-stepping.

6. Side-step to your right. "Freeze!" Side-step to your left. Show me how you can side-step across the play area, changing directions at will. Remember to watch out for others and keep sideways. Can you side-step in the same direction while changing the leading foot?

7. Find a partner and, holding hands, skip side by side, changing pathways and directions on my drumbeat signal. Explore other ways of skipping together: backwards; around in a circle holding hands; linking elbows and skipping in opposite directions. Now explore galloping together side by side, one behind the other. How many different ways can you side-step together?

8. Make a skip-gallop-side-step story.

MA-16 SLIDING, CRAWLING, AND CREEPING

FOCUS: Space awareness

EQUIPMENT: Benches;
chairs;
table;
parachute;
hoops;
folding mats

ORGANIZATION:

- "Sliding" is the action of moving the whole body in as low a position as possible. "Crawling" is the action of moving on hands and knees at a medium level. "Creeping" is the action of moving one body part slowly after another. Check for good understanding of movement vocabulary and good usage of space.

- Have the class place several obstacles throughout the play area: benches, chairs upright or upside down; table; parachute spread out along the floor; folding mats in "tent" shapes; hoops. Children begin in a free space.

DESCRIPTION OF ACTIVITY:

1. How can you slide on different body parts? Use big or small surfaces: tummy; back; seat and feet; feet; etc. Repeat, moving in different directions.

2. Show me how you can crawl forward; backwards; sideways. Who can crawl slowly? Now crawl quickly.

3. Can you crawl around the obstacles; under the obstacles; over the obstacles? How can you crawl through a low, narrow opening?

4. Show me how you can creep forward; backwards; sideways. Creep as slowly as possible; creep quickly.

5. Who can creep on hands and feet? on your knees and elbows? with the same side of your body moving forward? with opposite sides of your body moving forward or backwards? Can you show me another way to creep?

6. Creep over the obstacles; creep through them; creep under the parachute.

7. How many different ways can you slide along a bench? Slide along other obstacles; under them; over them.

8. *How Do These Animals Move?* (This game relies on a question from you, then a verbal and movement response from the players. For example: *Question*—"How do frogs move?" Players respond by jumping and saying "ribbit, ribbit!") "How does a . . . move?" rabbit (hopping); caterpillar (sliding with a hump;) snake (slithering); kangaroo (bounding); deer (leaping); turtle (crawling); snail (creeping); puppy (scampering); kitten (pouncing); eagle (gliding); horse (galloping); You! (variety of locomotor movements!)

MA-17 LOCOMOTION STATIONS

FOCUS: Space awareness; locomotor movements

EQUIPMENT: Hoops; cone markers; benches; chairs; low box; large and small mats; beanbags; play balls; ropes; climbing apparatus

ORGANIZATION:

• Children explore the different locomotor movements learned in a variety of stations such as those suggested below. Encourage them to change directions, levels, pathways, and speeds while using the equipment. Have the children set up the stations and put the equipment away. Divide the class equally, depending on the number of stations, and have them rotate to another station every five minutes. Remind children to move safely at all times.

DESCRIPTION OF ACTIVITY:

Station 1 (Scatter several hoops in different patterns.) Hop or jump in and out of the hoops.

Station 2 (Scatter several cone markers in one area. Place a basket of beanbags nearby.) Gallop around the cones, carrying a beanbag. Change directions and the body part holding the beanbag. Repeat sliding.

Station 3 (Set up the climbing frame and place safety mats under it.) Travel in different pathways and directions on the frame. Crawl through the frame. Move across the beam in different ways. Jump off from a low level.

Station 4 (Scatter several chairs in this area and place a cart of balls nearby.) Get a ball and walk while bouncing the ball in and out of the chairs. Run while bouncing the ball. Can you skip and bounce the ball while travelling? Roll the ball under the chairs and run to retrieve it.

Station 5 (Use benches, low box, chairs, mats, hoops, and ropes to set up an obstacle course.) Travel along the bench in different ways; jump on and off the bench in different ways; leap over a low box or hurdle; hop back and forth over a rope; roll along the mat; roll in a different way along another mat; crawl through a hoop; run in and out of the cones.

MA-18 MAKING MOVEMENT SEQUENCES

FOCUS: Sequence-making; space awareness

EQUIPMENT: Posterboard; marking pen (or chalkboard and chalk)

ORGANIZATION:

• A "Sequence" is a "movement sentence" with a beginning, a middle part, and an ending. Children perform locomotion sequences using the actions they have learned, and then add levels, directions, pathways, speed. At first, children try to do some sequences that you have made; then they invent their own locomotion sequence. Put the action words sequence on posterboard or chalkboard. Encourage and praise children as they put together their own sequences. Provide opportunity for children to observe each other.

DESCRIPTION OF ACTIVITY:

1. Try the following movement sequences:
   — RUN–LEAP–HOP; SKIP–SIDE-STEP–CRAWL; WALK–LEAP–GALLOP.
   — Move quickly forward in a zig-zag pattern at a high level.
   — Move slowly backwards, in a straight pathway, at a low level.
2. Make up a three-action word sequence of your own. Practice it. Then perform your sequence for the rest of the class.

MA-19 EXPLORING BODY PARTS

FOCUS: Body awareness; familiarization; left-right discrimination   **EQUIPMENT:** None

ORGANIZATION:

- Children learn to identify different parts of the body, explore moving isolated body parts in personal space and then in general space, and discriminate between right and left.
- To begin, have them find a home space.

DESCRIPTION OF ACTIVITY:

1. Let's see how many different body parts we can name. (Point to a child, in turn, and ask him or her to name a body part and touch it. Have the rest of the class repeat the name and touch that body part.)

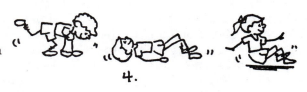

2.

2. What body part do you: [Do the action as well.]
   — Hear with . . . ?   — Snap with . . . ?
   — Smell with . . . ?   — Crawl on . . . ?
   — Talk with . . . ?   — Wave with . . . ?
   — Blink with. . . ?   — Shrug with . . . ?
   — Clap with . . . ?   — Jump with . . . ?
   — Print with . . . ?   — Kneel on . . . ?

3.

3. Now show me how you can:
   — turn your head   — twist your neck
   — bend your elbows   — snap your fingers
   — wiggle your nose   — shrug your shoulders
   — circle your wrists   — bend your knees
   — blink your eyes   — open-close your mouth
   — clap your hands   — stamp your feet

4.

4. Move in general space using two hands and one foot; knees; tummy and hands; seat and feet; back and feet; toes or heels; etc. Now move on your feet in general space. On one drum beat, stop on one body part; on two drum beats, stop on two body parts; on three drum beats, stop on three body parts. (Repeat several times.)

5.

5. Now wave to me with your left hand. Shake right hands with a partner. Put your right foot forward and shake it all about. Do this with your left foot. Cover your right eyes with your right hand and point with your left hand. Reverse this. Snap your left fingers; wiggle your right fingers.

6. Move on all fours with right side moving together, then left side. Now move with opposite sides moving together. Which feels more natural? Try this while crawling, walking, skipping. How do your hands and feet like to move?

6.

7. *Simon Says:* Stand tall in your home. If I say "Simon says . . . ," then you must do the task given. But if I give you a task to do without first saying "Simon Says . . . ," do not do it! Continue to do the task you were doing before. *Examples:* wiggle your toes; stamp your feet; nod your head; snap your fingers; wave your left hand high in the air; circle your arms; hop on left foot in place; put your hands behind your back and turn around; rise up on your toes; place your left elbow on the ground.

MA-20 RELATIONSHIPS OF BODY PARTS

FOCUS: Body awareness

EQUIPMENT: Set of "body parts" cards

ORGANIZATION:

- Children explore the relationships of different body parts to each other and to their environment. Create a "Body Part" deck by clearly printing each name of a body part on a file card.
- To begin, children move on any four body parts to a home space.

DESCRIPTION OF ACTIVITY:

1. Let's explore touching a body part to another body part. Try the following:

— nose to knee	— wrist to ankle
— chin to chest	— foot to leg
— ear to shoulder	— heel to heel
— hands to hips	— sole to sole
— elbow to knee	— hand to back
— toe to nose	— elbow to stomach
— fingers to shoulders	— your choice!

2. Now let's explore touching different body parts to our surroundings:

— head to floor	— ankle to wall
— nose to rope	— elbow to chair
— back to black line	— chest to desk
— ear to chalkboard	— knee to bench
— seat to corner	— shoulder to book
— finger to mat	— hip to ball

3. ***Body Part Card Game:*** I will ask one player to draw two cards from the "Body Part" deck. Aloud, as clearly as you can, read the name of the body part on each card. Everyone, quickly find a new partner each time and touch your partner's body part named. The game continues in this way.
   - Add "right" or "left" to the appropriate body parts on the Body Part deck.
   - Create a second set of cards which contains the names of various elements in the play area. Call this the "Environment" deck. Spread each deck on the floor. Select a player to flip a card from each deck. Everyone makes the appropriate touch, then returns home to await for the next two cards to be drawn.

ELBOW TO ELBOW

MA-21 CROSS-LATERAL COMBINATIONS

EQUIPMENT: None

ORGANIZATION:

- Children explore different ways of putting left and right body parts together and moving in this way.
- Observe children's movements, noting any difficulties.

DESCRIPTION OF ACTIVITY:

1. Lie down on your back, feet together, and hands at your sides. At the same time, lift your right hand to meet your left foot; then return to starting position. Now repeat with your left hand and your right foot.
2. Now sit up with your legs wide apart. Reach with your right hand toward your left toes; then reach with your left hand to your right toes.
3. Stand tall. Show me how you can hold your left foot with your right hand behind, and hop in any direction. Good! Now repeat, holding your right foot with your left hand behind, and hop in a different direction.
4. In the squat position, grasp ankles with opposite hands. Show me how you can travel in different directions in this position.
5. Play "Simon Says" using cross-lateral combinations.

MA-22 EXPLORING BODY SHAPES

FOCUS: Space and body awareness   **EQUIPMENT:** Drum

ORGANIZATION:

- Children explore "Body Shapes": long; narrow; wide; rounded; twisted; crooked; small; tall; pointed; flat; in personal and general space, at different levels. Have half of the class observe the other half's shapes. They then explore letting different body parts lead. Offer encouragement and praise for good effort.
- To begin, have children travel with their elbows to a home space.

DESCRIPTION OF ACTIVITY:

NARROW   WIDE   1.   ROUND   TWISTED

1. In your home, show me a long, narrow shape (like a pencil) at a high level; at a low level. Now change your shape to a wide shape (like a wall). Change from low level, to medium, to high level. How can you make a round, curled shape (like a ball) at a medium level? at a low level? Who can show me a twisted shape (like a corkscrew) at a high level? at a low level?

2. How can you make a flat shape? a pointed shape? Travel in general space, changing from a large shape to a small shape.

POINTED   2.   FLAT

3. Travel about in general space, choosing the direction, pathway, level, and body parts at will. On signal "Freeze!" (one drum beat), hold a shape. (Repeat several times so that children can experiment with different shapes and levels.)

4. Travel about in a high, wide shape. "Freeze!" in the same shape.

   — Now travel in a medium, curled shape. "Freeze!" in the same shape.
   — Travel in a low, narrow shape. "Freeze!" in this shape.
   — Finally, travel in a high, twisted shape to your home. "Freeze!" in this shape in your personal space.

4.

5. *Shape Story:* Create your "Shape Story" which has a beginning, middle, and ending, changing shapes, levels, directions, pathways, and body parts in personal and general space.

6. *Statue Tag:* (Choose two players to be IT. All other players scatter throughout the play area and stand in a long shape at a high level.) On signal "Move!" IT give chase. If you are tagged by an IT, you must freeze in a wide shape. To be freed, another player must copy your shape in front of you. (After a while, choose two new ITs and a different "freeze" position.)

6.   IT

7. *Leading Body Parts:* Travel in general space with your right hand leading you. Freeze in a flat shape. Travel with your elbows leading. Freeze in a small round shape. Travel with your head leading. Freeze in a large twisted shape.

8. *Trip to the Moon:* Astronauts, put on your space suits, boots, special gloves, and then helmet. Climb into your space ship, feet first, and buckle yourself into the seat. Check over all the instruments. Everything is "A-okay!" Prepare for take-off 10-9-8-7-6-5-4-3-2-1-BLAST-OFF! (Jump in the air with hands leading, in a pointed shape.) Land on the moon with a Crash! (seat first, twisted shape). Get out of your space ship, head first. Walk lightly with your knees leading. You are almost weightless. Oh-oh, a space creature is coming toward you. Quickly hide by curling up into a very small shape. Be still on four body parts; then crawl slowly backwards into your space ship. Blast off!

BLAST-OFF!

MA-23 EXPLORING STATIC AND DYNAMIC BODY SHAPES

FOCUS: Body and space awareness

EQUIPMENT: One mat per child

ORGANIZATION:

- Children explore making shapes using a variety of body part combinations as supports or bases. Explain the four basic shapes that the body can assume while moving or balancing: A "round" shape is created by curling all body parts close in to the center so that movement can be forward, backwards, and sideways as in rocking or rolling. A "narrow" shape is created by stretching long like a pencil and is used in jumping, vaulting, balancing, and rolling. A "wide" shape is created by extending the right and left side of the body away from the midline. A cartwheel and certain jumps and balances are examples of moving in this shape. A "twisted" shape results from turning body parts in opposite directions or from holding one part of the body while rotating other parts.
- Have each child collect a mat and find a home space.

DESCRIPTION OF ACTIVITY:

1. With your feet on the floor, make any interesting shape on your mat. Now try to make the same shape resting on another part or parts of your body. For example, make a wide shape on your feet; on your seat; back; tummy; your shoulders with your feet in the air. These body parts on which you support yourself are called "bases."
2. Can you make a long narrow shape on one body part base? two body parts? three body parts? Can you make a round shape on one body part? two body parts? three body parts? Show me a twisted shape on your mat. Change your base and make another twisted shape.
3. Can you make a wide shape with your upper body and a long shape with your lower body? Now try a long top and wide bottom; a twisted top and round bottom.
4. In your home space, start from a round shape, stretch to a long shape, then to a wide shape, and finish in a twisted shape.
5. In your home space, make your body into a wide stretched shape at a high level. Show me how many different ways you can move in that shape (forward, backwards, sideways, turning around and around). Find ways of moving in a curled round shape in your home.
6. Can you travel about in general space changing shapes? For example, skip in a wide shape; roll in a long, narrow shape; jump and land in a twisted shape.
7. Try this **Shape Story.** Jump from a crouched position; stretch to a wide shape in the air; land softly in a curled shape. Then make a Travelling Shape Story of your own.
8. **Partner Shapes:** Find a partner and place your mats together. Show me how you can make a wide shape together on two body parts. Make the same shape using four different bases, such as feet, seat, head and knees; or hands and feet. (Repeat, changing shapes and bases of support.)
9. **The Shape Game:** In your home space, show me how you can make the shape of the letter "T," "Y," "X"; the number "7," "6," "2"; the first letter of your name; your favorite number, etc.
   — Find a partner and together create the shape of the letter "W"; the number "8"; the word "O-N," "I-T," "A-S"; etc.
   — Get into groups of three or four. Together form simple three- or four-lettered words such as "C-A-T"; "B-I-R-D"; "S-U-N"; "M-O-W."

MA-24 EXPLORING STATIC BALANCES

FOCUS: Body awareness; weight-bearing

EQUIPMENT: One mat per child

ORGANIZATION:

- Children explore stationary or "static balances" on different bases, and discover which bases of support create more stable bases.
- Have children get a mat and find a home space.

DESCRIPTION OF ACTIVITY:

1. Find one body part to balance on. Change your one body part balance to another part (seat, one foot, tummy, back). Balance on two body parts; three parts; four parts. Which balance gives you a better base of support? Try to hold your balances for three seconds.

   — Can you discover a balance that gives you an uneven base (resulting in the tipping of the body)? For example, knee and shoulder.

   — Show me how you can balance on two parts that are on the same side of your body; on different sides of your body.

2. Balance on your feet. Keeping this base still, move the rest of your body by swaying, twisting, curling. Can you change the level of your body? Balancing on one foot, how can you change the position of your arms, your seat, the other foot?

3. Now let's explore changing the position of your base; for example, balance on your feet. Move them close together; far apart; one in front of the other. Repeat with three body part balances; four body part balances.

4. **Balance Story:** Change from a one body part balance to a two body part balance to a three body part balance. Hold each balance for three seconds. Create your own Balance Story.

5. **Partner Balances:** Find a partner about your size. Find ways of balancing on a total of two body parts; three parts; four parts; five parts.

6. Let's explore different ways of getting yourself "upside down." Place your hands in front of you on your mat. What parts of your body can you take higher than your hands? Can you raise your feet into the air?

   — Show me how you can kick your legs while in the air.

7. How many different ways can you come down from your hands: a bridge; a roll; a twist; step one foot down, then the other.

8. Take your weight on your hands and forehead. Now try to curl your body up and lift your feet off the floor. Explore putting your hands near your head; further away. Which position is best?

9. **Partner Bridges:** One partner make a four-point bridge while the other partner explores ways of travelling around, over, under, and through the bridge. Change roles. Repeat, creating other bridges.

MA-25 EXPLORING DYNAMIC BALANCES

FOCUS: Body awareness; weight-bearing; weight transfer

EQUIPMENT: Several benches;
mats;
chairs;
box horse;
climbing apparatus

ORGANIZATION:

- Children explore "Dynamic Balances" or travelling in balanced positions; stopping in different balanced positions; and transferring weight from body part to body part. Emphasize controlled movements! Discuss "Points and Surfaces": A point is a small area such as the elbow or knee; whereas a surface is a large area such as the tummy and back.
- To begin, children find a home space.

DESCRIPTION OF ACTIVITY:

1. Travel about in general space in different directions, pathways, and speed. On signal "Freeze!" stop immediately in a balanced position on one body part. Can you hold your balance for three seconds? (Repeat several times, having children stop on two body parts; three parts; four parts. Encourage them to travel in a different way each time.)
   — Repeat, stopping in different shapes: curled; stretched; long; twisted.
   — Repeat, stopping at a high level; medium level; low level and holding the balance.
2. Travel about in general space on one body part; two body parts; three parts; four parts. On "Freeze!" hold your balance on your travelling base.
3. Can you put your weight on different points: elbows, knees, head, hands, feet? Now put your weight on different surfaces: back, tummy, side. Show me how you can move from one surface to another; from points to a surface (foot to back). How smoothly can you move from one position to another? Travel on two points and one surface; one point and one surface.
4. Show me how you can make a bridge on or over the bench you are near. Can you move from a four-point bridge to a three-point bridge? Travel in a two-point balance along a bench? four-point?
5. Travel to a bench. Show me a low balance on your bench. Jump off, landing softly in a balanced position. Now travel in a different way to another bench. Show me a medium balance on your bench. Jump off, making a twisted shape in the air. Travel to yet another bench. Show me a high balance on your bench. Jump off, making a wide shape in the air.
6. *Travelling Balance Story:* Hop on one foot; walk on hands and feet; then slide on your seat and feet. Take your "Travelling Balance Story" and perform it on a bench. Create your own "Travel Balance Story."
7. *Apparatus Balance Game* (Have children set up apparatus throughout the play area.) On signal "Travel," move on, off, over, under, around, and through the apparatus. On signal "Balance," perform a balance task on the nearest apparatus; for example, "balance on one body part at a high level."

MA-26 EXPLORING ROCKING AND ROLLING ACTIONS

FOCUS: Body awareness; transference of weight

EQUIPMENT: One mat per child; one hoop per pair; one cylinder-shaped object

ORGANIZATION:

- Children explore rocking and rolling actions in personal and general space, with a partner, and using manipulative equipment. "Rocking" is the action of smoothly and gradually transferring from one body part to another. This action is best performed on a rounded body part, with arms, legs, and body movement helping to gain momentum. "Rolling" is the smooth and continuous transfer of weight (usually involving the spine) from one body part to another.
- Have children get a mat each and take it to free space.

DESCRIPTION OF ACTIVITY:

1. In how many different ways can you rock? Think of a rocking chair. Try standing position; sitting; lying on your back. Try rocking in different shapes: curled; stretched; twisted. Which shape rocks best? (curled)

2. Rock on different body parts. Lie on your back and rock. Try rocking with your hands and feet far from your body; near your body. Lie on your tummy and rock. How many different ways can you rock, holding your ankles?

3. Show me how you can rock in different directions: forward; sideways; backwards. How far can you rock in one direction before starting back in the opposite direction? Start with a small rocking motion and gradually make it bigger and bigger. Rock slowly; rock quickly. Keep the action smooth!

4. Now watch the cylinder roll along the floor. Show me how you can make a long stretched shape, like a cylinder, and roll. Can you roll in a stretched shape from one end of your mat to the other with your hands by your sides? with your hands stretched over your head? with your arms and legs crossed? Roll slowly in a stretched shape. Roll quickly. Repeat in a curled shape.

5. Can you roll in a curled shape in different directions: forward; sideways; backwards? Try to start your roll with a different body part on the mat: hands; knees; back; feet.

6. Explore rocking in different ways while holding a hoop.

7. ***Rock 'n Roll Story:*** Can you start with a rocking action and move into a rolling action, back to a rocking action?

8. ***Partner Rocking and Rolling:*** Find a partner. Explore different ways of rocking together: feet interlocked; hands joined; hands and feet touching; side by side. Now explore rolling together in these ways. One partner roll up in a curled position. Other partner show me how you can roll the "ball" (curled partner) in any direction. Take turns. Collect a mat and a hoop. One partner hold a hoop just off the mat, while the other partner rolls through. Take turns.

MA-27 EXPLORING NON-LOCOMOTOR ACTIONS

FOCUS: Body awareness; non-locomotor actions   **EQUIPMENT:** None

ORGANIZATION:

- In this segment, the non-locomotor actions of "bending" and "stretching" are explored. "Bending" is a movement of a joint; whereas "Stretching" is a movement that makes the body parts as long or wide as possible. Both actions should occur through the full range of motion, smoothly with no jerkiness.

- Have children begin by standing in a home space.

DESCRIPTION OF ACTIVITY:

1. Let's explore different ways your body can bend (fingers; arms; toes; legs; whole body itself!). Your body bends at joints. Can you bend two body parts at the same time; three parts; four parts? Show me how you can bend forward; then backwards. Now bend sideways—to the right; to the left. How many body parts (joints) can you bend above your waist; below your waist?

2. You have been exploring different ways that your body can bend while you are standing. Now sit down in your home and explore different ways of bending. Lie on your back; lie on your front and bend in different ways.

3. How would you bend to look happy? To look unhappy? Bend a body part quickly, then slowly. Try this with other body parts. Make different shapes while bending two body parts; three parts; four body parts.

4. Show me how you can stretch as tall as a giraffe; as wide as a hippopotamus; as long as a snake. How many different body parts can you stretch: arms, hands, legs, back, feet? Why is it so important to stretch every day?

5. How many different ways can you stretch in the sitting position? Now in back-lying position, show me how you can stretch your feet in one direction and your hands in another. Standing in your home, try bending one arm while holding the other still. Show me how you can bend one arm while unbending (stretching) the other. Repeat with your legs.

6. Make a "Bend and Stretch Story."

7. Find a partner. Explore stretching together in different ways. Explore making big bends together; little bends. Explore bending and stretching together.

MA-28 TWISTING AND TURNING

FOCUS: Body awareness; non-locomotor actions

EQUIPMENT: Climbing frame and ropes;
heavy posterboard;
marking pens;
box horse;
benches;
chairs

ORGANIZATION:

• Children explore twisting and turning actions in personal and general space and on apparatus while travelling, balancing, and transferring weight. "Twisting" is a rotation of a body part around its own axis. This action can only happen at the neck, shoulder, spine, hip, and wrist joints. "Turning" is a rotation or circular movement of the body or body parts around in space, in a CW or CCW direction. Whereas turning focuses on the space in which the body part turns, twisting is the action around the body part itself. Demonstrate this twisting action by screwing the lid off a jar, dialing on a telephone, using a screwdriver.

• Have children begin in a home space.

DESCRIPTION OF ACTIVITY:

1. Let's pretend your feet are glued to the floor. Can you twist your body to the right? to the left? Twist it slowly; quickly. Can you bend and twist it at the same time?

2. Let's explore keeping a body part still while twisting another body part. Keep your body still while you twist your head gently around. How far can you go? Now hold your head still and twist your shoulders around.

3. Try twisting two or more body parts at the same time; one body part around another. How can you twist a body part in one direction while twisting another body part in the opposite direction? Can you twist the lower half of your body without twisting the upper half? Try to do this in reverse!

4. Show me how you can turn your whole self to the right in a CW direction; to the left in a CCW direction. Can you make two full turns? Now make a quarter-turn to the right. Continue making quarter turns until you are facing the starting direction. Repeat to the left. Repeat using half turns.

5. Standing on one foot, turn your body around quickly; slowly. Repeat in the opposite direction. Repeat with the other foot. On what other body parts can you turn around? Try turning while in sitting position; lying on your tummy; while lying on your back.

6. Can you turn around while walking? running? skipping? Jump up and turn around in the air. Try a quarter-jump turn; half-jump turn; full-jump turn!

7. Make a "Turning" Story. Make a "Twisting" Story. Can you create a "Twist and Turn Story"?

8. *Partner Twists and Turns:* Explore twisting and turning actions with a partner.

9. *The Alphabet Twister* (Make the "Alphabet Grids" on heavy 9 feet by 3 feet posterboard as shown above. Divide the class into groups of four and assign each group a set of words and an Alphabet Grid.) In your group, take turns making the selected word by placing different body parts in the squares; examples, "work," "play."

10. *Apparatus Tasks:* Explore twisting and turning actions on the benches and mats. Jump off the box horse or bench with a turning action, land, and hold a twisted balance. Travel on the climbing frame twisting as you go; twist your body around a climbing rope.

MA-29 EXPLORING EFFORT

FOCUS: Effort awareness; body control **EQUIPMENT:** Drum

ORGANIZATION:

- The factors of "Effort Awareness" are "Time," "Weight," "Space," and "Flow." This activity focuses on the Time and Weight factors. Children explore the basic elements of speed or the rate at which the body moves: slow, medium, fast, acceleration, deceleration, and rhythms. Children also explore how the body moves in space with force: strong, medium, or weak actions; sudden or explosive movements, sustained or smooth movements. They explore creating force (quick starts, sustained powerful movements, held balances) and absorbing force (sudden controlled stops, gradual "give").
- Tasks demanding changes of speed or force may be formulated from any of the previous themes on travelling, locomotion, transference of weight, step-like actions, and non-locomotor actions.
- Have children begin by hook-sitting in a home space.

DESCRIPTION OF ACTIVITY:

1. Stand up very slowly, and then quickly sit down. Now stand very quickly, and then slowly sit down. Show me how you can slowly curl into a ball in your home space. Slowly stretch out. Curl quickly back into a ball. Quickly stretch out again. Now slowly stand up.
2. Let's explore travelling at different speeds. Run slowly; run at a medium speed; run quickly. On the drum beat, freeze on three body parts and hold your balance. (Repeat using other locomotor movements.)
3. How many body parts can you use to move slowly? (tummy, hands and knees, seat, back) Can you travel on hands and feet, showing a change in speed?
4. Let's make a sequence. Travel in a forward direction from your home by galloping at a medium speed; slowly walk backwards in a zig-zag pathway; then quickly skip back to your home. Now make a sequence of your own showing me changes of speed.
5. Now stand very still in your home space. Move slowly from your home; gradually increase your speed, until you are moving quickly (accelerating). Now gradually slow down again (decelerating). Finally come to a stop in your home space.
6. Create a "Change of Speed Story." In general space: *beginning*—roll slowly; *middle*—skip quickly at a high level; *ending*—decelerate to a slow crawl. In personal space: Turn quickly in place; curl slowly into a ball; stretch out to a low level. Now create your own story!
7. Can you show me different ways of being strong? What actions can you do that require strength? (Jumping, lifting heavy objects) Now can you show me an action that does not take much strength to do—a weak action? (blinking an eye) Make a strong swinging action with your arms. Now try to make this same action weak. Repeat with a kicking action.
8. Stand still. Suddenly burst into speed. Then suddenly stop in control. (Repeat several times.)
9. Let's make a sequence. Run lightly in general space as if you were "floating"; then run heavily; stop suddenly in control.
   — Jump up as high as you can. Land softly in balance. Quickly dart into another space. Stop suddenly again.
   — Make your own sequence.

MA–30 EXPLORING PARTNER RELATIONSHIPS

FOCUS: Partner work; copying, mirroring; interacting

EQUIPMENT: Beanbags; deckrings; hoops; benches; mats; chairs; tables; box horse; climbing apparatus

ORGANIZATION:

- Children explore actions of copying, leading, following, shadowing, meeting and parting, and mirroring. Discuss the term "mirroring": copying an action, but as if you were looking into a mirror. Have one pair demonstrate "mirroring." At first, allow children to choose their own partners. Later, arrange the children in pairs according to size. Encourage children to work with a variety of different partners, including boys with girls.

DESCRIPTION OF ACTIVITY:

1. One partner be the leader; the other partner be the follower. Leader, travel in different directions and pathways. The other partner, follow and copy the movements. Change roles often.
2. Follower, can you copy the Leader's movements, staying as close as possible to the leader? Take turns. This is called "shadowing."
3. *Partner Copying Story:* Create a sequence of three different movements. One partner lead while the other follows; then change roles.
4. *Meeting and Parting:* Start together in a home space. Travel in the same way, moving apart from each other, and then meeting again. Continue in this way, watching out for others as you travel. On signal, find a new partner and repeat.

5. *Follow the Leader* (Set up a variety of apparatus such as mats, benches, hoops, tables, chairs, box horse, climbing ropes, and frame throughout the play area.) Partners, take turns being the Leader as you travel in the same way around, along, across, over, under, through, on, and off the apparatus.

6. *Face-to-Face Mirroring:* Stand, facing your partner. One partner be the leader; the other partner, copy the leader's actions: hand-clapping; foot-stamping; hopping in a circle; snapping fingers under a leg; jiggling legs; swaying upper body; stretching, curling, or twisting body parts; etc. Change roles and repeat.
   — Change to other body bases (sitting; kneeling; front-lying) and do face-to-face mirroring actions.
7. Explore face-to-face mirroring while travelling in general space, taking turns at leading and following: side-stepping; rolling; hopping; jumping; travelling on other body parts, with different parts leading.
8. *Side-by-Side Mirroring:* Travel in a variety of ways, such as walking backwards; skipping; galloping; leaping; rocking and rolling. Change directions, pathways, levels, speeds, and body parts.
   — Explore side-by-side mirroring in personal space: bending, stretching, twisting, turning.
9. *Equipment Mirroring:* Select a piece of equipment. Take turns being leader and follower. Copy your partner's actions while facing; while side by side. For example, toss a beanbag or deckring from hand to hand; roll a hoop along the floor; travel along the bench or mat side by side.

MA–31 CREATIVE MOVEMENTS 1

FOCUS: Space awareness; imitating

EQUIPMENT: None

ORGANIZATION:

- Creativity can be developed by children taking on the identity of a familiar creature, character, or object and then interpreting its movements:
  - —Animals (dogs, snakes, seals, frogs)
  - —Mythical creatures (dwarfs, fairies, giants, witches)
  - —People (boxers, cowboys, firefighters, ballet dancers)
  - —Play Objects (balls, spinning tops, robots, swings)
  - —Machines (planes, trains, racing cars, lawn mowers)
  - —Circus (clowns, tightrope walkers, jugglers, lion tamers)
  - —Nature (sunsets and rises, rain, wind, clouds, leaves)
- The following tasks provide a variety of movement experiences from the above categories and can be used throughout this section at your discretion. Let half the class observe the other half from time to time.
- Have children begin in their homes.

DESCRIPTION OF ACTIVITY:

1. **Scamper** like a frisky puppy. Oh-oh, you have a sore paw. How can you move now? What sounds would you make?

2. **Slither** like a snake, making "hissing" sounds. **Wriggle** like an earthworm.

3. **Waddle** like a duck, making "quacking" sounds. **Strut** like a proud rooster. What sounds will you make?

4. **Leap** like a frog trying to "zap" a fly. How does a frog sound? **Jump** like a kangaroo, moving in and out of each other. **Spring** like a cat about to pounce on a mouse.

5. **Drag** yourself like a seal just coming out of the water. How do you move on land? What sounds do you make? Now be a crab coming out of the water and travelling along the sand.

6. **Kick** like a wild horse. How will you sound?

7. **Glide** like a butterfly, landing on a flower, flapping your wings, and then moving on to another flower. **Stretch,** ever so slowly, like a sleepy cat waking up.

8. **Animal Charades:** Get into groups of four. Take turns imitating different animals. The other members of your group must guess what you are.

MA-32 CREATIVE MOVEMENTS 2

FOCUS: Locomotion; space and effort awareness   **EQUIPMENT:** None

ORGANIZATION:

- Children explore various travelling, step-like actions and non-locomotor actions. Remind children to look for open spaces. Encourage and praise.

DESCRIPTION OF ACTIVITY:

1. You are a Boeing 747 about to take off. Travel down the runway, gathering speed. Now you are flying high in the sky, moving in a straight pathway. Zoom with your arms out, swoop, turn and glide. Come in for a landing in a spiral pathway, slowing down and landing softly on your front. Repeat, flying a different flight path.
2. Roll like a pig in mud. Rock like a rocking chair, slowly at first, and then quickly. Crawl like a curious baby, changing directions often. Creep like a mouse past a big sleeping cat.
3. Skate like your favorite hockey player. Make quick starts and stops, changes of direction, pathways, and speeds. Now you are a star figure skater. Turn around on one skate; change body shapes and levels.
4. Travel like an angry giant; a frightened dwarf; a cackling witch on her broom; lightly on your tippy-toes as a fairy. Be a tightrope walker. Move with tiny steps; move sideways; sway to the right, to the left; jump-turn.
5. Twirl like a helicopter blade. Twist about in a washing machine; then stretch out and curl up in the dryer as you spin around and around. Jump like popping corn; sizzle like bacon in a frying pan.

MA-33 CREATIVE MOVEMENTS 3

FOCUS: Body and effort awareness   **EQUIPMENT:** None

ORGANIZATION:

- Children explore different body actions as they imitate play objects, machines, and people.
- Have children scatter and find a home.

DESCRIPTION OF ACTIVITY:

1. Be a *Rag Doll.* Be a *"Jack-in-the-Box."* Be a *Robot,* programmed to vacuum the rug. Be a pair of *Scissors* cutting paper.
2. Be a *Boxer.* How will your arms and feet move? Show me your best karate kicks. Be a *Sword Fighter* making jabs and slashes through the air.
3. You are a *Balloon* slowly being blown up—get bigger and bigger. Now I let you go! Then I will blow you up again. Oh-oh, I blew you up so much that you burst! Be a *Spinning Top.* When will you come to a stop? Now be a *Yo-Yo.* How will you go-go!
4. Be a *Speed Boat* travelling through rough water. Watch those turns! Look out for others! Be a *Rocket Ship* blasting off to the moon. Land on the moon with a crash. Be a *Moon Machine.*
5. *Invention Game:* Get into groups of three. Think of all the different machines that we use daily. Can your group become one of these machines? Let's see if the other groups can guess what machine you are! Now invent a "wacky machine" of your own!

FOCUS: Space awareness; dramatization   **EQUIPMENT:** None

ORGANIZATION:

- The following ideas stimulate the imagination, enhance creative expression, and foster good listening skills. Provide opportunity for children to observe each other. Offer constant encouragement and praise good effort.

- Have children scatter and find a home space to start.

DESCRIPTION OF ACTIVITY:

1. You are **Baby Chick** inside its shell and are trying to hatch out. You finally hatch! Explore your new world. Try to walk on your wobbly legs.

2. Take your large **Pet Dog** for a walk. Suddenly your dog spies a cat and the chase is on! Now you are a little **Fly** buzzing around. Land on a piece of sticky bubble gum. Oh-oh! You are stuck!

3. You are **Lion Hunters** moving about in a dark, thick scary jungle looking for the lions who prowl around in the shadows. Show me what happens when you meet each other! Oh-oh! You fall into a trap! Struggle and struggle to get out of the trap. Finally you free yourself but are covered from head to foot with ants! Shake and shake every part of you to get rid of the bugs.

4. You are a **Firefighter.** The fire alarm sounds. Quickly put on your coat, boots, and firefighter hat. Jump onto the fire engine and hang on. You arrive at the scene of the fire. Grab the hose and climb the ladder, aiming your hose at the flames. Rescue someone who is trapped.

5. **Summertime Fun:** Let's go fishing! Put a worm on your hook; throw out your line. Give the line a tug; feel the line pull. Looks like you've got a big one. Reel it in! Don't let it get away.

6. **Wintertime Fun:** Find a partner and make a snowman together. Now show me how you can toboggan together. Throw imaginary snowballs at each other and show me how you would dodge them. Play follow the leader as you skate on ice.

7. **Visit to the Zoo:** Imitate the different animals in the zoo, such as Monkeys, Polar Bears, Seals, Elephants, Tigers, etc.

8. **Quiet Halloween** (Divide the class into four groups: the Ghosts, the Witches, the Monsters, and the Scary Bats. Assign each group to a corner of the play area.) Listen for the name of your group; then show me how you would travel toward the center of the play area. Move in the center area near to each other but without touching each other or making a sound. Quickly and ever so quietly disappear to your corner as I call another group's name.

MA-35 CREATIVE MOVEMENTS 5

FOCUS: Space and body awareness; creative expression; listening

EQUIPMENT: Stuffed animal named "Sniggles"; different colored paper; crayons; drawing paper

ORGANIZATION:

- Children act out different fairy tales such as "Jack and the Beanstalk"; "Billy Goats Gruff"; "Wizard of Oz"; "Snow White and the Seven Dwarfs"; "Little Red Riding Hood"; "The Three Pigs"; "Goldilocks and the Three Bears."
- They are also introduced to "Sniggles" and create an Action Story about him. Have children draw their own Sniggles.

DESCRIPTION OF ACTIVITY:

1. **Simon Says Warm-Up:** Perform the actions only when I say "Simon Says . . ." first; otherwise, continue what you were doing beforehand. Stretch up on your toes; swing your arms together; twist one leg around the other; pull yourself along the floor; bend from side to side; stand on your right foot and turn twice around; push yourself off the floor; balance on your elbows and knees; travel on your seat and feet; curl into a ball and rock forward and back; make a shape with body parts far from each other.

2. **Jack and the Beanstalk:**
   - —Jack in his yard   *Skipping, playing*
   - —Jack plants a bean and it grows into a beanstalk   *Bean—growing*
   - —Jack climbs the beanstalk   *Climbing*
   - —Jack sees the giant's castle, creeps up and sneaks inside   *Creeping*
   - —Jack hears the giant coming and hides   *Hiding*
   - —The giant searches angrily for Jack and says: "Fee, Fie, Fo, Fum! I smell a boy and he smells yum!"   *Giant—searching*
   - —Jack flees back to the beanstalk and climbs down. The giant follows closely behind.   *Fleeing*
   - —Jack chops down the beanstalk.   *Chopping*
   - —The giant falls with a loud "thud" to the ground.   *Giant—falling*
   - —Jack jumps for joy.   *Jumping*

3. **Sniggles:** I have a friend to introduce to you. His name is Sniggles. Show me how Sniggles moves when he is happy; sad; tired; angry; scared; excited.
   - How do you think Sniggles feels when he sees different colors? What does this color make him want to do? (Hold up different colored sheets of paper.)
   - Sniggles is a "warm fuzzy"; not a "cold prickly." What does this mean? Find a partner and show me how you can be a "warm fuzzy": shake hands, friendly hugs, kind comments.
   - Sniggles decides to go on a "Hiking Expedition." Let's make up an Action Story about what happens to Sniggles.

Rhythms and Dance

The Rhythms and Dance activities are meant to develop creative expression, rhythmic movement, musical appreciation, and active listening skills. They improve muscular growth and coordination; space, body, and effort awareness; and social skills in an atmosphere of fun. Specific music suggestions are provided through the dance section. Lively popular music is suggested.

This section presents 35 Rhythms and Dance activities, including:

RD-1 FUNDAMENTAL RHYTHMS—INTRODUCTION

FOCUS: Teacher guidelines

EQUIPMENT: None

ORGANIZATION:

- In this section the four basic themes of "Movement Awareness"—namely, Space Awareness, Body Awareness, Effort Awareness, and Relationships—are rhythmically developed. Children explore even and uneven rhythms, create rhythmic movement sequences, interact in singing movement songs, simple folk and novelty dances; and use manipulative equipment to develop rhythm patterns.
- Rhythmic movements can be accompanied by: *your voice; percussion instruments*—drums, tambourines, lummi sticks, maracas, castinettes, bells, and cymbals; *children's voices; selected contact sounds*—snapping fingers, clapping hands, stamping feet; *visual stimuli*—pictures, toys, balloons, elastic bands, ice cubes, candles, playdough, tools, live animals, colors; *language stimuli*—action words, action poems, dramatic stories, and folk tales—dance oriented, not drama; *nature stimuli*—clouds, rain, lightning, fire, sun rising and setting, egg hatching, seed growing.

RD-2 EVEN RHYTHMS—WALKING

FOCUS: Fundamental rhythms; listening skills

EQUIPMENT: Drum or tambourine; music with an even rhythm; tape or record player

ORGANIZATION:

- Begin with children in a listening circle.

DESCRIPTION OF ACTIVITY:

1. Listen to my drum beat. Can you clap your hands in time to my drum? Good! Now let me see you clap your hands and walk your feet to a home space to the drum beats; then clap your hands and walk your feet in place.

2. Show me how you can walk in general space, keeping in time to my drum. Move in and out of others but don't touch anyone! Freeze on two loud beats; walk in place and snap your fingers to the beat. Walk in different directions to the drum beats: forward, backwards, sideways, diagonally. Change direction on the loud beat. Change direction every eight beats; every four beats. Walk in different pathways—curvy; straight; zig-zag—changing on every loud beat.

3. Can you walk in time to my drum beat, at a high level for eight counts? at a medium level (natural walk) for eight counts? at a low level (grasp your ankles) for eight counts? On two loud beats, walk in place, snapping your fingers for eight counts.

4. How many other ways can you walk to my drum beat? stiff-legged; with a limp; lifting your knees high (marching); crab-walk; puppy-dog walk; walk toed-in; walk toed-out; tippy-toe walk; heel walk.

5. ***The Marching Dance:*** Walk freely in general space to the music being played. On two loud drum beats, walk toward another dancer, pair up, and continue to march together side by side. On three loud drum beats, form a circle of three, all holding hands, and continue walking around in a circle to the music. On four drum beats, form a file of four (in a follow-the-leader formation) and march to the music. On one drum beat, drop hands and walk to the music by yourself.

RD–3 DID YOU EVER SEE A LASSIE?

FOCUS: Rhythm walking; listening

EQUIPMENT: Music reference—E-Z 78902A; tape or record player

ORGANIZATION:

- Singing Movement Songs ("Singing Games" or "Action Songs") offer a wide variety of moods and subjects, including the interpretation of an old story or fable, a festive occasion, or some specific task. They are designed to develop physical fitness, coordination, agility, and rhythm and enhance purposeful listening, memory, and creative expression. Singing movement songs have been interspersed through this section.
- Briefly and simply tell the children something about the song—its name, nature, and meaning. Have children listen to the music and clap to the beat; teach them the verses and chorus so that they can sing along, but one verse at a time; then add the action to that verse before learning the others. Write the song on the chalkboard or chart paper. Offer encouragement and praise quality performance.

DESCRIPTION OF ACTIVITY:

Did You Ever See a Lassie? (Scotland) Have children form a single circle, join hands, and all face left. Select one dancer to stand in the center. Skills involved are walking and pantomiming.

—Did you ever see a Lassie, a Lassie, a Lassie?
Dancers walk eight steps to the left.

—Did you ever see a Lassie, do this way and that?
Dancers walk eight steps to the right.

—Do this way and that way and this way and that way.
Center dancer performs some action. Circle dancers stand still.

—Did you ever see a Lassie, do this way and that?
Circle dancers imitate the action. Center dancer then points to one of the circle players, who is doing the action. This dancer becomes the new center dancer. Repeat dance.

RD–4 MULBERRY BUSH

FOCUS: Singing movement song

EQUIPMENT: Tape or record player; music reference—RCA 45 416151; tambourine or drum

ORGANIZATION:

- "Mulberry Bush" involves the basic step of walking and pantomiming. Have dancers form a single circle, join hands, and face inward.

DESCRIPTION OF ACTIVITY:

1. Chorus:
   — Here we go round the Mulberry bush, the Mulberry bush, the Mulberry bush. Here we go round the Mulberry bush, so early in the morning.
   Walk left around the circle during the chorus.

2. Verses (Repeat chorus after each verse.):
   — This is the way we wash our hands, wash our hands, wash our hands. This is the way we wash our hands, so early in the morning. Chorus.
   Show me how you would "wash your hands" (washing action). On the words, "so early in the morning," drop hands and turn yourself once around in place.

3. Other verses (repeat chorus after each verse):
   — This is the way we "eat our breakfast."
   — This is the way we "brush our teeth."
   — This is the way we "do our exercises."
   — "stretch our body"; "comb our hair"; "skip to school."

"BRUSH YOUR TEETH."

RD-5 EVEN RHYTHMS—RUNNING

FOCUS: Fundamental rhythms; listening

EQUIPMENT: Drum or tambourine; lively music in 4/4 time; tape or record player

ORGANIZATION:

- Running is a smooth, rhythmical action, performed on the balls of the feet; upper body relaxed, head up, arms swinging back and forward instead of sideways, and knees lifting. Emphasize that children should make good use of space—always watching where they are going. Check for good sense of rhythm.
- Have children find a home space to start.

DESCRIPTION OF ACTIVITY:

1. Listen to the beat of my drum. Clap this beat with your hands. Show me how you can keep in time with light running steps in place.

2. Now run in general space, keeping in time to my drum. Remember to watch out for others. On one loud beat, jog in place, snapping your fingers to the drum beat.
   — Now run, changing directions every eight beats. Can you do this changing directions every four beats? Jog in place when you hear the loud beat.

3. Return to your home. Show me how you can stamp one foot in place for four counts; then the other for four counts.
   — Now move around in general space, stamping your feet and changing direction every eight counts.

4. Can you run with small steps forward, keeping the beat? (Use quick, steady drum beats.)
   — Run with large steps forward (slow, steady beats).
   — Run with small steps backwards to your home. Then run on the spot, lifting your knees high. Keep in time to my drum beats!

5. *Hickory, Dickory, Dock* (Introduce action poem without drum at first. Encourage children to sing the words while doing the actions.)
   — Hickory, dickory, dock
     Run on the spot, lifting your knees high.
   — The Mouse ran up the clock.
     Run with small steps in space.
   — The Mouse ran down,
     Run backward to starting place.
   — Hickory, dickory, dock.
     Stamp in place.

6. *Rhythm Running Sequence:* Stamp in place for four steps; run forward for eight steps; stamp in place for four steps; run backwards for eight steps; walk in a circle for eight steps; then run in a figure-8 for eight steps; stamp in place for four steps.

7. Listen to the music I am playing. Create a "Running Dance" of your own. Your dance should have a definite beginning, middle, and ending.

VARIATION: Have children learn "Dance of Greeting," RD-25; Music Reference—Folkraft 1187 or Hoctor Products, *Folk Dancing—Kindergarten and Early Primary,* HLP-4026.

RD-6 EVEN RHYTHMS—JUMPING AND HOPPING

FOCUS: Fundamental rhythms; listening

EQUIPMENT: Tambourine or drum; tape or record player

ORGANIZATION:

- Review the basic locomotor skills of "jumping" and "hopping": jump with both feet; hop on one foot at a time. To avoid undue stress to the legs, have children change hopping foot every four hops. Emphasize landing lightly on the balls of the feet, bending at hips, knees, and ankles.

DESCRIPTION OF ACTIVITY:

1. Find a home space. Listen to my tambourine. Show me how you can jump in place to the beat. Can you clap your hands and jump your feet to my drum?
   — Jump from side to side; forward and back to my drum.
   — Jump in a pattern: circle; triangle, favorite letter.
2. In your home space, hop in time with my drum, changing your hopping foot every four hops. Can you change your hopping foot every two hops? Now travel and hop, changing foot and direction every four counts.
3. Let's create a Rhythm Story, using jumping, hopping, walking, running, and stamping actions: jump from side to side in place for eight counts; run forward for eight counts; walk backwards for eight counts; hop forward for eight counts (change hopping foot every four hops); stamp in place for four counts. Repeat.
   — Create your own Rhythm Story using these loco- motor actions.
4. ***Hitch Hiker*** (DANCECRAFT DC73304—This sim- ple American foot-pattern dance involves the basic steps of jumping and walking. Have dancers scatter.)
   — Jump, jump
   With feet together, jump back twice.
   — Hitch, hitch
   With your right thumbs, make a hitch-hiking action.
   — Jump, jump
   Jump backwards two more times.
   — Hitch, hitch
   With your left thumbs, make a hitch-hiking action.
   — Jump, jump
   Jump backwards two more times.
   — Hitch, hitch
   With both thumbs, repeat hitch-hiking action twice.
   — Walk 2-3-4- . . . -8.
   Briskly walk forward eight steps.
   — *Repeat dance from the beginning.*

VARIATIONS:

a. In Hitch Hiker, have dancers pair off and face each other.
b. Have children learn "Jump Jim Jo" (Merit Audio Visual, Folk Dance Fundamentals, MAV 1041 or Folkraft 1180); and "Seven Jumps" (All Purpose Folk Dance). See activities RD–29 and RD–30 for the words and actions.

RD-7 UNEVEN RHYTHMS—SKIPPING

FOCUS: Fundamental rhythms; listening

EQUIPMENT: Tambourine or drum; music in 4/4 time

ORGANIZATION:

- Review the basic locomotor skill of "skipping": step and hop on one foot, then step and hop on the other foot; bring the knees up on each hop. Stress smoothness and lightness of step.
- Have children find a home space to begin.

DESCRIPTION OF ACTIVITY:

1. Listen carefully to my tambourine. Clap this rhythm. Now skip to this rhythm in general space. Remember to watch where you are going.

2. Show me how you can skip in some different way, keeping the rhythm: skip backwards; skip in a circle; skip in a figure-8; etc.

3. Let's create a Rhythm Story using walking, running, stamping, jumping, hopping, and skipping:

   — Skip forward for eight counts; walk backwards for eight counts.

   — Run in place for eight counts; jump from side to side for four counts; then stamp your feet and clap your hands four times.

   — Skip in a circle for eight counts; then hop all the way home!

4. *Circle Up*

   — Listen to the music being played and clap to its rhythm.

   — Show me how you can skip freely in general space to the music.

   — On two loud beats, skip toward another dancer, pair up, and continue to skip together. Are you keeping in time to the music?

   — On three loud beats, form a circle of three dancers, all join hands, and continue to skip in time CW around the circle.

   — On four loud beats, skip in a circle of four dancers.

   — On one loud beat, drop hands, and continue skipping to the music in general space, by yourself.

   — Repeat routine from the beginning each time.

VARIATION:

Have children suggest other ideas for the "Circle Up" routine.

4.

RD-8 THE FARMER IN THE DELL

FOCUS: Singing movement song

EQUIPMENT: Tambourine or drum;
music reference—Folkraft 1182;
tape or record player

ORGANIZATION:

- These English songs involve the basic step of skipping and rhythm clapping. Have children form a single circle, join hands, and all face inward. Select one dancer to stand in the center (Farmer or Muffin Man).
- Teach the tune and words of the song first; then add the actions.

DESCRIPTION OF ACTIVITY:

1. The farmer in the dell; the farmer in the dell;
   Hi, ho, the dairy oh, the farmer in the dell.
   Circle dancers skip for 16 counts CW, while the Farmer in the center skips CCW.
2. The farmer takes a wife; the farmer takes a wife;
   Hi, ho, the dairy oh, the farmer takes a wife.
   Farmer, choose a wife, join hands, and lead her into the circle center; skip CCW around the inside of circle.
3. The wife takes a child; the wife takes a child;
   Hi, ho, the dairy oh, the wife takes a child.
   The wife, choose a child, and the three of you join hands and skip CCW around the inside of the circle.

"THE FARMER TAKES A WIFE..."

4. *Repeat with the following verses:*
   The child takes a nurse . . . ; The nurse takes a cat . . . ;
   The cat takes a rat . . . ; The rat takes the cheese . . .
   Each dancer chosen, in turn, join the center group.
5. The cheese stands alone; the cheese stands alone;
   Hi, ho, the dairy oh, and we'll all take a bite.
   Everyone gather around the cheese and clap your hands overhead; then pretend to take a bite!

RD-9 THE MUFFIN MAN

FOCUS: Singing movement song

EQUIPMENT: Music reference—Folkraft 1188

ORGANIZATION:

- See activity RD-8.

DESCRIPTION OF ACTIVITY:

1. Oh, do you know the Muffin Man, the Muffin Man, the Muffin Man?
   Oh, do you know the Muffin Man, who lives in Drury Lane?
   Circle dancers stand still, clapping and singing the words, while the Muffin Man skips around the circle (first line). Then Muffin Man, choose a partner and skip in place in front of him or her. Muffin Man and partner, join hands; skip to the center (second line).
2. Oh, yes we know the Muffin Man . . .
   Repeat the action above, except the two center dancers, skip around in the circle, then each choose a new partner, join hands, and skip to the center.
3. Four of us know the Muffin Man . . .
   Repeat the action with four skippers and four partners being chosen.
4. Eight of us know the Muffin Man . . .
   Continue this pattern for the remaining verses, until all the dancers have been chosen.
5. Sixteen of us know the Muffin Man . . .
   All of us know the Muffin Man . . .
   All dancers skip around in general space, singing the words to the song.

RD-10 UNEVEN RHYTHMS—GALLOPING, SIDE-STEPPING

FOCUS: Fundamental rhythms

EQUIPMENT: Tambourine or drum; music with an uneven rhythm; tape or record player

ORGANIZATION:

- Children further explore uneven rhythms. Review the locomotor movement skills of "galloping": one foot leads, while the other follows in a forward direction; and "side-stepping": the movement is sideways, to the right or to the left.
- Have children find a home to begin.

DESCRIPTION OF ACTIVITY:

1. Listen to the beat of my tambourine. Can you clap this rhythm? Show me how you can gallop with your right foot leading, in general space, keeping in time to the beat. "Freeze!" on the loud beat and march in place. Now let your left foot lead. Travel when you hear my tambourine again. Can you change your leading foot every eight counts? then every four counts?

2. Still keeping the rhythm, gallop and change directions every eight counts. Gallop in a circle pattern: a rectangular pattern; a figure-8; a spiral; a winding pathway.

3. Show me how you can side-step in general space to my tambourine's beat. Change direction every eight beats. "Freeze!" on the loud beat and stamp your feet for four counts. Side-step in different pathways: curvy; triangular; diamond; circular.

4. Find a partner and stand side-by-side. Join hands and gallop together to the music being played, in general space, with the same foot leading; with opposite foot leading. Remember to move to the music.

5. Now face your partner, hold hands lightly, and side-step together in one direction for eight counts; then in another direction for eight counts. "Freeze!" on the loud beat and stamp your feet for four counts. (Repeat this pattern.)

6. Can you and your partner create a Rhythm Story that involves galloping and side-stepping? Use hand claps or finger snaps if you wish.

7. *Action Poems:* "Run, run all around, Skip, skip to the town, Hop, hop on a line, Jump, jump, jump up high! Gallop, gallop up to nine."

8. *Singing Movement Song:* "Yankee Doodle" (*Singing Games and Folk Dances*, Album 3, Bowmar Records, Inc.—This popular American circle dance involves the basic steps of galloping and side-stepping. Have dancers form a single circle, all facing CCW.)
   - Yankee doodle went to town, riding on a pony,
     All gallop eight times CCW.
   - He stuck a feather in his cap, and called it macaroni.
     All stop, face center, point to the cap; then bow on "macaroni."
   - Yankee doodle, Ha, Ha, Ha. Yankee doodle dandy.
     All join hands and take six side-steps to the right; then stamp your feet two times on the word "dandy."
   - Yankee Doodle, Ha, Ha, Ha. Buy the girls some candy.
     Side-step six times to the left; then clap your hands two times on the word "candy."

RD-11 TOUCH YOUR TOES

FOCUS: Singing movement song

EQUIPMENT: Music reference—*Multi-Purpose Singing Games,* Educational Activities Inc. N.Y.; tape or record player

ORGANIZATION:

- The Fundamental Rhythms are further reinforced through this song, which goes to the tune "Are You Sleeping" ("Frère Jacques"), if the music is unavailable.
- To begin, have children stand in a large circle, facing you in the center. Teach the words and encourage children to sing along.

DESCRIPTION OF ACTIVITY:

"DO A LITTLE JUMPING...!"

1. Touch your toes, touch your toes,
   Bend over to touch your toes, then straighten.
   Turn around, turn around.
   Turn around in place.
   Do a little JUMPING, do a little JUMPING,
   Jump lightly, keeping the rhythm.
   Squat down low; up you go!
   Squat down low, then spring up ready to begin again.
2. Repeat the song, substituting other locomotor movements: hopping; skipping; climbing; swimming; dancing.

RD-12 TEN LITTLE INDIANS

EQUIPMENT: See activity RD-11

ORGANIZATION:

- For this American traditional children's song, have dancers stand in a single circle, all facing center; except for one dancer who is the "Chief" and stands on the outside of the circle.
- The locomotor movements involved are running and side-stepping. Repeat the dance using the skipping step.

DESCRIPTION OF ACTIVITY:

1. *Verse:*
   One little, two little, three little Indians,
   Four little, five little, six little Indians.
   Seven little, eight little, nine little Indians,
   Ten little Indian boys and girls.
   The "Chief," run around the outside of the circle and tap a dancer on the shoulder as each of the numbers is called. Tagged dancer remember your number; then skip four steps toward the center, and join hands.
2. *Chorus:*
   Tra, la, la, la, la, la, la, la, . . .
   Dancers of the inside circle, with hands joined, side-step together CW around the circle; outside circle dancers side-step CCW around the circle.
3. *Verse:*
   Ten little, nine little, eight little Indians,
   Seven little, six little, five little Indians,
   Four little, three little, two little Indians,
   One little Indian boy.
   Inside circle dancers return to outer circle in reverse order.
4. *Chorus: All dancers join hands and side-step CCW around the circle. Then repeat from beginning.*

RD-13 BODY PART RHYTHMS

FOCUS: Rhythmical body movements

EQUIPMENT: Drum or tambourine;
music in 4/4 time;
tape or record player

ORGANIZATION:

- Children explore moving different body parts in rhythm in personal and general space.
- Have children find a home space to start.

DESCRIPTION OF ACTIVITY:

1. Listen to the rhythm of my drum. In your home space, show me how you can move different body parts to the drum beats (regular steady beat):
   — Hands—shake, clap, slap knees, punch
   — Fingers—snap, flick, squeeze and open
   — Elbows—point, jab
   — Heads—shake, nod
   — Feet—stamp
   — Arms—circle, move up and down
   — Hips—circle, swing from side to side
   — Knees—bend and straighten
   — Shoulders—shrug

2. Listen to the music. Show me how you can move your feet in your personal space and, at the same time, move another body part of your choice, to the music. Repeat moving other body parts with your feet. Can you move three different body parts at the same time to the music? four different parts?

3. Now skip in general space and at the same time clap your hands to the music. Can you change the way your feet are moving and use a different body part with your feet?

4. *Head and Shoulders* (Perform to the tune "London Bridge.")
   Head and shoulders, knees and toes; knees and toes, knees and toes
   Head and shoulders, knees and toes; clap your hands and round you go.
   Touch your elbows and your nose; touch your ankles and your clothes.
   Touch you seat, reach out wide; shake yourself from side to side.
   Touch your hips and touch your heel; touch your chin, how does it feel?
   Touch your ears and touch your thigh, One, two, three—now jump up high.

5. *Looby Lou* (Singing Movement Song—RCA 45 41-6153) Have children all join hands and form a large circle. Teach them the tune and words to the song; then add the actions.

   — *Chorus:* Here we go Looby Lou, Here we go Looby Light,
     Here we go Looby Lou, All on a Saturday night.
     Walk CW in a circle for eight steps. Change direction after eight counts; then circle back to the starting position for eight counts.

   — *Verses* (For each verse, have children stand in place and do the actions):
     I put my right hand in, I put my right hand out,
     I give my hand a shake, shake, shake; And turn
       myself about. *Chorus.*
     I put my left hand in . . . *Chorus.*
     I put my right foot in . . . *Chorus.*
     I put my left foot in . . . *Chorus.*
     I put my two hands in . . . *Chorus.*
     I put my head in . . . *Chorus.*
     I put my whole self in . . . *Chorus.*

" I PUT MY RIGHT FOOT IN . . ."

RD-14 RHYTHMS IN SPACE

FOCUS: Rhythmical locomotor movements; directions

EQUIPMENT: Tambourine or drum; four sets of colored banners

ORGANIZATION:

• Children explore moving rhythmically in personal and general space, using a variety of locomotor movements, and in different directions.
• To begin, have children find a home space.

DESCRIPTION OF ACTIVITY:

1. In your home, clap your hands and at the same time bend your knees in time to my tambourine for eight counts; then turn around in your home for four counts; turn the opposite way for another four counts; march in place for eight counts. (Repeat this sequence.) Explore other actions such as forward and backward arm swings; turning upper body from side to side; etc.
2. Pretend that you are a **Dancing Horse.** Show me how you can gallop forward, keeping in time to my drum (lively uneven beats). On the loud beat, prance in place to my drum beat. On two loud beats, gallop forward again, but in a different direction. (Repeat several times.)
3. Now let's be a **Slider.** Point your finger and side-step along in that direction, following your finger. Are you moving to the rhythm of my drum (uneven beats)? Freeze on one loud beat. Side-step in the opposite direction on two loud beats. Let your pointer finger lead the way. (Repeat several times.)
4. You are a **Skipper.** Show me how you can skip to my drum. Skip in place on one loud beat. Change direction on every two loud beats. Skip forward; skip backwards, changing every eight counts.
5. **Rhythm Colors** (Divide the class into four groups; each group wears a different set of colored banners: yellow, red, blue, and green.) The group, whose color is called, move to my tambourine in general space, while the other three groups move only in personal space. On the two loud beats, all groups freeze. Listen carefully for the next color called. Now I will call out two or three colors at a time and ask you to move in a certain way: "Green, gallop; Red, walk backwards; Yellow, skip." Remember to keep in time to the beat.

6. **Rhythm Exchange:** Red and Blue groups stand on this endline, facing the Yellow and Green groups, who stand on the opposite endline. Make sure you are well spaced apart. On signal, move toward each other (by walking, skipping, side-stepping, galloping . . . to my drum beats), pass each other, without touching, to the opposite endline.
7. **Rhythm Square** (Position each group on one side of a 4-meter [16-foot] square.) Listen carefully for the colors I call. Exchange sides, moving to my tambourine's beat. (Vary the locomotor movements and directions.)
8. Show me how you can join the actions of side-stepping, skipping, and galloping together to make a Rhythm Directions Story. Remember, your story should have a beginning, middle, and ending. Show me your starting position if you are going to be a Skipper (a knee ready to lift); a Slider (a pointer finger ready); a Galloper (one foot in front).

RD-15 RHYTHMS AND PATHWAYS

FOCUS: Rhythmical locomotor movements

EQUIPMENT: Drum or tambourine; music in 4/4 time; tape or record player

ORGANIZATION:
- Children explore moving rhythmically in different pathways, directions, and levels.
- Have them begin in a home space.

DESCRIPTION OF ACTIVITY:

1. You are my **Magical Paintbrushes.** Dip your feet into the paint and travel to my tambourine (steady shaking), painting wiggly lines all over the floor. Can you paint wiggly lines while moving backwards to your home? Show me how you can stamp a straight line on the floor, moving forward; backwards; sideways.

2. Now put some imaginary paint on your nose. How can you draw a circle? a curvy line? a straight line that goes up and down; that moves from left to right? a wiggly line? Put some paint on your "belly button." What kind of patterns can you paint now? Let your head be the paintbrush; one foot; one hand.
3. Listen to the music being played. Can you make a Painting Dance? Think of all the different pathways and patterns you can paint: straight, winding, curvy, zig-zag, spiral, figure-8, circle, triangle, diamond pattern. Remember to paint in time to the music!
4. Find a partner and together paint a picture. Take turns being the leader and the follower. Keep in time to the music.

RD-16 RHYTHMS AND LEVELS

FOCUS: Rhythmical locomotor movements

EQUIPMENT: Drum or tambourine; music in 4/4 time; tape or record player

ORGANIZATION:
- Children explore moving rhythmically in different pathways, directions, and levels.
- Have them begin in a home space.

DESCRIPTION OF ACTIVITY:

1. Stand tall in your home. Show me how you can change from a high level to a low level in eight counts. Now take eight counts to change to a high level. (Repeat, using four counts.)
2. With my drumbeat, travel in general space at a high level in a winding pathway; freeze on the loud beat at a medium level; travel in another pathway at this level. Freeze on the next loud beat, at a low level. Travel in another direction and pathway at this level. (Repeat several times.)
3. Let's pretend that you are **Skyhorses.** Gallop to my soft drum beats, changing directions. Leap from cloud to cloud on the loud beats. At what level are you moving? (*high level*) Now you are **Sand Crabs** scurrying sideways across the sand. At what level are you moving now? (*medium level*) Show me how you can wiggle and squiggle and roll in the mud as **Mud Bugs.** At what level are you moving? (*low level*)
4. Create a High-Low Dance with a partner. Decide who will be "high" and who will be "low" to start. First partner travel high to my drum beat. Freeze high on the loud beat. Now second partner travel low. Freeze low on drum signal. Then first partner travel low; freeze low on drum signal. Second partner travel high; freeze high. Continue in this way.
   — Now travel together, one high and the other low. Freeze at that level on the loud drum beat. Then travel again, but switching levels. Continue in this way.

RD–17 RHYTHMS AND RANGES

FOCUS: Space awareness

EQUIPMENT: Tambourine and cymbals; appropriate music; tape or record player, two large balloons

ORGANIZATION:

- Children explore moving rhythmically in large and small areas in personal and general space, using the body actions of shrinking, curling, spreading, and growing.
- Have children begin in a home space.

DESCRIPTION OF ACTIVITY:

1. Stand tall in your home. Show me how you can slowly shrink until your body is small. Now grow and grow until you are big again. (Strike the cymbals together. As the sound fades, have the children slowly shrink to the floor. Strike the cymbals again to signal the growing action.)

   — Shrink again. How can you slowly spread until you take up as much space as possible? Are most of your body parts far away from each other?

2. Run anywhere in free space in time to my tambourine (lively, regular beats). Freeze on the loud beat. Take eight counts to make your body as small as you can by curling into a tight ball and tucking all parts in. Take another eight counts to grow and grow and grow. Run in a different way to my tambourine. "Freeze!" See if you can take up even less space this time on different body parts. Grow again.

3. Skip in free space. Freeze on the loud beat. Now make yourself as big as you can. Now skip in a different way. "Freeze!" and use a different body surface to spread yourself, taking up even more space.

4. Create a ***Shrinking-Growing Story:*** Travel to my tambourine's beat, staying as big as you can (slow, even beats). Stop when the tambourine stops. Let your body shrink until you are very small. Be very still. (Gently shake tambourine.) Now slowly spread-and-spread, taking up a lot of space. (Gently and slowly shake tambourine.) Grow bigger and bigger, and travel in your big shape.

5. ***Big and Small:*** Listen carefully to the music being played. Can you hear music that tells you to be very big or to be very small? Can you make up your own "Big and Small Dance"?

6. ***Betty Balloon*** (action poem). Look at my balloon. It takes up only a small space. Watch what happens as I blow it up: it takes up a bigger and bigger space! Now I will let my balloon go. Watch the path it takes as the air escapes out of it. Listen for the sound.

   — Betty Balloon was thin as could be
   Then got a bit bigger when blown up by me.
   Bigger and fatter, and then one more blow . . .
   Fattest of all, . . . and then I let go.
   Zoopedy, zoopedy, zoopedy, zoop!
   Zoopedy, zoop, zoop! Then Betty went d-r-o-o-p!
   More air in Betty, until fatter than fat!
   I tied a string on and kept her like that.
   She floated around and around and around.
   But then she went POP! and dropped to the ground.

"ZOOPEDY, ZOOP!"

RD-18 RHYTHMS AND BODY PARTS

FOCUS: Rhythmic movement; space and body awareness **EQUIPMENT:** Tambourine or drum

ORGANIZATION:

- Dancers explore moving rhythmically on different body parts and using different body parts to lead.
- To begin, have dancers walk to the rhythm of your drum to a home space.

DESCRIPTION OF ACTIVITY:

1. Listen to the rhythm of my drum. Can you clap this rhythm with your hands? Repeat echo clapping, using hand and knee (1-2-3-4); hand and hip (1-2-3-4); feet and hands (1-2-3-4); feet only; etc.

2. Now show me how you can travel in general space, keeping in time to the drum beats, and changing directions and pathways, on:
   — two parts (run, skip, jump, gallop, dart, side-step, hop, etc.)
   — four parts (crawl, creep, pounce)
   — whole body (slither, roll, wiggle)

3. Travel in general space to the rhythm of the drum, with a body part leading you. Freeze on one loud beat in a flat shape (pointed shape, small shape, large shape). On two loud beats, change the way you are travelling and let a new body part take over:
   — Walk backwards with your seat leading.
   — Skip in a circular pattern with your elbows leading.
   — Run forward with your head leading.
   — Side-step with your knee leading.
   — Add your own idea!

4. How can you travel about, letting one body part lead for eight counts, and then let another body part lead for the next eight counts? Can you continue in this way?

5. *Action Ideas* (Accompany with tambourine or drum to a steady rhythm [1-2-3-4]):
   — Little pony galloping
   — A frog jumping from lily pad to lily pad
   — Crawling through a low tunnel
   — Creeping up on someone . . . to surprise them
   — Rolling to get rid of . . . a bug on your back
   — Curious puppy dog sniffing . . . for a bone

6. Can you make up a Body Part Dance which begins on two body parts, moves to four body parts in the middle, and then ends with the whole body moving?

7. *Monster Dance:* Listen to the music being played. Can you create a Monster Dance which uses different body parts to move in personal and general space? Try to use changes of levels, directions, pathways, and leading body parts. (Let small groups of five or six, in turn, perform their dances for the rest of the class.)

RD-19 RHYTHMS AND BODY SHAPES

FOCUS: Body and space awareness

EQUIPMENT: Tambourine or drum; mood music; tape or record player

ORGANIZATION:

- Children explore changing shape while moving rhythmically in personal and general space. Review the four basic body shapes: "narrow," "wide," "rounded," and "twisted."
- Have children find a home space to begin.

DESCRIPTION OF ACTIVITY:

1. Move in general space to my drum. Freeze in a wide shape for four counts. Move in another way. Freeze in a narrow shape (1-2-3-4). Travel; freeze in a rounded shape. Travel; freeze in a twisted shape. Can you change the level of your shape on each freeze? (Repeat several times.)

1.

2. In your home space, show me how you can change to a different shape each time you hear a drum beat: shape-shape-shape-shape. "Freeze!" (Repeat.)

3. Back-lying in your home space, take four counts to bring your hands and feet together. Take four counts to bring your feet and hands wide apart. Take four counts to round yourself into a ball; and four counts to stretch yourself out.

3.

4. Show me how you can travel to my drum, moving from a large shape to a small shape; from a small shape to a large shape; from a rounded shape to a flat shape.

5. Listen to the music being played. Make a Body Shape Dance using the four basic body shapes.

6. *Halloween Magic* (Children explore action words: floating, flying, twirling, twisting, leaping and galloping in an action story about Witches.) You are a Halloween Witch who is:
   — old, crouched, and has gnarled fingers
   — peering around, taking long steps
   — stirring your magic brew in a big black pot
   — sweeping cobwebs from the roof
   — leaping, twirling, and suddenly stopping; crouch low; then suddenly stretch up waving hands above your head and hisssss!

7. *Witches, Elephants, Goblins, and Fairies:* Divide the class into four groups: Witches, Goblins, Elephants, and Fairies. Have each group begin in a certain space in the play area.
   — Witches, ride your broom in the sky and cackle.
   — Sneak up on the Goblins who are floating in the sky. Watch their Spooky Dance as they twist and twirl into different shapes.
   — Fly over a zoo where you see Elephants eating hay.
   — Change the Elephants into Ducks!
   — Ducks try to fly—but you are too heavy!
   — Witches cackle and dance in glee.
   — Fairies come to the rescue. Frighten the witches away. (Witches fly to their starting space.)
   — Fairies change the ducks to boys and girls, who ride away on white ponies to their home space.

8. Listen to the music I am playing. Can you create your own Monster Dance to the music?

RD-20 RHYTHMS AND TEMPO

FOCUS: Effort awareness; even and uneven rhythms; speed   **EQUIPMENT:** Tambourine or drum

ORGANIZATION:

- Children explore the element of time as they move rhythmically to "even and uneven rhythms" that are slow, steady, or fast tempos. Discuss the meaning of "tempo" or the speed at which the music moves. Check for good understanding of movement vocabulary.
- To begin, have children find a home space.

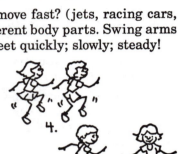

DESCRIPTION OF ACTIVITY:

1. What does slow mean to you? (not active, not lively, no spirit) What things can you think of that move in a slow way? (turtles, snails, worms, caterpillars, . . .) In your home, show me some slow movements with different body parts: using your hands, your feet; changing from one level to another; changing body bases. (For slow movements, shake or scrape the tambourine slowly.) Can you tell me what things move fast? (jets, racing cars, bullets, . . .) In your home, show me some quick movements using different body parts. Swing arms quickly, slowly; open and close your hands quickly, slowly; stamp your feet quickly; slowly; steady!

2. Listen to the drum. (Play a fast, even beat [1-2-3-4]; a slow even beat; then a steady beat.) Can you hear the difference? Now listen to the beat, then "echo clap" with your hands. (You play the rhythm; dancers copy it by clapping.) Echo clap using different body parts (feet, knees, elbows, head, hips, arms, etc.) Repeat several times.

3. Listen to the slow even rhythm of my drum. Show me how you can walk to this rhythm (16 counts). Walk to my fast even rhythm; steady, even rhythm. Now listen to the quick, light beats of the tambourine. Run in general space, keeping in time to this even rhythm. (Repeat using jumping and hopping movements.)

4. Listen to the uneven rhythm of my drum. Show me how you can skip to the beat (eight slow counts); now skip to the quick, uneven rhythm (eight counts); then skip to the steady rhythm. (Repeat using galloping, side-stepping.)

5. Listen carefully to the drum beats—show me how you would move. Change from even to uneven rhythms, using steady beats. (Can children react correctly to the changes in rhythms?)

6. **Slow/Fast Dance:** Create a dance that has a slow beginning, a steady middle part, and a fast ending, using different locomotor movements. (Run forward for eight beats; skip in a circle for eight steady beats; slowly walk backwards for eight beats.) You may wish to change the slow and fast parts of your dance. Practice; then we will watch your dance.

7. **The Toy Shop:** Have you ever wondered what toys do when they come alive? Today we are going to visit a toy shop where the toys are alive! Everyone, up on your feet! Open the door.
   - See the **Ragdolls** dance. Their arms hang, legs bend and wobble, and heads bob (slow uneven beats on drum). The **Soldiers** march right, left, right, left, swinging arms high at their sides (steady even beats).
   - **Ballerina Dolls** or **Karate Kids** side-step over the floor, twirling, swishing, kicking (quick uneven beats).
   - **Jack-in-the-Box** laughs and sways, then jumps up high, squats down low, jumps up high (strong even beats).
   - Over in the corner, we see **Little Train** chugging across the floor. Be the train as it moves along, slowly at first, then gathers speed (uneven slow-quick beats).
   - In another corner, red and blue **Balls** are doing a "bouncing dance." Bounce low, bounce high, roll and bounce (slow-quick even beats).
   - **Spinning Tops** are the last toys we see. Sit on the floor and spin yourself around and around (quick even beats).
   - Close the door quietly; it's time to go. Tip-toe slowly back to the listening circle. Shhh . . . (light even beats).

RD-21 RHYTHMS AND ENERGY

FOCUS: Effort awareness; rhythmic movement

EQUIPMENT: Drum, triangle, bells, or finger cymbals, or tambourine; "spooky" music in 4/4 time; tape or record player

ORGANIZATION:

- Children explore strong and light rhythmic actions in personal and general space. Discuss the terms "strong" (powerful) and "light."
- To begin, have children find a home space.

DESCRIPTION OF ACTIVITY:

1. Show me how strong you can be: grip one hand; grip the other hand. Grip one foot; grip the other. How can you grip your whole body? (by squeezing as tightly as you can) Grip a different body part each loud drum beat.

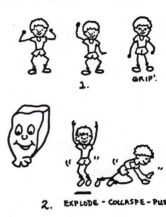

2. Let's explore strong actions. "Explode!" (Accompany the actions with a steady drumbeat building into a loud double bang, or hold a sustained ring on the cymbal, followed by a crash.)

   — Collapse to the floor (two counts); then push yourself up with your hands (four counts). Repeat, using the back as the base of support.

   — You are a paper bag that I am blowing into. Get tighter and tighter, until finally you burst! Collapse on the floor. (Repeat.)

   — Can you join four strong actions together to form a sequence? GRIP-EXPLODE-COLLAPSE-PUSH.

3. Now let's explore light actions which travel quickly and turn. Show me how you can quickly flee on your toes. (Accompany with a soft ringing sound of the triangle, bells, or cymbals.) Look for an empty space. Remember to stay on your tip-toes. Freeze on the loud drumbeat. (Repeat this FLEE-FREEZE sequence several times.)

4. Show me how you can flit lightly from place to place as if you were a hummingbird! I'm listening, don't let me hear your feet!

   — Who can twirl high into the sky? twirl low? Remember to twirl in both directions so you don't get dizzy!

5. Pretend that you are dragonflies, dancing in the sunlight. Move ever so silently, but quickly, as you flit from leaf to leaf. Flee over the pond, chasing an insect. Twirl about in fun, then flee away.

6. **Action stories—Barnyard Ghosts.** Listen to the following poem:

   "Ghosts are flying through the air; softly, slowly, . . . everywhere!
   Twirling . . . Leaping . . . Skipping around . . . ever so lightly, with not a sound."

   Now you are a ghost. Show me how you fly ever so quietly in general space, changing directions and pathways often, to the beat of my tambourine. Fly sometimes high; sometimes low. Fly around people, coming very close; then fly off at the last moment.

   — Show me how you can twirl in the air to my tambourine. Can you start slowly and gradually twirl faster and faster? Now twirl high; then slowly change to twirling low. Run, leap, and twirl in the air. (Repeat several times.) Remember to land lightly, bending at your knees and ankles.

   — Now let's join these movements together as you act out the poem. Boys first, while girls observe; then girls, it will be your turn. Take your starting ghost shape. If you can, say the poem with me as you do the actions we have explored.

7. Make your own Light and Strong Dance.

RD-22 RHYTHMS AND TIME

FOCUS: Effort awareness

EQUIPMENT: Drum; two rhythm sticks

ORGANIZATION:

- Children explore the elements of "Flow" through sudden and sustained action words using the whole body and body parts in personal and general space. Discuss sudden movements: balloon bursting, alarm clock ringing, door slamming shut. Discuss sustained movements: plant growing, snail crawling, slow-motion walking.
- Dancers begin in a home space.

DESCRIPTION OF ACTIVITY:

1. Listen to the quick beats of my rhythm sticks. Clap your hands in time. Snap your fingers to the beat. Pick the space around you (like picking imaginary apples from a tree). Pick high, pick low, pick behind you, in front, other side. Now hide your fingers; then flick them out! Try this sequence (do four counts of each): CLAP-SNAP-PICK-FLICK.
2. Stand in your home space. Quickly dart to a free space for eight counts (eight light even drum beats). "Freeze!" (on the loud drum beat). Snap your fingers 1-2-3-4; then dart for another eight counts; "Freeze!" Snap fingers 1-2-3-4. Repeat this sequence several times.
3. Now you are a balloon floating in the air. Move in time to the shaking of the tambourine (eight counts). Now take four counts to slowly sink to the floor. Take another four counts to slowly rise and float again (eight counts). Repeat sequence several times; then have dancers "float" to their home space.

RD-23 EXPLORING TIME AND ENERGY

ORGANIZATION:

EQUIPMENT: Drum; cymbals

- Now dancers explore strong, sudden actions; strong, slow actions; light, sudden actions; and light, slow actions in personal and general space.

DESCRIPTION OF ACTIVITY:

1. In your home curl up tight for four counts. Poke out your elbow; poke your knees; your head. Poke out a different body part each time you hear the drum. This is a strong, sudden action. Now flick your elbow, your fingers, your knees. This is a light, sudden action.
2. Listen to the quick, strong beats of my drum. Use sudden, strong jumps to travel to another free space (eight counts). Freeze on the loud beat and grip up tight (four counts). Repeat. Now travel across the floor with slow, strong stepping actions (eight slow counts). Can you keep a strong-looking body at the same time? Freeze and punch slowly into the air (four counts). Repeat.
3. When you hear the sound of the cymbal, twirl about. Glide up high in the sky; glide down low. Now twirl for eight counts; then glide for eight counts. Repeat. Flit from place to place. Be light and happy. Try this sequence: FLIT-FLIT-TWIRL-GLIDE.
   — Now take eight counts to melt to the floor. Let just one body part slowly rise for four counts; then on the loud drum beat, it suddenly collapses. Repeat.
4. *Eggshell Dance:* Curl up tight inside your shell. Begin to poke, trying to break out. You are out, but you feel so jerky. Flick out your wings, your feet, your beak. Pick the air. Now test your wings as you glide up in the sky. Flit from tree to tree. Twirl about. Glide to land lightly on a branch. Curl up tight. Sleep.

RD-24 RHYTHMS AND RELATIONSHIPS

FOCUS: Partnerwork; rhythmic movement; copying

EQUIPMENT: Drum; music in 4/4 time; tape or record player

ORGANIZATION:

- Children, working in pairs, move rhythmically while leading or following, then approaching and retreating, and finally parting, meeting, and travelling together.
- Have the dancers choose partners and each pair skip to your drum beats to a home space.

DESCRIPTION OF ACTIVITY:

1. One partner be the Leader; the other, the Follower. Listen to my drum. Show me how you and your partner can skip together in general space, one leading, the other following, and both keeping in time to the beat (16 counts). "Freeze!" on the loud beat (two counts); join hands and skip in a circle for six counts. Change roles on four counts, then skip again in another direction (16 counts). Repeat this sequence several times.

2. Repeat, using other locomotor rhythms such as walking, running, jumping, hopping, galloping, and side-stepping, travelling in different pathways. Have dancers freeze on the loud beat and change partners.

3. Now leader, cut a pattern on the floor (eight counts); then stop to watch your partner copy it. (Dancers could travel at a certain level; travel by taking giant steps or small steps, changing speeds.)

4. Find another partner and choose who will lead first. Leader, move in personal space to the music while your partner copies your moves. Can you change your base of support while your partner mirrors your every move?

5. **Siamese Dance:** I will call out a body part to which you are both attached: tops of heads, hips, shoulders, seat, legs, etc. Listen to the music being played. Show me how you can move in time with the music, keeping attached. Do not release until I give you the signal. Find a new partner, and repeat.

6. **Approaching and Retreating** (Position yourself in the center of the play area): Listen to my drum beats. Run to the beat toward a corner of the play area (16 counts). Freeze on the loud beat. Stamp and turn in place until you are facing me (four counts). Now walk to the beat toward me (16 counts). Freeze and snap your fingers in place. Repeat, using other locomotor movements, travelling in different directions, pathways, and levels.

7. Now, boys, stamp loudly away from me (16 counts); while girls lightly tip-toe toward me. Girls, as soon as you get near to me, change your direction and move away by stamping your feet. Some of you will be moving toward me, while others will be going away. Try to move in time with the drum beats. (Use a variety of locomotor movements.)

8. Now find a partner. In time with the music, travel away from each other in different directions (16 counts); then travel toward each other (16 counts). Meet and clap each other's hands for four counts, then travel together side by side (16 counts); then part ways again. (Continue this sequence using different locomotor movements.)

RD-25 DANCE OF GREETING

FOCUS: Folk dance

EQUIPMENT: Music reference—Folkraft 1187 or Hoctor Products HLP-4026;
tape or record player

ORGANIZATION:

- This simple Danish folk dance uses the following actions: clapping, bowing, stamping, and running. Have children form one large circle, facing center.

DESCRIPTION OF ACTIVITY:

1. Clap, clap, bow. Clap, clap, bow.
   Stamp R, stamp L; Turn R around 1-2-3-4.

   Everyone clap your hands twice then bow. Then stamp your feet twice (right, left). Then turn around to the right with four light running steps.

2. Run L-2-3-4- . . . -16; Run R-2-3-4- . . . 16

   All join hands in a circle and run 16 light steps to the left; then 16 steps to the right.

VARIATION: This dance could be done with a double circle formation in partners: boys on the outside; girls on the inside.

RD-26 BIRD DANCE

FOCUS: Novelty dance

EQUIPMENT: Music reference—Dance, Dance, Dance Album with the Emeralds, K-Tel NC 634, K-Tel International Ltd.;
tape or record player

ORGANIZATION:

- This popular dance involves the basic steps of skipping and swinging. Have dancers pair off, then scatter around the play area, with partners standing and facing each other in a free space. Make sure that everyone can see you clearly.

DESCRIPTION OF ACTIVITY:

1. Part A (Repeat Part A four times.)
   — Cheep, cheep, cheep, cheep.
     Make "pecking" actions with your fingers.
   — Flap, flap, flap, flap.
     Hook your thumbs under your arms, and make flapping movements.

   CHEEP-CHEEP!.   FLAP-FLAP!

   — Wiggle, wiggle, wiggle, wiggle.
     Sway hips from side to side.
   — Clap, clap, clap, clap.
     Clap your hands.

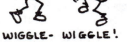

CIRCLE R...

WIGGLE- WIGGLE!.   CLAP-CLAP!.

2. Part B (Repeat Part B twice.)
   — Circle R-2-3-4-5-6-7-8.
     Join hands with your partner and skip CW in a circle for eight counts.
   — Circle L-2-3-4-5-6-7-8.
     Join hands with your partner and skip CCW in a circle for another eight counts.

CIRCLE L...

VARIATIONS:

a. On part B, have children hook right elbows, then skip CW in a circle for eight counts; then hook left elbows and circle CCW for eight counts.

b. Have children choose a new partner each time the dance is repeated.

RD-27 CHIMES OF DUNKIRK

FOCUS: Folk dance

EQUIPMENT: Music reference—Folkraft 1159 or Hoctor Products, HLP-4026; tape or record player

ORGANIZATION:

- This simple folk dance from Belgium uses the basic steps of running, stamping, and side-stepping. Have children form a double circle, with boys on the inside facing girl partners on the outside.

DESCRIPTION OF ACTIVITY:

1. Stamp L-stamp R-stamp L; Clap-clap-clap

   Turn-2-3-4-5-6-7-8.

   Everyone stamp your feet three times; then clap your hands three times. Partner join hands and circle CW in place for eight running steps.

2. Side-step right-2-3-4-5-6-7-8.

   Side-step left-2-3-4-5-6-7-8.

   Partners join hands and side-step CCW around the circle to the chorus. Then repeat from beginning.

VARIATION: Have children skip instead of side-step in part 2.

RD-28 TURKEY IN THE STRAW

FOCUS: Folk dance

EQUIPMENT: Music reference—Folkraft 1067; tape or record player

ORGANIZATION:

- This American folk dance uses the basic steps of walking, skipping, side-stepping, and elbow-swinging. Have dancers pair off and form a single circle; everyone joins hands and faces the center.

DESCRIPTION OF ACTIVITY:

1. Side-step-2-3-4- . . . -8; Side-step-2-3-4- . . . -8.

   Beginning with the left foot, move eight side-steps to the left; then beginning with the right foot, move eight side-steps to the right.

2. Walk-2, Stamp, Stamp, Stamp;

   Walk-2, Stamp, Stamp, Stamp.

   Beginning with the left foot, walk two steps toward the center and stamp three times; then beginning with the right foot, walk two steps back to place, and stamp three times.

3. Turn-2-3-4; Skip-2-3-4.

   Hook right arms with your partner and turn in place with four skips; then the left dancer of each pair, skip in a CCW direction with four skips to meet a new partner. Repeat dance from beginning.

3.

RD-29 JUMP JIM JO

FOCUS: Folk dance mixer

EQUIPMENT: Music reference—Folkraft 1180; tape or record player

ORGANIZATION:

- This American circle dance involves the basic steps of jumping, walking, running, side-stepping, and stamping. Dancers pair off and form a large circle, with partners facing and hands joined. (This dance can also be done without partners.)

DESCRIPTION OF ACTIVITY:

1. Jump, jump, jump Jim Jo; Take a little turn and away we go.
   Do two slow jumps in place; then three quick jumps in place. Drop your hands and each dancer turn in place to the right with four slow walking steps.

2. Slide, slide, and stamp just so
   You're a sprightly little fellow, when you jump, Jim Jo.
   Join hands and take two side-steps to the inside partner's left; then stamp three times in place. Drop your hands and each dancer turn in place to the right with four light running steps; then jump three times in place. (For Mixer, have partners take four running steps to the right to meet new partner; then together jump three times in place.)

RD-30 SEVEN JUMPS

EQUIPMENT: Music reference—RCA LPM 1623, *All Purpose Folk Dance;* tape or record player

ORGANIZATION:

- This Danish folk dance uses the skipping step and seven different body positions. Have dancers form one large circle, join hands, and face CCW.

DESCRIPTION OF ACTIVITY:

1. Right-2-3-4-5-6-7-Jump; Left-2-3-4-5-6-7-Pause
   Beginning with the right foot, skip to the right for seven counts, followed by a jump. Then skip left for seven counts, followed by a pause. Drop hands.

2. Raise right knee, then lower.
   Raise your right knee on the first held note. On the second held note, lower it. Join hands. Repeat part 1.
   Raise left knee, then lower.
   Repeat part 2. On the first held note raise and lower the right knee, then quickly raise and lower the left knee on the second held note. Join hands. Repeat part 1.

3. Kneel on the right knee, stand.
   Repeat parts 2 and 3; then kneel on the right knee of the third held note. Stand up, join hands, and repeat part 1.
   Kneel on both knees, stand.
   Repeat parts 2, 3, and 4; then kneel on both knees. On the fifth held note, stand up, join hands, and repeat part 1.

4. Place right elbow on floor, stand.
   Repeat parts 2, 3, 4, and 5. On the fifth note while still kneeling, place the right elbow on the floor. On the sixth held note, stand up, join hands, and repeat part 1.
   Place both elbows on the floor, stand.
   Repeat parts 2, 3, 4, 5, and 6. On the sixth held note, place the left elbow on the floor as well. Stand on the seventh held note, join hands, and repeat part 1.

5. Place forehead on floor, stand, bow.
   Repeat parts 2, 3, 4, 5, 6, and 7. On the seventh held note, place your forehead on the floor. Stand, bow to the center.

RD-31 KINDER-POLKA

FOCUS: Folk dance

EQUIPMENT: Music reference—Folkraft 1187 or Hoctor Products HLP-4026; tape or record player

ORGANIZATION:

- This German folk dance means "children's polka" and involves the basic steps of step-close, stamping, clapping, and step-turning. Have dancers learn and practice the step-close step individually; then facing a partner.
- Have dancers pair off and form a single circle of couples, with partners facing.

DESCRIPTION OF ACTIVITY:

1. Step-close, step-close; stamp, stamp, stamp.

   Step-close, step-close; stamp, stamp, stamp.

   Very slowly, take two step-closes toward the center of the circle; then stamp your feet in place three times. Then take two step-closes away from the center, and stamp feet three times. Repeat this pattern again.

1.

2. Slap knees; clap hands; clap partner's 1-2-3.

   With both hands, slap your knees once; clap your own hands once; then clap your partner's hands three times. Repeat this pattern again.

3. Shake right finger; shake left finger.

   Hop on your left foot, and reach your right heel forward; then shake your pointer finger three times at your partner. Repeat the "scolding" pattern with your left foot and left pointer finger.

2.

4. Turn, turn, turn, turn;

   Stamp, stamp, stamp, pause.

   Turn in place with four steps; face your partner and stamp your feet three times.

3.

4.

VARIATIONS:

a. *Kinder-Polka Mixer:* Partners facing CCW move past their partner to meet a new partner after each repetition of the dance.

b. Substitute "jump-turns" for step-turns in part 4.

RD–32 RHYTHM INSTRUMENTS—"THE BAND"

FOCUS: Exploring rhythm instruments

EQUIPMENT: Variety of rhythm instruments;
whistle;
music in 4/4 time;
tape or record player

ORGANIZATION:

- Children explore moving rhythmically while using different rhythm instruments.
- If possible, give each child a rhythm instrument and have children find a home space. Discuss the importance of looking after their instruments.

DESCRIPTION OF ACTIVITY:

1. In your home space, explore the sound your instrument makes. Listen carefully to it. Listen to my drum beat. Can you echo this beat using your instrument?

    — Keep rhythm to my drum and explore moving your instrument into different spaces around you: to one side or the other; in front; behind; above.

    — Try moving your feet as well as the instrument in rhythm to my drum beat.

2. Now keeping in time to the music with your instrument, all march in and out of each other. March in place when you hear two whistles and trade your instrument with someone else; freeze on one whistle. Continue when you hear the music again. (Repeat several times.)

3. Can you create a little dance with your instrument? Your dance should have a beginning, middle, and an ending.

4. All those with the *rhythm instruments* such as the drums and claps, form Group 1; those with *shaking instruments* such as the tambourine and wrist bells, form Group 2; those with *ringing instruments* such as the cymbals or triangle, form Group 3. When I call your Group number, can you show me the sounds of your instruments? Listen carefully.

5. ***The Travelling Band:*** Now Group 1 lead the other two groups in general space, keeping time to the music, by marching. Group 2, lead the other two groups by skipping and shaking your tambourines. Group 3, lead by sinking on two beats and rising on two beats. (Exchange groups so that children get to use different instruments.)

RD-33 DANCING SCARVES

FOCUS: Rhythmical manipulation; space and body awareness

EQUIPMENT: Drum or tambourine; one light, nylon scarf per dancer; one ribbon per dancer; lively music in 4/4 time; tape or record player

ORGANIZATION:
- Have each child get a scarf and find a home space. (Scarf Play is introduced in Section 6, "Game Skills," activities GS–22 and GS–23.)
- Provide opportunity for children to observe each other's scarf dances.

DESCRIPTION OF ACTIVITY:
1. In your home, show me how you can move your scarf to the music: around you; above you; behind you; in front of you; on either side of you. Can you make your scarf dance from a low level to a high level; from a high level to a low level? Can your scarf dance up and down?
2. Run with your scarf in general space, changing directions and pathways. Explore holding your scarf at different levels as you travel: trailing above you; trailing behind you; zig-zagging through the air; moving beside you; moving around you.
3. *Dancing Scarf Story:* Put your three favorite scarf movements together to create a dancing scarf story in personal space; then in general space.
4. *Partner Scarf Dance:* Find a partner. One partner lead while the other partner follows and copies the leader's movements.

RD-34 DANCING RIBBONS

FOCUS: Rhythmical manipulation; space and body awareness

EQUIPMENT: Ribbon; long dowel; fishing line; screw-eyes; lively music in 4/4 time; tape or record player

ORGANIZATION:
- Rhythmic ribbons can be made by attaching a 3- to 4-meter (9- to 12-foot) length of plastic, synthetic, or silk ribbon to a 40-centimeter (16-inch) long dowel. Use a fishing line swivel and trace, screw-eye, and about 30 centimeters (12 inches) of fishing line between the two parts, as shown. Have each dancer get a ribbon and find a home. Ensure that children are well spaced so that ribbons do not become entangled. Have children use one hand, then the other.

DESCRIPTION OF ACTIVITY:
1. Show me how you can swing your ribbon in front of you from side to side like *windshield wipers.* Now try to swing your ribbon forward and back on one side of you; then on the other side of you.

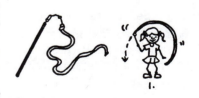

2. Show me how you can make your ribbon travel in a circular pattern: in front of you like a *propeller;* above you like a *helicopter;* on either side of you like a *spinning wheel.*
3. Who can make their ribbon move in a figure-8 pattern? in front of you like a *butterfly;* above you like a *ribbon;* on either side of you like *bows?* How can you make your ribbon look like an *air snake;* a *floor snake?*

4. Explore making *spirals*—bigger and bigger circles with your ribbon; making smaller and smaller spirals with your ribbon.
5. Listen to the music I am playing. Can you make a Ribbon Dance Story?

RD-35 RHYTHM STICKS

FOCUS: Rhythm patterns

EQUIPMENT: Two lummi sticks per child; drum or tambourine; tape or record player

ORGANIZATION:

- Children explore rhythm patterns using lummi sticks. Rhythm sticks can be made from 25-millimeter (1-inch) dowelling, cut into 30-centimeter (12-inch) lengths. (Lummi Stick Play is introduced in Section 6, "Game Skills," activities GS–18 and GS–19.) Have each child get two lummi sticks and find a home space.

DESCRIPTION OF ACTIVITY:

1. Listen to the rhythm I am tapping out. Can you tap this same rhythm with one lummi stick? (Repeat several times as this provides excellent auditory training. Have dancers tap out pattern using either hand.)

2. Let's explore rhythm patterns using two sticks in your home space:
   - Tap the sticks on the floor in front of you four times; to the sides four times; tap sticks behind you four times.
   - Tap the sticks together in the air four times; tap the ends of your sticks together, alternating your palms up and down four times.
   - Cross your arms in front of you and tap sticks to the floor.
   - Try this sequence: tap in front; tap to sides; cross and tap floor; tap sticks together (four counts for each).
   - Can you flip each stick over, in turn, and catch it?
   - Try this sequence: tap front; together; flip and catch.

3. Listen to the music. Show me how you can use your stick like a conductor of an orchestra. Now create your own Tapping Story, choosing any three or more tapping actions. Your story should have a beginning, middle, and ending.

4. Listen to the drum's rhythm. Holding a lummi stick in each hand, show me how you can march in place and tap your sticks together in time to the drum beats. Now march in general space, tapping your sticks as if you were a drummer in a marching band. March forward, backwards, sideways; march in different patterns. Who can march and twirl your sticks like a baton twirler?

5. Skip in a circle and tap sticks together in front of you. Gallop and tap sticks above your head. Side-step, tapping sticks together on the opposite side of your leading foot.

6. ***Partner Rhythms:*** Find a partner and sit cross-legged, facing each other. Listen to the music being played. Tap out this rhythm pattern in time to the music:
   - Tap the floor in front four times; tap your sticks together.
   - Tap partner's sticks in the air; trade sticks with your partner.
   - Cross hands and tap sticks to floor; tap sticks together.
   - Tap partner's sticks in the air; trade sticks with partner; then flip each stick in turn and catch.

7. Create a Partner Tapping Story with your partner. Let one partner be the leader; the other, the follower. Change roles and repeat.

Play Gymnastics

The Play Gymnastics activities progressively build muscular strength and endurance, flexibility, balance, and overall coordination. They also develop children's self-confidence and improve their posture and safety awareness.

This section provides 49 different activities organized into the following areas: Locomotion; Supporting and Balancing; Rotation Around the Body Axes; Springing and Landing; and Climbing, Hanging, and Swinging.

PG–1 ANIMAL WALKS

FOCUS: Weight-bearing; locomotion   **EQUIPMENT:** None

ORGANIZATION:

- Children explore weight-bearing on different body parts through novelty walks. Teach them the names of the different "walks" and use them as Breaks (see Section 2's activities FA–1 through FA–5) between different activities in the lesson.

DESCRIPTION OF ACTIVITY:

1. *Pussy-Cat Walk:* Start on all fours. Walk softly and smoothly like a cat. Stop, "meow," stretch! Here comes a mouse! Can you catch him?

2. *Puppy Run:* Take your weight on all fours, bending your arms and legs slightly. Keep your head up. Show me how you run forward, run backwards, run sideways. Run and chase after some of the other "puppies." Can you bark as you chase them? Can you roll over like a dog and get right back up on your hands and feet again?

3. *Lame Dog Walk:* Can you walk like a lame dog? Who can run like a lame dog? Place both hands and one foot on the floor.

4. *Bear Walk:* Start by taking your weight on all fours, with your hands and feet on the floor. Now show me how you can walk like a bear. Can you swing your hips, moving the arm and leg on the same side at the same time? Sniff around looking for that honey!

5. *Donkey Walk:* Kneel on hands and knees with your head bent forward, and hunch your back. Now raise your head upwards and hollow your back as you move. Continue in this way. Can you make a sound like a donkey? "Hee-Haw! Hee-Haw!"

6. *Crab Walk:* Sit on the floor with your hands behind you and your palms flat on the floor. Raise your body off the floor and take your weight on your hands and feet. Show me how you can move forward, backwards, sideways.

PG-2 NOVELTY STUNTS

FOCUS: Weight-bearing; locomotion   **EQUIPMENT:** None

ORGANIZATION:

- The children explore more weight-bearing activities through fun novelty stunts.

DESCRIPTION OF ACTIVITY:

1. *Inch Worm:* Go down into the squat position with your arms shoulder-width apart and hands on the floor. Without moving your hands, take tiny steps with your feet until your toes are near the backs of your hands. Now without moving your feet, take short steps forward on your hands until your legs and back are straight. Can you "Inchworm" your way across the play area?

2. *Leap Frog:* Start in squat position. Spring forward and land in your starting position. Can you make frog-like sounds as you move in this way? "Ribbet! ribbet!"

3. *The Lizard:* Begin in a front-leaning position. Walk your feet through your hands, using tiny steps until your body is straight and your back is now to the floor. Turn yourself over to the front-leaning position again and do another "Lizard."

4. *Emu Walk:* Place your hands on the floor. Place one foot in front and between your hands and stretch the other foot way out behind you. Switch feet positions as you move across the play area in this way.

5. *Chicken Walk:* From your standing tall position, bend down and place your hands between your legs, behind your ankles, and around to grasp in front of your shins. In this position, walk like a "Chicken." Can you walk backwards? Show me what sounds you will make: "Beep! beep!"

6. *Midget Walk:* (Do this on mats.) Start in a kneeling position on the mat. Arch your back; reach back and grasp your legs just above the ankles. Show me how you can take short steps forward. Who can move sideways, backwards, turn in place?

PG–3 WALK THROUGH THE ZOO

FOCUS: Locomotion; weight-bearing   **EQUIPMENT:** None

ORGANIZATION:

- Have the children find a home and stand facing you. Explain that you are going on a visit to the Zoo and as you mention the animals, you want them to show you how that animal moves.
- Allow the children to interpret first; then have them do the following movements together.

DESCRIPTION OF ACTIVITY:

1. *Camel Walk:* Stand with one foot ahead of the other. Bend forward at the waist and raise your hands behind you to lock fingers. This is the camel's hump. As you take a step, raise or lower your head. Can your camel walk backwards; sideways; go down on his knees; gallop?

2. *Kangaroo Hop:* Bend your arms, holding your hands limply in front of you at chest height. Lean forward, bend your knees, and jump forward and upwards to land lightly on your feet. Continue to "bound along" in this way. Can you hold a "joey" (a baby kangaroo) in your pouch near your bellybutton as you move?

3. *Crocodile Crawl:* From a front-lying position, bend your arms, taking your weight on your hands, elbows high. Now crawl forward, moving your right arm and left leg at the same time, and then your left arm and right leg (cross-lateral movement).

4. *Gorilla Walk:* Start on all fours. Turn your hands inward toward each other. Walk like a gorilla. Look like a gorilla. Can you sound like a gorilla?

5. *Elephant Walk:* From a standing position, bend forward at the waist. Let your arms hang down; then clasp hands together, to be the elephant's trunk. Walk with your knees slightly bent, your back rounded, and with your arms swinging from side to side. Can you make your trunk touch the floor as you walk? What noises does an elephant make?

6. *The Circus:* Let's form a large circle, with everyone facing the center. This will be the "Circus Ring." I will be the "Ringmaster" and stand in the center of the ring. Now everyone, think of an animal that you might find at the circus. When I call your name, I want you to come into the ring, tell us the name of your animal, do the actions and make the sounds for your animal. Then we will all do your actions together with you. Now I will choose another "animal" to come to the center. If someone uses your animal, try to think of another, or use the same animal and do something different.

VARIATION:

Have circle players guess the animal that has entered the "Circus Ring." The player with the correct guess then comes into the center. Ensure that everyone gets a chance to be an animal.

PG–4 BALANCING CHALLENGES

FOCUS: Exploring stationary balancing; body control; listening   **EQUIPMENT:** None

ORGANIZATION:

- Have the players find a spot alone facing you.

DESCRIPTION OF ACTIVITY:

1. Can you balance on the right foot and the right hand? Balance on the left foot and the left hand. What can you do with the other hand to help you balance?
2. Show me how you can balance on one knee and the opposite hand. Now try to balance on the right knee and the right hand; balance on your left knee and your left hand. Which way was easier? Why?
3. Balance on one knee and the toe of the other foot. How can your arms help you balance?
4. Who can balance on your head and two feet? Balance on your seat and one foot. Balance on one hand and two feet. Now try a balancing stunt of your own.

PG–5 STANDING BALANCES

              EQUIPMENT: None

ORGANIZATION:

- Have the players find a spot alone so that they are standing on a line.
- Have them do each of these balances three times, holding each balance for a slow count of five. Repeat all one-legged balances on the other leg. On all balances, have the players look ahead at their own height at a focal point; for example, a spot on the wall.

DESCRIPTION OF ACTIVITY:

1. **The Stork Stand:** Stand, and then lift one foot off the floor and place the sole of that foot against the knee of the standing foot. Hold both arms out sideways. Try these variations:
   — Hold your arms down by your sides.
   — Fold hands across your chest; place on your head, on your hips.
   — Close your eyes and hold the stork stand.
   — Try all these on the other leg.
2. **The Airplane:** Stand on one foot; lean forward and raise one leg off the floor backwards; raise both arms sideways for balance and hold for five counts.
3. **Leg-Lift Balances:** Stand; raise one knee forward to waist height and point the toe downward. Straighten the leg so that it is pointing straight out in front of you. Return to the bent-knee position, and then to the standing position again. Now try it on the other leg. Try these variations:
   — Raise the straight leg to the side.
   — Raise the straight leg to the back without leaning forward.
   — Raise one leg and cross it over in front of the other. Touch your hand (opposite hand to the raised leg) to the raised foot's toes and return. Repeat with the other leg.

PG–6 WALKING BALANCES

FOCUS: Balancing while moving

EQUIPMENT: Balance benches; lines on the floor

ORGANIZATION:

- Have the players run to stand on a line on the floor.

DESCRIPTION OF ACTIVITY:

1. Begin with both feet on the line; one foot in front of the other with your arms out sideways for balance. Look straight ahead, with good posture.
   — Walk forward, placing the toe and then the heel on the floor.
   — Walk forward on your tippy-toes.
   — Walk forward so that the heel touches the toe on each step.
   — Now walk backwards so that the toe touches the heel on each step.
   — Walk forward, with one foot always leading and the other following.
   — Walk sideways, with your arms raised in front for balance. Can you stay on the line?
   — Walk sideways, crossing one foot in front of the other. Now move back, crossing one foot behind the other.
   — Explore other ways of "balance walking" such as swinging legs upwards as you walk forward.

1.

2. **Balance Bench:** Get into groups of five to six, collect a balance bench, and place it in your space with the narrow side up. Take turns as you explore "walking balances" on the balance bench. Travel from one end to the other with a different "walk" each time. Invent your own bench walk!

2.

PG–7 BUILDING BRIDGES

FOCUS: Supporting and balancing; body control

EQUIPMENT: One mat per player

ORGANIZATION:

- Have players collect a mat and place it in a free space.

DESCRIPTION OF ACTIVITY:

1. Who knows what a bridge is? Can you all show me how you can make a bridge with your body? Can you make a bridge on your hands and feet? Show another way of making a bridge using hands and feet.
   — Make a bridge over your mat.
   — Make a bridge, using two hands and one foot.
   — Make a bridge, using two feet but only one hand.
   — How far apart can you move your hands and feet and still balance?
   — Try to balance with your hands wide apart and feet close together; then your hands close together and feet wide apart. Which way is easier?

1.

2. Now put three of your favorite bridges together, changing from one to the other.
3. Find a partner. Explore different ways of building bridges together. (Let half the pairs observe the other pairs' bridges.)

3.

PG–8 BALANCING AND SHAPE-MAKING

FOCUS: Balancing; weight-bearing; body control

EQUIPMENT: One small mat per player; background music; tape or record player

ORGANIZATION:

- Have the children each pick up a mat, put the mat in a home space, and stand on it. Check that the mats are well spaced apart. Emphasize good body control and stillness on all balances. Have children hold their balances for a slow count of 1, 2, 3.

- Allow the children time to explore and experiment. Make suggestions only when necessary.

DESCRIPTION OF ACTIVITY:

1. *Mat Balance Warm-up:* On the signal "Go," run to a different mat and balance on your "seat" on the mat. Remember, only one person on a mat at any time! Now run to another mat and balance on one foot. Run to a different mat and balance on one foot and one hand.

   — Balance with feet on the mat and hands off.

   — Balance with hands and one foot on the mat.

   — Balance on any three body parts, all on the mat.

   — Balance on four body parts, all off the mat.

   — Balance on two body parts, one part on the mat; the other, off.

1.

2. Go to your mat. Place both hands on the floor and throw both feet up into the air. Try to hold a balance. Land on both feet. Repeat and land on one foot.

3. Try balancing on your back. Can you lift your legs high? Now try balancing on your shoulders. How can your arms help? Who can lift your hips off the mat?

3.

4. *Making Shapes:* Can you make a shape, taking all your weight on four parts of your body? Slowly change to another shape. Suggestions: two hands, two feet; two hands, one foot, head; two hands, two knees; two feet, seat, one hand. . . .

5. Now try to make a shape on your mat taking all your weight on three body parts. Can you change slowly to another three-point shape? Suggestions: two hands, one foot, forehead; one foot, seat, one hand; one knee, one hand, one elbow; one knee, one foot, head. . . .

5.

6. Who can make a shape, taking all your weight on two parts? then on one part? Try to hold your shape for five seconds. Suggestions: one hand, one foot to one foot; two knees to one knee; seat and one foot to seat only.

7.

7. Find a partner. Can the two of you make a shape with you both in it, where you only balance on three body parts? Try it another way! Explore balancing together on two body parts; four body parts; five body parts. . . .

PG-9 MORE BALANCING CHALLENGES

FOCUS: Supporting and balancing; coordination

EQUIPMENT: One beanbag per player; mats (optional); one wand or folded jump rope per player

ORGANIZATION:

• Have the players find a home space and stand facing you.

DESCRIPTION OF ACTIVITY:

1. *Two Feet Sit:* Stand, look straight ahead, raise your arms forward, and then sit down as gently as possible without moving your feet. Stand again without moving or crossing your feet, kneeling, or placing your hands on the ground.

2. *The Bird Dog:* Kneel on the floor. Stretch your right leg backwards in the air and the left arm forward. Balance on one knee. Hold this position. Repeat with the left leg backwards and the right arm forward. It helps to fix your eyes on a spot directly in front of you. Try this stunt again, but raise your left arm forward and right arm back. Can you raise both arms forward and still keep your balance?

3. *Finger Touch:* Stand; put one hand behind you with your pointer finger pointing straight down. Grasp the wrist with the other hand. With your feet shoulder-width apart, can you squat down and touch the floor with your pointer finger? Return to the standing position without losing balance. If you can't do this, try touching a book on the floor behind you. Can you pick up a beanbag and return to the standing position?

4. *Greet the Toe:* Stand on both feet. Lift one foot, grab your free foot, and try to touch your toe to your forehead. Repeat with the other foot.

5. *Toe Touch Balance:* Place a beanbag about 30 to 60 centimeters (one to two feet) in front of a line. Stand behind the line, balance on one foot, with arms out sideways for balance, and reach forward to touch the beanbag with the other toe. Return to the starting position without losing your balance. Can you reach sideward? backwards? Can you move the beanbag farther away? Remove your sneakers and socks. Who can pick up the beanbag with your toes?

6. *Thread the Needle:* Stand, looking straight ahead. Join your hands together, interlocking fingers. While balancing on one leg, try to step through your clasped hands with one leg, then the other. When you stand up, your clasped hands will be behind you. Do not let go of your grip. Can you now get back to your starting position?

7. *Thread the Needle, Lying Position:* As above, but start by lying on your back holding a wand, ruler, or folded jump rope. Thread your legs through the loop; then return to the starting position. Repeat.

8. *Knee Up:* Place both hands on the floor, with one foot back and the other forward. Change to the standing position and balance on one foot by making a big push-off from the forward foot and hands. Keep the rear foot still as you rise and grasp the forward knee. Try to maintain your balance throughout the change.

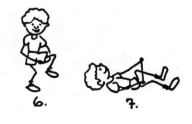

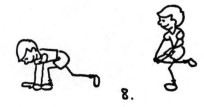

PG-10 BALANCE AND SUPPORT STUNTS

FOCUS: Supporting and balancing; coordination

EQUIPMENT: One beanbag per child; mats

ORGANIZATION:

• Have the children find a spot alone and stand facing you.

DESCRIPTION OF ACTIVITY:

1. *Ankle Hold Stand Up:* Begin in long-sit position, holding your right ankle with your right hand. Can you stand up while still holding your ankle? Repeat holding the left ankle with the left hand.

2. *Standing-Lying-Standing:* From the standing position, lie down on your back and stand again without your hands touching the floor. Stand in one continuous motion. Can you stand with your arms folded across your chest?

3. *Corkscrew Stand:* Stand with feet shoulder-width apart. Fold your arms across your chest. Without moving your feet from the spot, pivot on the balls of both feet, do a half-turn in place, and end up facing the opposite direction. Your legs will automatically cross. Lower your body to sit; then rise again to the starting position. Do this stunt again, turning in the other direction.

4. *Balance the Bag:* Lie on your back on the floor with a beanbag balanced on your forehead. Try to stand up. You may use your hands to help.

5. *High Arch:* Lie on your back on a mat with knees bent. Your hands reach overhead, just under the shoulders, and palms rest downward on the mat. Can you press upward with your feet and hands, making a high arch with your body? Try to hold this balance for five seconds.

6. *"L" Sit:* Sit on the floor with the legs straight and the toes pointed. Place your hands on the floor, just ahead of the hips. Lift yourself completely off the floor by pushing down with your hands. Keep the toes pointed and the legs straight. It helps to lean forward slightly and to look straight ahead, not down. (If children are having difficulty, place books or wooden blocks under their hands.)

PG–11 SUPPORTS ON THE HANDS

FOCUS: Supporting and balancing; upper body strength   **EQUIPMENT:** None

ORGANIZATION:

• Have the children find a home, and then lie down in the front-lying position.

DESCRIPTION OF ACTIVITY:

1. *Circle Hand Walk:* Begin in the front-support position. Keeping your feet still, show me how you can walk on your hands around in a large circle. Walk in one direction, then in the other. Keep your head up, your back straight, your arms and legs straight.

2. *The Compass:* (Designate North, South, East and West around the play area.) Start in the Circle Hand Walk position. Your head is the point of the compass. When I call North, without moving your feet, walk your hands slowly around in a circle until your head is pointing North. (Continue for the other directions.)

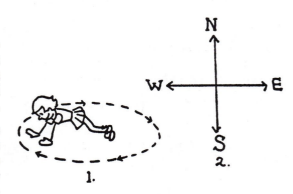

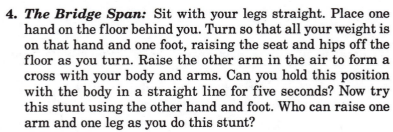

3. *The Wall Walk:* Stand with your back to a wall, with your shoulders against the wall and your feet about one step out from the wall. Place your hands over your shoulders with your fingers pointing downward. Look up at the ceiling and arch your back as you walk your hands down the wall. How far can you go? Walk your hands back up until you are in the standing position.

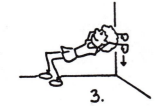

4. *The Bridge Span:* Sit with your legs straight. Place one hand on the floor behind you. Turn so that all your weight is on that hand and one foot, raising the seat and hips off the floor as you turn. Raise the other arm in the air to form a cross with your body and arms. Can you hold this position with the body in a straight line for five seconds? Now try this stunt using the other hand and foot. Who can raise one arm and one leg as you do this stunt?

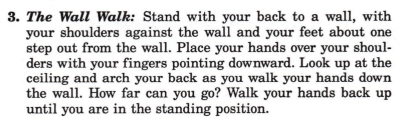

5. *The Coffee Grinder:* Start with one hand on the floor and the weight supported on that hand and both feet. Stretch your body out, with one side to the floor in a side-leaning position, keeping the arm straight. Walk your feet around your hand, making a complete circle while keeping your body straight. Use your supporting hand as the point of pivot. Try this stunt again, placing the other hand on the floor.

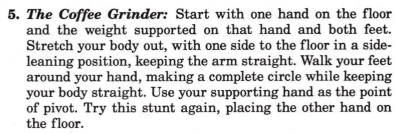

6. *The Pilot's Test:* Do you think you would make a good pilot? Then take this test: Lean forward and place your right "pointer" finger on the floor. Without moving your finger, run around your finger in a CW direction until you have made five complete turns. Then quickly stand up in the "Stork Stand" position, on one leg with arms out sideways. Can you hold this position for five seconds or longer? After the turns, stand and try to walk a straight line for ten steps. Do the "Pilot's Test" using the left pointer finger.

PG–12 PARTNER SUPPORTS

FOCUS: Supporting and balancing; cooperation

EQUIPMENT: One small mat per player

ORGANIZATION:

- Have children find a partner, get a mat, and place it in a free space.

DESCRIPTION OF ACTIVITY:

1. Stand on the mat with your partner. Explore different ways of supporting your body weight between you on two body parts.

2. Can you use three body parts to support yourselves?

3. Try supporting on four body parts; five body parts.

PG–13 SUPPORTS ON APPARATUS

FOCUS: Balancing and supporting; body control

EQUIPMENT: Climbing frame;
chairs;
benches;
hoops;
mats;
tables;
box-horse top

ORGANIZATION:

- Place an assortment of equipment and apparatus out in the play area. Use any type of apparatus with a flat upper surface.
- Divide children into groups of three or four and assign each group a piece of equipment or apparatus on which to work. Rotate groups so that everyone gets to use the different equipment.
- Encourage children to be patient and to wait for turns. Explain that they should place their weight evenly on all supports. Caution children not to interfere with others and to work carefully.

DESCRIPTION OF ACTIVITY:

1. Can you do a four-point support on your own, without touching another person on the apparatus or equipment?

2. Show me how you can do a three-point support on your equipment.

3. Now, let us try a two-point support. Can you do a two-point support with one of the supports on the floor and one on the equipment?

4. Who can do a three-point support with one point on the equipment and two points on the floor; two points on the equipment and one point on the floor?

5. Show me a four-point support over your piece of apparatus or equipment.

PG-14 INTRODUCTION TO ROCKING

FOCUS: Transference of weight; flexibility   **EQUIPMENT:** One mat per player

ORGANIZATION:

- "Rocking" involves the transference of weight onto adjacent body parts and then the reversal of weight along the same supports. Rocking leads very naturally into rolling. It is important that the body be formed into as rounded a figure as possible. Feet can be brought near the seat so that a smooth movement from spine, to heels, to feet can take place.
- To begin, have each player get a mat and take it to his or her home.

DESCRIPTION OF ACTIVITY:

1. Lie on your mat and show me how you can rock. Show me another way! Can you show me a third way of rocking? Very well done!

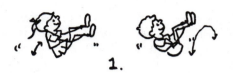
1.

2. Did anyone think of rocking like this?
   - Lie on your front, hold your toes, rock from side to side.
   - Lie on your front, hold your toes, rock forward and backwards.
   - Rock from side to side taking all your weight on your hands.

   - Lie on your back, lift your feet over your head to touch the mat behind you, and then rock forward to touch your toes on the mat. Can you get to your feet without touching the mat with your hands?
   - Lie on your back; bend your knees up to your chest. Rock your knees from side to side to touch the mat.
   - Lie on your back, raise your legs straight overhead to touch the mat on one side, and swing them over to the other side.
   - Lie on your tummy with your arms above your head. Rock back and forth like a rocking chair.

2.

   - Lie on your mat and show me how you can rock with your feet crossed. Good work!
   - Can you think of a different way of rocking?

3. **Tangle Foot:** Lie in the front-lying position (on your tummy). Bend your knees and cross your feet, so that your feet are touching your thighs. Can you reach behind you to grab your right foot with your left hand and your left foot with your right hand? Now try to rock from side to side.

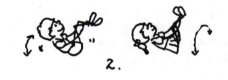
3.

4. **Rocking Chair:** Lie on your back. Keep your knees bent and your feet crossed. Hold your feet. Rock forward and backwards until you can stand on your knees without letting go of your feet. Repeat.

4.

5. **Reach and Roll:** Start by kneeling with your hands on the floor and your feet crossed. Reach under and across your body with one arm and twist over onto your back. Can you roll right over to the kneeling position again? Try reaching and rolling the other way.

5.

PG-15 INTRODUCTION TO ROLLING

FOCUS: Rotation around the body axes; sequence building

EQUIPMENT: One small mat per player

ORGANIZATION:

• Have the players collect a mat each and take it to their homes.

DESCRIPTION OF ACTIVITY:

1. Show me three different ways of rolling. Did you try rolling in different directions: forward, backwards, sideways?

   — Can you do your three different rolls, one after the other? Keep it going. Try to let the movement flow smoothly, without stopping.

2. Form groups of three players. Place your three mats in a straight pathway and roll from one end to the other end of the mats.

   — Place the mats in a zig-zag pathway and do a different roll on each of the three mats.

   — Place the three mats on a curved pathway and explore rolling on the mats.

3. Form groups of six players. Place the six mats in a circular pathway. Take turns at being the Leader. Follow the Leader around the circle, copying the roll that the Leader does.

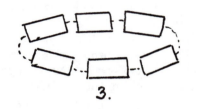

4. **The Log Roll:** Lie in a stretched-out position on your tummy with your arms "extended" overhead and your hands clasped. Make yourself as long as you can; roll sideways over onto your back and then onto your tummy again.

   — Can you do three Log Rolls, one after the other?

   — Show me how you can roll back the other way.

   — Can you Log Roll so that your feet and hands do not touch the mat?

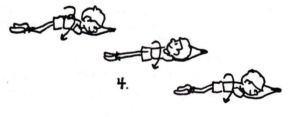

5. **The Egg Roll:** Lie on your back. Hug your knees to your chest, elbows in to your sides, chin tucked between your knees. Roll sideways so that you finish on your knees. Push with your elbows and knees as you roll.

   — Try Egg Rolling to the other side.

   — Do an Egg Roll, followed by a Log Roll, then another Egg Roll.

   — Do a Log Roll, an Egg Roll, and finish holding a balance for five seconds.

6. **Sequence:** Develop a sequence of your own. For example, do a Log Roll, followed by a rocking action, and finish with a Balance. You choose the order in which you want to do them. Remember how you did that sequence. Practice!

ROLL   6.   ROCK   BALANCE

PG–16 LOG ROLLING STUNTS

FOCUS: Rolling around the longitudinal axis; partnerwork   **EQUIPMENT:** One mat per pair

ORGANIZATION:

- Make sure the players are properly warmed up. Have players find a partner, get a mat, and go to a free space. Arrange the mats so that the players are always in view.

DESCRIPTION OF ACTIVITY:

1. *Log Roll in Pairs:* Lie on your tummies facing each other on the mat. Link hands and roll in the same direction. How many times can you roll like this? Can you roll so that your feet do not touch the mat?

2. *Log Roll with Feet Locked:* Lie down on the mat on your backs so that your feet are touching; then lock your feet together. Now roll slowly in the same direction with your feet locked.

3. *Leap the Log Roll:* (Divide the class into groups of six to eight players. Each group splits into two half groups, the "Rollers" and the "Leapers." The Rollers stand in single file at one end of the mat; while the Leapers stand in single file at the opposite end. Use one group to demonstrate.) On the signal "Go," the Rollers, start rolling down the mat, well spaced apart. At the same time the Leapers, leap over the approaching Rollers. Rollers, when you reach the end of the mat, you become Leapers, and Leapers, you become the Rollers.

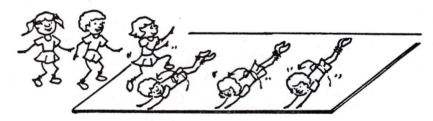

4. Can you and your partner create a Log Rolling stunt?

PG–17 ROCK 'N ROLL STUNTS

FOCUS: Transference of weight; rotation

EQUIPMENT: One small mat per player

ORGANIZATION:

• Have each player get a mat and take it to his or her home. Check for good spacing.

DESCRIPTION OF ACTIVITY:

1. *Rock to Stand:* Begin in hook-sit position. Clasp your hands in front of your ankles. Roll backwards so that your feet are in the air, and then rock forward until all your weight is on your feet. Keep your hands clasped and do it again. On the last try, rock right up to the standing position and hold for five seconds.

2. *The Oyster:* Sit on your mat with legs crossed, and grasp both feet. Roll backwards to touch the floor overhead with both feet.

3. *Human Ball:* Sit on the mat. Bring your knees up to your chest and keep your feet flat on the floor. Reach your arms under the inside of your legs to lock fingers around the ankles. Roll backwards; to the side, sit up, and then roll to the other side and onto your back again. Continue rolling around in a circle. Remember to stay curled into a little ball and to tuck your chin as you roll.

4. *Shoulder Roll:* (The Shoulder Roll involves an asymmetrical movement.) Squat down with your feet wide apart and one foot forward. Place one arm forward so the back of your hand is on the mat. The hand should be placed outside the front foot. Tuck your head to your chest, turning your head in the direction of the hand. Roll forward, keeping your chin on your chest, to land on the back of your shoulder. Roll diagonally across your back to finish in the standing position.

   — Start in the standing position.

   — Use an extra thickness of mats while learning the Shoulder Roll.

   — Walk into the Shoulder Roll.

   — Run into the Shoulder Roll.

   — Place mats end to end and do a series of Shoulder Rolls.

PG-18 LEAD-UPS TO THE FORWARD ROLL

FOCUS: Forward rotations

EQUIPMENT: One mat per player

ORGANIZATION:

• These stunts are small step progressions toward learning the Forward Roll. Have the players get a small mat and take it to their homes.

DESCRIPTION OF ACTIVITY:

1. *The Rocking Chair:* Sit in a crouched position hugging the knees tightly to the chest. Rock backwards onto the neck and head; then roll forward again to the starting position. Roll back and forth rhythmically. As you roll forward, try to get to your feet.

2. *The Bunny Hop:* Start in the squat position with your hands flat on the floor in front of your feet. Leap forward by pushing with the feet and lift the hands off the floor. Catch the weight on the hands, and then try to bring the feet past the hands.

3. *The Seal Walk:* Start in the front-support position with hands shoulder-width apart and directly under the shoulders. Walk by pulling the body along with the hands only. The feet should drag behind with the toes pointing outward. Keep the back straight and the head up. Swing the hips freely.

4. *Run and Squat:* Run in an open space. When I signal "Stop" each time, listen for my call:

   — Squat like a rabbit.

   — Bounce along on two feet, and then squat.

   — Run in a circle and then squat.

   — Run, jump up high, and then squat.

5. *Squat and Look Behind:* Start in the squat position. Raise your hips up overhead. Tuck your chin onto your chest and your head under, to look back between your legs. Can you see a friend? Who can see the wall?

6. *Tip Over:* Begin in the squat position. Tuck your chin under between your legs. You should be able to see the ceiling (sky) as the back of your head touches the mat. Raise your hips up until they tip you over to roll on your back. Finish in the sitting position. Can you hold your knees as you roll?

PG-19 FORWARD ROLL—TECHNIQUE AND VARIATIONS

FOCUS: Technique; spotting; sequence-building

EQUIPMENT: One mat per pair

ORGANIZATION:

- In performing the forward roll, emphasize that the head should be well tucked out of the way and that the landing should be made on the tops of the shoulders and the back of the neck, not the head.
- When performing the forward roll, players may need assistance. This is called "spotting." Teach players how to properly spot for their partners. Advise children with long hair to tie it back so that their performance is not hindered.
- Have players find a partner, get a mat, and find a free space.

DESCRIPTION OF ACTIVITY:

1. *Technique:* Begin in the crouch or squat position, with your weight on your toes. Place your hands on the mat slightly ahead of your toes, shoulder-width apart and fingers facing forward. Round your back by tucking your head between your knees. Your chin should be touching your chest. Push off from your toes, raising your seat as you roll forward, with your chin tucked to your chest. Land on the tops of your shoulders and push with the hands as you roll forward to the squat position, keeping your heels wide and close to your seat. Hug your shins with your arms while rolling onto your feet.

2. *Spotting for the Forward Roll:* Kneel on one knee alongside your partner. Place your leading hand on the back of your partner's neck and the other hand under the near ankle. As he or she rolls forward, assist by lifting with the leading hand and pushing forward with the back hand.

3. *Forward Roll Variations:*
   — Squat with your arms folded across your chest. Do a Forward Roll and return to the squat position.
   — Squat with your arms wrapped around your lower legs. Do a Forward Roll without using your hands. Land on the top of your shoulders. Make sure you keep your head well tucked under; it should not touch the mat.
   — Start in the standing position. Do a Forward Roll and finish in the standing position. Hold for three seconds.
   — Forward roll with legs crossed. Can you do a series of these along the mats?

4. *Forward Roll Sequences:*
   — Forward roll to a squat position; rock backwards onto your neck and shoulders and clamp your feet under you; roll forward onto your feet and do another Forward Roll.
   — Forward roll to a stand; forward roll to a stand; forward roll to a stand.
   — Start with your legs crossed. Cross-legged forward roll to a cross-legged stand; turn and repeat.

PG–20 FORWARD ROLL PROGRESSIONS

FOCUS: Sequence-building; reinforcing technique   **EQUIPMENT:** One mat per pair

ORGANIZATION:

- Have players find a partner, collect a mat, and find a free space.
- Have them take turns at performing and spotting. Emphasize that players should try for control rather than speed.

DESCRIPTION OF ACTIVITY:

1. From the standing position, do a Forward Roll. As you come out of the roll, go into a walk. Do another Forward Roll. This time as you come out of the roll, go into a Log Roll (Egg Roll, Shoulder Roll).

2. From the standing position, do a Forward Roll; jump high into the air, make a half-turn, land, and repeat in the opposite direction.

3. Stand on one leg. Do a Forward Roll to finish standing on both legs. Can you stand on the other leg and repeat?

4. *Angel Roll:* From the standing position, and holding your arms out to the sides, do a Forward Roll to stand on the mat. Your heels must be kept close to your seat. As you come out of the roll, thrust your arms forward, vigorously.

   — Place your arms sideways on the mat.

   — Do a Forward Roll followed by an Angel Roll.

5. *Squat-Bridge-Forward Roll:* Squat down, reach forward to place hands in the front support position. Form a high Bridge on your hands and feet. Spring forward from the bent-knee position to a Forward Roll with Tuck, keeping in a tight roll. As you come up to the standing position, shoot the arms forward; do not grab the ankles. Try to hold your balance for three seconds.

6. Partners, stand at opposite ends of the mats. Both do a Forward Roll past each other, then stand up, turn, and repeat.

7. Practice any type of roll on your mat. (Observe performers and comment on technique.)

PG-21 FORWARD ROLL—SEQUENCES

FOCUS: Variations; sequence-building

EQUIPMENT: One mat per pair; one hoop per pair

ORGANIZATION:

• Have the players find a partner, get a mat, and take it to a free space.

• Have the players take turns at performing and spotting for the following Forward Roll sequences.

DESCRIPTION OF ACTIVITY:

1. Squat down, do a Forward Roll, squat, stand, and hold your balance.

2. Squat down with your feet crossed, do a Forward Roll, and finish in the squat position, with the feet still crossed.

3. Get a hoop. First player, hold the hoop upright on the mat while the other player does a Forward Roll through it. Try this with the hoop lifted slightly off the mat.

4. Squat down, holding the outside of your ankles. Do a Forward Roll while holding the ankles. Open your knees wide, keeping the chin well tucked in.

5. Do a Bunny Hop, and then a Forward Roll to a Frog Jump.

6. Do a Leap Frog over your partner; then do a Forward Roll on the mat.

7. Do a Forward Roll to a stand; then leap into the air and land in the crouch position.

8. Have children do any two of these Forward Rolls in a row. Explore different combinations. Then try for three in a row; four in a row!

9. Can you do a Log Roll, an Egg Roll, and finish the sequence with a Forward Roll?

PG-22 LEAD-UPS TO THE BACKWARD ROLL

FOCUS: Rocking and balancing

EQUIPMENT: One mat per player; one beanbag per player

ORGANIZATION:

• These are natural and safe progressions to the teaching of the Backward Roll. Have each player get a mat and place it in a free space.

DESCRIPTION OF ACTIVITY:

1. *Back Balance:* Sit with your knees bent and your hands on the mat. Rock backward, raise your legs over your head, and balance there for five seconds.

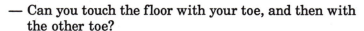

2. *Shoulder Balance:* Sit on the mat with your knees bent. Raise your elbows up and turn the palms of your hands toward the ceiling, fingers pointing backwards over your shoulders. Hold this position, and then rock backwards to balance on your shoulders using your hands on the floor to support yourself. Hold the balance for five seconds; then repeat. While in the Shoulder Balance position:

   — Can you touch the floor with your toe, and then with the other toe?

   — Try stretching your legs upward to the ceiling. Can you hold this balance?

   — Do the Shoulder Balance, starting in the squat position.

   — Start with a beanbag between your feet, and then place it on the floor behind your head.

3. *Backward Shoulder Roll from the Sitting Position:* Sit on the mat with your knees bent and one arm out to the side. Rock backwards to bring one leg overhead between the side arm and your head. Land on one knee, and then bring the other one over beside the first knee; lift the shoulders to bring you to the upright kneeling position. Repeat. Watch your outstretched hand all the time. Watch your feet as you roll.

4. *The Backward Shoulder Roll from the Squat Position:* Start in the squat position with the arms thrust forward, and knees to chest. Roll backwards, bringing both legs to the side of one ear. Your arms should lie straight along the mat. The roll is done across the shoulder, finishing on the lower legs. Practice rolling to one side, then to the other side.

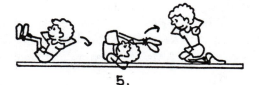

5. *Backward Forearm Roll:* Start in the squat position; hands clasped behind your head, elbows out to the sides. Quickly, overbalance backwards to sit down, roll across your back, and bring your knees up into your chest so you can gather speed. Take most of your weight on your forearms and elbows during the roll, to protect your neck.

FOCUS: Technique; spotting; sequence-building   **EQUIPMENT:** One mat per pair

ORGANIZATION:

- Have the players find a partner, and then get a mat and take it to a free space.
- Partners take turns at performing and spotting.

DESCRIPTION OF ACTIVITY:

1. *Technique:* Start in the squat position with your back to the mat. Place your hands pointing back over your shoulders with the palms up and the thumbs near your neck. Tuck your chin down onto your chest. To start the roll, sit down on the mat and push backwards with your toes, keeping in the tucked position. As you roll, bring your knees to your chest and roll onto your back. Push off the mat with your hands to land in the squat position on your toes, not on your knees. (Explain that players should keep in the squat position throughout the roll and that the weight should be taken on both hands and not on the head.)

2. *Spotters:* Position yourself at the side of your partner and kneel on the knee away from him or her. Assist by placing one hand under the head at the back of the neck and the other under the hip. Thrust in the direction of the roll. Help your partner gain enough speed to get the body weight over the hands.

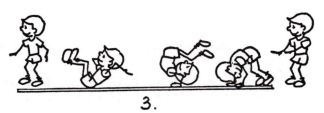

3. *Stand to Stand:* Start in the standing position. Sit, keeping your feet and knees in as close to your body as possible. As you roll back, push hard with the hands, and bring the legs over quickly to land in a standing position.

4. *Backward Roll from Sit to Squat:* Start the Backward Roll from the sitting position. To get speed, rock forward and then backward into the roll, giving a very hard push with the feet.

   — Can you finish with your feet together in a squat?

   — Can you finish with your feet apart?

5. *Forward Roll-Backward Roll:* Start with a Forward Roll from the squat position. Then do a Backward Roll to finish in the squat position.

6. *Backward Roll Series:* See how many Backward Rolls you can do in a sequence; then finish in the squat (tuck) position.

7. *Split-leg Backward Roll Series:* Starting in the feet astride position, roll backward to finish in the wide-astride position.

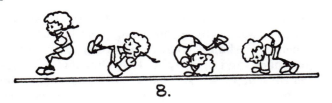

8. *Backward Roll with Legs Crossed:* Squat in the cross-legged position and remain in this position throughout the roll.

PG–24 FORWARD AND BACKWARD ROLL VARIATIONS

FOCUS: Rolling technique; spotting; sequence-building   **EQUIPMENT:** One mat per pair

ORGANIZATION:

- Children explore rolling from different starting and finishing positions. Have them find a partner, and then get a mat and take it to a free space. Partners take turns at performing and spotting.

- Remind spotters that they should protect the head and neck at all times. Children with long hair should tie it back so that performance is not hindered.

DESCRIPTION OF ACTIVITY:

1. *Forward Roll to a Cross-legged Stand to a Backward Roll:* As you roll to the finish of the Forward Roll, cross your legs, stand, and do a Backward Roll to the standing position.

2. *Forward Roll to Stand to Backward Roll to Stand:* Do a Forward roll; then stand up, Backward roll to stand. Repeat.

3. *Forward Roll to Stand to Jump and Half-Turn to Backward Roll:* Both rolls are performed while moving in the same direction.

4. *Forward Roll to Bridge to Backward Roll to a One-Foot Finish:* Forward roll to finish with feet wide apart, make a Bridge, and then Backward roll to finish standing on one foot only. Raise your arms sideways as you come to your feet to keep your balance.

5. Create your own Forward-Backward Roll sequence!

1.

3.

PG–25 SPRINGING AND LANDING STUNTS

FOCUS: Springing and landing—hands to feet

EQUIPMENT: Mats;
hoops;
beanbags

ORGANIZATION:

• When children are performing these springs, give them frequent rest periods; for example, have half the class perform while the other half watches; and then switch.

• To begin, have players find a home space. Check for good spacing.

DESCRIPTION OF ACTIVITY:

1. **The Bunny Hop:** Begin with all your weight over your toes. Place your hands on the floor, way out in front of your feet. Spring forward with your feet to bring them up to your hands. Spring forward to land on your hands, then your feet, then your hands to feet . . . just like a bunny!

— Can you hop quickly? slowly?

— Hop around in a circle.

— Hop along a bunny trail (any line on the floor).

— Can you get your feet high in the air as you Bunny Hop?

— Can you take more weight on your hands and arms?

— Bunny Hop, taking all your weight on your hands. Try to bring your feet past your hands.

— (Have half the class lie down on the floor.) Hop over all the "logs" you can see. Change and repeat.

1.

— Bunny Hop onto or over obstacles: mats, hoops, beanbags.

2.

2. **Leap Frog:** Find a partner and stand one behind the other. The front player, squat down keeping your head tucked and your weight on your hands. The back player, spread your legs and, from a half-crouch position, place your hands on your partner's shoulders. Then leap over your partner's back to land in the crouch position. Now your partner can leap over you. Remember, only touch your partner's shoulders lightly as you go over—do not put your full weight on his or her back! Continue leaping over each other in this way.

3. **Leap Frog Relay:** (Form groups of five or six in a line at one end of the play area. Each group should be well spaced apart from the other groups. In each line, players should be spaced two giant steps apart from the player in front of them. Have everyone squat down.) On signal, the back player, "leap frog" over each of your line players until you reach the front. Shout "Ribbit!", which is the signal for the next end player to go. Continue in this way until your whole group has reached the opposite end of the play area. Which group will finish first?

   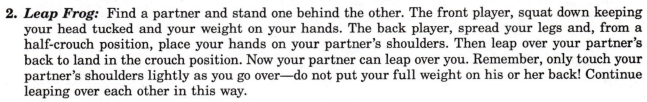

3.

PG–26 MORE SPRINGING AND LANDING STUNTS

FOCUS: Springing and landing—feet to feet   **EQUIPMENT:** One beanbag and ball per player

ORGANIZATION:

- As these springs can be strenuous, provide restful breaks in between springing tasks.
- Have players "Bunny Hop" to their homes and stand facing you.

DESCRIPTION OF ACTIVITY:

1. ***Kangaroo Hop:*** Bend down into the half-squat position with arms folded across your chest; body weight over your toes. Spring into the air, jumping upward and forward. Land in the half-squat position with the knees bent. Continue making big springs. Go as high and as far as you can. Remember to land softly and "give" with your knees to cushion your landing.

   — Try the Kangaroo Hop while holding your arms out in front like a kangaroo's forelegs.
   — Collect a utility ball and a beanbag and return to your homes. Place the beanbag between your ankles and "Kangaroo Hop" in a straight pathway; in a circle; figure-eight; etc. Can you hop with a ball held between your knees?

1.

   — Kangaroo Hop with a partner; in three's; four's.

2. ***Jack-in-the-Box:*** Crouch with your hands touching the floor. Jump up, raising your arms and legs sideways. Land on your toes, bending your knees as you return to the crouch position. Repeat.

   — Keep it going. Can you do four Jack-in-the-Box jumps in a row?
   — Can you move forward as you do Jack-in-the-Box jumps?
   — Show me how to do a Jack-in-the-Box, land softly, and then forward roll and spring to your feet.

2.

3. ***Pogo Stick:*** You are a Pogo Stick. Can you keep your body perfectly stiff and just spring on your toes with small jumps? Hold your hands out in front as if you are holding the Pogo Stick.

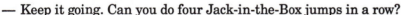

3.

   — Can you move forward? backwards? sideways?
   — Can you Pogo Stick your way around the play area without landing on a line?

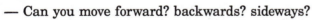

4. ***Bouncing Ball:*** Find a partner and a home space. Check for good spacing. Each player stand in the upright position with your hands down by your sides and your feet apart. Keep your back straight and your head up. Now take short up-and-down jumps, gradually lowering your body to the floor until you can touch with your hands—just like a ball coming to rest. Repeat the same action upward until you are standing again.

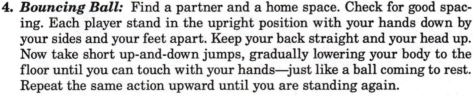

4.

5. ***Bounce Your Partner:*** One player be the "ball" and stay in the crouch position, as small as you can, with hands clasped around your knees. The standing player, place your hand on your partner's head and bounce him or her, "like a ball."

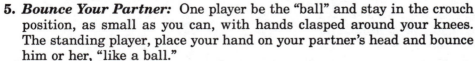

6. ***Head-to-Hand Jump:*** First player, stand on your tip-toes and hold your hand high. The other partner, start low in the crouch position, and then swing your arms upward quickly to spring up and touch your forehead to your partner's hand. Change roles.

5.

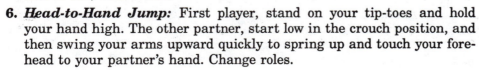

6.

PG–27 SPRINGING GAMES

FOCUS: Springing and landing—one foot only

EQUIPMENT: One mat per player;
one set of banners;
one flag per player;
three traffic cones per group

ORGANIZATION:

• Have the players find a home and face you. Check for good spacing.

DESCRIPTION OF ACTIVITY:

1. **Hoppo Bumpo:** Find a partner. Hold your right foot with your right hand behind, and then hold your right elbow with your left hand, behind your back. Face your partner. Try to bump your partner to make him or her lose balance. Play, the best out of three tries.

   — Find another partner and challenge him or her to a "Hoppo Bumpo" challenge.

   — Now reverse holds and repeat the "Hoppo Bumpo" challenge!

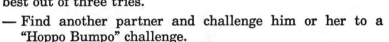

2. **Do the Rooster Hop:** Stand on one foot. Hold the other foot behind with the opposite hand to the raised foot. Show me how you can . . .

   — Hop four times in place.

   — Hop four steps forward; hop four steps backwards.

   — Hop four steps to the left, four steps to the right.

   — Hop in place and turn once around (four hops), saying "Cock-a-doodle-do!"

   — Repeat all of the above on the other foot.

   — Add your own Rooster Hop part!

3. **Rooster Hop Relay:** Form groups of four players and have each group stand single file behind a starting line, facing three turning cones. Space these cones about two giant steps apart. On signal "Cock-a-doodle-do," each "Rooster" in turn, hop in and out of your cones, around the end cone, and directly back to your single file. Tag the next Rooster with your free hand to repeat the zig-zag course. Who will be the first group to finish the relay and hook-sit in their file?

4. **Rooster Tag:** (Have each player collect a "nest" [mat], and scatter them over the play area. Choose one player to be the "Fox," who wears a banner and stands in the center of the play area. All other players are "Roosters," who wear a flag tucked into the back of their shorts with at least two thirds of the flag showing, and scatter around the play area.) Fox, the chase begins on your signal "Cock-a-doodle-do!" Try to tag as many Roosters as you can by pulling their flags. A Rooster whose flag has been pulled must put it on and become the Fox's helper. Roosters, you may run anywhere around the play area, leaping over the nests, but watch carefully where you are going! To be safe, you are allowed to "Rooster Hop" on any mat for five seconds; then you must get off the mat. The last Rooster to be tagged is the Fox for the next game. Start the game again with two Foxes.

PG–28 UPWARD SPRINGS

FOCUS: Springing for height; landing technique

EQUIPMENT: None

ORGANIZATION:

- Stress that players swing arms upward vigorously to gain more height when doing the upward springs. Remind players to look straight ahead all the time during these activities. Emphasize that players bring their legs up to meet their hands; don't allow them to drop their hands to meet the legs.

- Have players find a home space and stand facing you.

DESCRIPTION OF ACTIVITY:

1. **Heel Slap:** Stand with your legs apart and your arms turned sideways and to the back. Bend your knees and jump upward. Swing your arms back to slap your heels with the palms of your hands behind your seat. Land softly, bending at the knees to cushion your landing. Return to the starting position and repeat.

   — Slap your knees to the side.

2. **Heel Click:** Stand with your feet astride. Jump up to click both heels together in the air. Land in the starting position.

   — Click your heels to the left; to the right.

   — Try to click your heels two or more times in the air.

3. **Tuck Jump:** Stand. With a vigorous forward swing of the arms, jump as high as possible. At the height of the jump, grasp your knees in the "tuck" position, by pulling the knees up to the chest. Bring the legs down quickly to land in the crouch position. Remember to bend your knees to cushion your landing. Look straight ahead—don't look down. Repeat.

   — Try the Tuck Jump with a short run.

4. **Jackknife or Pike:** Stand erect with your feet shoulder-width apart. Spring up, throw your arms forward and slightly to the side, and at the same time, bring your toes up to touch your hands. Try to keep your legs straight when doing the Jackknife. Land in the crouch position, bending at the knees. How can you use your arms to balance you?

PG-29 FALLS AND LANDINGS

FOCUS: Falling and landing technique

EQUIPMENT: One mat per player

ORGANIZATION:

- Have the players get a mat and scatter over the play area.

DESCRIPTION OF ACTIVITY:

1. *Squash!:* Start in the kneeling position on the mat, with your weight on your hands and knees. On the signal "Squash!" quickly stretch out arms and legs to flop down on the mat. How can you use your arms and hands to cushion your fall? Try to keep your head up as you fall. Repeat.

2. *Fake Fall:* Stand facing the mat. Without moving your feet, dive forward into the lying position on the mat. Reach out with your hands and arms, bending at the elbows to break your fall. Keep your head up and arch your back as you contact the mat.

3. *Imagination Stunts:* Imagine you are. . . .
   — Tackled from behind in football.
   — Hit in the face while boxing.
   — Diving into a lake.
   — Falling while skating.
   — Jumping off a moving train.
   — Falling off a galloping horse.
   — Rolling down a steep hill.

1.

2.

BOXING

FALLING

ROLLING

3.

PG-30 SEQUENCE-BUILDING

FOCUS: Rolling; springing and landing; falling; balancing

EQUIPMENT: One mat per player; one chair per pair

ORGANIZATION:

- Allow players time to experiment and practice their sequences. Be on hand to offer suggestions when needed. Have players demonstrate their sequences to the class. Praise good efforts.
- To begin, have players get a mat and place it in a home space. Ensure that mats are well spaced.

DESCRIPTION OF ACTIVITY:

1. Can you make a sequence combining a spring, a landing, and a roll?

2. Show me a sequence of your own, which includes a spring, a balance, a roll, and finish standing up.

3. Begin with a roll to a balance and finish with a spring to a landing.

4. From a fall, go into a roll and finish with a low balance.

5. Find a partner, get a chair, and place in a home space. Check for good spacing. Take turns to make up a sequence which includes springing from the chair, landing, falling, rolling, and balancing. Teach your partner your routine. Steady the chair for your partner during springs.

2.

PG–31 INTRODUCING THE SPRINGBOARD AND TAKE-OFFS_____

FOCUS: Springing and landing from apparatus   **EQUIPMENT:** Springboard, beatboard or mini-tramp; mats

ORGANIZATION:

• Children familiarize themselves with the springing action of the board by taking off from the end of the board. In activity PG–32 a running approach to the board is introduced.

• Explain the safety guidelines; demonstrate the technique of springing from the board and landing safely.

• Arrange the class in small groups if you have more than one springboard. Designate three spotters and have them demonstrate the equipment set-up and spotting technique.

DESCRIPTION OF ACTIVITY:

SEAT KICK

JACKKNIFE

3.

1. *Spotting Technique:* (Always use three spotters: one on either side of the springboard and the third who stands in front, ready to assist players who overbalance.) Spotters, place mats in front of the springboard with the short edge closest to the end of the board. Place a mat on either side of the board; then take up your position. Performers, have three turns at each task; then change roles with a spotter.

2. *Springing Technique:* Stand on the springboard with your toes slightly over the edge and look straight ahead. Bend at the knees, take your arms back. Quickly throw your arms forward and upward, spring up, and push off. Cushion your landing by bending at the knees (hips and ankles) and use your arms to balance you. Straighten and extend your arms and hands upward, holding your balance for three seconds.

3. *Springboard Challenges:*

   — Bounce the board three times; bounce off on the third time. Look straight ahead so that you do not overbalance. Land and hold your balance for three seconds.

   — Explore landing with your feet close together; further apart.

   — Stand on the end of the springboard. Bounce and slap both knees while in the air. Finish with a safe landing. Can you slap your knees twice? Can you cross your arms then slap your knees?

   — Can you do a "Heel Click" off the springboard? "Heel Slap"? "Tuck Jump"?

   — "Seat Kick": Stand on the end of the board. Bounce up and kick your heels backwards to kick your own seat. Bring your legs down to a safe landing. Hold your arms out sideways as you do the Seat Kick.

   — "Toe Touch": Stand on the end of the board. Bounce up to touch your toes (bring your toes up to your hands, not your hands down to your toes). Snap your legs down to a safe landing.

   — "Jackknife": Stand on the end of the board. Bounce upward and forward. Bring your legs up straight in front; reach forward to touch your shins or toes. Land and hold your balance.

PG–32 SPRINGBOARD—RUNNING APPROACH

FOCUS: Run-in; springing and landing

EQUIPMENT: Springboard, beatboard or mini-tramp; mats

ORGANIZATION:

- Children learn how to spring off the board from a running approach. Review the safety guidelines for springing from the springboard and doing a "safe landing": knees, hips, and ankles bend (give); arms are stretched upward and forward; eyes look straight ahead. Demonstrate the technique of the "run-in" from a short approach first so that children will master the correct footwork.

- Arrange the class in small groups if you have more than one springboard. Designate three spotters, and have them demonstrate the equipment set-up and spotting technique.

DESCRIPTION OF ACTIVITY:

1. **Spotting Technique:** (Always use three spotters: one on either side of the springboard and the third who stands in front, ready to assist players who overbalance.) Spotters, place mats at the sides and in front of the springboard. Performers, have three turns at each task; then change roles with a spotter.

2. **Approach Technique:**

   — "Short Approach" (for a right foot take-off): Starting with the left foot, step Left-Right-Left to step right foot on the first part of the board; then push off to land both feet at the far end of the board. Bring your arms down and back as you bend at the knees and hips.

2. R   L   R

   — "On the Jump": Straighten the body out; stretch upward vigorously with the arms to gain height. Land softly on the mat on two feet—bend at the hips and knees, and take your arms down and back to a safe landing. Stand still and hold your arms upward and out to the sides for three seconds.

   — Now take a longer approach, practicing the correct footwork.

360 SPRING TURN

3. **Springboard Challenges:**

   — Run in, spring, and land without overbalancing and hold your balance for three seconds.

   — Run in, spring, and land with your feet close.

   — Run in, spring, and land with your feet wide apart.

   — "Knee Slap": Run in, spring off the board, slap both knees while in the air, and finish with a safe landing. Slap your knees twice. Cross your arms then slap your knees.

   — "Spring Turns": Run in, spring off the board, and turn in the air so that you land facing the board (180° Spring Turn). Run in, spring off the board, and turn around completely once so that you land facing in the direction of your take-off (360° Spring Turn).

TUCK JUMP

   — "Heel Clicks," "Seat Kicks," "Heel Slap," "Tuck Jump," "Toe Touch."

PG–33 SPRINGBOARD—STUNTS AND SHAPES

FOCUS: Run in; springing and landing

EQUIPMENT: Springboard, beatboard or mini-tramp; mats

ORGANIZATION:

- Designate three spotters. Have them set up the springboard and mats with the short side of the mat to the end of the springboard and then take up positions: one spotter on each side of the springboard and the third in front ready to assist players who overbalance. Give everyone a turn at being a spotter.
- Caution the players to look ahead while in mid-air. Explain that if you "look up, you stay up; if you look down, you fall down."

DESCRIPTION OF ACTIVITY:

1. Run forward, and spring from the board. At the height of your jump, clap your hands overhead. Land in a safe landing.
   — Clap your hands behind your back while in the air. Land softly in control.
   — Clap your hands above your head and then behind your back.
   — While in the air, *clap your hands under one leg* and then under the other leg.
2. *Salute the Captain:* While in the air, give a salute.
3. *Star Spring:* While in the air, stretch your legs and arms out to the sides, making a "star shape."
4. *Robin Hood:* While in the air, use your bow and arrow.
5. *Boxer:* While in the air, pretend you are a boxer. What other sporting types could you be: Dancer, Baseball batter?
6. *The Monkey:* Scratch yourself like a monkey while in the air. Can you think of another animal to imitate while in the air?
7. Create your own springing stunt.

PG–34 SPRINGBOARD—SEQUENCE-BUILDING

FOCUS: Run-in approach; springing and tumbling

EQUIPMENT: Springboard, beatboard or mini-tramp; mats

ORGANIZATION: See activity PG–33.

DESCRIPTION OF ACTIVITY:

1. *Run in, Spring, Land, Bunny Hop:* Run in, and spring from the board to land on the mat in a safe landing. Squat down, reach out in front, and do a Bunny Hop on your hands. Stand; hold balance for three seconds with arms out sideways. Kick your feet high as you do the Bunny Hop. (Caution the players to land first, count "1-2-3," then proceed with the next stunt; otherwise, they may go into their next stunt directly from the board.)
2. *Run in, Spring, Heel Slap, Forward Roll:* Run in, spring to slap heels behind you, then land on the mat, then do a Forward Roll. Hold balance from standing.
3. *Run in, Spring, Seat Kick, Bunny Hop:* Run in, spring from the board to do a Seat Kick, land, then squat down to do a Bunny Hop, stand and hold balance.
   — Do a Forward Roll after the Bunny Hop, and hold balance.
   — Throw your arms overhead as you do the Seat Kick.
4. Create your own sequence!

PG–35 INTRODUCTION TO THE BALANCE BENCH

FOCUS: Teaching and safety guidelines; balance and control

EQUIPMENT: Balance benches; mats

ORGANIZATION:

- During balance bench activities, have players use bare feet; curl fingers around the edges to grip the bench for mounts and dismounts; move along the bench in one direction only unless you state otherwise; focus eyes ahead and hold arms out at sides for balance; step off the bench if they lose balance rather than wait to fall off; bend at hips, knees, and ankles to land softly after dismounting. Have one group demonstrate the correct lifting, carrying, and anchoring of the bench. Emphasize the importance of safety at all times.
- These activities should be attempted on the wide surface of the bench first, and then on the balance beam.

DESCRIPTION OF ACTIVITY:

1. ***Lifting and Carrying the Bench:*** Use six carriers for each balance bench. Carry the bench this way: two players at each end and two on either side, facing the same direction.
   - Bend knees and lift together; hold the back flat and the head up as you straighten the knees.
   - Walk in step, moving quickly and quietly; then bend the knees, hold the back flat and head up, as you lower the bench to the floor.
2. ***Safety Mats:*** Use four mats per bench; one at each end and one on each side.
3. ***Anchoring the Bench:*** For stability, have two players anchor each bench: one player at each end sitting facing the middle. When working in pairs only, one player straddle-sits the bench while the other performs the task.

4. ***Bench Travels:*** Form groups of four to six players. Arrange the benches alongside each other, with mats at both ends and sides. Have each group stand in a line at one end of the bench. As soon as a player reaches halfway on the bench, the next player may begin. When a player reaches the opposite end of the bench, he or she jumps off, landing lightly, and then joins the line again. Players should take turns being the anchors for the bench.
   - Can you keep one foot on the floor and the other on the bench and move along the bench? Next time, travel with the opposite foot on the bench.
   - Let me see you explore ways of getting on and off the bench, over the bench, under the bench, across the bench, from one end to the other.
   - Walk forward along the bench to the other end; next time, walk backwards along the bench.
   - Run forward along the bench to the other end; next time, jump your way to the other end.
   - Gallop forward with the right foot forward to the opposite end; next time, gallop with the left foot forward.
   - Starting at one end, jump up on the bench, jump forward off the bench and to one side, jump up again, then off to the other side. Can you move along to the end of the bench this way?

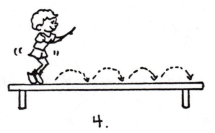

PG–36 BENCH TRAVELS

FOCUS: Travelling; body positioning; balance

EQUIPMENT: Balance benches;
mats;
beanbags

ORGANIZATION:

- Form groups of four to six players. Arrange the benches with mats at both ends and sides. Review the procedure for anchoring the benches and appoint anchors for each bench. Perform these tasks on the wide surface of the bench, and then on the narrow side. Performers should remove shoes and socks for a better feel as they travel along the bench. Emphasize that performers hold their arms out to the side for balance and look ahead at their own height (not look down). Stress good body position and a steady balance while walking. Have the spotter walk alongside the performer with arm raised and palm up, under the hand of the performer.

DESCRIPTION OF ACTIVITY:

1. Walk forward carefully with small steps, toe touching heel as you go. Walk backwards, heel to toe.
2. Walk sideways, on the balls of the feet.
3. Walk forward; turn around and walk backwards to the end. Walk forward, turning as you go.
4. Walk forward. Bend your knees to touch your hand to the bench. Walk forward and repeat. Can you pick up three beanbags along the bench as you go? It helps to look straight ahead all the time.
5. Walk in a crouch position; turn around and walk backwards. Jump off using your hands.
6. Walk forward. At about halfway, balance on one foot, walk forward, stop, balance on the other foot, and walk to the end. Jump off with a light landing.
7. Create your own way of walking on the balance bench.

PG–37 BENCH WALKS

EQUIPMENT: Balance benches;
mats

ORGANIZATION:

- Form groups of four to six players. If possible, arrange two benches alongside each other for each group. Use the wide surface of the bench only.

DESCRIPTION OF ACTIVITY:

1. Lie on your tummy along the bench. Show me how you can pull yourself along the bench. Lie on your back along the bench. Can you push yourself along using your hands and feet? using your feet only?
2. Move along the bench on body part points: hands and feet; seat and feet; knees; etc. Let a different part lead: head, seat, feet, hand, elbow.
3. Start in a stretched-out position. Can you move along the bench being stretched, then curled, then stretched . . . right to the end?
4. Travel along the bench by twisting and turning to the end; first on your tummy, then on your side, on your back. . . . Show me another way of travelling along the bench.

PG–38 BENCH TRAVEL STUNTS

FOCUS: Body control; strength

EQUIPMENT: Balance benches; mats

ORGANIZATION:

- These activities should be performed on the wide surface of the bench. Form groups of four to six players. Arrange the benches alongside each other, with mats at both ends and sides. Review the procedure for anchoring the benches, and appoint anchors for each bench. As soon as one player reaches halfway on the bench, the next player may begin. Remind the players to take turns at being a performer and an anchor.

DESCRIPTION OF ACTIVITY:

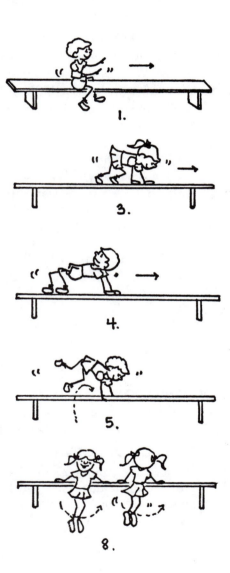

1. *Sit Walk:* Straddle-sit on the bench at one end with your feet touching the floor. Face the opposite end of the bench. Can you move along the bench from one end to the other without using your hands? Now try this again, but travel backwards.

2. *Duck Walk:* In squatting position, "waddle" your way to the end of the bench. Can you sound like a duck as you move?

3. *Cat Walk:* In all-fours position, walk like "a cat on a fence" to the other end.

4. *Crab Walk:* While in the back support position with hands on the floor, feet on the bench and tummy facing up, Crab Walk to the end of the bench.

5. *Bunny Hop:* Grip both sides of the bench. Push off with one foot, jump over the bench, with the opposite foot landing first and then the other. Move your hands forward and hop back over the bench to the other side. Continue to the end. Can you straighten your legs out as you jump? How high can you get your legs?

6. *Over and Under:* Lie on your tummy along the bench. Roll sideways to alternately go underneath and up the other side without touching the floor, or the underneath part of the bench.

7. *Pencil Walk:* Place your hands on the bench and your feet on the floor. Keep your body stiff and straight. Move sideways along the bench, taking your weight on your hands and feet.

   — Repeat, but this time travel with your hands on the floor and your feet on the bench.

8. *The Windmill:* Start with both hands on the bench and both feet on the floor in the front support position. Roll over and over along the bench, taking your weight on your hands and feet as you turn over and over to the end of the bench. It helps to keep your body and elbows straight.

PG-39 BENCH DISMOUNTS

FOCUS: Dismounting and landing technique; body control; sequences

EQUIPMENT: Benches; mats

ORGANIZATION:

• Place mats at the sides and ends of the benches. To begin, choose two anchors per bench. Ensure anchor sits safely away from the performer dismounting.

DESCRIPTION OF ACTIVITY:

1. Working from either end of the bench, perform these dismounts:

   — Standing on both feet, jump off the bench and land on the mat.

   — Do a backwards jump to land on the mat.

   — Jump as high as you can before landing.

   — Jump for distance. Go as far as you can.

   — Jump a quarter-turn and land.

   — Jump a half-turn and land.

   — Jump a full-turn and land.

   — Jump making a big shape; a long shape.

2. Walk with giant steps to the end of the bench. Long jump off the end to land in the crouch position.

3. Do a **Frog Jump:** Stretch upward with the arms as you jump; land on the feet and then hands.

4. Do a **Star Jump** from one end of the bench. Remember to bend at the hips, knees, and ankles when landing. Be in control on your landing; hold your balance for three seconds.

BACKWARD JUMP

FULL-TURN JUMP

1.

2.

4.

5. Stand facing the bench from the side. Jump to stand on the bench. Jump off backwards to land in the crouch position on the mat. Move along the bench in this manner.

6. Create your own safe dismount!

7. **Sequences:**

   — Walk backwards along the bench to halfway; then walk sideways, jump off the end in a big shape.

   — Skip forward along the bench and jump off backwards, landing on both feet.

   — Gallop forward with one foot leading; do a pivot-turn at the opposite end, and then gallop back with the other foot leading; dismount with a Heel Slap.

   — Now invent your own "travel and dismount" sequence!

PG-40 BENCH STATIONWORK

FOCUS: Balance; control; strength

EQUIPMENT: Four benches;
twelve mats;
eight hoops;
four beanbags

ORGANIZATION:

- Form the class into four equal groups. Arrange the benches in a square, with ample room between each. Have each group start at a different bench and travel along each bench in a clockwise direction. Place mats at the ends and sides of each bench. Make sure the benches are anchored and that all anchors have a turn at all activities. Stress that when walking along the bench, the arms should be held out sideways for better balance and that children should keep their heads up and look straight ahead. To start, have each team appoint two anchors for each station.

DESCRIPTION OF ACTIVITY:

1. *Bench No. 1:* Explore different ways of travelling along the bench using different body parts. For example: crawl on your hands and knees, pull yourself along on your tummy, travel along on your back, use your seat and feet, spin around on your seat only.

2. *Bench No. 2:* Walk along the bench with a beanbag on your head. Walk along the bench, tossing and catching the beanbag to yourself as you move. Find other ways to travel along the bench with your beanbag.

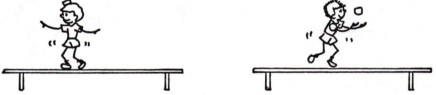

3. *Bench No. 3:* Walk along the bench. Step through the hoop (or hoops) held vertically by other group members. Try to step through without touching the hoop. Now take the hoop and step through like a skipping rope as you move along the bench. Can you walk along the bench and twirl the hoop on one hand; on the other hand? Find other ways of using your hoop as you travel along the bench.

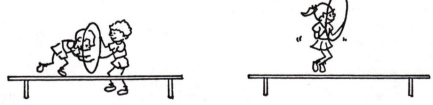

4. *Bench No. 4:* Travel across your bench using different locomotor movements: walk forward, sideways, backwards; gallop, skip, run, jump. Then try your own special way of jumping off: forward, to the side, backwards, turning in the air, rolling on the mat after landing.

PG-41 INTRODUCTION TO THE BALANCE BEAM—BALANCE BEAM WALKS

FOCUS: Balancing; control; strength

EQUIPMENT: Balance beam or balance bench;
four mats;
one ball;
two beanbags per group

ORGANIZATION:

• These activities may be performed on the balance beam, the narrow side of the balance bench, or the climbing frame beam. Place mats at the side and ends of the beam. Form groups of four to five performers. Have children take turns at being a performer and a spotter. Spotters, when necessary, should walk alongside the performer, extending their hand under that of the performer. Performer should dismount with a safe landing, bending at the knees to cushion the impact. Encourage a variety of dismounts.

DESCRIPTION OF ACTIVITY:

1. Walk forward along the beam. Keep your head up. Hold your arms in different positions as you move slowly: behind your back; one up, one down; both up; arms held sideways. Which way gives you the best balance?

2. Walk forward slowly along the beam to the middle. Turn on the balls of your feet and walk back. Keep your head up. Your partner may spot for you as you walk.

3. Shuffle-step sideways along the beam, balancing on the balls of the feet. Shuffle one foot up to the other. Look ahead as you go.

4. **Squat Balance:** Walk to the middle, squat on your toes, and raise your arms sideways. Hold the balance for three seconds, and then continue to the other end.

5. **Foot Dips:** Walk slowly along the beam, and then bend the supporting leg while the other leg dips just below the beam. It now becomes the supporting leg while the other leg dips below the beam. Continue in this way.

6. **Knee Balance:** Balance on one knee and both hands. Can you raise the other leg backwards and high?

7. **Hands and Toes Balance:** Show me how you can balance on the beam in the "push-up" position, on the toes and hands. Look up as you hold the balance.

8. **Cat Walk:** Walk forward on all-fours. Move smoothly.

9. **Side-Stepping:** Step sideways along the beam, balancing on the balls of the feet. Cross one foot over the other. Look ahead as you go.

10. **Beanbag Pick-Up:** Place a beanbag on the beam. Walk forward to pick up the beanbag; place it on your head and continue to the end.

11. **Backwards Walking:** Walk backwards, while balancing a beanbag on the back of each hand. Can you turn around in the middle without dropping the beanbags?

12. **Ball Carry:** Walk forward slowly along the beam, carrying a ball out and away from your body. Try this walking backwards, sideways.

PG-42 INTRODUCTION TO CLIMBING APPARATUS—CLIMBING FRAME

FOCUS: Grips; arm/shoulder strength; travelling safely

EQUIPMENT: Climbing frame; horizontal or parallel bars; several folding mats

ORGANIZATION:

- *Safety Procedures:* Check the frame. Make sure it is safe and secure at the top and bottom. Use mats under the frame. Players should be in bare feet or gym shoes, and pockets should be empty. The ideal is four to five players per station. Do not permit players to storm the frame. Caution players not to interfere with others. Stand so that you can see all groups at the same time. Skill is impaired by fatigue—watch for the signs. Permit groups to work at stations for a maximum of four minutes.
- Sit the players on the floor facing the climbing frame. Explain the parts of the frame. Train all players in the technique of moving and erecting the frame and attachments, and discuss the safety procedures involved. Explain some of the activities which may be done on the frame: climbing, hanging, swinging, sliding, crawling, pulling, balancing, twisting, turning, jumping and landing. Demonstrate the two safety grips: Over Grip and Under Grip. Teach these grips first. Divide the class into groups of four or five players and have the groups move to a station.

DESCRIPTION OF ACTIVITY:

1. *The Over Grip:* When hanging from the bar, place the thumb underneath and the fingers on top. You should be able to see your knuckles.

   The Under Grip: Grasp the bar with fingers and thumb pointing toward you.

   — Move to the bar. Practice hanging using either grip.

   — Practice swinging using the Over Grip.

   — Try pulling yourself upward using either grip.

2. Now explore your station, moving in different directions: climb, crawl through or over, hang, pull.

3. Can you travel up one side and down the other?

4. Climb diagonally up the frames and come straight down, and jump off with a safe landing. As you climb, move only one body part at a time: a hand, then the other hand; a foot, then the other foot; or a hand, then a foot. Keep three out of the four body parts in contact with the frame.

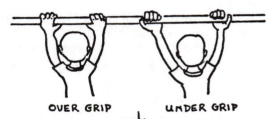

OVER GRIP   1.   UNDER GRIP

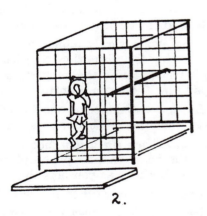

2.

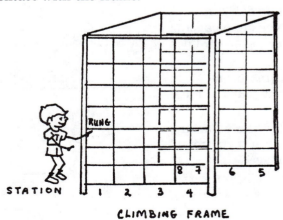

STATION   1   2   3   4

CLIMBING FRAME

PG–43 CLIMBING FRAME CHALLENGES

FOCUS: Climbing; hanging; swinging

EQUIPMENT: Climbing frame; climbing bar and ladder; several mats

ORGANIZATION:

- Set up the climbing ladder and bar on the climbing frame. Check that the apparatus is secure. Arrange four stations on the frame as shown and place mats under each station. Divide the class into four even groups and assign each group to a station. Review the Over Grip and the Under Grip. Remind players to move with control and not to interfere with others. Encourage players to go only as high as they can safely manage and feel confident. Watch for fatigue. Have players rotate stations about every four minutes.

DESCRIPTION OF ACTIVITY:

1. **Climbing Frame:**
   - Find a spot on the frame. Hold with right hand and right foot. Raise the left leg outward and hold the ankle with your free hand. Try this holding with the left hand and left foot.
   - Hang from your spot using only two body parts; only one body part.
   - Climb up with your back to the bars. Move slowly, and then come down the same way.
   - Climb, twisting and turning as you go. Find a spot, hang, and twist your body as you hang.
   - Lie on the floor, feet tucked under the lowest bar, knees bent. Sit up to touch your knees with your elbows. How many "sit-ups" can you do?
   - Add your own idea!

2. **Climbing Ladder:** Take turns travelling across the ladder in different ways: on hands and knees; on hands and feet; using hands only.
   - Hang on a ladder's rung. Can you pull yourself up so that your chin touches the rung? Try this again!
   - Hang onto the rung and swing yourself back and forth like a pendulum.
   - Add your own idea!

3. **Climbing Bar:** Explore different ways of hanging on the bar: two hands; two hands and two feet; sideways; upside down.
   - Hang and pull yourself up so that the bar is just below your chin; then lower yourself. Repeat.
   - Travel along the bar using only your hands, no feet!
   - Add your own idea!

1.

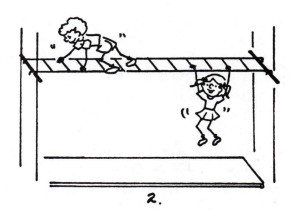

2.

3.

PG–44 INTRODUCTION TO CLIMBING ROPES

FOCUS: Safety guidelines; lifting and climbing

EQUIPMENT: Climbing ropes; several mats

ORGANIZATION:

- Teach children how to arrange the ropes and the mats underneath the ropes ready for activity: demonstrate and provide practice time for this. Discuss the safety guidelines, and teach the correct procedures for climbing and descending the rope. Number the players from one to (number of climbing ropes). Number each of the ropes. Have players sit in a line facing their climbing rope, at a safe distance away.

DESCRIPTION OF ACTIVITY:

Safety Guidelines:

- Use the ropes only when told to do so by your teacher.
- Stand well away from the ropes when others are using them, unless spotting.
- Do not tie knots in the ropes.
- Do not climb a swinging rope.
- Climb, hand-over-hand going up and hand-under-hand coming down.
- Do not slide down the rope, as this causes rope burns.
- Do not interfere with others who are using the ropes.
- When climbing, look up and hold tight.
- Always place mats under the climbing ropes when in use.
- Never leave a swinging rope; stop the swinging first!

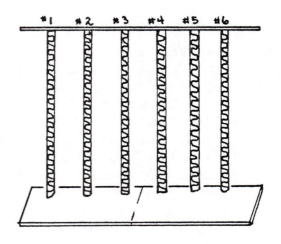

1. Lie on the mat under the rope. Reach up, grasp the rope as high as you can and try these tasks:

   - Walk on your heels, forward, backwards, around in a circle, around the other way.
   - From the lying position, pull yourself up, hand-over-hand until you are standing. Lower yourself hand-under-hand to the sitting position.

2. **Chin the Rope:** Reach upward to grasp the rope; then pull up so that your chin touches your hands.

3. **The Snail:** Grasp the rope a little lower; curl your knees up to your chest. Continue to curl so that your feet touch the mat behind your head. Uncurl and start again.

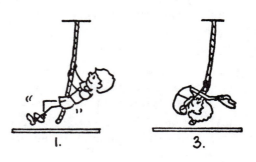

4. **Bicycling:** Stand near your rope so that it falls down between your knees. Grasp the rope as high as you can with both hands. Can you raise your feet off the mat? Who can raise your knees and move your legs as if you were "riding a bike in the air"?

5. **The Clutch:** Stand near your rope. Jump upward, grasping your rope as high as you can. Grip the rope with your feet and hang in this position for a ten-second count. (Everyone in your group can count with you!)

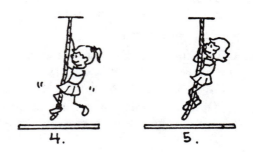

PG–45 CLIMBING ROPES—SINGLE ROPE TASKS

FOCUS: Hanging; climbing technique

EQUIPMENT: Climbing ropes; several mats

ORGANIZATION:

• Place mats under the climbing ropes. Divide the class into groups (equal to the number of climbing ropes). Assign a climbing rope to each group, corresponding with the number of the group. Have members of each group sit in a line just behind their rope, at a safe distance away.

DESCRIPTION OF ACTIVITY:

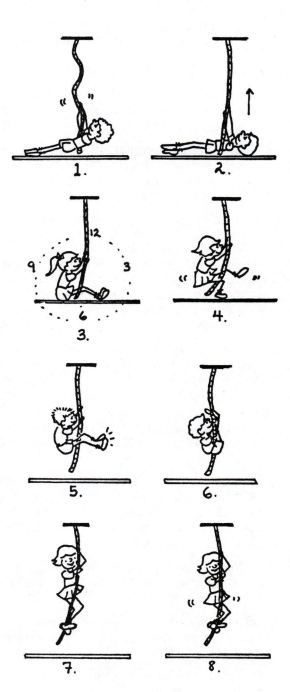

1. *Ring the Bell:* Lying on your back under the rope, reach up to grasp the rope. Wave the rope from side to side; around in circles.

2. *Lazy Lift:* Lie on your back. Grasp the rope as high as possible. Without moving your feet, climb upward with your hands, hand-over-hand, until you are standing. Keep your body rigid. Can you let yourself back down slowly? Remember to lower yourself hand-under-hand!

3. *The Clock:* Sit on the mat. Grasp the rope as high up as possible. Pull up to raise your seat off the mat. Using tiny steps, shuffle your feet around to the 9 o'clock position; 3 o'clock; 12 o'clock; 6 o'clock.

4. *Rope Dancer:* Sit, holding the rope as high as possible. Pull up so that your seat is off the mat. Hanging on to the rope, kick your legs, one at a time, out in front.

5. *Clappers:* Reach up to hang on the rope. Can you raise your legs off the mat, lift them straight out in front, and clap your feet together?

6. *Leg Lifts:* Stand and grasp the rope up high. Push off to lift your knees up to your chest and hold them there. Can you grip the rope with your toes from this position?

7. *Foot Leg-Lock:* Rope should hang in front of body and between legs. Hook your right leg around the rope so that it passes over the top of your right foot. Stand on the rope with left foot to lock the rope into position.

— Stand near your rope. Reach up as high as you can on the rope and grasp the rope. Lock your feet into position on the rope.

8. *The Climber:* Pull up with hand-over-hand, allowing the rope to slide through your feet and knees. Lock feet on the rope after each pull, straighten legs, and reach hands up for another pull. Practice locking feet after each pull.

— To descend, lock feet in position; move hands down rope hand-under-hand. Lock feet into new position and lower hands again. Do not slide down the rope.

— Practice three hand-over-hands; four hand-over-hands; five hand-over-hands; etc.

PG-46 ROPE SWINGING CHALLENGES

FOCUS: Hanging and swinging technique

EQUIPMENT: Climbing ropes;
safety mats;
four benches;
one beanbag;
one hoop per group

ORGANIZATION:

• Place mats under ropes. Divide the class into equal groups based on the number of available ropes. Assign each group to a climbing rope and a mat-covered bench. Teach the basic swing first from the floor level, and then have children swing from a bench.

DESCRIPTION OF ACTIVITY:

1. *Pivot and Swing:* Hold the rope at head height, place both feet together under the rope, and lean back.

   — Can you swing yourself around in a circle without moving your heels off the spot? Can you swing yourself around the other way?

2. *Basic Swing:* Grasp the rope up high and push back to gather speed. Hang on to the rope, grip with your feet, and swing back and forth four times across the mat. Gently let go of the rope as you land on the mat, bending at the knees, and stop the rope from swinging. (If needed, give the performer a gentle push to get a swinging action.)

3. *Bench Swing:* (Position benches about one meter [three feet] behind the climbing ropes [as shown].) Stand on the bench, grasp the rope high, get a firm grip with your hands and feet, and swing out across the mats and back to land on the bench. Can you swing back and forth four times and then land on the mat? Remember to stop the swinging rope!

4. *Hoop Landing:* (Place a hoop about one meter [three feet] in front of the rope and safety mat.) Swing from the bench, across the mat, and land in a hoop. Can you swing from the hoop back to the bench?

   — Now hold a beanbag between your feet; swing and drop the beanbag in the hoop, and then return to land on the bench.

5. *Sitting-Swing Challenge:* Swing from the bench. Hang freely in the sitting position. Do not knot the rope.

6. *L-Swing Challenge:* Hold the legs in the "L" position as you swing.

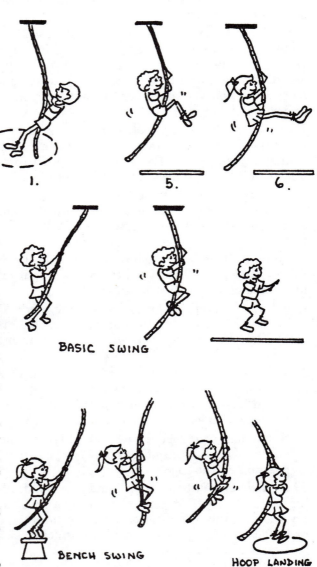

1.　　5.　　6.

BASIC SWING

BENCH SWING　　HOOP LANDING

PG-47 TWO CLIMBING ROPES CHALLENGES

FOCUS: Hanging; arm and shoulder strength

EQUIPMENT: Climbing ropes; safety mats

ORGANIZATION:

• For eight climbing ropes, divide the class into four equal groups. Assign each group two climbing ropes and have each group place a mat directly under the climbing rope. For each performer, have a spotter positioned on each side of the performer.

• To begin, each group sits in a line behind the climbing ropes.

DESCRIPTION OF ACTIVITY:

1. How many different ways can you hang from the two ropes?

2. What shapes can you make as you hang from the ropes?

3. Can you climb from one rope to the other and then to the floor?

4. Can you hang onto the two ropes and let your feet "run in the air"?

5. *The Twister:* Twist yourself into different positions while hanging onto the two ropes.

6. *Hula:* Stand; jump up to grasp the ropes as high as you can. Pull up so that your arms are bent. Can you swing your hips around in a circle to do the "Hula"? Swing your hips the other way.

7. *Still Rope Swing:* Stand holding both ropes as high as you can so that your feet do not touch the mat. Pull up so that your arms are bent and your legs straight. Can you swing your legs forward and backwards without swinging the ropes?

8. *The Grasshopper:* Stand; jump up to grasp the ropes as high as you can. Spring off your feet; place one foot forward and the other foot back. Continue to alternate feet in this way.

9. *L-Sit Hang:* Grasp the ropes as high as you can. Can you raise your legs in the "L" position as you hang?

10. *Inverted Hang:* Grasp the ropes as high as you can; push off and swing yourself upside down, hooking your feet around the rope. Can you hold this inverted position for five seconds?

11. Invent your own "Two-Rope Hanging Stunt"!

FOCUS: Springing and landing from a height

EQUIPMENT: Box horse;
benches;
tables;
mats;
beanbag;
hoop;
crash pad;
climbing rope

ORGANIZATION:

- Set up five different stations using box horses, benches, tables, crash pad, and climbing rope. Place mats under all landing areas. Make sure apparatus is well spaced apart and stable. Anchor the benches by having a player sit on each end; prevent table from moving by having a player on each side holding it securely.
- Rotate groups through the stations every four minutes. Emphasize safe landings: bend at the hips, knees, and ankles, and look straight ahead while dismounting. Appoint three spotters: one on either side, and one on the mat facing the performer.

DESCRIPTION OF ACTIVITY:

1. **Station 1:** Low box horse and landing mat.

   Place your hands flat on the top of the box and spring onto it with a two-foot jump. Get your balance and control; then spring off the box high into the air with arms raised upward, to a safe landing.

2. **Station 2:** Bench and landing mat.

   Explore springing off the bench, getting as much height as you can. Land correctly and safely, and then do a roll: forward roll, log roll, shoulder roll.

3. **Station 3:** Table and landing mat. Ensure table is secure.

   Explore springing off the table and doing a stunt while in the air: click your heels together; slap your heels behind you; touch your toes, hug your knees. Remember to land correctly, bending at the knees.

4. **Station 4:** Box horse and crash pad.

   Explore springing off the box horse, making a wide shape in the air, landing and rolling. Now try making a narrow shape; a twisted shape. Can you spring off and do a half-turn in the air; do a full turn?

5. **Station 5:** Box horse, climbing rope, safety mat.

   Explore different ways of swinging out from the box horse and swinging back to land on the box horse. Can you hold a beanbag between your ankles, swing out from the box horse, drop the beanbag into a hoop in the center of the safety mat, and then return back to the box horse?

STATION 1   STATION 2

STATION 4   STATION 5

PG-49 APPARATUS SIGNALS

FOCUS: Listening; moving in control; space awareness

EQUIPMENT: Climbing frame; climbing ladder; climbing ropes; parallel bars; box horse; tables; chairs; benches; balance beam; springboard; mats

ORGANIZATION:

• This activity involves all the apparatus used in this section. Throughout the activity, emphasize the importance of listening well, moving safely, always being in control, watching out for others. Scatter the apparatus over the play area. Place mats under the apparatus and landing areas.

DESCRIPTION OF ACTIVITY:

1. We are going to do **Apparatus Signals.** Listen carefully for the signal I call, and the instruction for it. Move safely, watching out for others and always being in control of your movements! On signal "Freeze!" stop immediately and wait for the next signal.

2. **Apparatus Signals:**
   — On signal **Around,** move around as many different types of apparatus as you can without touching anything or anyone!
   — On signal **Under,** move under as many different types of apparatus as you can, watching out for others.
   — On signal **Over,** move over as many different types of apparatus as you can.
   — On signal **Through,** move through as many different types of apparatus as you can.
   — On signal **On-Off,** move on and off as many different types of apparatus as you can.
   — On signal **Hang,** hang on different types of apparatus. Hang for a five-second count on each one!
   — On signal **Across,** move along as many different types of apparatus as you can.
   — On signal **Climb,** climb up, down, along different types of apparatus.
   — On signal **Swing,** swing on different types of apparatus. (Have boys "Swing" while girls "Hang" to disperse the performers.)
   — On signal **Hands and Feet,** move over the apparatus using your hands and feet only.
   — On signal **Body Part Travel,** move over the apparatus on different body parts: tummy, hands and knees, seat, back. . . .
   — Add your own ideas!

3. **Follow-the-Leader:** Follow your leader. Do whatever your leader does: climbing, swinging, hanging, balancing, springing, rolling. Change your leader on my signal "Change!" Remember to move carefully, watching out for other groups.

Games
Skills

Game Skills activities develop the abilities children need to participate in most traditional games, such as soccer, volleyball, basketball, softball, and football as well as more innovative games, such as parachute play, scooter play, and juggling.

The 108 Game Skills activities in this section are arranged in units which you might teach over a two- or three-week period.

GS–1 HOOP BALANCES

FOCUS: Body awareness; balancing

EQUIPMENT: One hoop per child

ORGANIZATION:

- Children explore balances and body shapes inside and outside of their hoops in personal space. Provide opportunity for children to observe each other's balances and shapes.
- Have each child get a hoop, lay it flat on the floor in a home space, check for good spacing, and then try the following tasks.

DESCRIPTION OF ACTIVITY:

1. Stand in your hoop and show me how you can balance on one foot; balance on the other foot, keeping your eyes closed.

2. Let me see you make a low balance and hold it for three seconds.

3. Can you make a three-body-part balance in your hoop? Show me a different three-body-part balance.

4. How can you make a balance bridge over your hoop using four body parts? Show me another way of making a bridge over your hoop.

5. Now try to balance on five body parts, with three parts inside the hoop and two parts outside. Can you make a balance with two body parts outside your hoop and one part inside?

6. Show me how you can balance your hoop on as many body parts as you can!

7. Can you make a curled shape inside your hoop? Place one or more body parts on the hoop and make a wide, stretched shape.

8. **Change Homes:** Leave your hoop. Run (skip, gallop, hop, crawl, walk backwards) around the play area without touching any of the hoops. Listen to the number signal I will call. When you hear "One!" quickly find a new home and stand on one leg inside the hoop. On "Two!" find a new home and put two hands in the hoop and two feet out. On "Three!" find a new home and curl up inside.

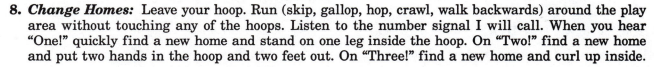

VARIATIONS:

Change Homes:

a. Add another signal "Four!" Have children make a bridge over the hoop.

b. Change the positions for the number signals called. For example, on "One!" have children hop up and down on one leg in a hoop (change hopping foot every four hops); on "Two!" have children pair up and stand back-to-back inside a hoop; on "Three!" have children group together in three's, join hands, and slide-step around the hoop.

c. Have the children suggest what they will do for each number signal.

GS-2 HOOP STUNTS

FOCUS: Manipulation; weight-bearing   **EQUIPMENT:** One hoop per child

ORGANIZATION:

- Have each child get a hoop, find a home space and lay it flat on the floor, and then stand inside of it. Check for good spacing.

DESCRIPTION OF ACTIVITY:

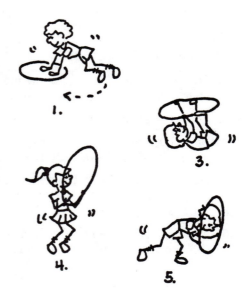

1. Put your hands in the hoop and your feet out. Let me see you walk your feet around the hoop in one direction; then in the other direction. Now place your feet in your hoop and your hands out. Show me how you can walk your hands around the hoop.

2. In your home space, show me how you can pass your hoop around your body, passing it from one hand to the other.

3. Lie on your back and hold the hoop with your hands and feet. Try to rock back and forth; rock from side to side. Now step inside your hoop, pick it up, and hold it above your head. Who can drop it to the floor without letting it touch your body? Try again!

4. How can you use your hoop like a jump rope? Stand your hoop on edge in the upright position. Can you step through head first? Go through it backwards?

GS-3 HOOP SPRINGING

FOCUS: Jumping and landings   **EQUIPMENT:** One hoop per child

DESCRIPTION OF ACTIVITY:

1. Jump with two feet out of your hoop and land outside on two feet. Jump back in, landing on one foot. Jump out, landing on the other foot. Touch a wall (or boundary line); then run toward your hoop. Take off with one foot and land inside on two feet. Did you remember to make a "soft landing," bending at your knees?

2. Now jump forward out of your hoop. Can you jump backwards into your hoop? Let me see you jump backwards out of your hoop; then jump forward into your hoop. Repeat this jumping sequence again!

3. Show me how you can jump sideways out of your hoop; sideways into your hoop; then sideways (to the other side) out of your hoop, and sideways into your hoop again. Repeat.

4. Now try to jump in and out of your hoop, travelling all the way around it! Find another way to travel around your hoop.

5. Can you hop all the way around the outside of your hoop on one foot? Change hopping foot, and hop around in the opposite direction.

6. *Frog in the Pond:* Let's pretend that your hoop is a lily pad and you are a frog. Show me how far you can jump off your lily pad. Land softly with a "splash!" Now turn around and jump back onto your lily pad, landing in a crouch position. Can you sound like a frog ("Ribbit!") as you Frog Jump from one lily pad to another? How would you catch a flying insect as you jump about?

GS-4 HOOP SPINNING AND ROLLING FUN

FOCUS: Manipulation; spinning and rolling techniques

EQUIPMENT: One hoop per player

ORGANIZATION:

• Have players get a hoop and take it to a home space.

DESCRIPTION OF ACTIVITY:

1. Show me how you can make your hoop spin. Begin by holding your hoop with both hands so that the hoop is standing upright. Place your favorite hand on top of the hoop, grasping it between your thumb and forefinger. Spin the hoop by a quick flick of your wrist in a circular motion.

2. Can you spin your hoop like a top, touch a wall; then return to grab your hoop before it drops to the floor? Who can spin it and touch two walls? touch three walls?

3. Show me how to spin it CW; CCW; with your right hand; with your left hand. Who can keep the hoop spinning the longest?

4. See if you can spin your hoop like an eggbeater, and then run around it once and catch it before it falls to the floor. Repeat, running around it in the other direction. How many times can you run around it before it falls?

5. *Hula-Hoop Challenge:* Step inside your hoop and hold it around your waist. Show me how you can spin your hoop around your waist. How long can you keep it going? Now try to do the hula-hoop spin in the other direction. Can you walk while doing the hula-hoop spin?

6. *Arm Spinner:* Show me how you can spin your hoop around your right arm. Can you spin it CW? then CCW? Now spin it on the other arm. Who can spin the hoop on your arm while walking around?

7. Now let's explore rolling the hoops. Stand so that your hoop is on your right side with your left hand on top of the hoop to hold it upright. Place your right hand behind on the hoop with the palm against the hoop, and your fingers pointing slightly downward. Push the hoop forward with your right hand so that it rolls upright. Run after your hoop and try again. Always roll your hoop into open spaces.

8. Change sides so that your hoop is on your left side; your right hand is on top holding it upright; and your left hand pushes the hoop forward.

9. Can you roll your hoop forward; then run ahead of it, and catch it on one hand? Try again, catching it on the other hand. Who can roll your hoop forward, and then circle it two or three times before it stops?

10. Roll your hoop forward, allow it to fall; then jump into it before it stops moving. Jump out again without touching your hoop. Can you roll your hoop forward; then jump through it while it is moving without touching it? Who can jump back through it?

11. Roll your hoop forward and keep it rolling by gently pushing it forward. How far can you roll your hoop before it falls? Find a partner. Put one hoop away. Explore rolling your hoop back and forth to each other.

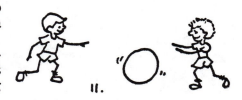

GS-5 HOOP GAMES

FOCUS: Spacial awareness; listening; cooperation

EQUIPMENT: One hoop per child;
four or five cone markers;
lively music;
tape or record player

ORGANIZATION:

• Have children get a hoop each; then find a home space. Check for good spacing.

DESCRIPTION OF ACTIVITY:

1. *The Car Game:* (Scatter four or five cone markers on the lines of the play area.) Pretend your hoop is a giant steering wheel. Show me how you can steer your hoop, twisting and turning it as you travel on a winding mountain road. Remember, always watch where you are going!

   — Now your hoop is a Car, and you are the Driver. Step inside your hoop and hold it at waist level. The lines on the play area are the Roads. How careful a Driver can you be? Drive on the roads slowly. As you drive, can you make a car noise? Let me hear your horn, "Honk! Honk!" From a slow start, step on the gas. Now slow down again. Whenever you come to a Stop Sign (cone marker) you must Stop! Look both ways! and Listen! Then drive on carefully. Stay on the right side of the road as you pass another car. A Pedestrian (teacher) has the right of way. What does this mean?

2. *Race Car Driver:* Be a race car driver. Can you make the sounds of a car turning sharp corners? Go fast! Go slow! Make quick changes of direction. Stop quickly on the signal "Freeze!" and make a balance using your hoop.

3. *Musical Hoops:* (Take away a hoop so that there is one fewer than the number of players.) Scatter your hoop throughout the play area. When you hear the music, move around the play area as I signal "Skip!" When the music stops, quickly try to land in a hoop. The player without a home, you give the next movement signal (run, gallop, walk backwards, hop, jump, crawl, side-step, crab-walk, puppy-dog walk); then rejoin the game. Who will be the next player without a home?

4. *High Tower:* Find a partner. Holding hands, skip with your partner in between the hoops without touching them. On signal "Tower!" quickly form a "high tower" over a hoop by joining hands overhead with your partner and standing on tip-toes. (Repeat using other locomotor movements.)

5. *Horse and Buggy:* One partner step inside a hoop and hold it on either side at waist level. You are the "Horse." The second partner hold onto the hoop from the outside, just behind the partner in front. You are the "Driver." Together, gallop around the play area. On signal "Switch," change roles and continue to gallop. Remember to watch where you are going.

VARIATIONS:

a. In Musical Hoops, have players land in different ways in the hoops: land on three body parts, crouch down low, be a statue.

b. In The Car Game, add Stop Lights signals (either verbally or using colored paper): Green to drive; Yellow to jog in place; and Red to stop immediately. Discuss car safety. Did you remember to fasten your seatbelts?

1.

2.

4.

5.

GS–6 HOOP RELAYS

FOCUS: Cooperation; agility

EQUIPMENT: Several cone markers; five hoops per team

ORGANIZATION:

• Divide the class into teams of six players per team. Use cones to mark out a starting line. Have each team stand in single file formation behind the starting line and facing a row of five hoops that are equally spaced two meters (six feet) apart. Ensure that teams are well spaced apart.

• Use a starting signal and have teams finish in a certain position, such as sitting cross-legged. Emphasize fair play and quality movement.

DESCRIPTION OF ACTIVITY:

1. *Zig-Zag Hoop Relay:* Zig-zag your way around each hoop. When you have rounded the end hoop, run back to tag the next player, who does the same.

2. *Stepping Stone Relay:* Land in each hoop. Jump out of the end hoop and run back to your team to tag the next player, who repeats the action.

3. *Leaping Hoop Relay:* Leap over each hoop; then run back to your team to tag the next player, who repeats the action.

4. *Hoop Caper Relay:* Run to each hoop, in turn, put it over your body, and then run back to your team to tag the next player, who does the same.

5. *Hoop Tunnel Relay:* Each team forms a circle, with players well spaced apart. Each team player holds a hoop vertically in front of the body with the bottom of the hoop touching the floor. On your signal "Go!" the first player drops the hoop; then crawls through all of the other hoops. As soon as the first player has picked up his or her own hoop and holds it upright, the second player may go. When everyone on the team has had a turn and each player is sitting cross-legged inside a hoop, the relay ends. Which team will be the quickest?

6. *Locomotion Hoop Relay:* (Have children in each team pair up; team leaders get a hoop each. Then each pair stand side-by-side in their team files behind the starting line, facing a turning line 20 meters [60 feet] away.) The first pair hold a hoop between you, with your inside hands at waist height. Your hoop should be level with the floor. Skip together in this way to a turning line and back. Hand over the hoop to the next pair, who repeats the task. When each pair has gone twice, then everyone must sit cross-legged in pairs behind the starting line. (Repeat relay, using the galloping step; using the slide-step; and each pair holding the hoop waist level with both hands.)

7. *Horse and Buggy Relay:* (Refer to Section 7, "Special Games," activity SG–13 for set-up.) One partner step inside the hoop and hold it on either side at waist level. You are the "Horse." The second partner hold onto the hoop from behind. You are the "Driver." Together gallop in this way to the turning line, change roles, and then gallop back to your team file. Give the hoop to the next pair in line. Continue until each pair has gone twice.

GS–7 HOOP GROUP GAMES

FOCUS: Cooperation; alertness; jumping skills

EQUIPMENT: One hoop per player;
six banners;
eight to ten cone markers

DESCRIPTION OF ACTIVITY:

1. *Obstacle Hoops:* (Divide the class into two equal groups: 1 and 2. Have Group 1 lay their hoops aside; Group 2, stand in a free space and hold hoops upright on or just above the floor.) On signal "Hike!" Group 1 skip around in general space climbing under, over, through, or around the hoops. On signal "Switch!" change roles. (Reverse roles often.)

2. *Hoop Pattern Jumping:* (Form groups of six to eight players and have each player get a hoop. Assign each group to a certain area. Ensure that groups are well spaced.) Place your hoops in a straight line on the floor so that they are touching each other. Taking turns, jump with feet together into each hoop. Show me another way to travel through your hoops (hopping on right foot, hopping on left foot, stepping into hoops, moving on hands and feet into hoops).

   — Now place your hoops in a different pattern. How many different ways can you travel through this pattern?

   — Create a new hoop pattern and explore different ways of travelling through it. Visit another group's hoop pattern and travel through it. Continue until you have visited each group's pattern.

3. *Circle Hoop Game:* (Have each group equally space seven hoops about two meters [six feet] apart, in a circle pattern on the floor, then place one hoop in the center of the circle. Have one player stand in the center hoop, while the other players stand in the circle hoops.) When you hear the music, circle players, change places with other circle players without getting caught in the center. Center player, try to get into a circle hoop as well. The player caught without a circle hoop when the music stops must start in the center.

4. *Space Shuttle:* (Form teams of six or eight players. Have each team stand in a file behind a starting line at one end of the play area. The Leader of each team stands inside a hoop, holding it at waist level. Place a cone marker in front of each team, about 10 meters [30 feet] away. Ensure that teams are well spaced apart.) On the signal "Go!" Leader, holding your hoop, run around the cone marker and return to your team to pick up the second player. Both players run together, with the leader inside the hoop and the second player outside, holding onto the hoop from behind. Travel around the cone and back to your team. Once you reach your team, drop off the Leader, second player step inside; then pick up the third player. Continue in this way; dropping off and picking up, until all players have had a turn. The first team to sit cross-legged in a file behind your Leader with the hoop is the winner.

2.

1.

GS–8 ADVANCED HOOP TRICKS

FOCUS: Manipulation; tossing and catching; back-spin technique   **EQUIPMENT:** One hoop per player

ORGANIZATION:

- Have each player get a hoop, take it to a free space, and hold the hoop vertically. Check for good spacing. Demonstrate the back-spin several times so that children can see the entire action.

DESCRIPTION OF ACTIVITY:

1. *Hoop Toss and Catch:*

   Hold your hoop in your favorite hand. Use an underhand toss to send the hoop into the air. By flicking your wrist as you let go, the hoop should spin backwards. Keep watching the hoop while it is in flight. Catch it with both hands.

2. Now show me how you can . . .

   — Toss the hoop with your favorite hand and catch it with both hands ten times.

   — Toss the hoop with your other hand and catch it with both hands ten times.

   — Toss and catch the hoop with your right hand ten times.

   — Toss and catch the hoop with your left hand ten times.

   — Toss and catch your hoop while walking.

   — Can you find another way to toss and catch your hoop?

3. *The Back-Spin Technique:*

   — Stand behind your upright hoop with one hand holding the top, the palm facing down, and fingers around the hoop.

   — Bring your hoop backwards and to the side. Throw the hoop forward quickly, flicking your wrist upward to create a backwards spin and pull the hoop downward toward the floor as you let go. The hoop should roll forward and then return to you. Practice on your own.

4. *Back-Spin Challenge:* Who can make their hoop back-spin over the longest distance?

GS-9 INTRODUCING BEANIE

FOCUS: Familiarization; manipulation

EQUIPMENT: One beanbag per player;
one hoop per player;
music with a lively 4/4 beat;
tape or record player

ORGANIZATION:

- Children explore manipulating and moving with beanbags in many fun and challenging ways, and learn the fundamentals of throwing and catching. Beanbag Play is an excellent lead-up to Ball Play because the beanbags are much easier to handle. Introduce "Beanie" to the class: Draw a happy face on a beanbag with a marking pen.

- Throughout the section, several dispersal and collection ideas will be given; use your own ideas as well! Scatter the beanbags over the floor. On your signal, have players each get a beanbag and take it to a home space.

DESCRIPTION OF ACTIVITY:

1. I want you to meet "Beanie." Can you give Beanie a big welcome? "Hello Beanie!" On how many different parts of your body can you place your Beanie? (head, forehead, nose, shoulder, hand, fingers, elbow, tummy, back, knee, foot) Stand with Beanie on your head. Can you kneel down without having Beanie fall off? Can you sit? Now squat; then try to stand up without touching Beanie with your hands. Who can turn around in your home without Beanie falling off your head?

2. Let me see you take Beanie for a little walk on your arm; on your shoulder; on your head; on the back of your hand. In what other ways can you give Beanie a ride? (Move in different directions and levels.)

3. Put Beanie on the floor in a free space. Check your space: stand in front of it; stand beside it; stand behind it. Now let me see you jump forward over Beanie; jump backwards over Beanie; jump sideways over Beanie. Hop on one foot around your Beanie. Find another way to move around your Beanie.

4. Build a bridge using four body parts over your Beanie. Make a different bridge using four body parts. Make a three-point bridge over Beanie. Who can touch your belly button on Beanie?

5. *Statue:* When you hear the music, skip (walk backwards, run, gallop, side-step, crab-walk) around the Beanies scattered on the floor. When the music stops, land on a Beanie and make a statue. Remember to watch where you are going!

6. *Steal the Hats:* Get a hoop, find a space, and stand inside the hoop, with Beanie (the Hat) on your head. When the music starts, walk or run about the play area. Try to steal other players' hats and put them in your hoop. If your hat is stolen, you cannot get it back, but you can still try to steal other hats. You are not allowed to touch the hat on your head or steal hats from other homes. If your hat falls off, quickly pick it up and put it back on your head. Who will collect the most number of hats before the music stops?

7. It is time to put Beanie away. Pick Beanie up, give it a gentle pat, and then put it on your head. Walk around the play area. As you pass the beanbag basket in the middle, nod your head forward so that Beanie drops in. Return to the Listening Circle.

GS-10 BEANBAG CHALLENGES

FOCUS: Manipulation; coordination   **EQUIPMENT:** One beanbag per player

ORGANIZATION:

- Children explore manipulating beanbags while in different body positions. Have the girls get their beanbags first; then the boys. Reverse the order when collecting the beanbags at the end. Challenge the players to take Beanie to a home space in a creative way.

DESCRIPTION OF ACTIVITY:

1. Stand in your home. Place Beanie on the floor. Show me how you can move Beanie along the floor using different body parts: feet, hand, one finger, an elbow, one knee, nose, head, etc.

2. Now put Beanie on your forehead and lean backwards slowly until Beanie falls to the floor behind you. Without moving your feet, try to pick up your Beanie. Do this stunt again.

3. Sit in the wide-sit position and hold Beanie in one hand. Let me see you use Beanie to draw a big circle around you on the floor. Reach out as far as you can. Try this again in standing position; knee-sit position, back-lying position.

4. Show me how you can lift your Beanie off the floor without using your hands or mouth! Can you lift up Beanie in another way? Use different body parts.

5. *Beanbag Rescue:* Place Beanie on your head and balance it there. Place one hand behind your back. Move in this way around the play area. Try to tip-toe up to another player and knock the beanbag off his or her head. When your Beanie is knocked off or falls off, you are frozen. You can be unfrozen by another player who picks up your Beanie and places it on your head, without losing his or her own Beanie! How many Beanies will you knock off? How many rescues will you make?

6. *Beanbag Signals:*
   - On signal "Toss and Walk!" walk around in general space, tossing Beanie upward with your favorite hand, and catching it in two hands. (Repeat, using other locomotor movements such as running, skipping, galloping, side-stepping.)
   - On signal "Freeze!" let your Beanie fall to the floor and stand on it holding a balance.
   - On signal "Leap!" run and leap over as many beanbags as you can before the next signal is called.
   - On signal "Jump!" jump sideways back and forth over your beanbag.
   - On "Hop!" hop around the beanbags; change hopping leg often.
   - On "Bridge!" make a bridge over a beanbag.
   - On "Home Beanie!" pick up Beanie, toss and catch it as you run once around the play area. As you pass the basket, drop your beanbag in.

VARIATION: Use deckrings instead of beanbags.

GS-11 BEANBAG TOSSING AND CATCHING

FOCUS: Underhand throwing technique; right–left dexterity   **EQUIPMENT:** One beanbag per player

ORGANIZATION:

- Children learn the underhand toss-and-catch technique using their dominant hand, then their non-dominant hand in personal space, and later, general space.
- Number the players off by four's; then call each group in turn to get a beanbag each, and find a home space.

DESCRIPTION OF ACTIVITY:

1. *Underhand Tossing:* Today we are going to learn how to toss and catch your Beanie. A toss is a one-hand underhand throw.
   - Hold Beanie in the palm of your tossing hand and grip your fingers around it. Don't hold it by the corners! Put the foot opposite your throwing hand, forward.
   - Swing your throwing hand down and back, as you take your weight on your back foot. Then swing the throwing hand forward and upward, as you step forward onto your front foot.
   - When you let your Beanie go, your hand follows Beanie in the line of direction. Let your eyes follow the toss, too!

2. *Catching:* To catch Beanie, we will use two hands first, and later just one hand.
   - Watch the Beanie as it comes toward you. Don't take your eyes off of it until you feel it in your hands! Line yourself up so that you are directly in front of the beanbag.
   - If Beanie is coming toward you below your belly button, then make a "basket" with your hands, palms up, so that the little fingers are touching.
   - If Beanie is coming toward you above your belly button, then make your basket with the thumbs touching. Reach forward with your basket and keep your fingers relaxed. Let the Beanie fall softly into your hands; then close your fingers over it. Bring your arms in toward you ("give") to make a soft catch.

3. Show me how you can toss Beanie with your favorite hand and catch it in two hands. Remember to keep your eyes on Beanie and make a "catching basket." Try not to make a sound when you catch Beanie! Repeat ten times. Toss Beanie up with your other hand and catch it in two hands. Repeat ten times.

4. Toss Beanie up, clap once, and catch it in two hands. Toss Beanie up, clap two times, catch; toss, clap three times, catch; etc. Keep going! Use your other hand to toss and repeat the toss-clap-catch pattern.

5. Let me see you toss and catch Beanie with your right hand ten times. Then toss and catch Beanie with your left hand ten times. Can you toss Beanie with one hand and catch with the other: toss right, catch left; toss left, catch right?

6. Toss Beanie up, touch your shoulder, and catch it in two hands. Toss Beanie up, touch your other shoulder, catch. Toss Beanie up, touch your knees, catch. Toss Beanie up, touch . . . , catch.

7. Who can toss Beanie up, touch the floor, and catch it? Can you toss Beanie up, turn right around, and catch it? Show me another way you can toss and catch your Beanie using your favorite hand; using your other hand.

GS-12 BEANBAG TARGET TOSSING

FOCUS: Accurate throwing; right–left dexterity

EQUIPMENT: One beanbag per player; one wall target per player; one hoop per player; one large plastic garbage pail

ORGANIZATION:

- Children, working in pairs, practice the Underhand Throw for accuracy. Introduce the step forward with the foot opposite the throwing hand as the beanbag is tossed.
- Wall targets can easily be made by taping 50-centimeter (20-inch) squares about 1.5 meters (5 feet) from the floor. If possible, "Happy Faces" could be painted on the walls and used as targets.
- Have the taller partner get a beanbag first, then get a hoop; while the shorter partner gets a hoop first, then a beanbag. To start, each player stands inside the hoop and holds a beanbag.

DESCRIPTION OF ACTIVITY:

1. *Hoop Tossing:* Walk two giant steps away (2 meters or 6 feet) from your hoop, turn, and face it. Let me see you toss your Beanie into the hoop and make it stay inside! Start with your feet together and hold Beanie in your favorite hand. Step forward on the foot opposite to your throwing hand, as you toss Beanie toward the hoop. Toss upward and out. Keep your eyes on the target and let your hand follow Beanie on its way to the hoop! After five tries with your favorite hand, repeat tosses with your other hand.
   — Now take one step further away from the hoop and toss again with each hand, in turn. How far away from the hoop can you toss Beanie?

2. *Wall Target Tossing:* Find a partner and stand two giant steps away (2 meters or 6 feet) from a wall target. Take turns, tossing your Beanie at the target. Remember to step into your throw! Make five tosses with your right hand; then five tosses with your left hand.
   — Take one step back away from your target and toss again. How many times can you hit your target?

3. *Partner Tossing:* Find a partner. Stand back-to-back and walk two giant steps away from each other, turn, and face your partner, who is your "target"! Toss one Beanie back and forth to each other. Remember to make your "catching basket" with your hands. Count the number of catches you can make without dropping the beanbag.
   — Practice tossing with your right hand; then with your left hand.
   — Practice catching with two hands; then with one hand.

4. *Toss Away:* (Place a large plastic garbage pail in the middle of the play area and have the class form a large circle about 3 meters [10 feet] from it.) Toss your beanbag in the pail. If you miss, do three jumping jacks, and then try again, until your Beanie lands in the pail.

GS-13 BEANBAG STUNTS AND TOSSING GAMES

FOCUS: Visual tracking; manual dexterity; tossing and catching; dodging

EQUIPMENT: One beanbag per player

ORGANIZATION:

- Have all children wearing a certain color get a beanbag and find a free space. Continue calling out colors until everyone has a beanbag. Call out colors again to return beanbags to the storage container.

DESCRIPTION OF ACTIVITY:

1. Hold your Beanie as high as you can with both hands. Drop it, and catch it. Do this again, but this time try to catch it below your belly button! Can you clap once before you catch it?

2. Now hold Beanie with your right hand as high as you can. Drop it, and catch it in two hands. Can you catch it in your right hand? Can you catch it in the left hand? Hold Beanie in your left hand and catch it in your left. Catch it in your right hand.

3. Put Beanie on your head, nod Beanie off your head, and catch it. Put Beanie between your feet, jump up, and toss Beanie into your hands.

4. Who can toss Beanie up, kneel down, and catch it? From squatting position, toss Beanie up; then stand up and catch it.

5. Find a partner and stand back-to-back. Pass the Beanie overhead; then through your legs to each other. Pass the Beanie from one side to the other side. Pass in the opposite direction.

6. Invent another stunt that you can do with your Beanie!

7. *Beanbag Egg Toss:* (Have players pair off; then have the partner with the bigger feet get a beanbag, while the other partner finds a free space.) Partners, stand back-to-back and take two giant steps away from each other, turn, and face. Toss your Beanie back and forth to each other. If no one drops the Beanie after five tosses, then both players take one step back; otherwise continue passing and catching until you complete the task.

   — Which pair can toss and catch the furthest distance?
   Game 1: Toss with best hand, catch in two hands.
   Game 2: Toss with other hand, catch in two hands.
   Game 3: Toss with one hand, catch in that hand.
   Game 4: Toss with one hand, catch in the other hand.

   — Challenge: If one player drops the Beanie, the pair must begin again!

8. *Dodge the Beanbag:* (Form groups of three. Number off 1, 2, and 3 in each group; then have the first player get a beanbag. Scatter in your groups throughout the play area. Have each group mark out a confined area in which they will play the game. Increase the size of this area as ability improves.) The first and second players stand about 4 meters (12 feet) apart, facing each other; the third player stand between them. The two outside players, use an Underhand Toss with either hand, to try to hit the middle player below the waist. Middle player, try to dodge the beanbag. If hit, you must exchange places with the player who made the hit. Remember to stay in your area and not interfere with any of the other groups.

GS-14 BEANBAG RELAYS

FOCUS: Manipulation; cooperation

EQUIPMENT: One beanbag per team;
one wall target per team;
one container per team;
floor or wall tape;
several cone markers;
five hoops per team

ORGANIZATION:

- Three beanbag relays are suggested here. Refer to Section 7, "Special Games," for other relays using beanbags. Encourage fair play and good cooperation.

DESCRIPTION OF ACTIVITY:

1. *Beanbag Balancing Relay:* (Form teams of four and have each team stand in a file behind a starting line, and face a turning line 10 meters [30 feet] away. The Leader of each team has a beanbag.) On the signal "Go!" each player, in turn, balance Beanie on your head as you walk to a turning line and back. If Beanie falls off, quickly pick it up, put Beanie back on your head, and continue. When you cross the starting line, nod Beanie off your head into the hands of the next player. (Repeat relay having players balance Beanie on different body parts: shoulder, back of hand, back, tummy.)

2. *Beanbag Passing Relay:* (Form teams of six players and have each team stand in a circle, with the Leader holding a beanbag.) Pass Beanie quickly around the circle in a CW direction. If someone drops the beanbag, your team must do five jumping jacks. Each time Beanie returns to the Leader, count one. Which team can get to ten and sit cross-legged the quickest? (Repeat the relay, passing in a CCW direction.)

3. *Beanbag Target Toss Relay:* (Form teams of four and have each team, in single-file formation, face a wall target, 3 meters [10 feet] away. The Leader holds a beanbag to start.) Each player, in turn, try to toss Beanie into the target. Quickly pick up Beanie and hand it to the next player in line; then go to the end of your line. Count one every time Beanie lands in or on the target. Which team can get the best score at the end of two minutes? (Repeat relay, except have players toss into a floor target such as a hoop or container [cardboard box, garbage pail, or laundry basket].)

4. *Five-Hoop Relay:* (Form teams of five or six and have each team in single-file formation, with each Leader standing in a hoop and holding a beanbag.) On signal "Go!" Leader pass the beanbag to the player behind you, who passes it to the next player, and so on down the line. When the last player receives the beanbag, he or she runs in a CCW direction around the outside of each team and returns to stand in his or her team's hoop, and then starts passing down the line again. The relay ends when the Leader is back inside the hoop, holding the beanbag high, and all team members are sitting cross-legged.

2.

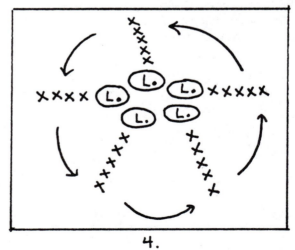

4.

FOCUS: Familiarization; manipulation

EQUIPMENT: One deckring per player; music with a lively 4/4 beat; tape or record player

ORGANIZATION:

- Deckrings help develop hand-eye coordination and object control. Most of the beanbag tasks can be repeated using deckrings. In the following activities, the children will explore and discover other ways of manipulating their deckrings.

- Introduce "Deckie" to the class; then roll deckrings out on the floor for the children to capture and take to a home space. Make sure that children are well spaced apart.

DESCRIPTION OF ACTIVITY:

1. The object that I am holding in my hand is called a deckring. Let's call it "Deckie!" As I roll the Deckies toward you, capture one and take it to your home space. Show me what you can do with your Deckie.

2. How can you make your Deckie roll along the floor? Remember to roll it into open spaces. To roll Deckie forward, place the palm and fingers of your favorite hand behind the deckring, pointing downward, and push Deckie away with your pointer finger. Practice with your best hand; then try to roll Deckie with your other hand.

3. Roll Deckie forward and show me how you can run in front of your Deckie and pick it up with one hand. Can you pick it up with the other hand?

4. Show me how you can jump over it as Deckie rolls along the floor. How many times can you jump over Deckie before it stops rolling?

5. Now try to run alongside Deckie and scoop it up with one foot. Can you use your other foot to do this? What other trick can you do?

6. Who can make Deckie spin in place, like you did with your hoops? Whose Deckie will spin the longest? Now show me another way to make Deckie spin.

GS–16 DECKRING TOSSING CHALLENGES

FOCUS: Visual tracking; manual dexterity

EQUIPMENT: One deckring per player

ORGANIZATION:

- Children explore different ways of tossing and catching a deckring individually, while stationary, and then while moving. To begin, scatter the deckrings on the floor around the play area. As a warm-up, do "Beanbag Signals," activity GS–10, using the deckrings. Emphasize that children must visually track the deckring, reaching with their hands toward it to make the catch with relaxed fingers! Give them plenty of time to practice these tasks.

DESCRIPTION OF ACTIVITY:

1. Find a Deckie and pick it up. This will be your home space. Let me see you do the following challenges:

   — Hold Deckie up with one hand, let it go, and catch it with both hands. Try this with your other hand. How low can you catch your Deckie?

   — Hold Deckie up with the right hand, let it go, and catch with the right. Do this again, using your left hand.

   — Hold Deckie up with your right hand, let it go, and catch with your left. Now hold with your left, catch with your right.

1.

2. Let's try these tossing-and-catching challenges:

   — Toss Deckie up with your best hand and catch it with two hands. Try this again using the other hand.

   — Toss Deckie into the air, clap once, and then catch it. Toss it again, clap two times, and catch it. Repeat the toss-clap-catch pattern. How many claps can you do?

   — Toss Deckie up with right hand and catch with right hand.

   — Toss Deckie up with left hand and catch with left hand.

   — Toss Deckie up with right hand and catch it with left hand.

   — Toss Deckie up with left hand and catch it with right hand.

   — Toss Deckie up in the air and catch it in the kneeling position; toss from the knee-sit position and stand up to catch Deckie.

   — How high can you toss your Deckie and still catch it?

   — Toss Deckie up, turn right around, and catch it.

   — Toss and catch your Deckie while walking in general space. Repeat while running; skipping; galloping; side-stepping.

3. Create your own tossing-and-catching trick.

CLAPPING

KNEE-SITTING

SKIPPING

GS-17 BEANBAG-DECKRING FUN

FOCUS: Visual tracking; manual dexterity; partnerwork

EQUIPMENT: One deckring per player; one beanbag per player

ORGANIZATION:

- By combining Beanbags and Deckrings in challenging tasks, children further develop hand-eye co-ordination, control and accuracy in underhand throwing at stationary and moving objects, and the ability to use the nondominant hand as well as the dominant hand.

- Have each child collect a deckring and a beanbag, and take them to a home space. Check for good spacing.

DESCRIPTION OF ACTIVITY:

1. Place Deckie on the floor in front of you. Hold Beanie just below your eyes. See if you can drop your Beanie into the Deckie. Do this with your right hand and then with your left hand.

2. Now place your Deckie about two giant steps away from you. Can you toss your Beanie into the Deckie? Use your right hand to toss; then your left hand. If you find this easy, then move back one step.

3. Hold Beanie in your favorite hand and Deckie in the other. Can you toss Beanie up and catch it through the Deckie? Try again, but this time hold Deckie in your favorite hand and Beanie in the other; then toss Beanie up and catch it through the Deckie. Invent a trick of your own using your beanbag and deckring.

4. *Partner Deckring Egg Toss:* (Have players pair up: The taller partner gets a beanbag, while the shorter partner gets a deckring; then each pair finds a free space.) Partners, stand back-to-back; then take two giant steps away from each other, turn, and face. Using just your Deckie, toss it back and forth to each other. Toss with one hand, then the other; catch with two hands, then one hand. Every time you make five catches in a row, each partner may take another step back! How far away from each other can you toss and catch your Deckie?

5. *Beanbag Basketball:* Partners, stand facing about four giant steps away from each other. One partner hold the deckring horizontally while the other partner toss the beanbag toward the deckring. Try to catch the beanbag through the deckring. Switch roles after every five tosses. Gradually increase the tossing distance as the task becomes too easy!

6. *Beanbag Horseshoes:* Get a beanbag each. Stand facing each other 10 meters (30 feet) apart. Place the deckring in the middle between you. Using an Underhand Toss, see which partner can toss the Beanie closer to the deckring. Play to five points; then trade partners and play a new game.

7. *Kill the Snake:* Collect a deckring and a beanbag each; then scatter around the play area. The deckring is the "Snake!" On signal "Go!" roll your Snake forward along the floor; then run after it and try to hit the Snake by tossing your Beanie at it. If you miss, run to pick up the beanbag and try again. Keep throwing your beanbag until you have "killed" the Snake; then start over. Remember to hit only your Snake and to watch where you are going!

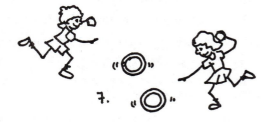

GS-18 LUMMI STICK FUN

FOCUS: Familiarization; manipulation   **EQUIPMENT:** One lummi stick per player

ORGANIZATION:

- Children manipulate lummi sticks in personal and general space. Lummi sticks can be made from 25-millimeter (1-inch) dowelling, cut into 30-centimeter (12-inch) lengths. As an art project, the sticks could be painted; then hung to dry.

DESCRIPTION OF ACTIVITY:

1. Today I am going to introduce you to "Lummi." As I gently tap you on the head, get your Lummi and take it to a home space. Let's explore different ways of using the lummi sticks.

2. Put Lummi on the floor. Show me different ways of jumping over it: forward and back; side-to-side; end-to-end.

3. Hop around three different lummi sticks, touch each with your nose; then hop around your own Lummi, and make a bridge over it. Make a three-point balance, with two parts touching Lummi. Balance on one foot, leaning over your stick as far as you can. Try this balancing on the other foot. How many different body parts can you balance Lummi: head, hand, shoulder, elbow, knee, tummy, back, foot?

4. Let me see you balance Lummi on some body part and walk around in general space. Find a different way to balance Lummi and move.

5. Show me how you can spin Lummi on the floor using your favorite hand; then spin it with your other hand.

6. Hold the Lummi straight up (vertically) in one hand and pass it back and forth without moving your head. Can you pass the lummi stick around your waist; knees; ankles? Who can pass the Lummi in a figure-8 pattern around your legs? Reverse the direction.

7. Show me how you can make your fingers climb the stick; climb back down! Try this with your other hand.

8. Now hold Lummi flat (horizontally) with one hand, like this. Roll it forward with your fingers; backwards. Try this with your other hand. Twirl the lummi stick like a baton.

9. What other tricks can you do?

GS-19 LUMMI STICK CHALLENGES

FOCUS: Manipulation; visual tracking; partnerwork

EQUIPMENT: Two lummi sticks per player; one deckring per pair; one tennis ball per pair; one bowling pin per pair

ORGANIZATION:

• Have each player get two lummi sticks and find a free space.

DESCRIPTION OF ACTIVITY:

1. Who can balance one lummi stick on a finger of your hand? Now try to balance the stick on a finger of the other hand. Create another balancing trick.

2. How can you blow against one stick to make it travel across the play area?

3. Hold one lummi stick vertically in each hand, drop one stick, let it bounce once, and catch it in the same hand. Drop the other stick and catch. Can you drop them at the same time and catch? Put one stick on the floor. Let me see you drop one stick, let it bounce, and catch it with the opposite hand.

4. Now hold one end of that stick with your right hand. Can you flip the Lummi over once and catch it at the same end, with your right hand? Repeat with your left hand. Who can flip the lummi stick once with one hand and catch it in the other hand?

5. Take two sticks, one in each hand. Show me how you can hold one stick (as if it were a nail), and hammer the stick through your hand. Switch hands and repeat. Hold each stick horizontally at one end. Try to tap the sticks together until they pass through your hands. Can you do this with your eyes closed?

6. *Lummi Stick Tugs:* Find a partner and stand in a free space. Each hold one end of the lummi stick and try to pull it away from your partner. Change hands and repeat. Grip the stick with both hands so that one of your hands is between your partner's. Try to pull your partner across a line. Hold the stick vertically; then hold it horizontally.

7. *Lummi Stick Hockey:* One partner get a tennis ball. Wide-sit facing each other, about three giant steps away. Use your sticks to pass the ball back and forth to each other. Put the ball away and get a deckring and a plastic pin. Put the pin in the middle between you. Use your stick to shoot the deckring at the pin and knock it over.

8. *Ring Toss:* One partner hold the lummi stick vertically in one hand; the other partner hold the deckring. Stand facing each other about two giant steps apart to start. Try to "ring the deckring on the stick." Change tossing and stick-holding hands after every five tries. Change roles after ten tosses.

9. Create a trick with your partner using the lummi sticks.

GS-20 INTRODUCING WANDS

FOCUS: Familiarization; manipulation

EQUIPMENT: One wand per player

ORGANIZATION:

- Wands are inexpensive manipulative equipment that can be cut from 12.5- to 16-millimeter (½- to ⅝-inch) dowelling or from PVC plastic piping, in lengths of 60 to 80 centimeters (24 to 32 inches), adjusting to ability level.

- Discuss the importance of handling the wands safely. Then hand out the wands and have children take them to a free space.

DESCRIPTION OF ACTIVITY:

1. **Wand Signals:** Place your wand on the floor. Check for good spacing. Show me how you can . . .

   — Leap over ten different wands; then return to your own and make a five-point bridge with two body parts on one side of it, and three body parts on the other side.

   — Skip around the wands. On signal "Freeze!" stop and build a low bridge over the nearest wand. Skip again. Build a high bridge over it.

   — Stand on one side of your wand. Jump sideways over it, from one end to the other end.

   — Stand just behind your wand. Show me how far forward you can jump from a standing position. Use your arms and bend at the knees to help you spring forward.

   — Hop all the way around your wand. Change feet and hop around in the opposite direction. Can you hop sideways over your wand from one end to the other?

   — Show me another way of travelling over your wand.

2. **Wand Balancing:** How many different ways can you balance your wand horizontally? (palm of your hand, back of your hand, two fingers, other hand, shoulder, knee, other knee, elbow)

   — Balancing your wand on the back of your hand, try to kneel, sit down, and then stand up again.

   — Who can place the wand horizontally on your foot, flip it up, and catch it?

   — Can you balance your wand vertically on the palm of your hand? Who can keep it balancing the longest? Try this with your other hand.

   — Let me see you balance the wand vertically on two fingers; one finger!

   — Can you show me another way to balance your wand?

GS-21 WAND STUNTS

FOCUS: Manipulation; coordination

EQUIPMENT: One wand per player

ORGANIZATION:

- Have each player get a wand and take it to a home space. Check for good spacing.

DESCRIPTION OF ACTIVITY:

1. **Thread the Needle:** Hold your wand horizontally with both hands, in front of you. Show me how you can step over it, then step back over, without letting go with your hands.

2. **Wand Cross-Sit:** Hold your wand horizontally with both hands, in front of you. Can you cross your legs and sit down? Now try to stand up again!

3. **Wand Pass:** Hold the wand vertically in front of you. Who can pass the wand from one hand to the other without watching it?

4. **Bouncing Wand:** Hold your wand vertically in front of you with your right hand. Let it drop and bounce once; then catch it in your right hand. Try this with your left hand. Can you drop it with one hand and catch it in the other hand?

5. **Falling Wand:** Use your right hand to stand your wand upright on one end; then let it go, spin yourself around once, and try to catch it in your right hand. Can you do this again using your left hand and spinning in the opposite direction?

6. **Dropping Wand:** Hold your wand at the bottom with your right hand. Let it go. Can you grab it at the very top with your right hand? Try this again using your left hand.

7. **Wand Tugs:** Find a partner. Grip a wand with both hands so that one of your hands is between your partner's. Try to pull your partner across a line behind you. Hold the stick horizontally; then hold it vertically.

8. **Creative Wands:** In your home space, show me how you can use your wand to do different activities. For example, let your wand be a:

   —walking cane   —paddle   —flute
   —telescope   —sword   —conductor's wand
   —baton   —baseball bat   —hammer

9. Invent a wand stunt of your own!

GS-22 TOSSING AND CATCHING WITH ONE SCARF

FOCUS: Visual tracking; manual dexterity   **EQUIPMENT:** One scarf per player

ORGANIZATION:

- Children explore and discover different ways of manipulating a scarf with their dominant and non-dominant hands. Because scarves float in the air, almost in slow motion, players can visually track them more easily. Buy inexpensive lightweight nylon scarves (45- to 60-centimeter or 16- to 24-inch squares, ideally) from any department store, choosing a wide variety of colors.

- Have each player get a scarf and find a free space. Check for good spacing.

DESCRIPTION OF ACTIVITY:

1. In your home space, show me what different things you can do with your one scarf. Now hold your scarf in your favorite hand. Each time you toss your scarf upward, try to catch it with a different body part: head, knee, back, foot, back of hand, tummy.

2. Toss your scarf into the air; then wait as long as you can to grab it before it touches the floor. Toss and catch with your right hand; then toss and catch with your left. Toss, wait, wait, wait, . . . grab!

3. Toss your scarf, clap once, grab it. Toss, clap twice, grab. Toss, clap three times, grab. How far can you go? Toss your scarf, touch the floor, and grab it. Toss scarf, touch a shoulder and a knee, and grab it. Toss scarf, touch as many different body parts as you can, and catch it.

4. *Basic Scarf Toss and Catch:* Hold your scarf in the "ghost position": Hold the middle of scarf with your thumb, pointer, and middle fingers. Raise your tossing arm as high as you can reach. Just before you reach the height of your toss, gently flick your wrist upward and let the scarf go. Watch it float downward; then grab it straight down with a "clawing action," catching it at waist level. Practice. Remember to keep your eyes on the scarf to make the catch. Repeat, using your left hand. Practice!

5. *Capture the Scarf:* Tuck your scarf into the back of your shorts so that most of it is showing. On signal "Go!" try to capture as many scarves as you can by pulling them out of the backs of other players. Use one hand to capture and the other to hold the pulled scarves. If your scarf is pulled, continue to try to capture others. Remember to watch where you are going! How many scarves will you capture? Who will still have your scarf tucked in the back when the game stops?

GS-23 TOSSING AND CATCHING WITH TWO SCARVES

FOCUS: Visual tracking; manual dexterity   **EQUIPMENT:** Two scarves per player

ORGANIZATION:

- Have players select two different-colored scarves; then find a free space.
- Emphasize that players watch the scarves, not their hands. Stress that the hands are not crossed when catching the two scarves. The first scarf tossed is the first scarf to be caught.

DESCRIPTION OF ACTIVITY:

1. ***One-Scarf Toss and Catch:*** Place one scarf on the floor near you, and hold the other scarf in your favorite hand in the "ghost position." Bring your arm across your body and at the height of the toss, let it go upward with a flick of the wrist. Watch the scarf as it floats down and grab it (with a "clawing action"), about waist level, with the other hand. Now toss the scarf with the other hand and catch it in your favorite hand.

   — Practice this pattern, saying "Toss-catch, toss-catch!"

2. Now hold a scarf in the "ghost position" in each hand. Can you toss both scarves in the air and catch them at the same time?

   — Who can keep both your scarves floating in the air by continuously sending them upward?

3. ***Two-Scarf Toss and Catch:*** Hold the first scarf in your favorite hand; the second, in your other hand in the "ghost position" about waist level. Raise your right arm across your body and at the height of the toss, let the scarf go with a flick of your wrist. Watch this scarf closely. When it is at the highest point, toss the scarf in your left hand toward the opposite shoulder. Your arms will make an "X" pattern across your chest. Let the scarves float down to the floor. Pick them up and repeat.

   — Now catch the scarves at waist level in this way: Catch the first scarf in your other hand with a "clawing action"; catch the second scarf with your favorite hand. Practice the pattern, saying "Toss, toss, catch, catch!"

VARIATION:

Call the colors of the scarves as the cues; for example, "Toss orange, toss yellow; catch orange, catch yellow."

GS-24 MANIPULATIVE EQUIPMENT STATION PLAY

FOCUS: Accurate tossing; visual tracking; manipulation

EQUIPMENT: Five or six hoops;
one beanbag per group member;
five or six plastic garbage or cardboard containers;
one deckring and lummi stick per group member;
one plastic bowling pin per group member;
two scarves per group member;
five or six wands;
eight to ten cone markers;
six chairs;
station signs;
floor and masking tape;
background music;
tape or record player

ORGANIZATION:

- Set up five stations using the manipulative equipment the children have worked with in the previous activities. Let them practice the skills introduced in those activities, and challenge them with new tasks.

- Divide the class into five groups and assign each group to a starting station: Group 1 to Station 1; Group 2 to Station 2; etc. Have groups rotate to the next station every four or five minutes. Use music to start and stop the activity.

- Circulate around to each of the groups, observing and offering guidance as needed. Some station ideas follow.

DESCRIPTION OF ACTIVITY:

1. *Hoop Play:* Roll hoop in and out of the cone markers.

2. *Beanbag Play:* Toss beanbags into the plastic garbage containers which are placed at different distances from a throwing line. Take turns throwing.

3. *Deckring-Lummi Stick Play:* Use your lummi stick to toss the deckring at the plastic bowling pin target and knock it over. There should be one target for every two players.

4. *Scarf Play:* Explore different ways of tossing and catching two scarves.

5. *Wand Hurdles:* Practice jumping, leaping, and moving under the hurdles.

6. *Wand Balance:* Explore different ways of balancing your wand on different body parts. Try to transfer your wand from one part to another!

GS-25 BALLOON PLAY

FOCUS: Striking; visual tracking

EQUIPMENT: One balloon per player; one whistle

ORGANIZATION:

- Balloons can be used to introduce and develop many of the skills required for major sports, such as volleyball, basketball, soccer, and baseball. Since balloons are inexpensive, purchase the more durable ones in bulk.

- The children will enjoy blowing up the balloons in class before their P.E. session. Knot the balloons and store them in a large garbage bag until you are ready to use them. Have extras on hand for those that pop.

- Continually check for good spacing of the children.

DESCRIPTION OF ACTIVITY:

1. Take your balloon to a home space. Show me how you can keep it up by tapping it gently with either hand; just your right hand; just your left hand. Can you keep the balloon in the air without letting it touch anything or anyone else?

2. Who can tap the balloon from one hand to the other hand? Can you keep the balloon in the air while kneeling; while sitting? Now tap the balloon up, let it fall; then hit it just before it touches the floor. Who can tap the balloon up, turn once around, tap it up again, turn once around in the other direction, tap it up again? Catch it in two hands when you hear my whistle signal.

3. Now show me how you can keep the balloon in the air a long time without touching it with your hands. Use your feet, head, elbows, shoulders, seat, knees, chest, back. . . .

4. Can you use just your knees to keep the balloon in the air like a soccer player? Use just your elbows to keep the balloon up; your feet; your head?

5. Let me see you keep the balloon up by striking it up with both hands. Keep your thumbs near each other and your palms up. Try to take it from your forehead. This is called volleying and is a volleyball skill.

6. Now interlock your fingers and keep your arms long in front of you. Show me how you can bat the balloon upward with your arms in this position. This is called bumping, another volleyball skill.

7. Can you bat the balloon as if your hand was a tennis racquet? How else can you strike your balloon?

GS-26 BALLOON CHALLENGES

FOCUS: Manipulation; visual tracking   **EQUIPMENT:** One balloon per player

ORGANIZATION:

• Have the balloons inflated ahead of time. Inflate several spare balloons in case of "accidents." Hand out one balloon per player.

DESCRIPTION OF ACTIVITY:

1. **Balloons in Space:** Everyone, bat the balloons into the air. Can you keep them all up without having any balloons touch the floor? Keep the balloon up using only your pointer finger.

2. **Partner Balloon Volley:** Find a partner. Can you volley the balloon back and forth to each other without it touching the floor? Try to tap the balloon near your forehead, with the thumbs and fingers of both hands. Which pair can keep two balloons going at the same time?

3. **Partner Feet Volley:** Can you and your partner keep one balloon in the air using only your feet?

   — Volley the balloon back and forth using only your heads.

   — Use only your elbows to volley the balloon.

   — Which pair can keep the balloon up using only your knees?

4. **Balloon Balance:** Each partner show me how you balance your balloon on the back of your hand; on two fingers; on your pointer finger.

   — With your partner, can you hold a balloon between your heads without using your hands? Try to move around the play area this way with one player leading and the other following.

   — Move around the play area with the balloon between your chest; sides; back; seats.

5. **Cloudburst:** Form groups of six to eight players. Now lie on your backs with your feet and hands in the air. When I throw a balloon up, try to keep it in the air as long as possible. You may use your hands or feet, but you must not move off your spot to reach the balloon. Can your group keep the balloon from reaching the floor?

6. With your partner, invent another balloon trick!

VARIATIONS:

a. In "Cloudburst" have groups try to keep two or three balloons up!

b. Have players use feet only—no hands—in "Cloudburst."

c. Have players sit in chairs and use hands and feet; then feet only.

GS-27 BALL FAMILIARIZATION

FOCUS: Manipulation; control; carrying and running

EQUIPMENT: One large play ball per player; four large plastic garbage containers or laundry baskets; one large cardboard box

ORGANIZATION:

- Children explore different ways of handling the ball in personal and general space. Use a variety of different types and sizes of balls.
- To begin, number the children off by four's.

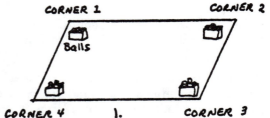

DESCRIPTION OF ACTIVITY:

1. I have placed a container of balls in each corner of the play area. Point at the corner as I call out the number for each corner: "Corner 1," "Corner 2," "Corner 3," and "Corner 4." Go to your corner which is the same number that you have, get a ball, and take it to a home space. Show me how you can cooperate and be considerate of others when getting your ball. Remember your corner so that you can return the ball to its proper container when I give you the signal.

2. Hold your ball up high with both hands; down low; far away from you; near you; behind you. Repeat with one hand, the other hand.

   — Keeping your hands near each other, show me how you can pass the ball from one hand to the other hand. Pass with your hands high, medium level, low. Watch the ball!

3. Place your ball on the floor and build a bridge over the ball. Can you lower yourself so that you just touch the ball? Who can make a bridge and hold the ball off the floor at the same time?

4. Pick up your ball and hold it in both hands. Let me see you sit cross-legged; then stand up without using your hands to help you.

   — Try this: Stand-kneel-sit-lie down-stand again.

   — Jump over your ball in different ways.

5. Find a partner about your size. With your partner, explore different ways of holding the ball between both bodies without using your hands or arms. Show me how you can move in this position.

6. *Pet Catcher* (This is an ideal game for collecting the balls [or any other manipulative equipment such as beanbags, deckrings] at the end of the gym class. Place a large container, such as a cardboard box, in the center of the play area. Select one player to be the Pet Catcher, who stands near the container. Have the other players each get a ball [favorite Pet], hold it in both hands, and scatter throughout the play area.) Pet Catcher, your job is to round up all the stray Pets. On signal "Go!" try to tag the others by touching them on the back with one hand. If you are tagged, you must put your Pet in the box and become the Catcher's helper. The last player with a Pet is the winner and becomes the Catcher for the next game. If a player drops the Pet, he or she must pick it up, drop it in the box, and become a Catcher's helper.

GS-28 ROLLING AROUND BODY PARTS

FOCUS: Manipulation; control

EQUIPMENT: One 20-centimeter (8-inch) ball per player; two ball containers

ORGANIZATION:

- Children explore manipulating a ball in their personal space. Have the girls each get a ball from one container and the boys each get a ball from the other container; then find a home space. Have the balls returned in the same way.
- Check for good spacing.

DESCRIPTION OF ACTIVITY:

1. Hold the ball in both hands. Feel it. Make it travel in a circle path in your hands; make it travel the other way. Turn it slowly; turn it quickly.
2. Now stand tall in your home space. Show me how you can make the ball travel around your body so that it touches you all the way around your waist. Can you roll it around your seat? your thighs? your knees?
3. Stand with your feet wide apart and roll it around one knee, then the other knee. Now lean down. Show me how you can roll the ball along the floor around your feet. Roll the ball in the opposite direction.
    — Stand with your feet wide apart. Who can roll the ball around one foot, then the other? Try to roll the ball in a figure-eight pattern in and out of your feet. Roll the ball in the opposite direction.
4. Hook-sit and roll the ball around you in one direction, then in the other. Can you roll the ball around you while long-sitting? Explore other ways of rolling your ball around body parts or with different body parts.

GS-29 ROLLING AND FIELDING—TWO HANDS

FOCUS: Technique; visual tracking

EQUIPMENT: One large ball per player

ORGANIZATION:

- Children discover how to properly roll and field a ball; then practice the technique, individually in general space and at a wall.
- To begin, have children find a home space and stand tall. Then roll the balls to the players, until each player is holding a ball in both hands. At the end of the class, have each player roll the ball back to you to put in the container.

DESCRIPTION OF ACTIVITY:

1. *Two-Hand Underhand Roll:* Stand with your feet shoulder-width apart, and one foot just ahead of the other. Hold the ball on its sides, with both hands, fingers spread. Bend forward at the waist. Bend at the knees as well. Swing the ball back between your legs with both hands; then swing the ball forward with an underhand motion. Push the ball smoothly forward with your fingers and let your hand follow the path of the ball.
2. *Fielding a Ball:* Face the ball coming toward you and keep your eyes on it! Bend at the knees. Lower your hands and cup them so that your fingers are pointing down. Keep your fingers relaxed. Watch the ball as it rolls into your hands and "give" with the ball. When you feel the ball in your hands, grip it firmly.

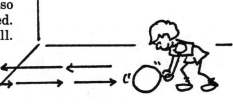

3. *Practice:* Stand about three giant steps away from a wall. Using two hands, roll and field your ball, making sure that the ball stays in contact with the floor throughout the roll and does not bounce. Take another step away from the wall and repeat.

GS-30 TARGET ROLLING CHALLENGES

FOCUS: Accurate rolling; fielding; visual tracking; partnerwork

EQUIPMENT: One large ball per pair; one large container; two cone markers or pins per pair; one bowling pin or plastic bottle per pair

ORGANIZATION:

- Children work in pairs, then in small groups, and practice rolling for accuracy and fielding.

- First, have children pair off. One partner gets a large ball, while the other partner finds a free space. As their rolling and fielding ability improves, gradually have them increase the rolling distance.

DESCRIPTION OF ACTIVITY:

1. *Partner Rolling Tasks:* Partners, wide-sit facing each other about four giant steps apart. Roll the ball back and forth to each other. Receiving partner make a target with your hands. Can you roll the ball right into your partner's hands? How can you make the ball go faster? (Push harder, use force!) Make the ball travel slower.

   — Now stand with your back to your partner. Roll the ball through your legs to your partner. Receiving partner make a target with your hands.

   — Now stand about eight giant steps from each other. Place two cone markers halfway between you, and about one meter (three feet) apart. Can you roll the ball back and forth to each other, sending it between the cones?

   — Partners take turns rolling a ball toward a bowling pin or plastic bottle which is placed near a wall.

2. *Bunny Jumps:* Form groups of three. The first two players stand about eight giant steps away from each other; while the third player stand in the middle, facing the outer player who has the ball. Outer players, roll the ball with both hands to each other. Middle player, jump over the rolling ball as it comes toward you. Change position after the middle player has made five jumps. Continue until everyone has had a turn.

3. *Hot Rock:* On my signal "five!" quickly get into groups of five and knee-sit in a circle, spaced about arm's length apart. Which group will do this the quickest? Choose a leader for your group and have him or her get a ball; then return to the group. The ball is a "Hot Rock." The leader will start the ball rolling to a player across the circle. As the ball comes near you, use both hands to gently bat it away from you before the ball can touch you. If the Hot Rock does touch your body, you have been "burned" and must run once around your group circle; then return to your place. Keep your eyes following the ball! Do not let the ball bounce along the floor. The ball cannot be batted to a player on either side of you or to a player who just sent it to you. (Add another ball and watch the action!)

4. *Keep the Ball Rolling:* Roll your ball with two hands along the floor. Can you keep all the balls rolling? Try not to let any ball stop. The game ends when a ball does stop; then we will start a new game. On my signal "Pick up!" quickly field your ball and carry it to touch each endline of the play area; then drop it in the ball container.

GS-31 ONE-HAND ROLLING AND FIELDING A BALL

FOCUS: Technique; visual tracking; right–left dexterity; agility

EQUIPMENT: One 15-centimeter (6-inch) utility ball per player

ORGANIZATION:

- Explain and demonstrate the technique of a one-hand roll and two-hand fielding.

- Have those children with birthdays in the first four months get a ball and find a free space about three giant steps from a wall; then those with birthdays in the next four months, and so on, until everyone has a ball. Reverse order for returning balls to storage container.

DESCRIPTION OF ACTIVITY:

1. *One-Hand Roll:* Begin by holding the ball in two hands. Keep your eyes on the target; line the ball up with the target. Swing your rolling arm back beside your body. Step forward with the opposite leg. Bend at the knees and swing your rolling arm forward to release the ball close to the floor. Follow through with your rolling hand pointing straight at the target.

2. *Fielding with Two Hands:* Face the ball coming toward you and keep your eyes on it! Bend at the knees. Lower your hands, cupping them so that your fingers are pointing down. Keep your fingers relaxed. Watch the ball as it rolls into your hands and "give" with the ball. When you feel the ball in your hands, grip it firmly.

3. Roll your ball with your favorite hand into an open space. Show me how you can run after it, get in front of the ball, and field it before the ball stops rolling. Try this again. Now roll your ball with your other hand and field it.

4. Roll your ball with your favorite hand again into an open space. Can you jump over it once; then pick it up before the ball stops? Try this again using your other hand. Who can jump over the ball two times; then field it?

5. Roll your ball along the floor. Try to stop it by putting one foot on it. Pick it up and start again. Roll with your right hand; stop the ball with your right foot. Roll with your left hand; stop with left foot. Roll with one hand; stop with the other foot. Show me another way to roll and field a ball.

6. *Wall Roll:* Stand about four giant steps from a wall. Roll your ball with your favorite hand, and field it with two hands. Roll the ball with the other hand, and field it.

   — Now try a one-hand roll using a moving approach. Face the wall in your own space. Take two steps forward; then roll the ball with your right hand. Field it. Repeat using your left hand.

FOCUS: Rolling and fielding; cooperation

EQUIPMENT: One utility ball per player; two cones or beanbags per player

ORGANIZATION:

- Have all those players wearing a certain color each get a ball first and take it to a home space; then players wearing another color get a ball. Continue until everyone has a ball. Have the balls returned to storage in the same way. Check for good spacing.

DESCRIPTION OF ACTIVITY:

1. ***One-Hand Pick-Up:*** Begin by rolling the ball with one hand into an open space. Keep your eyes on the ball as you run alongside it and catch up with the ball. When you are level with the ball, reach down, bending at your knees, and put the palm of one hand in front of the ball and the other behind it. Scoop the ball into the front hand with your back hand and hold it in both hands. Practice, using either hand to roll and field!

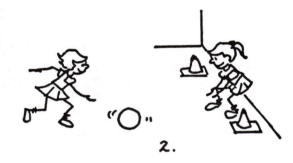

2. ***Goalie:*** Find a partner. Each pair collect a ball and two cones or beanbags. Make a goal against a wall by placing cones or beanbags about two giant steps apart. One partner be the Roller; the other, be the Goalie. Roller, start about three giant steps away. Using a one-handed roll, try to roll the ball past the goalie between the two cones. Goalie, stop the ball using your hands only; no kicking! Trade places after ten shots on goal. Trade partners and repeat the game. (Gradually increase the rolling distance as ability improves.)

3. ***Jump the Ball:*** Form groups of three, get one ball, and find a free space. Check for good spacing. Players A and C stand about five giant steps apart, and Player B stand in the middle between the other two players. Players A and C roll the ball toward Player B, trying to hit B below the knees with the ball. Player B escape being hit by jumping the ball. If hit, change places with the player who hit you. If Player B is not hit after ten rolls, players should change places to ensure that each one gets a turn in the middle. (Emphasize that the ball must be rolled, not bounced along floor.)

4. ***Beat the Ball:*** Line up at one end of the play area. I am going to roll a ball from your end to the other end of the play area. Can you race the ball to the endline? Girls first, then boys!

GS-33 MORE ROLLING GAMES

FOCUS: Rolling and fielding; cooperation; alertness

EQUPMENT: One bowling pin, bleach bottle, cone, or garbage can per group; one utility ball per group; floor tape or two long ropes

ORGANIZATION:

- Through small and large group play, rolling and fielding skills are further developed. In Game 1, use floor tape (or long ropes) to mark out each group's circle to avoid "creeping in." To ensure easier scoring, use a garbage can.

DESCRIPTION OF ACTIVITY:

1. *Guard the Pin:* Form groups of six to eight players. Each group collect a pin and a ball; then form a circle with one player standing in the middle to guard the pin in the center. Circle players, try to knock over the pin by rolling the ball toward it. If you knock over the pin, change places with the guard player. Guard player, you may only bat the ball away with your hands; no kicking.

2. *Tunnel Ball:* (Using floor tape or two long ropes, mark off a starting line and parallel back line, spaced 10 meters [30 feet] apart, or use the sidelines of the play area.) Each group of six to eight players, stand with your feet wide apart in a single-file formation behind a starting line. The last player must stand just behind a back line. The Leader at the front holds a ball to start. On signal "Go!" Leader, using both hands, roll the ball back through your legs to the player behind you, who keeps the ball rolling through his or her legs to the next player, and so on. Last player, you must field the ball behind the back line when it rolls to you. Then quickly pick it up and run to the front of the line, while everyone shuffles back one place. As the new Leader, start the ball rolling between your legs. The game continues in this way until the leader is back in his or her original position. The first team to finish and sit cross-legged wins.

VARIATIONS:

a. Vary the type and size of ball used for these games.
b. Do activity SG–10, "Down-and-Up Rolling Relay," from Section 7.

GS-34 TWO-HANDED TOSS AND CATCH

FOCUS: Technique; visual tracking; control

EQUIPMENT: One utility ball per player; music with a steady 4/4 beat; tape or record player

ORGANIZATION:

- Children explore different ways of tossing and catching a ball with two hands while stationary in personal space, and then while moving in personal and in general space. Teach the two-handed toss and catch; then have them practice and check for good technique.
- To begin, have players form an "Alphabet Line" (lined up in alphabetical order); then get a ball and take it to a home space for a few minutes of free play. Balls are returned to storage in the reverse order.

DESCRIPTION OF ACTIVITY:

1. Toss the ball to yourself and catch it using two hands. Can you toss and catch the ball without making a sound?

2. Now stand in your home with feet shoulder-width apart. Hold the ball in two hands, with your fingers spread on the sides of the ball. Toss the ball up in front of you and catch it with two hands. Keep your eyes on the ball. Let it drop into your cupped hands, fingers relaxed; then pull the ball in. Do not grab at the ball. Remember to catch the ball below your waist, your little fingers are near each other; to catch a ball above the waist, your thumbs are near each other! Practice tossing and catching the ball above and below the waist.

3. Let me see you kneel-sit, toss the ball up; then quickly stand up and catch it.

   — Who can toss the ball up while standing and catch it in the wide-sit position? Let me see you toss and catch the ball a little higher each time. How high can you go?

   — Can you toss the ball up, make a quarter-turn, and catch it? Try this again, making a half-turn. Turn CW; turn CCW.

   — Try to toss, clap, and catch the ball. Toss, clap two times, and catch the ball. Toss, clap three times, and catch the ball . . . Continue.

   — Can you toss the ball upward, let it bounce once, and catch it? Try this again. Now touch a shoulder before you catch it. Touch your knees; the floor; clap your hands behind your back; etc.

   — Who can toss the ball upward, let it bounce once while you quickly turn once around, and then catch it?

   — Invent your own tossing-and-catching trick!

4. In your home space, let me see you toss and catch the ball with two hands while walking in place; jogging in place; hopping on the spot; jumping on the spot; turning slowly around in place; turning in the opposite direction; dancing in place!

5. Now toss and catch the ball with two hands while walking in general space. At first, walk slowly; then gradually walk faster.

   — Who can toss and catch the ball while running slowly? running faster?

   — Can you toss and catch your ball while galloping? while skipping? while side-stepping?

6. ***Toss and Catch Game:*** When you hear the music, march around the play area tossing and catching your ball with two hands. As soon as the music stops, you stop; then toss and catch while marching in place, until you hear the music again. This time travel in your favorite way in general space while tossing and catching. When the music stops, continue to move in this way on the spot, still tossing and catching your ball.

GS-35 PARTNER TOSSING AND CATCHING

FOCUS: Accurate tossing; visual tracking; cooperation   **EQUIPMENT:** One utility ball per player

ORGANIZATION:

- Explain and demonstrate the two-handed Underhand Throw technique; then have players practice in pairs.
- To begin, have players pair up, get one ball, and find a free space.

DESCRIPTION OF ACTIVITY:

1. *Two-Handed Underhand Throw* (for right-handed player): Stand with feet shoulder-width apart; eyes on your partner, who is your target. Hold the ball in both hands in front of you, with elbows bent and fingers spread around the sides of the ball. Swing the ball back so that it is level with the right hip. Your right hand should be behind the ball; your left elbow bent, and left hand in front of the ball. Swing your arms forward as you step forward with the opposite foot, and throw the ball toward the target. Let your arms reach for the target to follow through.

2. *Partner Tossing and Catching:* Stand back-to-back and walk two giant steps away from each other, turn and face the other. Use a two-handed throw to send the ball back and forth to each other. Receiving partner, make a target with your hands. As the ball comes toward you, reach with relaxed fingers, catching it in two hands, and pull the ball in.

GS-36 TWO-HANDED TARGET TOSSING

EQUIPMENT: One utility ball per player;
one wall target per pair;
garbage pails, cardboard boxes, laundry baskets, and/or hoops;
floor tape

ORGANIZATION:

- Use floor tape to mark out circular or square wall targets on the walls, about 1.7 meters above the floor. Review the two-handed Underhand Throw technique; then have players practice at targets.
- To begin, have players pair up, each get a ball, and stand facing a wall target, about 3 meters (10 feet) away.

DESCRIPTION OF ACTIVITY:

1. *Wall Target Tossing:* Take turns underhand throwing the ball with two hands at your wall target. Remember to step forward with the opposite foot as you throw the ball, and keep your eyes on the target. Let the ball bounce once off the wall; then catch it with relaxed fingers in two hands.

2. *Floor Target Tossing:* One partner get a box, a hoop, a basket, or garbage pail, and place it just under your wall target, about 1 meter (3 feet) away from the wall. Take turns underhand throwing the ball into your floor target. On signal "Trade!" trade targets with another pair, and continue. Challenge: Who can toss the ball at the wall so that it bounces off the wall into the floor target?

VARIATIONS:

a. Vary the type of ball used.
b. Gradually increase the throwing distance as ability improves.
c. *Performance Checking:* Have each player take ten tosses and record the results. Repeat three times. Give the weaker players help and additional practice; then repeat this performance check.

GS-37 ONE-HANDED UNDERHAND THROWING

FOCUS: Technique; visual tracking; manual dexterity; partnerwork

EQUIPMENT: One 15-centimeter (6-inch) utility ball per player

ORGANIZATION:

- Review the Underhand Throwing and Catching technique using a beanbag (see activity GS–11). Have the children practice tossing a ball to themselves; then at a wall. Emphasize catching in two hands.
- To begin, have each player get a ball and find a free space.

DESCRIPTION OF ACTIVITY:

1. In your home space, using your favorite hand, toss the ball straight upward in front of you, and catch it in two hands. Remember to keep your eyes on the ball and catch in cupped hands with your fingers relaxed! Toss and catch ten times; then repeat using your other hand.

   — Toss the ball up with one hand, let it bounce once off the floor, and catch it. Now practice with your other hand.
   — Toss the ball up, let it bounce once, clap your hands, and catch it. Can you clap two times? three times? Practice with each hand.
   — Toss the ball up and catch it at head height with cupped hands and thumbs together. Toss the ball up, let it bounce once, and catch it below your belly button. Did you catch the ball with little fingers together? Practice with each hand.
   — Show me another way to toss and catch the ball to yourself.

2. Let me see you toss with one hand and catch the ball while walking; while jogging; galloping; side-stepping. Try to use your weaker hand to toss as well as your favorite hand.

3. Now face a wall about 3 meters (10 feet) away. Using the one-hand Underhand Throw, pass your ball to the wall and catch it after it bounces once off the floor. Keep your eyes on the ball as it comes off the wall, and your hands ready to make the catch. Catch with soft hands, fingers relaxed. Can you make ten perfect throws and catches using your favorite hand? using your other hand?

4. Find a partner and a free space, and stand facing each other three giant steps apart. Check for good spacing. Staying in your home space, show me how you can pass the ball, using the Underhand Throw to your partner. Use your favorite hand to throw; then use your other hand. Take one step away from each other after every five good tosses and catches.

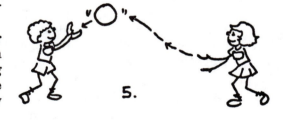

5. Can you toss the ball back and forth to each other while walking in general space?

6. **Throwing Copycats:** One partner, throw the ball to the other partner in different ways. Receiving partner, return the ball in the same way. Suggestions:

   — Throw high; throw low; throw waist level.
   — Throw quickly; throw slowly.
   — Place the ball on the floor between your feet. Lean forward and, with both hands, send the ball backwards to your partner, who is behind you.
   — Roll a ball to each other at the same time, without the balls hitting each other.
   — Invent a "copycat" trick of your own!

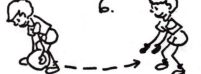

GS-38 PASSING AND CATCHING GAMES

FOCUS: Visual tracking; catching; alertness; cooperation

EQUIPMENT: One utility ball per group; one large ball container; lively music; tape or record player

ORGANIZATION:

- The skills of one-handed Underhand Throwing and two-handed Catching are reinforced through these small group games.

DESCRIPTION OF ACTIVITY:

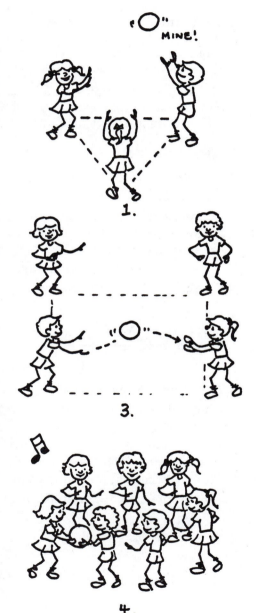

1. *Sky Ball:* Form groups of three players. Each group find a free space and stand in a triangle formation. Check for good spacing. One player get a ball and start the game by throwing it up high, over the heads of the other two players. Use the one-handed Underhand Throw. Whoever is nearest, try to catch the ball in both hands and at the same time call out "Mine!" (Continue the game in this way, so that everyone gets a chance to throw and catch the ball.)

   — *Challenge:* Score one point for every good catch. Who will get to five first?

2. *Triangle Pass:* Each group stay in your triangle formation, standing about three giant steps apart from each other. Pass the ball from player to player using the one-handed Underhand Throw and two-handed Catch. Pass the ball so that it is easy to catch. On signal "Pass!" pass the ball CW; on signal "Reverse!" change the direction.

3. *Square Pass:* In groups of four, repeat the above activity.

   — *Challenge:* Pass one ball around the square; then add a second ball as soon as the first ball is on its way.

4. *Hot Potato:* (Divide the class into teams of six or eight players.) Have each team form a circle, with players spaced arm's length apart and everyone facing inward. Each team Leader holds a ball to begin. When you hear the music, begin passing the ball around the circle, from player to player as if it were a "hot potato!" When the music stops, immediately stop the passing. The player "caught" holding the ball receives the first letter of the word "H-O-T!" When the music starts, continue the passing. The challenge is to NOT be the first player to receive all three letters of the word "H-O-T!"

5. *Keep the Basket Full:* (Place a large container in the center of the play area full of balls.) I am going to try to empty this container by tossing the balls out into the play area. Your job is to retrieve the tossed balls, one at a time, and return them with a toss into the container.

VARIATION:

Vary the size and type of object being passed: beanbag, large utility ball, basketball, volleyball, tennis ball, beachball.

GS–39 ONE-HAND UNDERHAND TARGET THROWING

FOCUS: Accurate throwing;
visual tracking; dexterity

EQUIPMENT: One target per pair (hoops, cardboard boxes, plastic garbage pails, several cone markers, plastic bleach bottles or pins); two benches; wall targets made with floor tape; one small utility ball per player

ORGANIZATION:

- Set up high and low targets, evenly spaced throughout the play area so that each pair will have a target to throw at. Have players pair off and each get a ball. Assign each pair to a starting target. Provide enough time at each target for partners, taking turns, to each have ten throws at the target. On your signal, have pairs rotate in a CW direction to the next target. For a large class, form groups of three or four and assign each group to a starting target.

- Circulate around the play area, checking for correct throwing technique. Make note of the weaker throwers and provide opportunity for additional help and practice. Gradually increase the underhand throwing distance as ability level improves.

DESCRIPTION OF ACTIVITY:

1. *Low Target Suggestions:*
   - Hoops on floor
   - Cardboard boxes against wall
   - Three bleach bottles or pins evenly spaced on a bench
   - Three cone markers in a pyramid
   - Plastic garbage pail near wall

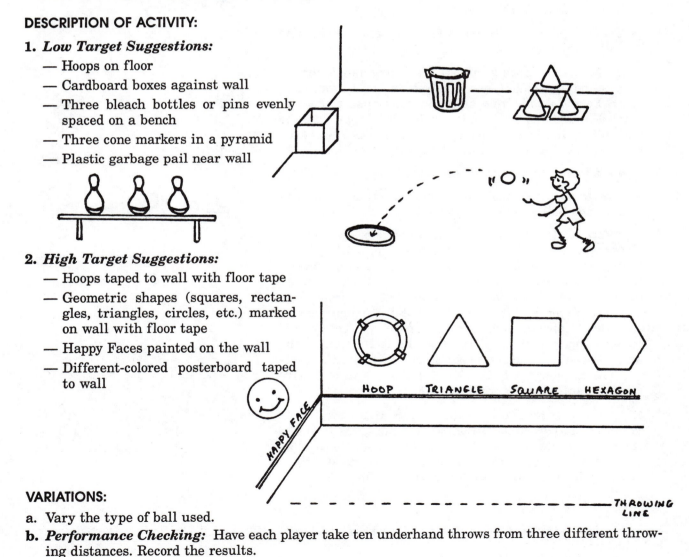

2. *High Target Suggestions:*
   - Hoops taped to wall with floor tape
   - Geometric shapes (squares, rectangles, triangles, circles, etc.) marked on wall with floor tape
   - Happy Faces painted on the wall
   - Different-colored posterboard taped to wall

VARIATIONS:

a. Vary the type of ball used.

b. *Performance Checking:* Have each player take ten underhand throws from three different throwing distances. Record the results.

GS-40 ONE-HAND OVERHAND THROW _____

FOCUS: Technique; visual tracking; left–right dexterity

EQUIPMENT: One beanbag per player; one small utility ball per player

ORGANIZATION:

- Introduce the Overhand Throw by having the children mime the action at first; then practice the skill using beanbags and small balls. Gradually increase the Overhand Throwing distance as ability level improves.
- To begin, have players get a beanbag, take it to a home space, and face you. Ensure that they can all see you clearly. Check for good spacing.

DESCRIPTION OF ACTIVITY:

1. Today, we are going to learn and practice the Overhand Throw. Put Beanie on the floor for now. Let's mime the overhand throwing action first; then put Beanie to work!
   - Turn sideways to the wall you are facing, with your feet shoulder-width apart. Keep your eyes on your target (the wall). Let your nonthrowing arm point to the target.
   - Swing your throwing arm back and take your weight on your back foot. Your elbow is bent and level with your shoulder; your throwing hand is near and behind your ear.
   - Whip your throwing hand forward and, at the same time, step onto your front foot. Your wrist should quickly snap forward and downward. Follow through with your throwing arm pointing toward the target. Practice! Throw with your favorite hand; throw with your other hand.

2. Now pick up Beanie, put it in your throwing hand, and stand sideways to a wall, about four giant steps away. Show me how you can use the Overhand Throw to hit an imaginary target on the wall. Throw with your favorite hand; then use your other hand. Repeat using a small ball. Can you catch the ball in both hands on the first bounce as it comes off the wall? Practice.

GS-41 OVERHAND TARGET THROWING AND CATCHING _____

EQUIPMENT: One beanbag per pair;
one small ball per pair;
one bowling pin, cone, or plastic bleach bottle per pair;
floor tape

ORGANIZATION:

- These activities help to develop accuracy in throwing and throwing for distance. Refer to activity GS–39 for a variety of high and low targets suggestions.
- To start, have players pair off. Have one partner get a beanbag.

DESCRIPTION OF ACTIVITY:

1. *One Step:* Face your partner about three giant steps away. Overhand-Throw the beanbag to your partner so that your partner can catch it without moving more than one step. Remember to step forward with the opposite foot as you throw. If a catch is dropped, both stay in your place. If you both make good catches, you take one step backwards. See how far away from each other you can go and still catch the beanbag.
2. *Target Challenge:* Each partner get a small ball; then stand behind a throwing line, facing a target (cone, bleach bottle, bowling pin) four giant steps away and near a wall. Throw your ball to hit the target. Field your ball, replace the target, and run back to the throwing line. Throw with your favorite hand; throw with your other hand. After hitting the target three times, take one step back and try from here!

GS-42 OVERHAND THROWING AT MOVING TARGETS

FOCUS: Accurate throwing; catching; dodging; team play

EQUIPMENT: One large utility ball per player; one beanbag per player; one small Nerf™, sponge or yarn ball per player; one hoop; one long rope or floor tape

ORGANIZATION:

- Throwing skills are further reinforced through the following related games. Ask players what the term "dodging" means: to quickly move aside.
- To begin, have each player get a beanbag and a large utility ball; then find a free space.

DESCRIPTION OF ACTIVITY:

1. **Bean the Ball:** Roll your ball along the floor into open spaces. As the ball rolls along, overhand throw your Beanie at this moving target! How many times can you hit the ball before I signal you to stop?

2. **Scramble:** (Place about 30 beanbags, sponge balls, and yarn balls inside a hoop in the center of the play area. Choose three players to be the Throwers. They must stand with one foot inside the hoop and one foot out. Have the rest of the class form a large circle around the center hoop, with players spaced arm's length apart and facing CCW.) On signal "Scramble!" circle players, begin to run CCW around the circle. Throwers, try to hit these moving targets, below the waist, with your balls. You are allowed to throw only one ball at a time. Circle player, if you are hit, hold the spot where you were hit and keep moving! Show me how brave you are. The game ends when all the balls have been thrown. Three new Throwers are chosen and the game begins again.

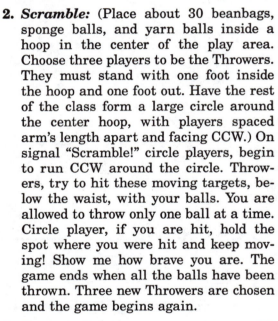

3. **Dodgeball:** (Form two equal teams. Have one team form a large circle, with players spaced arm's length apart and facing inward. The other team stands inside a 8-meter [24-feet]-diameter circle, marked off by a long rope or floor tape.) On signal "Go!" circle players, try to hit the inside players below the waist with the ball. You may use any type of throw, including rolling. Throws must be made from outside the circle. Circle players, you may pass to another circle player for a better shot. Inside players, if you are hit, change places with the thrower. The game continues in this way.

VARIATIONS:

a. **Scramble:** Set up two or three circles of throwers, with about six to eight circle players for each game. Vary the locomotor movements of the circle players. Have them skip, gallop, side-step, walk backwards.

b. **Dodgeball:** Use two balls. Have the circle and inside teams exchange places after a certain time.

c. Play "Wasps." (See activity IA-41.)

d. Play "Team Dodgeball" (activity SG-33) and "Squid" (activity SG-35) from Section 7; and "Nerf™ Tag" (activity IA-43) from Section 1.

GS-43 TWO-HANDED BOUNCING AND CATCHING TASKS

FOCUS: Technique; hand-eye coordination; visual tracking

EQUIPMENT: One large utility ball per player

ORGANIZATION:

- The two-handed and then one-handed bounce is explored through several challenging tasks in personal and general space. Check for correct bouncing and catching technique.
- Have each player get a ball and use two hands to bounce it to a home space.

DESCRIPTION OF ACTIVITY:

1. Hold the ball in both hands out in front of you. Drop the ball. How many times can you run around your ball before it stops bouncing? Now drop your ball again. Let it bounce; then catch it with two hands. Do this again!

2. Bounce your ball with two hands in your home space. Are you using your finger pads to push the ball downwards? How can you use your arms to pump the ball to the floor? Keep your fingers relaxed—don't slap at the ball. "Feel" the ball in your hands. Try this pattern: Bounce–catch; bounce–bounce–catch; bounce–bounce–bounce–catch; etc. How long can you keep your ball bouncing?

3. Bounce your ball in front of you; on one side; on the other side. Bounce your ball high with two hands. Bounce it low. Can you bounce your ball from high to low? from low to high?

4. Can you bounce the ball in two hands while kneeling on one knee; two knees? while wide-sitting? Who can move from standing to kneeling; then back to standing position while bouncing your ball with two hands?

5. Now try to walk in a circle around your ball as you bounce it with two hands on the spot. Can you skip around your ball while bouncing it?

6. How many different places can you look and still bounce the ball? Look up and tell me how many fingers I am holding up. Now how many fingers? Who can bounce the ball keeping your eyes closed?

7. Bounce your ball as high off the floor as you can, let it come down and bounce once, and then catch it in two hands. How high can you catch it? How low?

8. Bounce your ball with two hands as you walk in general space. Move into open spaces. Remember to watch where you are going. Find another way to move and still bounce your ball. Are you in control?

9. Show me a bouncing trick of your own. For example, can you bounce-clap, bounce-clap, etc.?

VARIATION:

Explore bouncing different types of balls.

GS-44 ONE-HANDED BOUNCE EXPLORATION

FOCUS: Bouncing and catching; right–left dexterity; partnerwork

EQUIPMENT: One large ball per child; one cardboard box or large garbage container per group of four; several cones, chairs, or hoops

ORGANIZATION:

- Have each player get a ball and find a home space. Check for good spacing.

DESCRIPTION OF ACTIVITY:

1. Show me how you can bounce the ball using your favorite hand. Now bounce using your other hand. Remember, push the ball downward with your finger pads; do not slap at it.

2. Can you bounce your ball slowly? quickly? in slow motion? Use your favorite hand; then your other hand.

3. Can you bounce your ball low? bounce it high? bounce it at medium level (waist height)? bounce it from high to low? from low to high? At which level is it easier to control? Try this with your favorite hand; then with your other hand.

4. How close to you can you bounce the ball? How far away? Can you bounce the ball kneeling on one knee; kneeling on the other knee? Try this with your favorite hand; then with your other hand.

5. Let me see you bounce the ball from one hand to the other hand.

6. Show me how you can walk forward while bouncing the ball. Can you walk backwards and bounce the ball? Let me see you move sideways and bounce the ball. Can you gallop while bouncing the ball? Try to travel in a curvy path while bouncing the ball. Bounce the ball in a circular path. Try this with the other hand. How else can you bounce your ball?

7. ***Partner Bounce Challenges:*** Find a partner and a free space. Get a ball and stand facing three giant steps apart. Bounce the ball with two hands back and forth to your partner. Catch the ball in two hands. Remember to keep your fingers relaxed. Step another giant step away from each other. Now bounce the ball with one hand to your partner and catch in two hands.

8. ***Bounce-Roll Combo:*** One partner bounce the ball to the other partner, who rolls the ball back. Switch after five rolls.

9. ***Bounce-Toss Combo:*** One partner bounce the ball to the other partner, who tosses the ball back. Switch after five throws. Invent another way of bouncing the ball to your partner with control!

10. ***Target Bouncing:*** Make a group of four and get a cardboard box (or large plastic pail.) Stand in a circle around the box, about two giant steps away. Take turns, bouncing your balls into the box. Use your favorite hand; then use the other hand.

11. ***Obstacle Bouncing:*** (Scatter several cones, chairs, or hoops around the play area.) Follow your partner as you each bounce a ball around the obstacles. Remember to watch the ball and where you are going!

GS-45 BOUNCING GAMES

FOCUS: Time awareness; throwing; rolling; visual tracking

EQUIPMENT: One 15-centimeter (6-inch) ball per player; one utility ball per game

ORGANIZATION:

- Body positioning, foot work, and sense of timing are developed through these games. Explain and demonstrate how to position directly in front of the ball to field the ball, hands ready, fingers relaxed!

DESCRIPTION OF ACTIVITY:

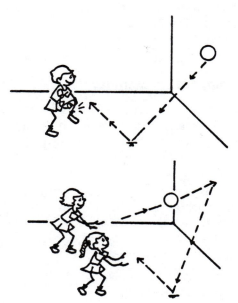

1. *Wall Bounce:* Collect a ball and scatter to find your own space at a wall. Stand about 5 meters (15 feet) from the wall. Throw your ball at the wall, higher than head height, do an activity, let the ball bounce once on the floor, and catch it. Try the following activities:
   — Clap your hands behind the back once; clap twice in front, three times!
   — Do a complete turnaround.
   — Touch the floor with both hands.
   — Lift your right leg and clap hands under.
   — Put two of these together; then catch.
   — Invent a new trick of your own!
2. *Partner Wall Bounce:* Find a partner, get a ball, and together stand facing a wall, about three giant steps away. Check for good spacing. One partner underhand toss the ball to the wall; other partner let the ball come off the wall, bounce once, and then catch it in two hands. Then you underhand-toss the ball back to the wall for your partner to catch. Continue in this way. After ten turns, take another giant step away from the wall and repeat.

GS-46 THROWING AND CATCHING CHALLENGES

FOCUS: Throwing accuracy; catching; visual tracking; right–left dexterity

EQUIPMENT: One ball per child

ORGANIZATION:

- To assess the performance level of children in throwing and catching, have each child perform the following challenges. Record the scores and make comments on ability level. Use the scores to determine the effectiveness of teaching and learning. Provide opportunity for weaker ball-handlers to get additional help.

DESCRIPTION OF ACTIVITY:

1. *One-Hand Underhand Throw to Self and Catch:* (Use favorite hand, then other hand.) In place—ten times; Walking—ten times; Running—ten times.
2. *Two-Hand Bounce and Catch:* In place—ten times; Walking—ten times.
3. *One-Hand Bouncing:* (Use favorite hand, then other hand.) In place—ten times; Walking—ten times; Running—ten times.
4. *One-Hand Throw at Wall and Catch:* (Use two hands to catch rebound on first bounce.) Right hand—ten throws and catches; Left hand—ten throws and catches.
5. *One-Hand Throw at Wall and Catch:* (Use two hands to catch rebound before ball bounces off floor.) Right hand—ten throws and catches; Left hand—ten throws and catches.

GS–47 FOOT DRIBBLING EXPLORATION _____

FOCUS: Foot-eye coordination; dribbling; trapping

EQUIPMENT: One large rubber ball per player; several cones, chairs, or hoops; one whistle or drum

ORGANIZATION:

- Children develop foot-eye coordination as they explore moving and stopping a ball with their feet in general space. Introduce the soccer terms: "dribbling" and "trapping." Emphasize good ball control. Check for good use of space. Is the nondominant foot as well as the dominant foot being used to move the ball? Emphasize no hands! Challenge the children to see who will not use their hands until told to do so.

- To begin, have each player get a ball and take it to a free space.

DESCRIPTION OF ACTIVITY:

1. Show me how you can move the ball with your feet in a small space; in a large space. Remember to move into open spaces. On my whistle signal, stop the ball by gently stepping on it with one foot. Next time you hear the whistle, can you use your other foot to stop the ball?

2. Now explore moving the ball with different parts of your feet, such as the inside of your feet; outside of each foot; toes of each foot; heel of each foot; front of each foot.

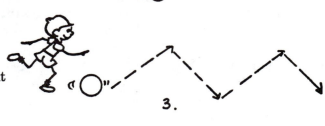

3. In how many different directions can you move the ball:

   — forward in a zig-zag pattern

   — sideways in a circle

   — backwards in a curving pattern

   — add your own idea

4. Now let's explore moving the ball at different speeds:
   — slow while walking
   — fast while running

5. **Obstacle Dribble:** (Scatter several cones, chairs, or hoops throughout the play area.) Show me how you can move your ball in and out of the obstacles. How can you keep your ball under control by tapping the ball lightly with your feet? This is called dribbling. On my whistle signal, stop the ball with one foot. This is called trapping.

GS-48 FOOT DRIBBLING AND TRAPPING CHALLENGES

FOCUS: Foot-eye coordination; control dribbling

EQUIPMENT: One large utility ball per player; two benches

ORGANIZATION:

- Have players stand in a home space. Check for good spacing. Roll a ball to each player, in turn, and have them trap the ball with the sole of either foot. "Round up" the balls by having the players dribble their ball into the "corral area" (two benches turned on the sides in one corner of the play area). Then choose two players to put the balls into the storage container.

DESCRIPTION OF ACTIVITY:

1. *Kick and Pick-Up Warm-Up:* Pick your ball up. Toss it up and catch the ball with two hands, place it on the floor, kick it, run after the ball and pick it up, and then start again: Toss–catch–kick–pick-up pattern.

2. *Kick and Trap:* Kick the ball along the floor slowly, into an open space. Can you run after it, get in front of it, and trap the ball with the sole of your foot? Bring the ball under control before you kick it again. Repeat! Don't forget to use either foot to trap the ball.

3. *Bubbles:* Dribble your ball ("bubble") around the play area. Do not let your bubble touch another bubble or a player; otherwise your bubble will "burst" and you must do ten jumping jacks before rejoining the game.

4. *Dribble Through the Forest:* All boys stand still in a home space holding your ball in both hands. You are the Trees. Girls, dribble through the forest without touching the trees or any other girls. On signal "Switch!" girls quickly become Trees, and boys dribble.

VARIATION:

Poison Trees: Play the game as for activity 4 above, except that if a dribbler's ball touches a Tree, then the dribbler becomes a Tree, or the two change roles; or a point is awarded to the "Tree" team.

GS–49 DRIBBLING WITH INSIDE OR OUTSIDE OF FOOT; SOLE-OF-THE-FOOT TRAP

FOCUS: Control dribbling; trapping technique; cooperation

EQUIPMENT: One ball per player; cones

ORGANIZATION:

- Have each player get a ball and dribble it to a home space.
- In "Follow the Leader," emphasize that players should watch the ball and the Leader at the same time. Encourage Leaders to dribble in interesting patterns: circle, zig-zag, square, circle.

DESCRIPTION OF ACTIVITY:

1. Show me how you can dribble the ball with the inside of one foot only. Now dribble with the inside of the other foot only. On the signal "Trap!" stop the ball by placing one foot on top of the ball. This is called the "sole-of-the-foot trap." On the signal "Dribble!" lightly tap the ball using your other foot, in a different direction. Remember to look for open spaces.

2. Now try dribbling the ball with the inside of your right foot; then dribble with the inside of your left foot. Move slowly, keeping the ball close to your feet, tapping it from right to left, left to right. Can you continue to dribble the ball with the insides of your feet at a walking pace? at a slow jog pace? At a faster pace? Be in control! Do not kick the ball!

3. Dribble the ball using the outside of your right foot; outside of just your left foot; then outside of either foot. How fast can you dribble, keeping the ball under control? On signal "Trap!" stop the ball with the "sole-of-the-foot" trap.

4. *Soccer in Motion:* Each collect two balls. Place them on the floor. By dribbling with the insides of your feet, can the whole class keep all the balls moving? Try not to let any ball "die" (stop)!

5. *Follow the Leader:* (Form groups of three players; each player with a ball. Have groups scatter and each group stand in file formation.) On signal "Dribble!" Leader, dribble the ball, using the inside or outside of your feet, in general space. Other two players, follow your Leader, copying the actions. On signal "Change!" Leader, dribble to the end of the line. The second player takes over as the new Leader. Continue until all have had a turn at being the Leader.

6. *Zig-Zag Cone Relay:* (Form teams of four players. Have each team stand in single file behind a starting line and face a row of four cones, spaced two meters (six feet) apart from each other. The Leader of each team has a ball.) On signal "Dribble!" each player in turn, dribble the ball with the insides of your feet, in and out of the cones, around the last cone, and directly back to your file, to pass the ball to the next player. Continue the relay until everyone has had two turns each. First team to finish and sit cross-legged is the winner.

6.

GS–50 INSIDE-OF-THE-FOOT KICK AND TRAP

FOCUS: Technique; foot-eye coordination

EQUIPMENT: One soccer-type ball per player

ORGANIZATION:

- Children explore kicking and trapping a ball using the inside of either foot, at a wall; then passing to a partner. Teach the stationary kick first; then introduce the "step and kick" approach as they move in toward the ball.

- Have each player get a ball and stand facing a wall, about three giant steps away.

DESCRIPTION OF ACTIVITY:

1. Show me how you can use the inside of your foot to kick the ball toward the wall. Can you trap the ball with the inside of your kicking foot as it rebounds off the wall?

   — Repeat, kicking the ball even harder toward the wall!

   — Now use the inside of your other foot to kick and trap the ball.

   — Can you kick the ball with one foot and trap it with the other?

   — Take another giant step away from the wall and do inside-of-the-foot kicks and traps.

2. Now dribble your ball back to where you started; then back up one giant step away from your ball and to the opposite side of your kicking foot. Show me how you can step toward your ball and kick it with the inside of your foot toward the wall. Remember to keep your eyes on the ball! How can you use your arms for balance? Can you trap the ball with the inside of your kicking foot as it comes off the wall? Now try using the other foot to kick and trap.

3. **Partner Passing:** Find a partner and a free space. Put one ball aside. Stand six giant steps away from each other. Show me how you can kick the ball back and forth to each other, using the inside-of-the-foot kick. Receiving partner, trap the ball with inside of your foot first; then kick the ball to your partner. Can you kick the ball so that your partner does not have to move? Can you use either foot to kick and trap the ball?

   — Now practice stepping into your kick. After you each make five good kicks, take one giant step further away and repeat.

4. **Partner Passing on the Move:** Stand alongside your partner, about three giant steps apart. Show me how you can move slowly in general space, passing the ball to each other with the inside or outside of either foot. Remember to move and pass into open spaces. Be in control!

GS–51 INSTEP KICK AND TOE KICK

FOCUS: Kicking technique; accurate kicking; partnerwork

EQUIPMENT: One soccer-type ball per player; targets: hockey nets, low wall targets, cones, plastic bleach bottles, boxes and chairs

ORGANIZATION:

- Children are introduced to the Instep and Toe Kicks, which are used for distance kicking. They practice these kicks at a wall, with a partner, and then at low targets for accuracy.
- Have each player get a ball and find a free space about four giant steps from a wall.

DESCRIPTION OF ACTIVITY:

1. Let's explore kicking the ball with the front or shoelace-part of your foot. This is called the "Instep Kick." Back up one giant step from your ball. Keep your eyes on the ball as you move in to take the kick. Step your nonkicking foot to the side and slightly behind the ball. At the same time, swing your kicking leg back. The knee of your kicking leg should be right over the ball. Swing your kicking foot forward and underneath the ball to contact the ball on the shoelace part. Let your kicking foot finish by pointing toward the target on the follow-through. Extend your arms out to the sides for balance. Practice, using your best foot; then using your other foot. Can you trap the ball with the sole-of-your-foot trap? or inside-of-your-foot trap?

2. Show me how you can kick the ball with the toes of your foot. This is called the "Toe Kick." Practice this kick as for the Instep Kick.

3. **Partner Kicks:** Show me how you and your partner can pass to each other, using the kicks you have learned. Remember to trap the ball, get control, and then pass it. Now kick-pass the ball to each other while both of you are moving in general space about three giant steps apart. Look for open spaces to avoid collisions with other pairs! Where should you kick the ball so that your partner can easily field it? (slightly ahead; called a "Lead Pass")

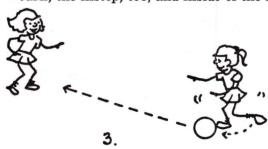

4. **Goal-Kicking:** (Have each pair collect two cones and place them one giant step apart on the floor. Each partner then paces three giant steps away from the cones.) Try to kick the ball between the two cones to your partner. Explore using the different kicks you have learned. Explore placing the cones closer together, or moving further away from the goal.

5. **Target Kicking Challenges:** (Use hockey nets, low wall targets, cones, plastic bleach bottles, boxes on their sides and open at one end, and chairs as targets. Pair off players, assign them to a starting target, and have them practice, in turn, the instep, toe, and inside-of-the-foot kicks.)

GS–52 INTRODUCING TACKLING

FOCUS: Tackling technique; dribbling; kicking; trapping; partner and group play

EQUIPMENT: One soccer-type ball per player; two cone markers, hockey nets, or plastic bleach bottles per pair

ORGANIZATION:

- Children discover different ways of taking the ball off an opponent or "tackling," through partner, small group, and large group play. Then dribbling, kicking, passing, and trapping skills are reinforced through small group games.
- To begin, have players pair up, one partner get a ball, and together find a free space.

DESCRIPTION OF ACTIVITY:

1. You have explored different ways of dribbling, trapping, and kicking the ball. Today we are going to learn how to take the ball off another player. This is called "Tackling." One partner start with the ball. Dribble toward your partner. Partner without the ball, keep your eyes on the ball as you move toward it. Using only your feet, show me how you can get control of the ball. Remember to stay in your own area.

2. *Keep Away:* Form groups of three; one player with the ball. Two players try to keep the ball away from the third player, who is IT. If the third player does get the ball, then that player who was tackled becomes IT.

3. *Pirates:* (Have everyone, each with a ball, scatter around the play area, except for four or five players, who are without a ball and stand in the center. These players are the "Pirates.") Players, start to dribble your ball around the play area. On the signal "Pirates are coming!" Pirates, try to tackle the ball away from the dribblers. Dribbler, as soon as you no longer have a ball, you become a Pirate! Remember to watch where you are going.

4. *One-on-One:* Find a partner, collect a ball and two cones, and then find a free space near a wall, if possible. Space the cones about two giant steps apart for the goal. Check for good spacing. One partner be the Kicker; the other, the Goalie. Kicker, take five kicks to try to score a goal. Goalie, try to trap the ball with your legs or feet.
   — *Two-on-Two Mini-Soccer:* Play as for game 1 above, except one pair challenges another pair.
   — *Three-on-Three:* A team of three players challenges another team of three. Have players rotate positions so that everyone has a turn at being goalie. Encourage players to pass the ball to each other.

5. *Keep It In:* (Form groups of six to eight players, who stand in a circle formation. Ensure that groups are well spaced apart. Have a Leader from each group get a ball.) Kick the ball across the circle to another player, who traps the ball first and then kicks it across the circle to a different player. Continue in this way, trying to keep the ball in the circle. Each time the ball comes to you, try to trap it, and then kick it, in a different way, using the traps and kicks you have learned. Can you play this game while moving CW slowly around the circle?

6. *Bull in the Ring:* (Form one large circle of 10 to 12 players, with players spaced about arm's length apart. Choose one player to be the Bull, who stands in the center.) Circle players, try to keep the ball away from the center player by passing it from one player to another using the kicks you have learned. If the ball goes outside the circle, or the Bull intercepts the ball, then the player responsible becomes the new Bull.

GS-53 KICKING SKILLS—STATIONWORK

FOCUS: Accurate kicking; control dribbling; trapping; groupwork

EQUIPMENT: Soccer-type balls; cone markers; nine plastic bleach bottles or bowling pins; six chairs; wall targets; three hockey nets; three large plastic containers or cardboard boxes

ORGANIZATION:

- Set up five or six stations around the perimeter of the play area. Number each station in clockwise order, and tape a sign to indicate the activity. Divide the class into groups of three or four players and assign each group to a starting station. After four or five minutes, use a stopping signal; then have groups rotate CW to the next station.
- Circulate around to the stations, observing children's performance and providing help as needed. Encourage players to use their nondominant foot as well as their dominant foot to kick the ball.

DESCRIPTION OF ACTIVITY:

1. *Soccer Hockey:* Take turns, kicking the ball into the net, using the different kicks you have learned. Increase your kicking distance to give you more challenge.
2. *Bleach Bottle Kick:* You may stand the bleach bottles any way you like; then try to kick the bleach bottles over. For example, stand the bottles in a triangle; make a pyramid; place them in a line; etc.
3. *Dribble Maze:* Dribble your ball in and out of the cones. Try not to let the ball touch a cone!
4. *Chair Goal:* Kick the ball between the two chairs to score a goal. Move the chairs closer together for more challenge!
5. *Box Kick:* Place a container on its side so that the open end faces you. Kick the ball into its "mouth" to score a goal.
6. *Wall Target Kick:* Kick the ball at a low wall target and trap it as the ball comes off the wall. Use either foot to kick and trap.

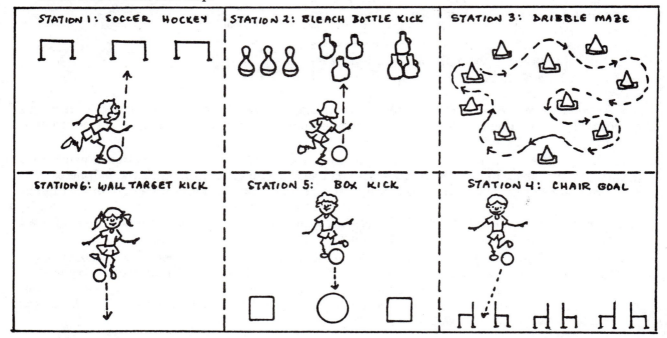

GS–54 THROWING, CATCHING, AND PITCHING

FOCUS: Visual tracking; manual dexterity

EQUIPMENT: One small ball per player; one carpet square per pair

ORGANIZATION:

- The fundamental skills of Underhand and Overhand Throwing and Catching are reviewed with this activity; then the "Underhand Pitch" is introduced. The softball terms "Pitcher" and "Back catcher" are also introduced through partner play.
- Review the fundamentals of a good underhand throw: Step into the throw with the opposite foot to the throwing hand, eyes on the target, and follow through in the direction of the throw. When catching the ball, remind players to keep their eyes on the ball, tracking the ball into their hands, giving with the ball, fingers relaxed. To catch a high ball, thumbs are together and fingers face upward; to catch a low ball, little fingers are together and fingers face downward.
- Have each player get a small ball and stand about two giant steps from a wall.

DESCRIPTION OF ACTIVITY:

1. Let me see you underhand-toss the ball to the wall with your favorite hand; let it bounce once off the floor; then catch it in two hands. Try underhand tossing with your other hand. Take another step away from the wall and do this task again. Repeat.

2. Can you overhand-throw the ball so that it hits the floor first, then the wall, and catch the ball in both hands as it comes off the wall? Try this task throwing with your favorite hand; throwing with your other hand.

3. **Partner Pitch and Catch:** Find a partner. Together collect a ball and a carpet square. Stand, facing each other about four giant steps apart. One partner squat down just behind the carpet square and make a target with your hands. You are the Back catcher. The other partner holding the ball, you are the Pitcher. Throw ten Underhand Pitches. Can you send the ball into your partner's hands each time? Change places and repeat.

VARIATION:

Vary the type of small ball used: sponge ball, tennis ball, plastic whiffle ball.

GS–55 FIELDING A GROUNDER

FOCUS: Ready position; fielding technique; visual tracking; partnerwork

EQUIPMENT: One ball per pair

ORGANIZATION:

- Discuss what it means to "field a ball" (to catch it, or stop it, to get control of the ball). Ask "what is a grounder?" (a ball that travels low along the ground) Guide players to discover what is the best "ready position" to field a grounder; then let them practice against a wall or with a partner. Use a variety of balls.
- To begin, have players find a home space and face you.

DESCRIPTION OF ACTIVITY:

1. Let's pretend that an imaginary grounder is coming toward you. How will you field the ball? Which is best:
   — standing tall, or *bending at the knees and leaning forward?*
   — feet together, or *feet shoulder-width apart and one foot just ahead of the other?*
   — *moving in front of the ball,* or moving to the side?
   — keeping your head down, or *head up and eyes on the ball?*
   — holding your hands with thumbs together, or *little fingers together?*
   — placing your hands on the ground, or *just off the ground?*
   — *letting the ball roll into both hands,* or just one hand?
   — keeping your fingers stiff, or *giving with the ball and fingers relaxed?*
2. Get a ball and stand about three giant steps from a wall. Toss your ball toward the wall so that it rebounds off the wall low, along the floor. Show me how you can field the ball as it comes toward you.
3. Find a partner. Practice fielding grounders with your partner. Start four giant steps away; then take another step back after you each field five grounders. Experiment fielding with different types of balls.

GS–56 FIELDING GROUNDERS—BODY STOP TECHNIQUE

EQUIPMENT: One ball per pair

ORGANIZATION:

- Review the "Ready Position" for fielding a grounder: positioning directly in front of the oncoming ball; eyes following the ball; feet shoulder-width apart, one foot slightly ahead of the other; leaning forward and bending at the knees; palms of hands facing upward, little fingers together.
- Have players pair off. The taller partner gets a ball, while the other partner finds a free space. Players stand facing you. Check for good spacing.

DESCRIPTION OF ACTIVITY:

1. Show me the "Ready Position" to field a grounder. To make sure that the ball you are fielding does not go right through your hands, let's explore how we can use our bodies to stop it.
2. Keep your eyes on an imaginary ball coming toward you. Get in front of the ball. This is called "fronting the ball." Kneel on one knee. Place your hands between your raised and lowered knee so that your hands are just touching the floor and your little fingers are together. Let the ball roll into both hands; then scoop it up. Your hands should be ready to catch the ball, but if you miss it, your body will be there to stop it! As soon as you have the ball in control, stand up, and throw an imaginary grounder toward me. How will you throw the ball so that it travels low along the floor?
3. Now with a partner, try to use the body stop to field the ball. Send the ball with an Underhand or the Overhand Throw. Start about four giant steps away from each other. Then move one step back after you each have fielded three grounders. First throw slow grounders; then try to make the ball travel faster.

GS–57 BASE RUNNING

FOCUS: Infield awareness; agility

EQUIPMENT: Four bases or carpet squares; four cone markers; one small utility ball

ORGANIZATION:

• Players are introduced to the Infield Base positions and to the softball terms "Diamond," "Infield," and "Outfield." They learn how to "tag up" (touch the inside of the base with one foot) through game play.

• To start, have players stand on one sideline facing the opposite side of the play area.

DESCRIPTION OF ACTIVITY:

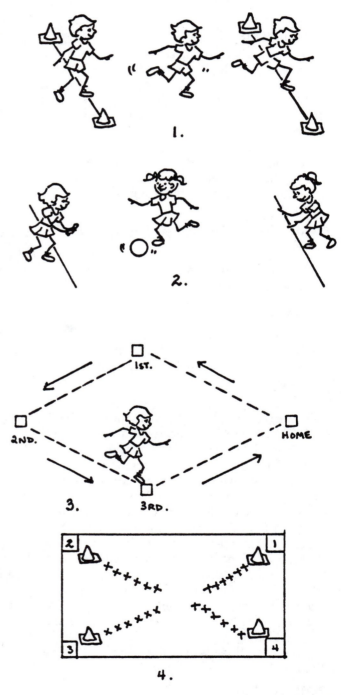

1. *Line Run Warm-Up:* (Use cones to mark off two parallel lines, spaced 10 meters [30 feet] apart.) Stand with your left foot behind the line, and your right leg on the line, which is your "imaginary base." On signal "Run!" take off as quickly as you can, run to the opposite line (or base), and "tag up" by having one foot touch the line. Now start with your left foot on this line. Wait for the signal to go.

2. *Line Ball Run:* (Choose one player with a ball to stand on the first line and another to stand on the second line, opposite the first player.) Runners, try to reach the second line before the player of the first line can roll the ball to the player on the second line. (Continue in this way changing the runners and rollers, frequently.)

3. *Base Running Follow the Leader:* Home base is our starting base. Now follow me to first, second, third, and then back to home base. (Repeat three times.) Show me how you can tag the inside of each base with one foot as you come to it.

 — In what direction are we travelling? (CCW)

 — What shape do the four bases make? (Diamond shape)

 — The area inside the four bases is called the "Infield." The area outside of the diamond is called the "Outfield."

4. *Base Running Relay:* (Place a carpet or base in each corner of the play area. Put a cone marker in front of each base. Form four even teams. Have each team line up in a file in front of a cone marker [see diagram].) On signal "Go!" each player, in turn, run CCW and touch all four bases with one foot; then return to your file to tag the next player. The first team to finish and sit cross-legged is the winner.

GS–58 BEAT BALL

FOCUS: Throwing; fielding; team play

EQUIPMENT: One 15-centimeter (6-inch) utility ball per game; two bases or cones per game

ORGANIZATION:

- For each game, mark off a large rectangular playing field about 20 meters by 10 meters (60 feet by 30 feet) in size. Then divide the class into two equal teams: Throwing team and Fielding team. Place a home base or cone in the middle of one end of the play area, and a second base or cone in the middle of the playing area, about 10 meters (30 feet) from the home base. Have the Throwing team stand just outside one sideline, near the home base endline. The Fielding team scatter throughout the play area, except for one player, who is the Catcher and stands just behind home base. Adjust the distance between home and second base according to the ability level of the children. Rotate the Catcher after every three Throwers.

DESCRIPTION OF ACTIVITY:

1. Each Thrower, in turn, stand with one foot on home base and throw the ball into the field area as far as you can; then run to the second base and home before the Fielding team can retrieve the ball and throw it to the Catcher at home base.
2. Thrower, if you beat the ball to home base, you score a run for your team. Fielder, if you catch an air ball, the Thrower is out. After each player of the Throwing team has had a turn to throw, the two teams then exchanges places.

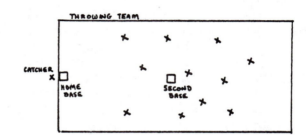

GS–59 ONE-ON-ONE KICKBALL

FOCUS: Lead-up game; kicking; base-running; fielding

EQUIPMENT: One 15-centimeter (6-inch) utility ball per game; four bases or cones per game

ORGANIZATION:

- Divide the class into two even teams: Kicking team and Fielding team. In each team, number the players consecutively 1, 2, 3. Have the Kicking team stand in a file just outside the base line between home and third base; and the Fielding team stand just outside the base line between home and first base.

DESCRIPTION OF ACTIVITY:

1. Player 1 of the Kicking team place a ball on home plate; then stand just behind it. Player 1 of Fielding team take up a fielding position within the boundaries of the infield.
2. Kicker, kick the ball and then run as quickly as you can around the bases, tagging each base in turn. Meanwhile Fielder, get the ball as quickly as you can and run to touch home plate with the ball. As soon as the Fielder touches home plate, Runner stop where you are.

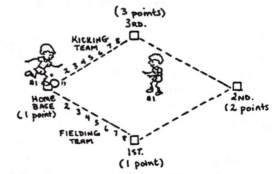

3. Kicking team, earn points from your team as follows: one point for first base; two points for second; three points for third; and four points for a "Home Run."
4. Now Fielder, go to the end of your Team; then player 2 of the Fielding team enter the infield. Player 2 of the Kicking Team step up to make the next kick. Play continues in this way. When everyone on Kicking team has had a turn, the two teams change roles.
5. A fly ball caught by the Fielder is an automatic out. A ball landing in the infield between and including the base lines is called a "fair ball." A ball landing outside of third or first baseline is called a "foul ball," and the Kicker gets another kick.

VARIATION: Have the Fielder roll the ball to the Kicker.

GS-60 MANOC

FOCUS: Lead-up game; kicking; fielding; base running; teamwork

EQUIPMENT: One slightly deflated soccer ball per game; four bases per game

ORGANIZATION:

- Divide the class into two even teams: Kicking team and Fielding team. Have each team number off consecutively for kicking order. The Kicking team should stand off to one side at a safe distance away; the Fielding team scatters throughout the diamond area.

DESCRIPTION OF ACTIVITY:

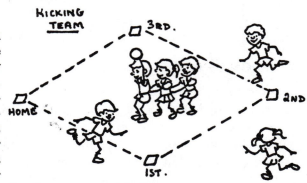

1. First Kicker, place the ball on home base; then kick the ball into the field. The ball must be kicked in a forward direction. Now run as quickly as you can around the bases until you reach home.
2. Meanwhile, one of the fielding team players retrieve the ball and quickly stand at that spot holding the ball up above your head. Fielders, this is your signal to quickly form a file behind the fielder with the ball, and stand with your legs wide apart and your hands holding onto the waist of the player in front of you. Fielders, you must not block or interfere in any way with the runner.
3. Kicker, if you can make it home before the Fielding team forms a file, then you earn one point for your team; otherwise, the Fielding team earns a point. I will record scores on the board. After everyone on the Kicking team has had a turn, the two teams exchange roles. Which team will earn the better score?

GS-61 KICKBALL

FOCUS: Lead-up game; infield positions

EQUIPMENT: Same as for activity GS-60, plus chalkboard, chalk, and eraser

ORGANIZATION:

- Divide the class into two even teams: Kicking and Fielding. Have the players in each team number off for batting order and field positioning. Teach and show on the chalkboard the infield positions: #1—Catcher, #2—Pitcher, #3—First Baseman, #4—Second Baseman, #5—Third Baseman, #6—Shortstop; and outfield positions: #7—Left Fielder, #8—Center Fielder, #9—Right Fielder. Have the fielding team take positions. If there are extra Fielders, evenly space them around the outfield. The Fielding team players rotate one position each time the team returns to field. Have the Kicking team players stand off to one side at a safe distance away.

DESCRIPTION OF ACTIVITY:

1. Pitcher, roll the ball toward the Kicker. The ball must roll along the ground; it cannot bounce. Kicker, kick the ball; then run to first base. If it is safe to continue to second base, do so. Can you make it to third base? Can you safely make a home run?
2. Fielding team, try to field the ball and throw it to first base to touch the base or the runner before he or she can tag up. Fielder, make a good throw to first base. First baseman, be alert to catch the ball!
3. Runner, you are not allowed to lead off your base or steal a base while the pitcher holds the ball. If you are not on your base, you can be put out by a Fielder tagging you with the ball or hitting you below the waist with a thrown ball. If a ball travelling through the air is caught by a Fielder, the Kicker is automatically out.
4. Each time a Runner tags up at home base, the Kicking team earns one point. Once the members of the Kicking team have all had a turn, the two teams change roles.

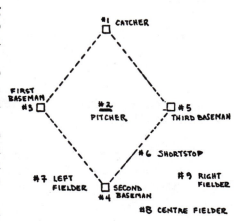

GS–62 INTRODUCING BATTING

FOCUS: Stance; grip; swing

EQUIPMENT: One bat per player; one base or carpet square

ORGANIZATION:

- Review the basic stance position, hands' position on the bat, and the swing. Check for cross-handed grips; that is, the incorrect hand is on top. Allow the weaker players to choke up (hold bat further up on the handle).
- Have each player collect a bat and a base and find a free space. Check for good spacing. If it is not possible to give a bat to each player, then have each player find a partner.

DESCRIPTION OF ACTIVITY:

1. *The Grip:*
   - Place both hands together on the bat, near the end.
   - Grip the bat with your favorite hand on top and swing the bat. Now try gripping the bat with your other hand on top and swinging it. Which way feels more natural? If you are right-handed, grip the bat with your right hand on top; if you are left-handed, your left hand should be on top.
   - Hold your bat firmly, not squeezed tightly, over your right shoulder if right-handed; left shoulder if left-handed. Do not let the bat rest on your shoulder. Check the trademark on the bat. It should be facing up!

1.

2. *The Swing:*
   - Keep your eyes on the ball until you hit it.
   - Begin your swing with a hip roll and short step forward into the ball.
   - Swing your bat level with the ground.
   - Follow through in the line of direction.
   - Make your swing smooth.

2.

3. *Stance:*
   - Put your base on the ground. Show me on which side of the base you should stand. If right-handed, stand with the front of your body facing the base and the left side of your body toward the pitcher.
   - Spread your feet shoulder-width apart, knees slightly bent.
   - How far away from the base should you be? Place your bat in the middle of the base; then stand as far away from the base as you can comfortably reach with your bat.

4. Practice taking your stance, gripping your bat, and swinging through an imaginary ball.

5. Play "Tee-Ball," activity GS–65.

3.

GS–63 TEE-BALL PLAY

FOCUS: Stance; grip; swing; cooperation

EQUIPMENT: One plastic bat per group; three whiffle balls per group; one batting-tee per group

ORGANIZATION:

- Batting skills are further developed through hitting the ball off a "batting-tee," which can be a purchased regulation batting-tee or a whiffle ball sitting on top of a cone marker. Demonstrate the positioning at the batting-tee plate; review the stance, grip, and swing. Stress safety—watch for the ball coming toward you. Check for correct stance, grip, swing and follow-through.

- Form groups of three and have each member of the group number off 1, 2, 3. Each group then collects a bat, three balls, and a batting-tee. Designate an area for each group to set up its batting-tee station. Check that groups are well spaced apart.

DESCRIPTION OF ACTIVITY:

1. First player, you are the Batter; second and third players, you are the Fielders. Your job is to field the hit balls and return them to the batting-tee.

2. Each batter, in turn, take three hits off the batting-tee. How far can you hit the ball? After you have made your three hits, rotate one position: batter go to the third player's position; third player go to the second player's position; second player to the batter's position.

3. Batter, do not crowd the plate or get too far away from it. Stand far enough behind the tee so that you can step forward into the swing.

   — Hit the ball in front of you.

   — Don't throw your bat after you hit the ball!

   — Keep your eyes on the ball!

4. *Batting-Tee Game:* Place a base or carpet square 4 meters (12 feet) to one side of home plate. Have the Batter hit the ball; then try to run to the base and back as many times as possible before the Fielders can retrieve the hit ball and either touch the Batter or home plate. Rotate positions after every three hits. Each Batter keep track of the number of runs you make in three hits.

BATTER

BATTING TEE

BASE

FIELDERS

GS–64 TWO BASES TEE-BALL

FOCUS: Batting; fielding; base running

EQUIPMENT: One plastic bat per pair;
one whiffle ball per pair;
one batting-tee or cone per pair;
two bases or carpet squares per pair

ORGANIZATION:

- Have players pair up and each pair collect a bat, a ball, a batting-tee, and two bases; then scatter around the playing field. Check for good spacing. Each pair sets up the bases about 10 meters (30 feet) from the other as shown. Check that the Batter stands far enough behind the tee so that he or she steps forward into the swing, hitting the ball slightly in front of him or her. Have the shortest bat first.

DESCRIPTION OF ACTIVITY:

1. Batter, hit the ball off the tee; then run to the long base and back to home base before the Fielder, your partner, can retrieve the ball and touch you with the ball or touch home base.

2. Score one run each time you run to the base and back home. Remember to drop your bat, not throw it, after hitting the ball!

HOME BASE   LONG BASE

GS–65 TEE-BALL

FOCUS: Lead-up game; batting; base running; throwing and fielding; teamwork

EQUIPMENT: One bat per game;
one batting-tee per game;
one small sponge ball per game

ORGANIZATION:

- Divide the class into two even teams: Batting and Fielding. Have the players in each team number off for batting order and field positioning. (See "Kickball's" Organization, activity GS–61.) You may wish to alternate boy-girl-boy-girl, etc. Then have the Fielding team take positions and the Batting team players stand off to one side at a safe distance away. Note that the Pitcher does not pitch but still takes up the fielding position. The Catcher does not enter the play until the ball is hit off the tee.

DESCRIPTION OF ACTIVITY:

1. Play the game using the same rules as you did for "Kickball," except that the Batter hits the ball off the tee; then runs to first base. Batter, remember to drop your bat, not throw it after you make the hit!

2. Fielding team and Batting team change roles after everyone on the Batting team has had a turn at bat.

3. When your team returns to field, everyone will rotate one position so that you get to know all the infield and outfield positions.

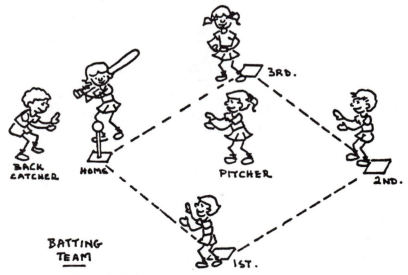

BACK CATCHER   HOME   PITCHER   3RD.   2ND.
BATTING TEAM   1ST.

VARIATION: Have the two teams change roles after every four outs.

GS-66 TENNIS BALLS AND TENNIS CANS PLAY

FOCUS: Hand-eye coordination; right–left dexterity; visual tracking

EQUIPMENT: One tennis ball per player; one tennis can per player

ORGANIZATION:

- To further develop and refine hand-eye coordination, introduce children to the challenge of tossing a tennis ball and catching it in the can! Used tennis cans and balls can be collected by asking parents and fellow teachers.

- Have each player collect a tennis ball and can and then find a free space.

DESCRIPTION OF ACTIVITY:

1. Show me how you can toss your tennis ball up with one hand, let it bounce once; then catch it in the can held by your other hand. Remember to keep your eyes on the ball until it lands in the tennis can and "give" with the ball to soften your catch. Try this trick several times. Switch hands and repeat the task.

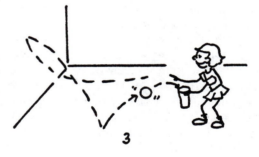

2. Now toss the tennis ball up again but try to catch the ball in the can without letting it bounce off the floor. Was this easier or more difficult? Try this task several times. Switch hands and repeat the task.

3. Go to a wall. Toss your tennis ball up and toward the wall. Let it bounce once off the floor; then try to catch it in the can. Practice! Switch hands and try this trick again.

4. Let me see you toss the ball up, kneel down, and catch the ball in the tennis can on the first bounce. Do this trick again. Switch hands and repeat the trick.

5. Hold the tennis can upside down and rest the tennis ball on bottom of the can. Show me how you can balance the ball in this way while walking; jogging; galloping; skipping; side-stepping.

6. Invent a trick of your own!

7. Find a partner. Can you Underhand Toss a tennis ball to each other and catch it in your tennis can on the first bounce? on no bounces? Invent a partner trick of your own! Trade tricks with another pair.

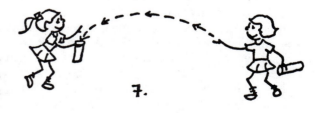

FOCUS: Accuracy in rolling, underhand and overhand throwing, kicking; visual tracking; cooperation

EQUIPMENT: Five wooden or plastic bowling pins; three 15-centimeter (6-inch) utility balls; three 20-centimeter (8-inch) utility balls; four benches; three beanbags; six cone markers; one tennis ball and can per player; three small garbage containers; three lightweight mats; three batting-tees and whiffle balls; floor tape

ORGANIZATION:

- This station activity reinforces all the balls skills learned to this point, including rolling, accurate underhand and overhand throwing, fielding, kicking and striking. See activity GS-53 for organization of these stations. If possible, set up two identical activities at each station to increase the participation level! Add station ideas of your own! Stations 5 and 6 are ideally suited for field play.

DESCRIPTION OF ACTIVITY:

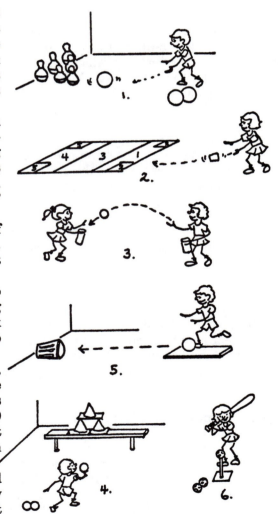

1. *Five-Pin Bowling:* (Near a wall, set up five bowling pins in a pyramid formation, and mark off a rolling line 5 meters [15 feet] away from the head pin. Place two benches on edge to act as the "sides of the bowling alley.") Each player, in turn, bowls three balls at the pins, trying to knock over as many as possible. Other players field the ball, clear pins away, and then reset them.

2. *Beanbag Shuffleboard:* (Use floor tape to mark out a simple grid on the play area floor, or use chalk on a tarmac. Number the grid as shown. Also mark out a tossing line 3 meters [10 feet] away.) Each player, in turn, toss three beanbags, using the one-handed underhand throw, toward the shuffleboard. How many points will you score? On your next try, toss with your weaker hand.

3. *Tennis Ball and Can Trick:* Explore different ways of tossing a tennis ball and catching it in the tennis can. Pair up and toss one tennis ball to each other, catching it in the can. What other trick can the two of you invent?

4. *Three for One:* (Balance one cone marker on top of two others on a bench. Use floor tape to mark out a throwing line.) Each player, take one overhand throw to try to knock all the cones off the bench. Use your favorite hand to throw; then on your second try, use your other hand!

5. *Three-Hole Golf Kicking:* (Set up three golf holes, around the perimeter of the play area. Place a garbage container on its side to act as the hole. Use a light mat as the "tee-off" place. Space the "hole" and "tee-off" about 10 meters [30 feet] away from each other.) Each player, count the number of kicks you will make to sink the ball in each hole. Try to equal or better your score for each hole.

6. *Batter's Box:* (Set up three batting tees; well spaced apart.) Each player hit three balls off the batting-tee. How far can you hit? Try to equal or better the distance hit each time.

GS-68 SHORT ROPES SAFETY

FOCUS: Teaching and safety guidelines

EQUIPMENT: One short rope per skipper; appropriate music; tape or record player

ORGANIZATION:

- *Rope Jumping* should be taught throughout the school year as a fitness activity or as the main focus of the lesson. Rope Jumping contributes significantly to the development of coordination, rhythm, timing, agility, aerobic endurance, and leg strength.

- *Beaded Ropes* should be used for skipping, if possible. These weighted ropes make turning easier, and the sound of the beads hitting the floor helps children pick up the rhythm. Remove some of the beads for a faster turning rope. Save extra beads for replacement purposes.

- *Speed Ropes* can be introduced when skippers have mastered the Basic Skipping Tricks.

- Store ropes by hanging them on hooks which can be easily accessed. Use colored tape on the handles to code the different lengths. Wooden floors, indoor/outdoor carpeting, or acrylic rubberized flooring are best as skipping surfaces.

- *Safety:* Ensure that skippers have enough space to turn ropes easily and safely. During activity, watch carefully for fatigue. Gradually increase activity time as fitness levels improve. Insist that skippers wear sneakers while skipping; no bare feet or socks!

- *Warm-Up* skippers by stretching arm and leg muscles for about five to eight minutes; *Cool Down* for three to five minutes by walking and stretching.

- To develop rhythmical jumping, use appropriate music with a steady beat, increasing tempo as ability improves.

ROPE JUMPING   BEADED ROPE

SAFETY CHECK

WARM-UP STRETCH

GS-69 STRAIGHT ROPE PATTERNS

FOCUS: Space and body awareness; listening   **EQUIPMENT:** One short rope per child

ORGANIZATION:

- Have children get a short rope, take it to a home space, and stretch it out along the floor. Ensure that ropes are well spaced.

DESCRIPTION OF ACTIVITY:

1. How many ropes can you leap over before I say "Freeze!"? Remember to watch where you are going! "Freeze!" (Repeat several times.) Quickly return to your own rope any way you choose and stand at one end.

2. Show me how you can jump back and forth across your rope from one end to the other end. Can you zig-zag jump backwards to your starting place? Stand on one side of the rope facing it sideways. Can you jump over the rope to the opposite end and back? Show me how you can keep your hands on the floor and jump back and forth across your rope.

3. Who can hop back and forth across the rope from one end to the other? Return to your starting place by hopping on the other foot. Repeat, facing sideways and hopping sideways.

4. Your rope is a tightrope. Walk forward on your rope; walk backwards; sideways, crossing one foot in front of the other; crossing one foot behind the other. Careful!

5. Show me how you can make a bridge over your rope. Try to move your bridge down the rope. Now make a new bridge. Move your new bridge back to the starting place.

6. Can you keep your hands on the floor and jump back and forth across the rope?

7. What other ways can you move on or over your rope? Try criss-cross walking to the other end as quickly as you can.

8. *Leap the Brook:* Find a partner. Place your ropes straight and alongside each other, about two giant steps apart. Take turns leaping over the ropes. Gradually increase the distance between the ropes. How far can you leap?

GS-70 CIRCLE ROPE PATTERNS

FOCUS: Space and body awareness; balancing; listening

EQUIPMENT: One short rope per child; music with a lively beat; tape or record player

ORGANIZATION:

• Have children get a short rope, take it to a home space, and make it into a circle shape on the floor. Ensure that ropes are well spaced.

DESCRIPTION OF ACTIVITY:

1. On the signal "Move!" travel around the play area without touching any of the rope circles. On signal "Shape . . . ," quickly stand inside a circle and perform the following:

   — Make your body as small as you can; as big as you can.

   — Make a one-foot balance; a tall balance; a low balance.

   — Touch your bellybutton to the floor in your circle.

   — Build a bridge across your pond using four body parts.

2. How can you put half of your body in the circle and half outside?

   — How many body parts can you touch inside the rope? How few?

   — Place one hand in the circle and your legs straight out. Can you move all the way around the circle, like a Grinder? Repeat with opposite hand in the opposite direction.

   — Balance with four body parts inside, one part out; two parts inside, one part out; three parts inside, one part out; one body part inside, one part outside.

3. Begin in the center of your home circle. Show me how you can move in and out of your rope: forward, backwards, sideways. Use two feet together; then one foot.

   — Make a quarter jump-turn; half jump-turn; full-turn in your circle.

4. Leap over your pond. How many different ways can you take off and land: two feet to two feet; two feet to one foot; one foot to one foot; one foot to two feet. While in the air, do a quarter-turn; half-turn; wide shape; stunt of your own.

5. *Musical Ropes:* When you hear the music, leave your home rope and move around the other ropes. When the music stops, quickly and safely find a rope to stand in. Each time I will remove one or more ropes. If you are caught without a rope to stand in, jog lightly in place until the game ends.

6. *Circle Rope Tag:* Find a partner and use two ropes to make one large circle on the floor. Play a game of tag with one partner trying to catch the other as you move around the outside of the circle.

GS–71 GEOMETRIC ROPE PATTERNS

FOCUS: Space and body awareness; creativity   **EQUIPMENT:** One short rope per skipper

ORGANIZATION:

• Have children get a rope and sit cross-legged in the Listening Circle.

DESCRIPTION OF ACTIVITY:

1. *Rope Shape Warm-Up:* (Divide the class into six different groups and give each group a name: Group 1, Squares; Group 2, Rectangles; Group 3, Triangles; Group 4, Circles; Group 5, Diamonds; and Group 6, Figure-Eight's. Make sure children know their group number and name; then have them scatter around the play area. Check for good spacing.)

1.

— Make your shape with your rope. What is your shape called?

— How many different ways can you hop in and out of your shape?

— Make a bridge over your shape; curl up inside.

— Leap over as many different shapes as you can. Watch where you are going!

— All Squares do quarter jump-turns; Rectangles be "Grinders" (put one hand inside and walk your feet around the outside of your rope). Triangles form three-point Bridges; Circles be Stepping Stones; Diamonds be Tap Dancers; Figure-Eight's be Skiers.

— (Have children trade shapes and repeat the tasks.)

2. *Number Shapes:* How can you use your rope to make your favorite number? Try making other numbers.

2.

— Can you add three and five together and draw the answer with your rope?

3. *Letter Shapes:* Make the first letter of your name; last letter of your name. Can you make the fifth letter of the alphabet; eighth; tenth?

3.

4. *Partner Rope Drawing:* Join with a partner and use your ropes to make your favorite giant number; make a two-digit number.

— Draw an Eskimo's home; an Indian's home; a home of your choice using your ropes; the world's largest bowtie; coolest moustache; longest braid.

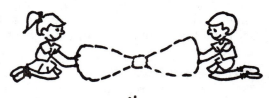

4.

— Add 6 and 3 together and draw the number; 8 and 5.

— Can you make a five-sided figure?

— Make a two-lettered word using one rope and your bodies.

GS-72 ROPE STUNTS

FOCUS: Coordination; listening

EQUIPMENT: One short rope per skipper

ORGANIZATION:

• Have children get a rope, check it for proper length, and then find a free space.

DESCRIPTION OF ACTIVITY:

1. **Rope Stretches:**
   — Hold a folded rope overhead and taut in both hands and stretch from side-to-side. Repeat, holding rope behind your head; in front.
   — Now put your folded rope behind your waist and pull for five seconds; then relax. Show me how you can step on one end of your rope and pull upward for another five seconds.
   — In the long-sit position, put a doubled rope around both feet and gently pull toward you for ten seconds. Repeat in the wide-sit position, with the rope around each foot, in turn.
   — How else can you stretch with your rope?

2. **Thread the Needle:** Holding your folded rope low and in front of you with both hands apart, "thread the needle" by stepping over it one foot at a time; then reverse.

3. **Swing and Jump:** Holding the folded rope with one hand, show me how you can swing it and jump over it.

4. **Rope Swings:** (Turn with best hand; then other.)
   — **Helicopter:** Hold the rope handles in both hands and swing the rope overhead like a helicopter's blades while jogging in place.
   — **Propellers:** Swing the rope in front with both hands like an airplane's propellers, while hopping in rhythm.
   — **Wheelers:** Swing your rope to either side and jump in rhythm as the rope hits the floor near your feet.
   — **Figure-Eight's:** Swing your rope in a figure-eight pattern in front of you. (Have children repeat these tasks swinging the rope with their dominant hand; then with their nondominant hand.)

5. **Rope Tugs:** Find a partner about your size. Fold a rope in half, and have a one-handed tug-o-war with your partner. Repeat using the other hand. Repeat using both hands.

6. **Tightrope Walk and Pass:** Stretch one rope out flat along the floor. Each partner, start at a different end of the rope and walk on the rope toward each other. Can you pass each other without losing your balance or letting your feet touch the floor?

HELICOPTERS   PROPELLERS

WHEELERS   FIGURE-8's

GS-73 INTRODUCING LONG ROPES

FOCUS: Rhythmical jumping; cooperation

EQUIPMENT: One long rope per group; music with a steady 4/4 beat; tape or record player

ORGANIZATION:

- Form groups of four skippers: two turners and two jumpers. Change roles frequently so that everyone has a turn at jumping and turning. Ensure that groups are well spaced around the play area. Use ropes that are 4 to 5 meters (12 to 15 feet) long. The rope length should suit the turners' ability. Using music will encourage skippers to turn the rope rhythmically and smoothly.

DESCRIPTION OF ACTIVITY:

1. *Ocean Waves:* Turners, ripple the long rope up and down along the floor. Each jumper, in turn, jump the rope once, travelling in a figure-eight pattern until you have made five jumps. Turners, gradually make the waves bigger. Can you still jump the waves?

1.

2. *Snake Jump:* Turners, wiggle your long rope from side to side along the floor. Each jumper, in turn, jump the rope once, travelling in a figure-eight pattern, until you have made five jumps.

3. *Mountain Climb:* One turner, while knee-sitting, hold the rope on the floor; other turner, stand holding the rope at waist height. The rope should be taut between you. Each jumper, in turn, jump the rope once at the low end, travel in a figure-eight pattern, and jump again higher up. Continue until you have jumped as high as you can go!

3.

4. *Blue Bells:* Turners, gently swing the long rope from side to side. Each jumper, in turn, jump in place over the rope. How long can you keep jumping before you stop the rope?

4.

5. *Ski Jumper:* Turners, hold the long rope flat and stretched out along the floor. Jumper, keeping your feet together, jump from side-to-side along the rope. Who can ski jump backwards to the starting place?

6. *Jump the Shot:* (Have skippers form one large circle and space themselves arm's length apart. Stand in the center and swing a long rope with a deckring securely tied to one end.) Jumpers, as the rope comes near you, try to jump the ring. If you are hit, jog once around the play area; then rejoin the game. If you are hit a second time, jog two times around the play area, and so on.

6.

7. *Spoke Jumping:* Form groups of four pairs of turners and four jumpers. Turners, position as shown in the diagram: First pair of turners do Ocean Waves; second pair, Snake Jump; third pair, Mountain Climb; and fourth pair, Blue Bells. Jumpers, jump from rope to rope in a CW pattern, completing the circuit twice.

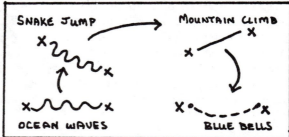

SNAKE JUMP → MOUNTAIN CLIMB

OCEAN WAVES — BLUE BELLS

7.

GS-74 LONG ROPE TURNING AND JUMPING

FOCUS: Turning and jumping technique

EQUIPMENT: One long rope per group; one deckring per group; music with a steady 4/4 beat; tape or record player

ORGANIZATION:

- Have skippers form groups of four: two turners and two jumpers. Each group then gets a long rope and scatters around the play area. Teach and demonstrate the basic technique of turning a long rope and jumping. Emphasize smooth, rhythmical rope turning and that turners watch the feet of the jumper.

DESCRIPTION OF ACTIVITY:

1. **Technique of Turning:** Turners, holding a rope handle each, hold the rope taut between you. With elbow at your side, turn the rope with your forearm, in toward the body. Now slowly walk toward each other until the rope touches the floor at the bottom of each swing. Listen to the rhythm of the rope as it hits the floor each time. Turn your rope with a high arch. Jumpers, can you clap your hands in time with the rope's rhythm? Change turners and repeat.

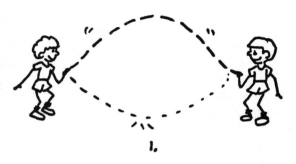

1.

2. **Long Rope Toe Catch:** Jumper, stand in the middle of the rope. Turners, turn rope overhead of Jumper. Jumper, try to catch rope with your toes as it touches the floor. Can you do this without looking at your toes?

3. **Long Rope Jump:** Jumper, stand in the middle of the rope. Turners, turn rope overhead of Jumper. Jumper, keeping your feet and knees together, jump the rope each time it passes under your feet. How many times can you jump the turning rope?

3.

4. **Jumping Rhymes:** Jumper, start in the middle of the rope. Turners, chant a Childhood Rhyme as you turn the rope; Jumper, jump the rope each time it passes under your feet and chant as well. Take turns.

5. **Jump the Shot:** (Combine two groups and have the members form a circle with a leader in the center, holding onto a rope with a deckring securely tied to one end.) Leader, gentle swing the rope CW around the circle along the floor. Jumpers, try to jump the ring as it comes near you. If you are hit, jog around the play area once; then rejoin the game. (If hit a second time, jog two times around and so on.) Change turners every 30 seconds. Continue until everyone has been a turner.)

5.

GS-75 JUMPING JINGLES

FOCUS: Rhythmical jumping; cooperation **EQUIPMENT:** One long rope per group

ORGANIZATION:

- Form groups of four or five skippers. Have each group get a long rope; then scatter around the play area. Ensure that groups are well spaced.

DESCRIPTION OF ACTIVITY:

1. *Tick Tock:*

   Tick Tock, Tick Tock,
   Give the time by the clock.
   One, two, three, . . . (to) Midnight.

2. *Lady, Lady:*

   Lady, Lady at the gate,
   Eating cherries from a plate.
   How many cherries did she eat?
   One, two, three, . . .

3. *Alphabet, Alphabet:*

   Alphabet, Alphabet,
   I know my A, B, C
   Alphabet, Alphabet,
   Listen to me! A, B, C, . . . Z.

4. *Teddy Bear:*

   Teddy Bear, Teddy Bear, turn around,
   Teddy Bear, Teddy Bear, touch the ground.
   Teddy Bear, Teddy Bear, show your shoe.
   Teddy Bear, Teddy Bear, jump-turn, too.
   Teddy Bear, Teddy Bear, go upstairs.
   Teddy Bear, Teddy Bear, say your prayers.
   Teddy Bear, Teddy Bear, turn out the light.
   Teddy Bear, Teddy Bear, say goodnight!

5. *Mother, Mother:*

   Mother, Mother, I am ill
   Call for the Doctor over the hill.
   First came the Doctor,
   Then came the Nurse,
   Then came the Lady with the alligator purse.
   Out went the Doctor,
   Out went the Nurse,
   Out went the Lady with the alligator purse.

6. I like milk, I like tea,
   How many boys (girls) are wild about me?

   (Pepper-Jump as turners turn the rope faster and faster!)

7. *Creative Jingles:* Each group create a Jumping Jingle of your own; then perform it for the other groups.

GS–76 FRONT DOOR PATTERNS

FOCUS: Entering; exiting; jumping; and rope turning

EQUIPMENT: One long rope per group; music with a steady 4/4 beat; tape or record player

ORGANIZATION:

- Skippers learn how to jump into and out of a turning rope. Demonstrate the Front Door technique of entering a rope turning toward the incoming jumper. Emphasize smooth rhythmical rope turning and that turners watch the feet of the jumper.

- Form groups of four skippers: two turners and two jumpers. Have each group get a long rope and scatter around the play area.

DESCRIPTION OF ACTIVITY:

1. *Blue Bells Warm-Up:* Turners, swing the rope back and forth like a pendulum. Jumpers, in turn, jump over the rope in different ways: both feet together, feet apart; one foot, then the other foot; a turn in mid-air. Rotate positions so that everyone has a turn at jumping and turning.

2. *Front Door Entry:* Turners, turn the rope toward incoming jumper. Jumper, stand near the right shoulder of the left rope turner. Watch the rope closely as it swings toward you, down, and away. As the rope passes your nose, enter and run through the "open window," exiting near the right turner's right shoulder. Re-enter front door near the right turner's left shoulder. Remember, run through—do not jump the rope! (Repeat pattern until each skipper has had four turns.)

3. *Front Door-Jump-Exit Pattern:* Jumper, do a Front Door entry, jump the rope once; then exit by the right turner's right shoulder. Re-enter front door near right turner's left shoulder. Remember to jump into the middle as the rope passes your nose. Repeat this figure-eight pattern four times. Take turns, doing this pattern with four jumps in the middle.

4. *Front Door Tasks:*
   — Run in Front Door, jump the letters in your last name; then exit; jump the letters in the alphabet; jump on one foot four times, then on the other foot four times. Repeat this pattern twice; then exit.

   — Run in Front Door, jump four quarter-turns in one direction; then exit.

   — Run in Front Door and jump in your own way in the middle of the long rope!

GS–77 INTRODUCING BACK DOOR ENTRY

FOCUS: Entering and exiting technique

EQUIPMENT: One long rope per group; music with a strong 4/4 beat; tape or record player

ORGANIZATION:

- Teach and demonstrate the Back Door technique of entering a rope turning away from the incoming jumper. Emphasize smooth, rhythmical rope turning and that turners watch the feet of the jumper.
- Form groups of four or five skippers and have each group get a long rope before scattering around the play area.

DESCRIPTION OF ACTIVITY:

1. *Call-In Warm-Up:* Turners, turn rope toward the incoming Jumper. Then first jumper, run in the Front Door and begin jumping. At random, call the name of another jumper, who will run in and jump with you three times. First jumper, then run out; second jumper, call another jumper's name at random and jump together three times. Continue until all skippers have called in another jumper. Change rope turners and repeat.

2. *Back Door Entry:* Jumper, stand near the right shoulder of the left turner. Watch the rope as it hits the floor and rises upward, away from you. When the rope is at the top, run through the open window; exit near the right turner's right shoulder. Re-enter near right turner's left shoulder, run through again, exiting near left turner's left shoulder; around that turner, ready to do figure-eight again. Remember to run through; do not jump the rope! Repeat this pattern until each skipper has gone twice.

3. *Back Door-Jump-Exit Pattern:* Each jumper start near the right shoulder of the left rope turner. Watch the rope as it hits the floor and rises upward. When the rope is at the top, run in; jump the rope as it hits the floor; and exit near the right turner's right shoulder. Re-enter back door near the right turner's left shoulder. Repeat this pattern until each skipper has gone four times. Repeat, jumping five times in the middle before exiting.

4. *Jumping Relay:* Each jumper, in turn, enter Front Door, jump five times; then exit. Continue until everyone in your group has had a turn at jumping. Which group will finish first? Repeat relay, jumping in Back Door.

GS-78 LONG ROPE JUMPING CHALLENGES

FOCUS: Rhythmical jumping; groupwork

EQUIPMENT: One long rope per group; music with a strong 4/4 beat; tape or record player

ORGANIZATION:

- Form groups of five skippers. Have one skipper get a long rope; then groups scatter around the play area. Ensure groups are well spaced.

DESCRIPTION OF ACTIVITY:

1. ***Copy-Cat Jumping Warm-Up:*** Turners, rhythmically turn the rope front door. Jumpers, stand in single-file formation behind one rope turner, with the leader at the head of the line. Leader, run in front door and jump the rope anyway you choose; then exit front door or back door. Other jumpers, in turn, try to copy the leader's action. If the leader stops the rope, the next jumper becomes the new leader, and the old leader goes to the end of the line. Change turners after each jumper has had a turn at being leader, and continue.

2. ***School Bells:*** Each jumper, in turn, try to complete the following sequence "to pass from Kindergarten to Grade Eight": Run through the turning rope Front Door to pass Kindergarten; enter Front Door, jump once, then exit, to pass Grade One; jump twice for Grade Two; three times for Grade Three, and so on. If you stop the rope, you become a turner.

3. ***Hot Pepper:*** Turners, begin by turning the rope slowly. Jumper, enter front door and jump the rope; on your signal "Pepper!" turners turn the rope quickly. How many times can you jump without stopping the rope? Repeat until everyone in your group has had a turn at jumping. Who in your group will be the "Hot Pepper Champ"? Who will be the class Champ?

4. ***Partner Stunts:*** Turners, turn the rope Front Door. Two jumpers, start in the middle together. Explore different ways of jumping together:
   - jump, facing each other and holding hands
   - jump, side-by-side, holding hands
   - jump-turn away from each other
   - run in Front Door together, if you can, and later exit
   - invent a partner stunt of your own

GS-79 INTRODUCING SHORT ROPES

FOCUS: Turning and jumping technique

EQUIPMENT: One short rope per skipper

ORGANIZATION:

- Skippers learn to size the rope for correct length, and they learn basic skipping form and basic jump. To begin, have skippers find a free space.

DESCRIPTION OF ACTIVITY:

1. *Skipping Warm-Up:*

   — Head-Turns: gently from side to side

   — Arm Circles: gently forward, crossing in front

   — Shoulder Shrugs and Rolls

   — Side Bends: gently bend to one side, then the other

   — Wrist Circles, Ankle Circles

   — Keeping knees and feet together, bounce lightly on the balls of your feet to the music. Pantomime rope turning as you jump by making little circles with your hands.

2. *Size the Rope:* Get a rope and check it for proper length by standing in the middle of it and drawing the ends up to your shoulders. The rope ends should just reach your arm pits. (If the rope is too long, undo the knots at the handles, remove some beads, adjust the length, and double-knot the ends.)

3. *Check the Spacing:* Take your rope anywhere in the play area and check that you have enough space to turn it easily without touching anyone.

4. *Basic Skipping Form:* Stand tall, knees slightly bent and head up. Hold the rope behind your heels, handles held loosely. Keep your elbows close to the sides; point forearms and hands slightly forward and away from your body. Keep your knees and feet together. Turn the rope using small, circular wrist movements.

   — *Toe Catch:* Start with rope behind you. Swing it overhead and forward, and catch it under your toes.

   — *Heel Catch:* Start with rope in front of you. Swing it overhead and backward, catching it under your heels.

   — Repeat, but jump once and then catch the rope.

GS–80 SHORT ROPE JUMPING PATTERNS

FOCUS: Basic jumps

EQUIPMENT: One short rope per skipper; music with a steady 4/4 beat; tape or record player

ORGANIZATION:

- Skippers learn single- and double-jump technique. Use lively music with a strong, steady beat to provide a jumping rhythm as skippers perform the following jumping patterns, turning rope forward and backwards.

- To begin, have skippers find a free space.

DESCRIPTION OF ACTIVITY:

1. *Pantomime Jumping Warm-Up:* Listen to the music. Show me how you can jump in place to its beat and pantomime the rope turning action. Jump once, every time you turn your imaginary rope. This is called "Single Jumping." Now do one jump; then a smaller jump. This is called "Double Jumping."

2. *Blue Bells:* Hold the rope, an end in each hand, in front of you. Let the rope gently swing back and forth, just off the floor. Can you jump the rope each time it passes under you?

3. *Basic Jump Technique:* Keeping feet together, make low jumps that are only three to five centimeters (one to two inches) from the floor; relax as you jump; bend your knees slightly and land softly on the balls of your feet; then lower heels to floor, rather than landing flat-footed; use your wrists rather than your arms to supply the power; turn and jump smoothly.

   — *Single or Pogo Jump:* Turn the rope once, jump once. Practice.

   — *Double Jump:* Turn rope once; jump lightly when rope is overhead; then jump when rope passes underneath. Practice.

4. *Short Rope Patterns:* Show me how you can do the following as you jump in time to the music:

   — Double-jump, turning rope forward; Single-jump.

   — Double-jump, turning rope backwards; Single-jump.

   — Double-jump, hopping on one foot, then the other as you turn the rope forward. Repeat Pogo Jumping.

   — Travel forward while turning your rope forward.

   — Show me another way that you can jump!

   — Create your own jumping pattern.

5. *Hot-Pepper Challenge:* How many times can you single-jump in 30 seconds?

GS-81 BASIC ROPE TRICKS

FOCUS: Mastering rope jumping basics

EQUIPMENT: One short rope per skipper; music with a strong 4/4 beat; tape or record player

ORGANIZATION:

- Have skippers get a rope, check that it is the correct length, and then scatter around the play area. Encourage and praise good effort.

DESCRIPTION OF ACTIVITY:

1. _Double-Side Swing:_ Hold one rope handle in each hand. Swing the rope to the right two times; then open it and jump over it. Do not cross your hands. Hands are close together when swinging the rope and far apart when jumping. Repeat to the left side. Practice this "swing right, swing right-jump-swing left, swing left-jump" pattern.

2. _Single-Side Swing:_ Swing the rope on only one side of your body; then open it and jump over it. Swing and jump on the other side. Practice this "swing right-jump, swing left-jump" pattern.

3. _Figure-Eight Side Swing:_ Side swing right; side swing left; side swing right; continue for eight swings.

4. _Figure-Eight Jump:_ Swing rope to right side of body; swing rope to left side of body; swing rope to right side of body; open it and jump over. Repeat pattern.

5. _Easy Rocker:_ Place one foot ahead of the other. Jump with weight on the front foot, leaning forward slightly. Shift weight to back foot and jump again, leaning backwards slightly. Practice with the rope turning slowly at first; then turn the rope faster as the rocker step becomes easier for you.

6. _Skier:_ Place rope stretched out along the floor and jump with feet together, from side-to-side, over it. Now add the rope. On the first turn, jump sideways to the right; on the second turn, jump sideways to the left. Imagine you are jumping side-to-side across a line each time you jump the rope.

7. _Boxer:_ Jump twice with your right foot; then twice with your left foot. Continue to jump twice on each foot.

8. _Jogger:_ Using a running step, step over the rope with first the right foot and then the left foot. Continue to alternate footwork, taking one jump for each step. Repeat, stepping over the rope with first the left foot; then the right.

9. _Side Straddle:_ Start with feet together. On the first turn of the rope, jump feet shoulder-width apart. On the second turn of the rope, jump feet together again. Say to yourself, "Apart," "Together."

10. _Forward Straddle:_ Start with feet together. On the first turn of the rope, jump feet apart so that your right foot is in front of your left. On the second turn of the rope, jump so that your left foot is in front of the right.

GS-82 PARTNER SKIPPING USING ONE ROPE_____

FOCUS: Cooperative rope jumping

EQUIPMENT: One short rope per pair;
music with a strong beat;
tape or record player

ORGANIZATION:

- To start, have skippers pair up with a partner about the same size and get a rope to share. To check that the rope is the correct length, have partners stand side-by-side on the rope; the ends should extend to their outer armpits. Pairs then scatter around the play area.

DESCRIPTION OF ACTIVITY:

1. ***Face-to-Face:*** Start by standing face-to-face. One partner turn the rope and both jump in unison. Take turns being the rope turner.

   — One partner, run in, face your partner, and match steps. Run out, then run in again, and jump in step with your partner. How many different tricks can you perform?

2. ***Side-by-Side:*** Partners, stand side-by-side, facing forward, with each partner holding one handle of the rope. You may wish to join inside hands or place an arm around your partner's waist or shoulders. In unison, turn rope forward with your free hands and jump. Can you turn the rope backwards and jump together? Now try the following tricks:

   — Skip forward; skip backwards; skip sideways together.

   — One partner, move out and back into position while continuing to turn the rope. Other partner, repeat; then both partners move out together and back into position again.

   — One partner, circle the other partner while continuing to turn the rope.

VARIATIONS:

a. ***Invent-a-Trick:*** Provide opportunity for pairs to create a new trick in the Side-by-Side and Face-to-Face positions.

b. ***Show-Off Time!:*** Provide opportunity for pairs to perform their tricks for the rest of the class.

GS-83 ROPE JUMPING STATIONS

FOCUS: Long and short rope jumping

EQUIPMENT: Several short ropes;
several long ropes;
recording paper and one pencil per group;
posterboard, marking pen, masking tape;
lively music with a strong 4/4 beat;
tape or record player

ORGANIZATION:

- Set up six skipping stations around the play area in a circuit. Post signs (and posters, if available) to designate each station. Put strong and weak skippers together in groups of four to promote peer-teaching. Every four to six minutes, have skippers rotate from station to station in a CW direction.

- Write to your State or National Heart Foundation for jump rope posters.

- Following are suggestions for jump rope stations.

DESCRIPTION OF ACTIVITY:

1. **Short Rope Tricks:** Practice the tricks you have learned. Work in counts of four or eight.

2. **Partner Skipping:** Practice rope jumping with a partner using one rope.

3. **Skill-Builder Idea:** Using the tricks you have learned, combine them to create new tricks. Give your new trick a name!

4. **Long Rope Tricks:** How many different Short Rope Tricks can you perform in a long rope? Practice!

5. **Jumping Jingles:** Can your group create a short rope-jumping jingle (poem) which will involve everyone making up a part of the jingle, a recorder writing up the jingle, and each skipper in your group, in turn, jumping in a long rope while your group recites the jingle in unison?

6. **Rope Challenger:** (Post posters of tricks the skippers have not as yet learned.) Choose a trick, read the description or helpful hints to go with the illustration, and try to learn it. You may get help from other skippers in your group and from me.

VARIATION:

Provide opportunity for skippers to "show off" their routines they have developed, the new tricks they have created, and the group jingle they have put together.

GS–84 INTRODUCING PARACHUTES

FOCUS: Teaching and safety guidelines; arm strength; cooperation

EQUIPMENT: One parachute per group

ORGANIZATION:

- Use parachutes indoors or outdoors, on play days, or as part of a lesson. Parachutes are great at any time because they require all players, regardless of skill or strength, to cooperate and to be vigorously and continuously involved throughout the activity. Parachutes of 7 meters (24 feet) in diameter are suitable for a class of 25 to 30 children. Smaller classes could use a 5-meter (16-foot)-diameter parachute, while larger classes could use either one 7-meter (24-foot)-diameter parachute or two 5-meter (16-foot) chutes.
- Have players stand around the edge of the parachute and grip the canopy at the seams.

DESCRIPTION OF ACTIVITY:

1. Hold the chute with both hands and roll the edge toward the center two or three times so that you get a better grip. If you have long fingernails, try not to pull too hard. Grip the edge of the chute at all times until you are told to let go.

UNDERHAND GRIP

2. Use any of the following grips:
   - *Overhand Grip:* Grip the edge of the chute with the palms facing down. The Overhand Grip is the most common parachute grip.
   - *Underhand Grip:* Grip the edge of the chute with palms up.
   - *Cross-Over Grip:* Cross the arms and grip the edge of the chute with the Overhand Grip.
   - *Alternating Grip:* Use the Overhand Grip with one hand and the Underhand Grip with the other hand.

OVERHAND GRIP   CROSS-OVER GRIP

1.

3. *Parachute Warm-up:* (Have children evenly space themselves around the parachute and hold onto the edge at waist level, using the Overhand Grip.) For *Ripples and Waves,* shake the parachute gently, making only ripples. Gradually, let your ripples get bigger, making little waves. Now let those waves get bigger and bigger. Show me how hard you can shake the parachute! Freeze!

4. *Merry-Go-Round Activities:* Hold the parachute with your right hand only and rest your left hand on your hip. Walk forward in a CW direction. Walk normally, holding the parachute as high as you can. Walk quickly. Walk backwards. Walk forward, gently raising and lowering the parachute on the signals "Up!" and "Down!"

3.

   - Change to a left Overhand Grip and jog forward CCW. On signal "Switch!" quickly grip the parachute with your other hand and jog in the opposite direction. (Repeat several times.)
   - Grip the parachute in your right hand again and skip forward in a CW direction, gently shaking the parachute. "Switch!" to your left hand grip and gallop forward in a CCW direction.
   - Using a right Overhand Grip and changing your hopping foot with every four hops, travel in a CW direction.
   - Hold the edge of the parachute with both hands, using the Underhand Grip, and side-step to the right; to the left. On signal, "Jump!" stop in place and gently bounce up and down.

5. *Stretch, Mr. Chute!:* Hold onto the edge of the parachute with both hands, using the Overhand Grip. On signal "Stretch!" gently pull the parachute tight for five seconds. Relax, letting Mr. Chute get floppy; then stretch it again.

GS–85 INFLATION FUN

FOCUS: Inflation technique and activities; cooperation

EQUIPMENT: One parachute per group; easy listening music (optional); tape or record player

ORGANIZATION:

- Review parachute grips. Then demonstrate and explain inflation action (to fill full with air) before practice. The inflation action is basic to most parachute activities. Establish definite signals such as "Ready—Begin," or "1, 2, 3,—Stretch!" so that everyone responds at the same time.
- Have players gather around parachute and hold it using the overhand grip. Check for good spacing.

DESCRIPTION OF ACTIVITY:

1. *Inflation:* Hold the canopy at waist level using the Overhand Grip. On the signal "Ready—Down!" squat and hold parachute to the floor. On signal "1, 2, 3,—Up!" stand and thrust arms overhead to allow as much air under the chute as possible. When the center of the canopy touches the floor, repeat, and try to get an even better inflation.

2. *Tenting:* Inflate parachute; then on the signal "In —1, 2, 3!" walk forward three steps. As the chute settles, on signal "Out—1, 2, 3!" walk backwards three steps.

2.

3. *Mushroom:* Inflate chute; then quickly pull the edge to floor to seal in the escaping air and make a mushroom shape. Continue to hold the edges down until canopy settles to floor. Try walking forward three steps before sealing parachute to the floor.

3.

4. *Igloo:* (Explain that you are now going to make the whole class disappear.) Hold the parachute using the cross-over grip, inflate it, and walk forward three steps. On signal "Turn!" quickly turn and duck under the parachute. Regrasp the inside edge, kneel (or sit), and seal edge to floor. Return to the outside and try again.

4.

5. *Peek-a-Boo Igloo:* Can you make an Igloo and seal it to the floor, leaving only your heads outside? Show me how you can make an Igloo, seal it to the floor, and then lie on your backs and poke only your feet outside!

6. *Fly Away:* Inflate the chute until it is totally inflated; then, on signal "Fly Away!" everyone let go at the same time. The chute should remain in the air for a few seconds before it settles down on top of you, but don't move off your spot!

7. *Sunflower:* Inflate the parachute. Now, quickly lower it to the floor and kneel on the outside edge to seal in the air. Raise arms sideways, join hands, and on the signal "In!" lean forward; on signal "Out!" lean backward. Pretend to be a sunflower closing and opening.

6.

VARIATIONS:

a. *Mushroom Challenge:* Using two parachutes, challenge each group to keep its "Mushroom" inflated the longest time.

b. On *Fly Away,* have children release parachute on your signal; then quickly move away from the parachute, watching it fall to the floor. Let them decide what kind of creature or monster shape the chute looks like after it settles on the floor.

GS-86 PARACHUTE MUSCLE-BUILDERS

FOCUS: Cooperation; arm and leg strength; listening

EQUIPMENT: One parachute per group; several balls such as beachballs, playground balls, tennis balls, whiffle balls; 12 to 15 beanbags; 10 to 12 skipping ropes; one stuffed toy; one plastic animal per player

ORGANIZATION:

• Have all players evenly space themselves around the parachute and hold it at waist level using the overhand grip.

DESCRIPTION OF ACTIVITY:

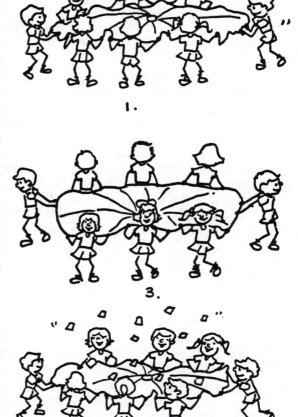

1. *Ocean Waves:* On signal "Ocean Waves!" slowly shake the parachute up and down; then shake a little faster . . . and faster (the wind is getting stronger and stronger . . . it's a hurricane!). Now make gentle waves as the wind is dying down . . . to a soft breeze! Create Ocean Waves in the kneeling position.

2. *Firefighter's Pull:* Holding the chute using the underhand grip, step one leg forward, plant both feet firmly, lean back, and straighten your arms. On signal "1, 2, 3—Pull!" pull the chute toward you without moving your feet or jerking the chute. Pull as hard as you can for ten seconds. Change to the Overhand Grip, kneel and repeat; then sit and repeat.

3. *Wild-Horse Pull:* Turn your back to the parachute and hold it using the Overhand Grip. Plant your feet firmly with one foot forward and the other back. On signal "Pull!" lean away from the chute, pulling as hard as you can for ten seconds. Repeat in the kneeling position.

4. *Ball Shake:* I will put different types of balls on the parachute, starting with a beachball. How many times can you make the beachball bounce up into the air? Repeat using a playground ball; then a whiffle or tennis ball. Which one will bounce the best?

5. *Snake Shake:* (Place the skipping ropes on the chute.) How long will it take to shake all the "poisonous snakes" off the parachute? Don't let a snake touch you; otherwise, you must jog once around the play area, holding your poisoned part; then rejoin the game.

6. *Popcorn:* (Place all the beanbags on the chute.) How long will it take to "pop" all the popcorn (beanbags) off the chute? Try again. Can you beat your best score?

7. *Critter Shake:* How many times can you make my "critter" (stuffed toy) bounce into the air? Now place your plastic critters (dinosaurs, small farm or wild animals) on the chute. Shake them off!

8. *Wrist Roll:* Hold the parachute at waist level using the overhand grip with your arms fully extended. Stretch the chute until it is tight. Then on signal "Roll!" slowly roll the edge toward the middle. When the parachute is completely rolled, it is ready to put away.

GS-87 PARACHUTE NUMBER GAMES

FOCUS: Cooperation; listening; alertness **EQUIPMENT:** One parachute per group

ORGANIZATION:

• Have players evenly space themselves around the parachute and hold the seam using the overhand grip.

DESCRIPTION OF ACTIVITY:

1. *Number Chase:* Count off by four's around the chute. Remember your number! Begin by gripping the seam in the right hand and jogging in a CW direction. Listen to the number I call out. If your number is called, immediately release your grip on the chute and run forward toward the next vacated place. You will have to put on a burst of speed to reach the spot left by another player with that number.

— Repeat game, travelling in a CCW direction.

— Vary the way the players move: walk quickly, walk backwards, run, skip, gallop, side-step.

2. *Number Race:* (Divide the class into two equal teams, and have each team number off, 1, 2, 3, etc. Position each team around one half of the parachute.) On signal, inflate the chute and listen carefully to the number I call. The player on each team whose number is called, run as carefully and quickly as you can in a CCW direction around the outside of the chute. Can you return to your place before the center of the chute touches the floor?

— Repeat game, but travel in a CW direction.

— Repeat game, but I will call two numbers.

3. *Number Exchange:* (Number off players by five as they stand around the chute.) On signal, inflate the chute. As it fills with air, I will call out a number. Listen carefully. Everyone with that number, leave your place on the chute; move under the chute to another open place before the chute touches you. Look where you are going so that no collisions occur!

GS-88 MORE PARACHUTE GAMES

FOCUS: Cooperation; alertness

EQUIPMENT: One parachute per group; two different-colored balls

ORGANIZATION:

- Have players space themselves evenly around the parachute and hold it at waist level using the overhand grip. In the game "Jaws," encourage players attacked by Sharks to call for help. Discourage players from looking under the parachute.

DESCRIPTION OF ACTIVITY:

1. *Jaws:* (Choose two players to be the Sharks, who position themselves under the middle of the chute on all fours.) On signal "Go!" standing players, shake the chute gently to create waves while the Sharks swim around under the chute. Sharks, gently grab the leg of a parachute player and pull that player under the chute. The two players change roles and repeat the game until everyone has been a Shark.

1.

2. *Moon Walk:* (Number off the players by four's around the parachute. Then have them kneel on one knee with the other knee up and hold the chute taut at floor level.) You are going to take a walk on the moon! Be ready to leave your place and walk on the chute when your number is called. As the space-walkers move across the chute, the rest of the class gently shake it up and down at a low level, keeping the chute stretched. When I call a new number, space-walkers carefully return to your place and new space-walkers begin your turn.

2.

3. *Mousetrap:* (Select six to eight children to be the "mice.") On signal "Inflate!" chute players inflate the chute. Mice, try to run under the chute, across and out the other side, before the chute players can trap you. Chute players, wait patiently until you hear the signal "Trap!" before sealing the chute to the floor. The trapped Mice must join the chute players. The game continues until there is one Mouse left. Six new Mice are chosen and the game begins again. Mice, look carefully where you are going at all times!

4.

4. *Hole in One:* (Divide the class into two equal teams with each team positioned around one half of the parachute. Assign each team a colored ball and roll the balls onto the chute.) On signal "Play!" each team try to shake your ball into the center pocket and keep the other team from putting its ball through the center. Score one point each time your team puts the ball in the hole.

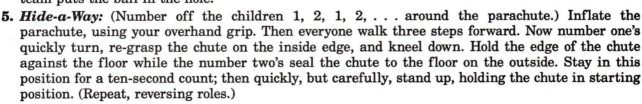

5.

5. *Hide-a-Way:* (Number off the children 1, 2, 1, 2, . . . around the parachute.) Inflate the parachute, using your overhand grip. Then everyone walk three steps forward. Now number one's quickly turn, re-grasp the chute on the inside edge, and kneel down. Hold the edge of the chute against the floor while the number two's seal the chute to the floor on the outside. Stay in this position for a ten-second count; then quickly, but carefully, stand up, holding the chute in starting position. (Repeat, reversing roles.)

GS-89 RHYTHMICAL PARACHUTE

FOCUS: Rhythmical movement; sequence-building

EQUIPMENT: One parachute per group; dance music of any type; tape or record player

ORGANIZATION:

• Working together, the children and you develop simple routines and dances that use the parachute as the focal point for movement. Try to incorporate all basic locomotor skills, different directions and levels, moving forward, backwards, and sideways, the exchanging of positions, and known dance steps.

DESCRIPTION OF ACTIVITY:

1. Let's make up a routine using our parachute:

   — Circle walk CW forward for eight steps, holding chute with right hands.

   — Circle walk CW backwards for eight steps.

   — Walk four steps toward the center, raising the chute upward.

   — Walk four steps away from the center, lowering the chute.

   — Gently shake the chute while you jump in place.

   — Side-step to the right for eight steps; then side-step to the left for eight steps.

   — Skip once around in a CCW direction, holding chute with your left hand.

   — Inflate and hide-a-way!

2. Modify dances such as "The Muffin Man," "Mulberry Bush," "Seven Jumps," "Jump Jim Jo," "Yankee Doodle," "Looby Lou," or any round dance from Section 4, "Rhythms and Dance," so that they can be performed around the parachute.

GS–90 INTRODUCING SCOOTERS

FOCUS: Teaching and safety guidelines; manipulation; control

EQUIPMENT: One scooter per player; one set of banners; several cone markers

ORGANIZATION:

• Relays and many other games can be adapted to scooter use if the size of the play area is reduced. One scooter per player is ideal; however, two players may share a scooter for many activities. Have each player get a scooter; then challenge players to try the following tasks on their own.

DESCRIPTION OF ACTIVITY:

1. *Safety:*
   — Scooters are not skateboards; do not stand on them.
   — Scooters are not missiles; with or without passengers, do not send them crashing into each other.
   — Watch your fingers! Do not drag your hands along the floor.
   — Before using your scooter, check that its casters fit tightly.

2. *Practice:*
   — Sit on your scooter, hold your feet off the floor, pushing only with your hands; can you move forward? Can you move backwards?
   — Now lower your feet to the floor. Try to propel yourself using only your feet. Move forward, then backwards.
   — Lie face down on your scooter, holding your feet off the floor. Show me how you can spin yourself around. Change direction and spin again!

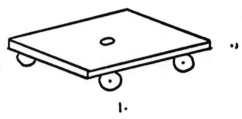

3. *Single Scooter Tasks:*
   — How can you kneel on your scooter and pull yourself forward? Now try to push yourself backwards. Can you push yourself around in a circle?
   — Show me how you can lie face down on your scooter and move forward using your hands and feet. Can you move forward using your feet only? Can you move backwards using your hands only?
   — Now gripping the sides of your scooter, show me how you can move forward; move backwards; move sideways.
   — Run into free spaces while holding the sides of the scooter. When you have gained speed, kneel on your scooter and glide as far as you can! Make sure you are always moving into open spaces.

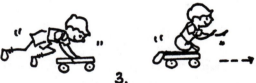

4. Show me your own way of moving on the scooter.

5. *Scooter Obstacle Course:* (Scatter cone markers throughout the play area.) Sitting on your scooter and using your feet only, zig-zag your way around the markers, moving forward at times and backwards at other times. Remember, watch your fingers; do not let them drag along the floor!

6. *Scooter Tag:* (Choose three players to be IT, who each wear a banner. All other players, in sitting position on their scooters, scatter around the play area.) On signal "Go!" IT players try to tag the others. A tagged player must put on a banner and help to tag, until all players are tagged. Who will be the last player to be caught?

GS–91 PARTNER SCOOTER FUN

FOCUS: Cooperative play

EQUIPMENT: One scooter per player

ORGANIZATION:

- Have players find a partner and get one scooter each before scattering around the play area.

DESCRIPTION OF ACTIVITY:

1. *Scooter Footwork:* Sit on your scooter in the following ways and show me how you can move forward, backwards, and sideways using your feet only:

I.

— Sit side-by-side with elbows linked.

— Sit back-to-back with elbows linked.

2. *Alligator Crawl:* Side-by-side with your partner, lie face down on your scooter and join inside hands. Show me how you can move forward; move backwards.

2.

3. *Pushcarts:* One partner, sit on one scooter and place your feet on the other. Have your partner push you in all directions. Change roles and repeat.

3.

4. *Pushcart Relay:* (Use cones to mark out a starting line and a turning line, 20 meters [60 feet] away. Ensure that there is ample turning room, away from any obstructions.) On signal "Go!" gently push your partner to the turning line. Once behind the line, carefully but quickly change positions, and return to your starting line. Which pair will cross the starting line first?

5.

5. Can you and your partner create another way of moving together?

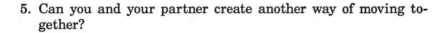

VARIATION:

Add On: Each player sits on a scooter and links elbows with another player. Each pair then links elbows with yet another pair to form groups of four, who then try to move together in this way without touching other groups.

GS-92 SCOOTER RELAYS

FOCUS: Cooperative activities; teamwork

EQUIPMENT: One scooter per player;
four cone markers per team;
one beanbag per team;
one ball per team

ORGANIZATION:

- Form equal teams of four players. Have each team stand in single-file formation at one end of the play area. Each of the first two players in each team has a scooter. Place a cone marker 10 meters (30 feet) from each team as a turning point.

- On the signal "Go!" each player in turn performs the following tasks as they move toward the cone marker, around it, and back to their team. As the first player crosses the starting line, the next player goes. The third player takes the first player's scooter and the first player goes to the end of the file. Have players upright any cone markers they knock over before returning to their team.

DESCRIPTION OF ACTIVITY:

1. **Two-Handed Relay:** Place two hands on the scooter, and run forward.

2. **Two-Hand, One-Foot Relay:** Place both hands and one foot on the scooter and push forward with your free foot. Change legs as you pass the cone marker.

3. **Kneeling Relay:** Kneel on your scooter and move forward using your hands only.

4. **Sitting Relay:** Sit backwards on your scooter and push forward with your feet.

5. **Lying Relay:** Lie face down on two scooters and push forward with your hands.

6. **Scooter File Relay:** (All players sit on scooters, spaced 1 meter [3 feet] apart, in a file. The last player holds a ball.) On signal "Go!" last player pass the ball to the player in front of you, who passes it to the next player, and so on. Front player, when you receive the ball, carry it on your scooter to the end of the file, and begin the passing from back to front again. The relay finishes when the front player is in original starting position. Repeat the relay with the front player starting the ball passing.

7. **Shuttle-Scooter Relay:** (All players sit on scooters, half the team facing the other half 10 meters [30 feet] away in shuttle formation. Player at the front of one file gets a beanbag.) On signal "Go!" player with the beanbag, move forward, hand the beanbag to opposite teammate, and go to the end of that file. Player with the beanbag, repeat the relay. Continue until all team members have had a turn. Repeat.

8. **Zig-Zag Relay:** (Place four cone markers in a row in front of each team, spacing them about 1 meter [3 feet] apart.) Each player in turn, zig-zag through the row of cone markers, circle the last cone in the row, and return directly to your team. Repeat.

9. **Siamese Twins Relay:** Each player sit on a scooter, in two's, side-by-side. First pair, linking elbows, move forward using your feet only. At the turning line, link other elbows together, and continue around the cone marker, back to your team. When you return to your team, the next pair may go. The relay ends when each pair has had three turns.

GS-93 SCOOTER GAMES

FOCUS: Cooperation; listening; alertness

EQUIPMENT: One scooter per player;
popular music;
tape or record player;
one whistle;
several banners;
one ball per game

ORGANIZATION:

• Have each player get a scooter and sit on it. Emphasize the importance of travelling safely on the scooters in open spaces.

DESCRIPTION OF ACTIVITY:

1. *Scooter Follow the Leader:* (Divide the class into groups of four to six players. Each group has a Leader and starts in a designated space of the play area. Encourage the use of a variety of body positions, different methods of propulsion, good use of space, and creativity.) Leader, when you hear the music, begin to move your team on their scooters in general space in any safe manner you choose. Other team members, imitate your leader's movements on the scooter. You must keep in contact with your scooter at all times! When you hear my whistle signal, then another player take over as leader. New Leader, can you move on your scooter in a different way for the rest of your group to copy? The activity is finished when everyone has had a turn at being leader.

2. *Frozen Tag:* (Choose three or four players to be IT, who wear banners and start in the middle of the play area. All other players scatter.) On signal "Go!" IT players, staying in the sitting position on your scooters, try to tag the free players. A tagged player is immediately "frozen" to the spot and must sit on his or her scooter, extending arms sideways. Another player can free the "frozen" player by passing under the extended arms. IT player, when you have made four tags, give your banner to the fourth player, who becomes the new IT.

3. *Scooter Ball Tag:* (Choose two or three players to be IT, have them start in the middle of the play area, and give them each a ball. All other players scatter around the play area.) On signal "Go!" IT player, try to tag a free player by touching him or her with the ball on the backside. Now tagged player, you are IT! Quickly retrieve the ball and begin the chase. Who can stay in the game the longest without being tagged?

4. *Scooter Team Tag:* (Form teams of five or six players.) The Leader of team one, give colored banners to your teammates. You are the IT team to start. Using a watch, I will time each team, in turn, as you try to tag all other players in one minute. Tagged players wheel slowly around the outside of the play area until the next game starts. Everyone must stay on your scooters throughout the game. The team making the most tags is the winner.

GS–94 STICK EXPLORATION

FOCUS: Manipulation; familiarization   **EQUIPMENT:** One hockey stick per player

ORGANIZATION:

- Children explore using a hockey stick in a variety of movement tasks, individually; then with a partner. Have each player get a stick and take it to a home space. Check for good spacing. Discuss the importance of using the stick safely at all times.

DESCRIPTION OF ACTIVITY:

1. Put your stick on the floor in front of you. Show me how many different ways you can travel along your stick:

   — Hopping back and forth over the stick.

   — Jumping from side-to-side over the stick.

   — Jumping forward and backwards over the stick.

   — Walking on the stick like a "tightrope walker."

   — Cross-walking along the stick from one end to the other.

   — Leaping over the stick and landing on two feet; on one foot.

   — Building a bridge over the stick with one part on one side, and one body part on the other side.

2.

2. Show me how you can "thread the needle" with your stick: hold it in both hands horizontally in front of you. Step one leg over the stick; then the other. Step one leg back, and then the other, without breaking your hand-hold.

3. Place one end of the stick on the floor and hold the other end upright. Show me how you can walk under your arm.

4. **Stick Tug-O-War:** Find a partner. Both grip one stick horizontally so that one hand is between your partner's hands. Try to pull your partner across a line between you.

4.

   — Hold the stick vertically and have a tug-o-war.

   — Grip the stick with one hand and pull; grip with the other hand and pull.

   — Challenge another player to the above tugs.

5. **Scottish Sticks:** On the floor, make a letter "X" with your sticks. Show me how you can move your feet in and out of the "X" without touching the sticks.

6. **Limbo Sticks:** One partner, hold the stick at different heights while your partner tries to move under the stick, keeping your belly button upward. How low can you limbo?

GS-95 THE GRIP AND CARRY

FOCUS: Holding the stick; footwork

EQUIPMENT: One hockey stick per player

ORGANIZATION:

- Children learn how to properly hold the stick; then they experiment with carrying the stick while they run in general space. Review the three main parts of the stick: the handle, the shaft, and the blade. Have each player get a stick and take it to a home space. Check for good spacing. As they perform the different tasks and challenges, observe how children stop and start. Do they lower their center of gravity (seat area) to stop? Do they push off with the back foot for a quick start?

DESCRIPTION OF ACTIVITY:

1. ***Holding the Stick:*** Place one hand at the top of the stick and the other hand down the shaft of the stick, about halfway down. Now change the position of your hands on the stick. Which way feels more comfortable to you?

2. ***Ready Position:*** Holding the stick with both hands, let the edge of the blade of the stick rest on the floor. Bend your knees slightly.

3. ***Carrying the Stick:*** Carry your stick in both hands, with the blade of the stick as low to the floor as possible. On my signal "Run—Straight!" run with your stick into empty spaces in a straight pathway. Try "Run—Curvy!"; "Run—Zig-zag!"

— Show me how you can run forward, backwards, or sideways, changing direction on my signal "Change!" On the signal "Freeze," stop immediately in the Ready Position. Remember to watch where you are going! (Combine two or more starting and stopping activities.)

— Can you begin running slowly; then suddenly burst into speed?

GS-96 STICK-HANDLING

FOCUS: Control; manipulation

EQUIPMENT: One hockey stick per player; one plastic ball or puck per player; several obstacles (cones or chairs)

ORGANIZATION:

- Players are introduced to the terms "carrying," "dribbling," and "stick-handling" the puck. In carrying the puck, the puck is always in contact with the blade, on one side only; in dribbling, the puck is moved with short taps in front of the body and in as straight a line as possible; in stick-handling, the puck is moved alternately from one side of the blade to the other, keeping the blade in front.
- Have each player collect a stick and a puck and take it to a home space. Sponge balls, tennis balls, and whiffle balls could be used as well as plastic pucks to ensure that each player has a puck or ball. In all these tasks, stress safety. Remind players to keep their heads up as they move around. Emphasize no body contact!

DESCRIPTION OF ACTIVITY:

1. You have learned to hold and carry your stick. Now you are ready to explore different ways of moving a puck or ball with your stick. Show me how you can move the puck along the floor so that it always stays touching one side of the stick blade. Can you "feel" the puck on your stick? This is called "carrying the puck."
   — Change directions on my signal "Change!" but keep your stick blade on the floor as you carry the puck.

2. Now show me how you can push the puck forward and in a straight line, using little taps. This is called "dribbling." Explore dribbling in different directions, always moving into open spaces.

3. Dribble the puck back to your home space. Staying in your home space, show me how you can move the puck from one side of the blade to the other. Do this slowly at first; then get faster. This is called "stick-handling."

4. All the boys freeze in your space. Girls, show me how you can stick-handle the puck in and out around the boys. Now girls freeze and boys stick-handle. Remember no body contact is allowed!

5. *The Obstacle Field:* (Scatter several cones and chairs throughout the play area.) Show me how you can control your puck as you carry, dribble, or stick-handle the puck through the obstacle field.

GS-97 STICK-HANDLING GAMES

FOCUS: Stick-handling control; alertness; defense

EQUIPMENT: One stick per player; one puck or ball for two thirds of the class; three cones or chairs per relay team

ORGANIZATION:

- This game reinforces the stick-handling skills and teaches players the concept of playing defense. For the first game, select one third of the class to be the Hockey Pirates, who each have a stick and stand in the center of the play area to start. Have the remaining two thirds of the class, the Free players, each get a stick and ball, and then scatter throughout the play area. Emphasize that absolutely no body contact is allowed!

- Players must play fairly. They cannot step on the puck or pin it against a wall.

DESCRIPTION OF ACTIVITY:

1. *Hockey Pirates:* On the signal "Pirates are coming!" Hockey Pirates, try to stick-handle the puck or ball away from the free players. Free players, as soon as you are without a puck or ball, you become a Pirate and must try to get the puck away from any Free player. Who will still have their puck or ball at the end of the game? Remember to look where you are going as you move around.

2. *Hockey Relay:* (Form groups of four. Have each group stand in a file behind a starting line and face a row of three cones or chairs spaced two meters [six feet] apart. Check for good spacing.) Each player, in turn, stick-handle in and out of the cones, around the last cone, and directly back to hand the puck off to the next player in the file. The relay finishes when everyone has had two turns and is sitting cross-legged in starting position.

GS-98 PASSING AND RECEIVING THE PUCK

FOCUS: Accurate passing; visual tracking; control

EQUIPMENT: One hockey stick per player; one puck or ball per player; two cone markers or chairs per player

ORGANIZATION:

- Players learn how to pass and receive the puck using their hockey sticks. Demonstrate the passing action: a smooth, sweeping motion with the blade following through in the line of direction. Demonstrate how to receive the puck: Keep eyes on the puck and cushion the pass as it touches the blade of the stick. Provide ample time to experiment and practice. Emphasize control!

- Have players pair up and each collect a hockey stick and one puck or ball between them; then find a free space.

DESCRIPTION OF ACTIVITY:

1. Face your partner and stand about 5 meters (15 feet) apart. Pass the puck back and forth to each other. Remember to stop and control the puck first before you pass it. After ten good passes, take one step back and continue to pass the puck back and forth. How far away can you pass and receive the puck with control?

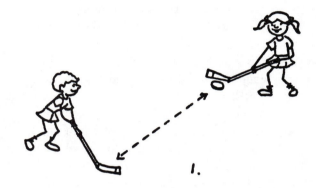

2. Now place two cone markers or chairs in the middle between the two of you. Experiment with spacing them far apart; then closer together as you try to pass the puck between the markers or through the chair's legs. Gradually move farther away from each other. Challenge your partner to make ten accurate passes first!

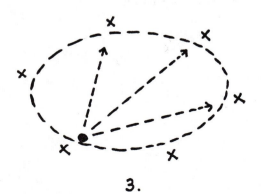

3. ***Pass-the-Puck Game:*** (Form groups of five or six players, who stand in a circle, spaced arm's length apart, and face inward. One player has the puck to begin.) Pass the puck to another player across the circle who is not on either side of you. How many passes can you make in two minutes?

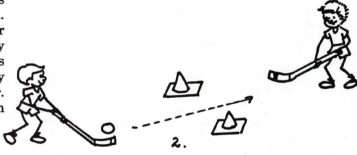

GS-99 SHOOTING THE PUCK/GOALTENDING

FOCUS: Technique; accurate shooting; goaltending

EQUIPMENT: One hockey stick per player; one puck or ball per player; two cone markers or pins per pair

ORGANIZATION:

- At first have children experiment with different ways of shooting the puck at a wall. Then introduce and demonstrate the "wrist shot" and "goaltending," or blocking a shot. Emphasize safety at all times! Have each player collect a stick and a puck or ball; then stand facing a wall four giant steps away.

DESCRIPTION OF ACTIVITY:

1. Shoot your puck or ball at the wall. Show me how you can field the puck as it comes off the wall. Shoot five times; then move one giant step away and repeat. Remember to stop the puck, get control, and then shoot it again.

2. One way of shooting the puck is called the "wrist shot."
   — Place the blade of the stick behind the puck so that it is touching.
   — Keep your eyes on the puck.
   — Use your lower hand to push the stick-blade through the puck. The puck should travel along the floor.
   — Let the blade follow through low and in line of direction; the blade of your stick should not follow through higher than hip level!
   — Practice this shot at the wall.

2.

3. *Goal-Scoring:* Find a partner. Together get two cone markers or pins. Space the cones a giant step apart, about one giant step from the wall. Take turns trying to shoot the puck through the cones to score a goal. Start three giant steps away from the cones. Take a look at your target; then keep your eyes on the puck as you shoot it.

3.

4. *Goaltending:* One partner be the goalie; the other partner be the shooter. Change roles after every ten shots. Goalie, place yourself between the cones in crouch position. Keep your eyes on the puck. Show me how you can use your stick and feet to stop the puck.

4.

GS-100 DECKRING SHOT

FOCUS: Lead-up game; hand-eye coordination

EQUIPMENT: One stick (no blade) per group;
three deckrings per group;
three plastic bleach bottles per group
two cone markers per group

ORGANIZATION:

- Divide players into groups of three and have each group collect three deckrings, three plastic bleach bottles, two cone markers, and one bladeless stick. Then have each group set up their equipment in a free space (near a wall of the play area, if possible). Check for good spacing. Allow children to experiment with the bottles being placed at different distances apart and gradually increasing the shooting distance.

DESCRIPTION OF ACTIVITY:

1. Place your three plastic bottles in a triangle formation about one giant step from a wall. Use the cones to mark off a shooting line four giant steps away from the bottles.

2. Each player, in turn, take three shots by placing the stick inside the deckring and pushing the deckring with your stick to try to knock over the bottles.

3. Players not shooting help by setting up the knocked-over bottles and sending the deckrings back to the shooter.

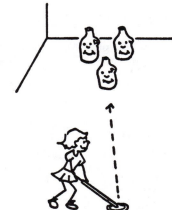

GS-101 MINI-HOCKEY

FOCUS: Lead-up game; stick skills; team play

EQUIPMENT: Four cone markers per group;
one hockey stick per player;
one puck or ball per group;
masking tape (optional)

ORGANIZATION:

- The skills of stick-handling, shooting, checking, and goaltending are reinforced in a game-like situation of three-on-three. Have each player get a hockey stick to start; then form groups of six. Each group collects four cone markers and one puck or ball. Using masking tape or the existing floor lines, divide the play area into five mini-courts (for a class size of about 30). Assign each group to a court and have them set up the goals at each end, using the cone markers. Each group of six plays a game of three-on-three in the assigned court. Observe the play closely, watching for dangerous swinging or raising of the sticks. Take immediate action!

DESCRIPTION OF ACTIVITY:

1. In your group of six, make two teams of three players. One player of the threesome is the Goalie; the other two players try to score a goal. Change roles often or after every goal that is scored.

2. Remember, there is no body contact! Don't bring your stick any higher than hip level or swing it dangerously. Always know where you are going and who is around you.

3. On my whistle signal, immediately stop the play. Rotate to the next court and play a game of three-on-three with the new team!

VARIATION: Divide the play area into three or four courts and play four-on-four mini-hockey.

GS-102 SIDELINE HOCKEY

FOCUS: Stick-handling; checking; shooting; goaltending; team play

EQUIPMENT: One hockey stick per player; one puck or ball per game; one whistle

ORGANIZATION:

- For each game form two equal teams and have each team line up on a sideline, facing each other. Have the players number off consecutively as shown. Then place a puck in the middle between the two sideline teams. Emphasize that no body contact is allowed and that sticks should not be raised higher than hip level

DESCRIPTION OF ACTIVITY:

1. When you hear your number called, the two players with that number run quickly to the puck, try to gain control, and then shoot it past one of the opposition sideline players to score a goal.

2. Sideline players, you are the "goalies." Stay just in front of the sideline and use your stick, feet, and free hand to prevent a goal from being scored.

3. When a Goalie makes a "save," I will blow the whistle. This is the signal for the play to stop, the puck to be returned to the middle, and players to return to their positions on the sideline. Then I will call a new number.

4. The team with the best score after all the numbers have been called is the winner.

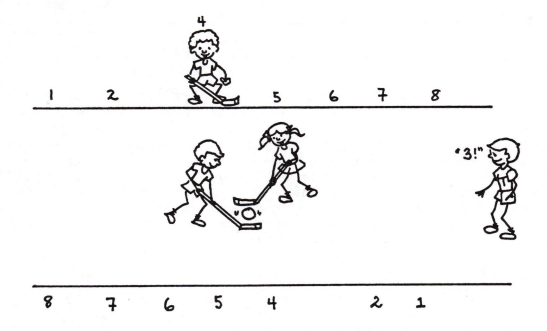

VARIATION:

Have two games going on at once to increase the participation.

GS–103 FOUR-STATIONS HOCKEY

FOCUS: Stick-handling; accurate shooting; passing; goaltending

EQUIPMENT: Four hockey nets;
seven deckrings;
six plastic bleach bottles;
eight bladeless hockey sticks;
six hockey sticks;
three folding mats;
three hockey pucks or balls;
floor tape or cone markers;
one whistle

ORGANIZATION:

- Partition the play area into four equal smaller areas and set up the suggested stations in each area. (If available, use benches turned over on their sides to mark off the four areas.) Then divide the class into four equal groups and assign each group to a station. Rotate groups every five to seven minutes on the whistle signal. Demonstrate the skill involved at each station. Emphasize safety at all times. At the finish, have each group put away the equipment.

DESCRIPTION OF ACTIVITY:

1. *Area 1, Ringette Hockey:* Play three-on-three or four-on-four hockey using a deckring, bladeless hockey sticks, and a net at opposite ends for each team.

2. *Area 2, Hockey Shoot:* (Position two nets in one quarter of the play area so that they are well spaced apart. Mark a shooting line 5 meters [15 feet] away from one net and another shooting line 6 meters [20 feet] away from the other net.) Take turns trying to score a goal, using the Wrist Shot.

3. *Area 3, Deckring Shot:* (Set up two identical stations with three plastic bottles in a triangle formation about one giant step from a wall. Use floor tape or cones to mark off the shooting line four giant steps away.) Take turns using the bladeless stick to send the deckring toward the bottles. How many bottles can you knock over in three tries?

4. *Area 4, Goalie Challenge:* (Position three folding mats, standing upright so they won't fall over, as goalie nets. Ensure that they are well spaced apart.) Each player, in turn, take five shots on goal to try and score. Goalie, how many saves can you make?

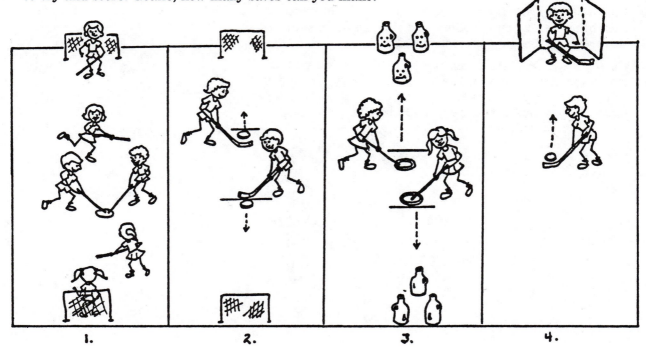

1.   2.   3.   4.

GS-104 BALLOON PADDLE PLAY

FOCUS: Grip; ready position; hand-eye coordination

EQUIPMENT: One paddle per player; one balloon per player

ORGANIZATION:

- Children explore using a paddle to strike different objects beginning with balloons; then the paddle is replaced by the "hand" striking a large playground ball. They also are introduced to the "ready position," which is basic for most racquet-type activities.
- To begin, have each player get a paddle and stand facing you in a home space. Check for good spacing.

DESCRIPTION OF ACTIVITY:

1. Turn to someone near you and shake that person's hand. Holding your paddle in your favorite hand, show me how you can "shake hands with it." Check that your thumb and second or index finger form a "V" which points to the edge of the "head" of the paddle.

2. Now turn and face me. Bend your knees slightly; keep your head up and back straight. Hold your paddle in front of you with your favorite hand in the "shake hands position" and your other hand on the "throat" of the paddle. This is called the "Ready Position."

3. On signal "Run!" run into open spaces. When I call the name of an object, quickly stop and face that object (door, climbing frame, ropes, blackboard, that wall) in the ready position.

4. Get a balloon and take it to your home space. Show me how you can use your paddle to bat the balloon. Don't let your balloon touch the floor! Can you hold the paddle in your other hand and keep the balloon up? Remember to keep your eyes on the balloon.

5. Find a partner and try to bat the balloon back and forth to each other using your paddle. Hold the paddle in your favorite hand; then in your other hand.

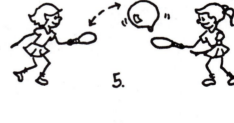

6. **Circle Balloon Bat:** Form groups of five or six players, who stand in a circle, spaced arm's length apart. How many times can your group bat the balloon before it touches the floor? Call "Mine!" if you are going to bat the balloon.

GS-105 BEANBAG PADDLE PLAY

FOCUS: Hand-eye coordination; visual tracking; right–left dexterity

EQUIPMENT: One paddle per player; one beanbag per player

ORGANIZATION:

• Have each player collect a paddle and a beanbag and find a free space. Check for good spacing.

DESCRIPTION OF ACTIVITY:

1. Walk with your Beanie on the paddle. Try to run; skip; gallop; side-step. Look for open spaces!

2. With your Beanie on the paddle, try to sit down; then stand up again without dropping the beanbag. Can you stand still and move the paddle all around your body; from hand to hand; high to low?

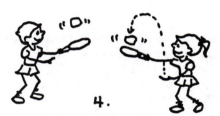

3. Place your beanbag on the paddle. Can you toss Beanie up off your paddle and catch it in your free hand? Can you catch Beanie between the paddle and your free hand? Switch hands and try this.

4. Who can toss the Beanie up with your free hand and catch it on the paddle? Can you toss it higher and still catch it? Can you use your other hand and still do this?

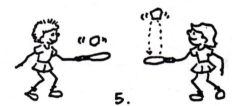

5. Show me how you can toss Beanie up off your paddle and catch it on your paddle. How many times can you toss and catch in this way without dropping the beanbag? Can you toss and catch the beanbag using your other hand?

6. Now try to toss Beanie up off your paddle as you hold it palm up (Forehand Position) and catch it on your paddle as you hold it palm down (Backhand Position). What other trick can you do using the paddle and your Beanie?

7. Find a partner. Stand facing each other about two giant steps apart. Place Beanie on your paddle. Can you toss Beanie back and forth and catch it with the paddle and hand? Can you catch it on the paddle only? Move one more giant step away from each other and do the activity again. Remember to watch the beanbag!

GS–106 BEACHBALL PADDLE PLAY

FOCUS: Manipulation; visual tracking; cooperation

EQUIPMENT: One beachball per pair; one paddle per player; several cone markers; several beachballs or light play balls

ORGANIZATION:

- Have players pair off. One partner gets a beachball (or light play ball) while the other partner gets two paddles; then each pair finds a free space. Check for good spacing.

DESCRIPTION OF ACTIVITY:

1. Show me how you can use your paddles to roll the beachball to each other. Use your favorite hand; then your other hand. Check your Handshake Grip.

2. Can you take turns bouncing the beachball with your paddle? Use your favorite hand; use your other hand.

1.

3. *Paddle Weave:* (Form teams of four players and arrange cone markers as shown. Have each player get a beachball or light play ball.) Follow the Leader, weaving in and out of the markers while rolling the ball. After your last marker, pick up the ball, place it on the paddle, and try to walk back to the start.

2.

3.

4. *Paddle Weave Relay:* (Form teams of four and have each team stand in a file facing a row of four cone markers or chairs. The leader has a paddle and a beachball to start.) On the signal "Weave!" each player, in turn, use your paddle to roll the beachball in and out of the cones, around the last cone and straight back to the file; then give the paddle and beachball to the next player, who does the same. After everyone has had two turns, sit cross-legged in your file. The first team to finish wins.

4.

GS-107 SMALL BALL PADDLE PLAY

FOCUS: Hand-eye coordination; manual dexterity

EQUIPMENT: One paddle per player; one small ball per player

ORGANIZATION:

- Use a variety of small balls such as tennis balls, sponge balls, rubber balls, and ping-pong balls. Encourage players to hold the paddle in their weaker hand as well as their favorite hand to perform these stunts. Have each player get a paddle and a small ball, and then find a free space. Check for good spacing.

DESCRIPTION OF ACTIVITY:

1. Hold the paddle in your "handshake" grip with the "V" between thumb and forefinger pointing toward the edge of the paddle. Try to balance the ball on your paddle while walking; running; galloping; side-stepping; skipping around the play area.

2. Put the ball on the floor. Show me how you can guide the ball into empty spaces over the play area. Can you use both sides of the paddle? Watch out for others!

3. How can you use your paddle to bounce the ball to the floor? Paddle-bounce the ball low; high; from high to low; from low to high. Who can paddle-bounce the ball while turning in a circle?

4. Now put the ball on your paddle. Try to tap the ball up, let it bounce once, and then tap it back up. How long can you keep this going? How many times can you bounce the ball on the paddle into the air without missing?

5. Stand near a wall, about three giant steps away. Turn yourself sideways to the wall, so that your weaker side is nearest the wall. Hold the ball in your weak hand, palm up, and the paddle in your favorite hand. Toss the ball slightly upward and out in front of you, let it bounce once, and then hit it with your paddle toward the wall. Repeat several times.

6. Now find a partner. Stand about four giant steps away from each other. Can you let the ball bounce once; then gently hit it with your paddle to your partner? Remember to watch the ball!

7. Invent a trick of your own using your paddle and ball.

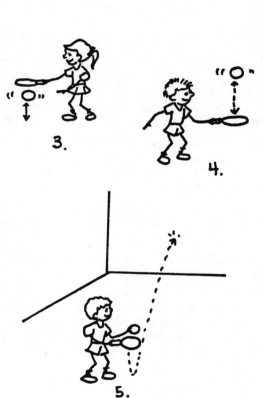

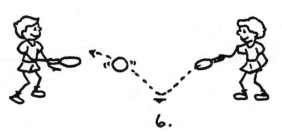

FOCUS: Striking; visual tracking; manual dexterity; footwork

EQUIPMENT: One 15-centimeter (6-inch) utility ball per player

ORGANIZATION:

- Children now explore using either hand to hit the ball to a wall. Have each player get a ball and stand facing a wall about three giant steps away. Check for good spacing.

DESCRIPTION OF ACTIVITY:

1. Show me how you can hit the ball to the wall with one hand. Let it bounce once; then hit it with your hand. Which part of your hand is the best to hit the ball? (Hit with the heel of the open hand.) How should you stand to hit the ball? (Stand sideways to the wall, with the non-hitting shoulder closest to the wall.) Can you let the ball bounce and as it comes up off the floor hit it with one hand? Practice. Remember to keep your eyes on the ball! Try to use your other hand to hit the ball to the wall.

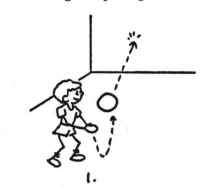

2. Now hold the ball in one hand and try to hit it off this hand with your other hand. Catch the ball as it comes off the wall, and try this again. Practice.

3. Can you hit the ball to the wall, let it bounce once off the wall, and then hit it back to the wall? How many times can you do this without missing?

4. *Handball Target:* (Tape targets on the wall so that two can share a target.) Try to hit the target with your right hand five times; left hand five times.

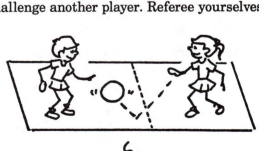

5. Find a partner and stand facing each other on either side of a line. Explore hitting the ball back and forth to each other.

6. *Two-Square:* (Use floor tape or paint to mark out as many 1-meter by 2-meter [4-foot by 8-foot] courts and a center line as needed. Have players pair off. Each pair gets a ball; players then stand facing each other on one side of the two-square court. Emphasize that players be in "Ready Position" and keep their heads up.) One partner, start the game by serving it: Drop the ball and hit it on the first bounce with your open hand into the other player's square. Continue hitting back and forth until one player misses. Play to five points. Then challenge another player. Referee yourselves and keep your own score.

   Rules:
   — On the line is in.
   — The ball must clear the center line and bounce in the other player's side.
   — Either hand or both hands may be used.
   — The ball must be hit after the first bounce.

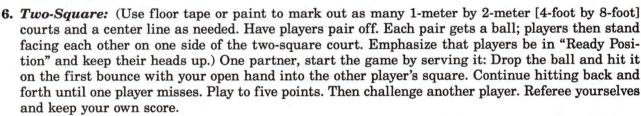

VARIATIONS:

a. *Two-Square:* Allow the ball to bounce twice before being hit.

b. Have pairs explore using different-sized balls: sponge ball, tennis ball, rubber ball, whiffle ball, etc.

c. Let each pair make up their own rules for the game.

Section 7

Special Games

Special Games activities develop leadership, cooperation, self-esteem, creativity, and a sense of fair play. The emphasis throughout these activities is on fun and teamwork, not winning or losing.

The 46 Special Games in Section 7 are organized into Relays, Low-Organized Games, and Play Day Activities. They include:

SG-1 SIMPLE LOCOMOTOR RELAYS

FOCUS: Basic locomotor movements; teamwork   **EQUIPMENT:** Four cone markers

ORGANIZATION:

- Use cones to mark the starting line and turning line, 10 meters (30 feet) apart. Form equal teams of four to six players and have each team stand in single file formation behind the starting line. Teams should be spaced at least 2 meters (6 feet) apart. Keep teams as small as possible to allow for maximum participation. If there is an unequal number of players in the lines, have a member of that line go twice.
- Emphasize that players wait behind the starting line until they receive the hand touch to go. Encourage team members to cheer for each other.

DESCRIPTION OF ACTIVITY:

1. On signal "Go!" the first player in each single file move forward to the turning line, touch it with your foot, and then run back to your file. Pass by on the right side of your file, touching the left hand of the next player in line, and then stand at the end of the file. (Have participants perform the following locomotor movements: running; hopping; galloping; slide-stepping; skipping; walking backwards; walking heel-to-toe; walking on heels only; galloping to turning point and then slide-stepping back.)

2. We will continue in this way until everyone has had a turn. The first team to complete the activity and sit cross-legged in their file is the winner.

TURNING LINE

VARIATIONS:

a. Assign a different locomotor movement to each team member: #1—Walk backwards: #2—Skip; #3—Slide-step; #4—Hop.

b. Repeat the relay in pairs.

c. Gradually lengthen the distance between the starting and turning lines.

d. **_Jump Relay:_** On signal "Jump!" the first player jumps as far as possible from the starting line, lands, and holds position. Then the second player places toes even with the first player's heels and jumps as far as possible. The relay continues in this way until each player has had a turn. Which team will jump the farthest? (Emphasize that players jump with both feet about shoulder-width apart, "pump" with their arms, and bend at the knees to cushion the landing.)

SG-2 ZIG-ZAG RELAYS

FOCUS: Agility; speed running; teamwork

EQUIPMENT: Cone markers, chairs, hoops, beanbags, deckrings or pins as obstacles; lively music; tape or record player

ORGANIZATION:

- Arrange each team of four to five players in single file formation behind a starting line and facing a row of four or five cone markers, spaced about 3 meters (10 feet) apart. If there is an unequal number of players in the files, have a member of that file go twice. Emphasize that players wait behind the starting line until tagged.

DESCRIPTION OF ACTIVITY:

1. On the signal "Go!" the first player of each team, run in and out of the cone markers, around the end cone, and back to your file. Tag the next team player, who runs the same course. Continue until every player has had a turn.
2. The first team to complete the course and sit cross-legged in their file is the winner.

VARIATIONS:

a. Have players carry an object such as a large ball while they zig-zag through the cones.
b. Have teams go through the course twice in pairs.
c. *Obstacle Relay:* Using chairs, tables, hoops, benches, high jump standards and poles, create a variety of obstacles to go around, under, over, through, on, and off.

SG-3 SHUTTLE RELAYS

FOCUS: Speed running; fair play; shuttle formation

EQUIPMENT: Four cone markers; lively music (optional); tape or record player

ORGANIZATION:

- Use cones to mark out two lines 20 meters (60 feet) apart. Form equal teams of four to six players. To arrange teams in shuttle formation, have half the players stand facing the other half behind each of the lines. Remind players to stay behind their starting lines until they receive the hand touch.

DESCRIPTION OF ACTIVITY:

1. On signal "Go!" the first player, run toward the other half of your team, give "ten!" (lightly slap both hands) to the second player, and go to the end of that file.
2. The second player run across to the opposite file, giving "ten!" to the third player, and go to the end of that file.
3. The relay continues until all players are in their starting positions and sitting cross-legged.

VARIATIONS:

a. Use a variety of locomotor movements: skipping; slide-stepping; hopping; walking backwards.
b. Have players carry an object (beanbag; deckring; baton; beachball) to the opposite player.
c. Challenge teams to see which team can make the most number of crossings in two minutes.

SG-4 ANIMAL WALK RELAY

FOCUS: Agility; arm-shoulder strength; teamwork   **EQUIPMENT:** Four cone markers

ORGANIZATION:

- Use cones to mark out a starting line and turning line that are 10 meters (30 feet) apart. Form teams of four or five players, who stand in single file formation just behind the starting line; each team about 2 meters (6 feet) from each other. Adjust the "walking distance" to the ability level of the players. If there are unequal teams, a player may have to go twice.

DESCRIPTION OF ACTIVITY:

1. Each player, in turn, perform an "Animal Walk" to the turning line and back to your file in this way:
   — First Player—"Puppy Dog Walk" on hands and feet, with your trunk facing downward.
   — Second Player—"Crab Walk" on hands and feet, with your trunk facing upward and feet leading.
   — Third Player—"Frog Walk" by leaping forward with hands together, and then feet together.
   — Fourth Player—"Seal Walk" by using only your hands and dragging your feet.
   — Fifth Player—"Bear Walk" by moving forward with your right hand and foot, and then your left side.

2. The first team to complete the relay and sit in cross-legged position is the winner.

VARIATIONS:

a. *Animal Walk Shuttle:* Arrange teams in shuttle formation and perform relay as above.

b. Include other "Walks" such as: "Spider Walk"—same position as for the Crab Walk but head leads; "Lame Dog Walk"—same position as for Puppy Dog Walk except that one foot is in the air.

SG-5 RESCUE RELAY

FOCUS: Speed running; teamwork   **EQUIPMENT:** Four cone markers; lively music (optional); tape or record player

ORGANIZATION:

- Use cones to mark a starting and turning line 10 meters (30 feet) apart. Form teams of four or five players in each team. Arrange teams in single file formation behind the starting line and spaced about 2 meters (6 feet) from each other. The leader of each team stands on the turning line, facing his or her team.

DESCRIPTION OF ACTIVITY:

1. On the signal "Go!" the leader, run to the first player of your team, grasp him or her by the wrist, and both run back to the leader's turning line.

2. While the leader remains at this line, the rescued player run back and get another player.

3. Continue the relay in this way until all the players are rescued. The first team to complete the task and sit cross-legged wins the relay.

VARIATION: Vary the way the players are rescued, such as: linking elbows; holding both hands while slide-stepping; hopping together on one foot each.

SG–6 THE COMPASS RELAY

FOCUS: Speed running; fair play

EQUIPMENT: One beanbag per circle;
lively music (optional);
tape or record player

ORGANIZATION:

- Form teams of six to eight players. Have each team stand in a circle facing outward, with members spaced arm's length apart. Players number off around the circle. The first player of each team holds a beanbag.

DESCRIPTION OF ACTIVITY:

1. On the signal "Go!" the first player, run CCW around the outside of the circle to your starting position and hand the beanbag to the second player, who repeats the circle run. Continue until everyone in your team has had a turn.

2. The first team to complete the activity and sit cross-legged in your circle is the winner.

VARIATIONS:

a. Have players run CW around the circle.
b. Repeat relay using other manipulative equipment such as deckrings, beachballs, and playground balls that must be handed off from one player to the next.

SG–7 AROUND-THE-WORLD RELAY

FOCUS: Speed running; ball control; fair play

EQUIPMENT: One ball per team;
lively music (optional);
tape or record player

ORGANIZATION:

- Form teams of five or six players. Have teams make one big circle, with each team being one quarter of the circle and all circle players facing outward, spaced arm's length apart. Each team numbers off its members: 1, 2, 3, . . . , 5 or 6. If there is an unequal number of players in the teams, adjust by having a player go twice for his or her team. Remind players that when passing another runner, go around the outside of that runner. Give the first player of each team a ball to hold.

DESCRIPTION OF ACTIVITY:

1. On the signal "Go!" the first player, bounce the ball CCW around the outside of the circle to your starting position. Give ball to the second player, who repeats the circle run. Continue until everyone in your team has had a turn.

2. The first team to complete the activity and sit cross-legged in their quarter of the circle is the winner.

VARIATION: Have players bounce ball CW around the circle.

SG-8 LEAPFROG RELAY

FOCUS: Coordination; cooperation; fair play

EQUIPMENT: Four cone markers

ORGANIZATION:

- Mark a starting line and a finishing line with cones and form teams of five or six players. Each team is in single file formation behind the starting line, with players spaced one meter (three feet) apart and kneeling on their knees and elbows, head tucked low. Remind players to keep their heads tucked until the last player has leaped over them. Emphasize that the last player may not go until he or she hears the signal.

DESCRIPTION OF ACTIVITY:

1. On the signal "Go!" the last player, "leapfrog" over each of the players until you reach the front of the file; then quickly yell out "Ribbit!" and sink down to the starting position.

2. Last player, as soon as you hear the signal "Ribbit!" perform the same leapfrog action.

3. Continue the relay in this way until all your team members are over the finishing line.

VARIATIONS:

a. *Leapfrog Race:* The first team to go through its file twice is the winner.

b. *Snake Crawl Relay:* The last player crawls under his or her team members' legs to the front of the file and gives the signal "HISS!" for the new last player to go.

SG-9 KANGAROO JUMP RELAY

FOCUS: Leg strength; coordination; fair play

EQUIPMENT: One small playground ball per team; four cone markers

ORGANIZATION:

- Arrange teams of six players in shuttle formation, with each half of the team in a file behind a line marked out with cones; lines 5 meters (15 feet) apart.
- The first player of each team holds a ball between the ankles or knees. Adjust the jumping distance to the ability level of the players. Allow players to use their knees instead of their ankles.

DESCRIPTION OF ACTIVITY:

1. On signal "Go!" each player, in turn, place the ball between your ankles and jump across to the opposite side, leave the ball in front of the first player there, and join the end of that file.

2. If the ball drops out, you must retrieve it, and then continue across to the opposite side from this point.

3. The first team to finish in starting position and sit cross-legged is the winner.

VARIATIONS:

a. Use beanbags instead of playground balls.

b. *Head Ball Relay:* Have team members pair off in shuttle formation. Pairs transport a beachball or large playground ball between their heads to the opposite pair.

SG–10 UNDER PASSING RELAY; OVERHEAD PASSING RELAY; OVER-AND-UNDER PASSING RELAY; DOWN-AND-UP ROLLING RELAY

FOCUS: Team work; ball handling

EQUIPMENT: One large ball per team; masking tape

ORGANIZATION:

- Tape two "X's," spaced about 5 meters (15 feet) apart, on the floor for each team, as shown. Arrange each team of four or five players in a single file formation, with the first and last players standing on the tape crosses and the other players equally spaced between these two players. The first player of each team holds a ball. All team members stand with feet wide apart.

DESCRIPTION OF ACTIVITY:

1. *Under Passing Relay:* On the signal "Go!" pass the ball through your legs to the player behind you until it reaches the last player. The last player, carrying the ball with you, quickly run to the front of the file to the tape mark and pass it down through the legs again; everyone else move one position backwards. Continue the relay in this way until you are in your starting positions. The first team to sit cross-legged is the winner.

2. *Overhead Passing Relay:* Repeat relay, but this time pass the ball overhead to the player behind.

3. *Over-and-Under Passing Relay:* The first player, pass the ball overhead to the second player, who passes it through the legs to the third player, who passes it overhead to the fourth player, and so on. The last player, carry the ball to the front, stand on the tape cross, and pass the ball overhead to the second player, etc.; everyone else move one position backwards. The first team to sit cross-legged in the starting position is the winner.

4. *Down-and-Up Rolling Relay:* The first player, start the ball rolling through each player's legs. End player, when the ball reaches you, yell out "Down!" All team members, squat down low so that the end player can straddle hop forward over you to become the front player. End player, when you reach the front tape mark, yell "UP!" Team members, quickly stand up with your legs wide apart so that the ball can once again be rolled through the legs to the new end player. Continue in this way until you are in your starting positions. The first team to sit cross-legged is the winner.

SG-11 DROP-AND-FETCH RELAY

FOCUS: Speed running; fair play

EQUIPMENT: One hoop and one beanbag per team; lively music; tape or record player

ORGANIZATION:

- Arrange each team of four or five players in single file formation behind a starting line, facing a hoop placed 6 to 9 meters (20 to 30 feet) away. The Leader of each team holds a beanbag. If there is an unequal number of players on the teams, adjust by having a player go twice for his or her team. Remind players to put the beanbag in the hoop; not throw it in.

DESCRIPTION OF ACTIVITY:

1. On the signal "Go!" the Leader, carrying the beanbag, run forward toward the hoop and drop it inside the hoop. Return to your team to tag the next player.

2. The second player, run forward to fetch the beanbag and return to your file to hand it to the third player, who runs to the hoop and drops the beanbag inside of it.

3. Continue dropping and fetching the beanbag until everyone has had a turn. The first team to finish and sit cross-legged wins the relay.

VARIATION: Substitute a bowling pin for the beanbag and stand it up inside the hoop.

SG-12 ROLL-AND-CATCH RELAY

FOCUS: Rolling and catching; teamwork

EQUIPMENT: One playground ball per team

ORGANIZATION:

- Form teams of five or six players, who stand in a single file formation. The Leader of each team holds a ball and stands out 3 to 5 meters (10 to 15 feet) in front of his or her team. Emphasize that the ball must be rolled, not thrown or bounced, with control.

DESCRIPTION OF ACTIVITY:

1. On signal "Roll!" Leader, roll the ball to each player in turn, starting with the first player in the file. Players, stop the ball with two hands, and then roll it back to your Leader and go to the end of your file.

2. Leader, when you have rolled the ball to everyone on your team, go to the end of the file, and the first player of the file becomes the new Leader.

3. When everyone has had a turn at being leader and the original Leader is holding the ball in starting position, you are finished. Which team will be the quickest?

VARIATION:

Bounce-and-Catch Relay: Players must bounce-pass the ball to each other.

SG-13 HORSE-AND-BUGGY RELAY

FOCUS: Speed running; partnerwork

EQUIPMENT: One hoop per team;
one cone marker per team;
two line markers;
lively music (optional);
tape or record player

ORGANIZATION:

- Use cones to mark out a starting line at one end of the play area. Form equal teams of six to eight players and have team members pair off. Each team stands in a single file behind the starting line facing a cone marker or turning point, 10 meters (30 feet) away. Have the first pair of each team get a hoop.

- Emphasize that pairs run safely together. Remind pairs to stay behind the starting line until they receive the hoop.

DESCRIPTION OF ACTIVITY:

1. On the signal "Go!" the first pair, gripping the hoop on either side, run toward the cone marker, around it, and back to your file. Hand the hoop to the next pair, who repeats the run.

VARIATION

2. The relay continues in this way until all pairs have had a turn. The first team to finish with pairs in cross-legged sit position is the winner.

VARIATION:

Have one partner step inside the hoop and hold it at the sides at waist level, while the other partner holds the hoop behind. Repeat relay as above.

SG–14 THREE-STUNT RELAY

FOCUS: Agility; strength; teamwork

EQUIPMENT: Eight cone markers;
one hoop per team;
lively music;
tape or record player

ORGANIZATION:

- Form teams of four or five players and have each team stand in single file formation behind a starting line. Mark three lines in front of and parallel to the starting line, all spaced three meters (ten feet) apart. Place a hoop on the first line in front of each team. The players will do a different stunt at each line.

DESCRIPTION OF ACTIVITY:

1. On signal "Go!" each player, in turn, run forward and perform a different stunt at each of the three lines; then return to your team to tag the next player in the file.

   Suggestions:

   — Jump in and out of a hoop four times at the first line.

   — Place one hand on the floor and pivot around it twice at the second line.

   — Kneel and touch left elbow and right knee to the third line.

2. Continue until all players have performed the stunts. The first team to complete the relay and sit cross-legged in file formation at the starting line is the winner.

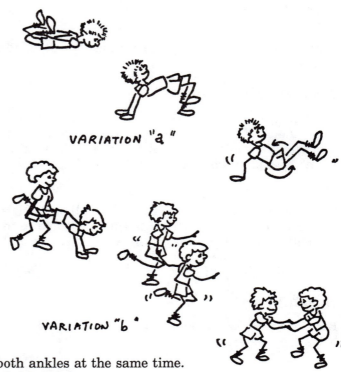

VARIATION "a"

VARIATION "b"

VARIATIONS:

a Ideas for other stunts include the following:
   —At the first line, lie face down and grasp both ankles at the same time.
   —At the second line, make a four-point back-bridge.
   —At the third line, hook-sit on the floor, and then spin around three times with your feet off the floor.
b. Have each player find a partner and repeat relay, performing partner-stunts at each line:
   —"Partner Wheelbarrow" to the first line.
   —"Partner Two-Leg Hop" to the second line.
   —"Partner Slide-Step" to the third line.

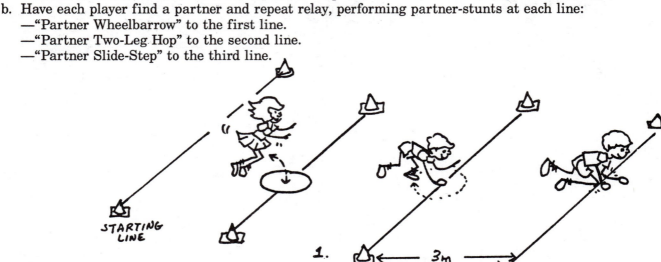

STARTING LINE

1.   ← 3m →

SG–15 MIDNIGHT

FOCUS: Running and dodging; alertness

EQUIPMENT: Two cone markers; masking tape or chalk

ORGANIZATION:

- Use cones to mark out two parallel lines that are 20 meters (60 feet) apart. Mark out a 2-meter (6-foot) square in the middle of the play area between the two lines. This is the Fox's Den. Choose a player to be the Fox, who stands in the den. Have players, the Chickens, stand on either line, facing the Fox.

DESCRIPTION OF ACTIVITY:

"TWO O'CLOCK!"

FOX'S DEN

1. Chickens, move toward the Fox's den and ask the question "What time is it?" throughout the game.
2. The Fox, answer "Three O'Clock"; "Ten O'Clock"; "Six O'Clock"; etc. Chickens, whatever time the Fox calls out, strut toward him or her, taking that number of walks.
3. When the Fox says "Midnight!" Chickens, run quickly back to your home line before the Fox can tag you with a one-hand touch. If tagged, you become a helper to the Fox and go to his or her den.

VARIATIONS:

a. Have players wear flags, tucked into the back of the waistband of their shorts, which can be pulled out to be caught.
b. Have the first player to be caught become the new Fox and start the game again.
c. Have more than one Fox.

SG–16 MOUSETRAP

FOCUS: Running and dodging; alertness

EQUIPMENT: None

ORGANIZATION:

- Divide the class into two equal teams. Have the players of one team join hands to form a circle and face the center. The other team players scatter around the outside of the circle. Circle players form the Mousetrap; the other players are the Mice. Emphasize that Mousetrap players listen carefully to the signals to make the trap effective. Warn Mice not to bump heads when they scamper in and out of the trap.

DESCRIPTION OF ACTIVITY:

1. On the signal "Go!" Mice, skip CCW around the outside of the circle, humming happily to yourself. Meanwhile, Mousetrap, move in a CW direction around the circle.
2. On the signal "Open!" the circle players, stop and set the trap by raising your joined hands to form arches. Mice, this is your chance to scamper in and out through the arches of the trap.
3. On the signal "Snap!" circle players, quickly drop your arms. All Mice inside are trapped and must join the circle.
4. Continue the game in this way until all the Mice are caught; then Mousetrap players and Mice exchange roles and a new game begins.

VARIATION: Vary the way the Mousetrap and the Mice move: slide-step, gallop, walk backwards.

SG–17 RED LIGHT

FOCUS: Alertness; fair play

EQUIPMENT: Four cone markers

ORGANIZATION:

• Use cones to mark out a starting line at one end of the play area and a finish line at the other end. Ensure that the finish line is located a minimum of 1.7 meters (8 feet) from any wall or obstruction. Have players, the Cars, stand in a line formation at one end of the play area, facing a Police Officer, who stands at the opposite end.

DESCRIPTION OF ACTIVITY:

1. Police Officer, you will tell the Cars when to move forward and when to stop, using the signals "Green Light" and "Red Light."

2. When you call "Green Light!" turn your back on the Cars, and slowly count to ten to yourself. Cars, move forward as quickly and quietly as you can.

3. Now Police Officer call "Red Light!" and then turn toward the Cars. Send any Car that you see moving back to the starting line. Cars, stop immediately on the signal "Red Light!" and remain frozen to the spot.

4. The first Car to cross the finish line becomes the new Police Officer for the next game.

VARIATION: Allow Police Officer to call "Red Light!" at any time he or she pleases.

SG–18 RED ROVER

FOCUS: Running; teamwork

EQUIPMENT: None

ORGANIZATION:

• Form two equal teams and have each team stand in line formation, hands joined, about 6 meters (20 feet) apart. Each team is given time to decide who will be called over.

DESCRIPTION OF ACTIVITY:

1. One team start the game by calling out together, "Red Rover, Red Rover, we call (name of a player from the other team) over!"

2. The player named, run across to the opposite side and try to break through the line in one try only. If you do so, you may choose any player from that team and take him or her back to join your team. If you are unsuccessful in breaking through, you must join the other team.

3. Teams, you will take turns calling a player over. The team having the most players at the end of the game wins.

VARIATION: Have one team call a boy over the first time, and then a girl the next time.

SG-19 FROG IN THE POND

FOCUS: Quickness; reaction time

EQUIPMENT: One hoop per team

ORGANIZATION:

- Form teams of five to six players per team. Have a leader, the Frog, for each team knee-sit inside a hoop, the Pond. Ensure that ponds are well spaced so that no interference occurs. All other players, the Flies, scatter around the pond.

DESCRIPTION OF ACTIVITY:

1. Flies, move around the pond, singing together:

   "Frog in the pond, how quick can you be?

   Frog in the pond, can you catch me?" (Step toward the Frog, daring it to tag you.)

2. Frog, reach out and try to tag one of the Flies without leaving your pond. A tagged Fly becomes the new Frog, and the game begins again.

VARIATION: If playing the game in a gym, use the basketball circles as ponds and have two or three frogs in each pond.

SG-20 CHARLIE OVER THE WATER

FOCUS: Alertness

EQUIPMENT: None

ORGANIZATION:

- Have players join hands to form a large circle. Choose one player to be Charlie, who stands in the center. (You could substitute the center player's real name for Charlie.) Remind players that they must keep their balance while squatting; otherwise, if they fall, they could be tagged.

DESCRIPTION OF ACTIVITY:

1. Circle players, skip around the circle in a CW direction, chanting:

   "Charlie over the water, Charlie over the sea,

   Charlie caught a bluebird, but can't catch me!"

2. On the word "me!" circle players, drop hands and quickly squat down, touching the ground with both hands.

3. Charlie, try to tag a circle player before he or she can squat down. A player tagged becomes the new Charlie, and the game continues.

VARIATIONS:

a. Vary the locomotor movements as players travel around the circle: slide-step; gallop; walk backwards.

b. Instead of squatting, use other positions such as crab-walk position; push-up position; balancing on one foot; dead-bug position (back-lying position with limbs in the air); front-lying position holding your ankles.

c. If played in a gym, players are safe only if they are standing on a bench (placed around the perimeter of the play area).

FOCUS: Listening; cooperation   **EQUIPMENT:** None

ORGANIZATION:

• Have players sit cross-legged in the listening circle. Explain the signals that will be used in this game, and have players practice the actions until they know them well; then play the game. Caution players to move carefully to avoid any collisions.

DESCRIPTION OF ACTIVITY:

1. I am going to be the **Fish Gobbler.** When I call out:

   — Ship!, run as quickly as you can toward this wall that I am pointing to.

   — Shore!, quickly change direction and run toward the opposite wall.

2. **Crabs:** Players stand back-to-back with a partner, bend over, and reach under your legs to hold your partner's hands. Now try to move sideways in either direction.

3. **Sardines:** Players, run to the middle of the play area, sit down there, and safely squeeze as close together as possible, like sardines in a can!

4. **Clams:** Quickly find a partner. One partner hook sit, while the other partner sits on your knees.

5. On the signal **Fish Gobbler,** quickly "hit the deck" (lie down on the floor) and link arms, legs, or bodies together with other players. I will move around the play area like a giant flying fish, trying to catch you. You are safe as long as you are linked together. If I catch you, you must do a special task for me; then you may rejoin the game.

6. When I see that everyone is safely linked together, I will call out **Rescue.** Quickly jump to your feet, join hands in a big circle, and yell as loudly as you can, "Tuna!" raising your joined hands overhead.

VARIATIONS:

a. **Fishnet:** Players, scamper up the climbing frame to a safe height and hang on, "caught" in the net.

b. **Sharkfin:** Players, get in groups of four and "swim" around in a circle.

c. **Fish Hook:** Let players decide what action this signal will be.

SG–22 MUSICAL HOOPS

FOCUS: Quick reaction

EQUIPMENT: One hoop per player;
lively music;
tape or record player

ORGANIZATION:

- Have each player get a hoop, take it to a home space, and sit cross-legged inside the hoop. Use music to start and stop the activity. Remind players to watch where they are going to avoid collisions. Emphasize that players cannot skip just around their hoop, but must skip into open spaces, and that only one player can stand in a hoop at a time. Explain the meaning of "fair play" and why players must be behind the line when the numbers are called.

DESCRIPTION OF ACTIVITY:

1. When you hear the music, leave your hoop and skip in and out of the other hoops on the floor. I will remove a hoop, or perhaps two hoops.
2. When the music stops, quickly jump inside a hoop; only one player to a hoop, please! Who will we catch without a "home"?
3. Homeless players, you will have to perform a task, and then you may rejoin the game. The game continues in this way.

VARIATION:

Cooperation Hoops: Each time the music stops, another hoop is removed so that players will have to share their hoop space with others. Challenge the class to see how many hoops will be needed to safely hold the whole class!

SG–23 WORM GRAB

FOCUS: Alertness; agility; fair play

EQUIPMENT: One short rope per player;
one hoop per game

ORGANIZATION:

- For each game, form two equal teams and arrange the teams in two lines about 6 meters (20 feet) apart, standing and facing each other. For a larger class, set up two games and conduct them simultaneously. Give each team a bird's name; for example, "Robins" and "Blue Jays." Have the players in each team number off: 1, 2, 3, etc. Use a 1-meter (3-foot) circle, or hoop, in the middle between the two lines. Place a rope in the circle.

DESCRIPTION OF ACTIVITY:

1. When I call out a number—for example, "3!"—the two players with that number, run to the circle and try to grab the worm (rope) first and return with it to your starting line.
2. Then I will add another rope to the circle and call another number.
3. When all players have had a turn (or several turns), each team will count the worms it has collected and we will see which team has more.
4. Let's play the game again!

SG-24 RUN, RABBITS, RUN

FOCUS: Running and dodging

EQUIPMENT: Two cone markers; one flag per player

ORGANIZATION:

- Use cones to mark a safety line, located a minimum of 1.7 meters (8 feet) from any wall or obstruction, at one end of the play area. Call the area behind this line the Rabbit Burrow and the area in front, the Woods. Divide the class into two equal groups: the Foxes who walk through the woods, and the Rabbits who stand side by side on their "home" line, facing the woods. Each Rabbit has a tail or a flag tucked into the back of the waistband of his or her shorts or sweats. Choose a leader of the foxes.

DESCRIPTION OF ACTIVITY:

1. Rabbits, quietly go out into the Woods to play. Can you hop like a bunny?
2. Leader of the Foxes, at any time, call out "Run, Rabbits, Run!" Rabbits, quickly head for your Burrow on this signal while the Foxes try to pull your tail to capture you. Any Rabbit whose tail has been pulled becomes a member of the Foxes' team.
3. Rabbits, again hop into the Woods to play. Leader of the Foxes, wait patiently, and then give the chase signal.
4. Continue the game in this way until all the Rabbits are caught. Play the game again and have Rabbits and Foxes change roles.

VARIATION: Play the game with fewer Foxes: two thirds of the class are the Rabbits; the remaining one third are the Foxes.

SG-25 BIRD CATCHER

FOCUS: Running and dodging

EQUIPMENT: Two 10-meter (20-foot)-long ropes; two beanbags

ORGANIZATION:

- Form a circle with each rope to mark out two Nests at opposite ends of the play area. (Choose one player to be the Mother Bird, who stands in one nest. A player who is unable to actively participate because of illness or injury could be the Mother Bird.) Select two more players to be the Bird Catchers, who stand between the two Nests, each holding a beanbag. Divide the rest of the players into Flocks of four to five Birds. Have each Flock decide what kinds of birds they will be; for example, Robins, Sparrows, Blackbirds, Blue Jays, Crows, Hummingbirds, and so on. The Flocks stand together, facing the Bird Catchers, in the opposite Nest.

DESCRIPTION OF ACTIVITY:

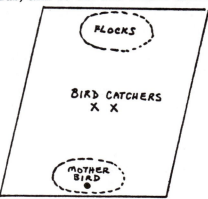

1. The Mother Bird, call the name of a Flock; for example, "Blue Jays, fly!" This is the signal for all the Blue Jays to "fly" across the player area from their nest to the Mother Bird's nest, without getting tagged by the Bird Catchers. Any bird touched with a beanbag becomes a Bird Catcher as well.
2. Continue the game in this way until all the Flocks have been called. Then repeat the game with a new Mother Bird, Bird Catchers, and Bird names.

SG-26 CIRCLE TAG

FOCUS: Agility; alertness

EQUIPMENT: None

ORGANIZATION:

- Have players join hands and form one large circle, except for one player who is IT and stays just outside the circle. Emphasize that circle players must not interfere with the runners.

DESCRIPTION OF ACTIVITY:

1. IT, run around the outside of the circle and tag one of the circle players by a gentle swat on the backside.

2. Tagged player, immediately chase IT around the circle. IT, if you reach the vacant spot without being tagged, you become a circle player and join hands with the players on either side of you. Tagged player, you become the new IT.

3. IT, if you are caught, you must go to the center of the circle and stay there until another player is caught; then you may join the circle. The chaser becomes the new IT, and the game continues.

VARIATION: For a large class, form two or more circles to provide more participation and activity.

SG-27 FLYING DUTCHMEN

FOCUS: Agility; alertness

EQUIPMENT: None

ORGANIZATION:

- Have players pair off and stand in couples, with inside hands joined, in one large circle. Choose one pair to be the Flying Dutchmen. Emphasize that pairs should pass each other on the right. Encourage the Flying Dutchmen to tag a different pair each time.

DESCRIPTION OF ACTIVITY:

1. The Flying Dutchmen, holding hands, run around the outside of the circle in a CCW direction. One partner of the pair, tag the joined hands of a circle pair.

2. The tagged pair, keeping your inside hands joined, run around the outside of the circle in the opposite direction to the Flying Dutchmen pair. Each pair try to get back to the empty place first.

3. The pair who reaches the place first becomes the Flying Dutchmen for the next time.

VARIATIONS:

a. Reverse the travelling directions of the two pairs.

b. Have pairs travel by joining inside hands and slide-stepping around the circle; skipping; or galloping.

SG-28 SQUIRRELS, TREES, AND FOXES

FOCUS: Running; alertness

EQUIPMENT: Flags

ORGANIZATION:

- Number off the class in four's. The one's and two's will be Trees; the three's, Squirrels; and the four's, Foxes (who wear the flags in their waistbands). The one's and two's pair off and scatter around the play area, forming trees by standing face-to-face with hands resting on the tops of each other's shoulders. Emphasize that Foxes are not allowed to guard Trees. Insist that the Trees accept the Squirrel that comes along. Caution players to watch where they are going to avoid collisions.

DESCRIPTION OF ACTIVITY:

1. On the signal "Scamper!" the Squirrels, dart from one tree to another, while the Foxes give chase. Only one Squirrel can stay in a tree at a time for a count of five seconds (one acorn, two acorn, three acorn, four acorn, five acorn).

2. Fox, if you tag a Squirrel with a one-hand touch, exchange roles.

3. After every two minutes, the four groups exchange roles and the game continues. Play until everyone has had a turn at each role.

SG-29 FOX AND GEESE

FOCUS: Cooperation; chasing and dodging

EQUIPMENT: Four cone markers

ORGANIZATION:

- Use cones to mark out a large rectangular play area.
- Divide the class into groups of three to four players per group, except for one player, who is the Fox. The players of each group are the Geese, who form a single file and hold onto each other's waists. Explain that a group of geese is called a "gaggle," and teach them how to spell the word. Have each Gaggle scatter about the play area. Emphasize that the Geese must stay together in their Gaggle and keep their waist-hold throughout the game. Insist that the groups stay within the boundaries of the play area. Remind groups to watch out for other groups to avoid any collisions.

DESCRIPTION OF ACTIVITY:

1. Fox, try to tag onto the last player of a group. The other players in the Gaggle, try to protect the Goose by swinging your file around to block the Fox's path.

2. If the Fox succeeds in holding onto the last Goose, the front Goose becomes the new Fox, and the game continues.

VARIATION:

Have two or more Foxes per game.

SG-30 IKE, MIKE, AND WILBER

FOCUS: Agility; teamwork

EQUIPMENT: Several beanbags; one hoop

ORGANIZATION:

- Arrange players in groups of three, evenly spaced around a large circle. In each group, players sit cross-legged, side-by-side, facing the center of the circle. The player on the right of each group is called Ike; the middle player is called Mike; and the player on the left is called Wilber. Scatter several beanbags (one fewer beanbags than the number of groups) inside a hoop placed in the center of the circle. During the game, insist that players place, not toss, the beanbags back into the hoop each time. Caution runners to pass other runners on the outside.

DESCRIPTION OF ACTIVITY:

1. Listen carefully. I will call out one of the three names; for example, "Ike!" All the Ikes, run CCW around the outside of the circle, go underneath the arch formed by the other two members of your groups, and into the center. Try to get a beanbag, and return to your group with it.
2. Now Ikes, return your beanbags to the hoop, and everyone listen for the next name I will call.
3. Groups, keep track of the beanbags you get. Which group will collect the most beanbags?

VARIATION: Use other objects to be picked up from the center such as deckrings, small balls, large balls, knotted short ropes.

SG-31 THE GREAT PUMPKIN

FOCUS: Halloween game; running and dodging

EQUIPMENT: Several cone markers; one flag per player

ORGANIZATION:

- Using the cones, mark out a large square with 10-meter (30-foot) sides. Choose one player to be the Great Pumpkin and stand in the middle of the square. Divide the remainder of the class into four equal groups: Witches, Bats, Monsters, Ghoulies. Have each group stand in line formation on one of the sides; everyone has a flag tucked into the back of the waistband of his or her shorts, with at least two thirds of the flag visible. Emphasize the importance of players moving into open spaces to avoid any collisions.

DESCRIPTION OF ACTIVITY:

1. I will call out the name of one of the groups; for example, the "Ghoulies." The Ghoulies, then try to run across the square to the opposite side without having your flags pulled by the Great Pumpkin.
2. If your flag is pulled, hand it to me, and join the Great Pumpkin in the middle as his or her helper. Now I will call the name of another group.
3. After I have called all the groups, we will select a new Great Pumpkin and play the game again.

VARIATIONS:

a. Allow each group to choose its own Halloween name.
b. Call two groups over at the same time, either from opposite sides or from adjacent sides.
c. At the end of each game, determine which group had the least number of players captured by the Great Pumpkin.

SG–32 SIMPLE DODGEBALL

FOCUS: Throwing accuracy; dodging

EQUIPMENT: One Nerf™ ball per circle; several cone markers or one 10-meter (30-foot)-long rope

ORGANIZATION:

- Mark out a 6-meter (20-foot)-diameter circle, using cone markers or a long rope. Have five or six players stand inside the circle, and the remaining players space themselves arm's length apart just outside the circle markers. Give one outside player a ball to start the game. Encourage circle players to take turns throwing the ball.
- Emphasize that the ball must be thrown from behind the circle markers; otherwise, a hit player will not have to change places with the thrower.

DESCRIPTION OF ACTIVITY:

1. On the signal "Go!" player with the ball, throw it at the players inside the circle and try to hit a player below the waist.

2. Ball-thrower, if you hit a player, change places with that player. Continue to play the game in this way. Who will stay in the circle the longest?

VARIATION: Make the circle slightly larger, and use two balls.

SG–33 TEAM DODGEBALL

FOCUS: Throwing accuracy; dodging

EQUIPMENT: Two Nerf™ balls per circle; several cone markers or one 10-meter (30-foot)-long rope

ORGANIZATION:

- Mark out a large 6-meter (20-foot)-diameter circle, using cone markers or a long rope. Form two equal teams, and have the players of one team stand inside the circle and the players of the other team space themselves arm's length apart just outside the circle markers. Give two circle players a ball each to start the game. Encourage circle players to take turns throwing the ball.
- Emphasize that the ball must be thrown from behind the circle markers; otherwise, a point will not be awarded for hitting a player below the waist.

DESCRIPTION OF ACTIVITY:

1. On the signal "Go!" players with the ball, throw it at the players inside the circle and try to hit them below the waist.
2. Score one point for every player you hit below the waist.
3. After three minutes, circle players and inside players change places, and play another three-minute game. Which team will have the best score at the end of the game?

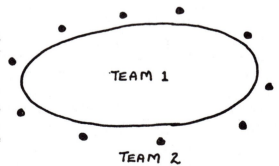

VARIATION:

For a large class, divide the class into four teams and have two games occurring at the same time.

SG–34 FISHNET

FOCUS: Running and dodging; teamwork

EQUIPMENT: Four cone markers; chalkboard and chalk

ORGANIZATION:

- Mark out two parallel lines, 20 meters (60 feet) apart. Divide the class into two equal teams: the Fish team, who stands in a line formation on one line, facing the Net team, who stands with hands joined in a line formation about 6 meters (20 feet) from the other line, as shown. Choose a captain for each team. Emphasize that the Net team keep the hand-hold throughout the game.
- Emphasize that players must play fairly and safely.

DESCRIPTION OF ACTIVITY:

1. Captain of the Net team, call out "Swim!" Fish, this is your signal to try to run toward the opposite line where you will be safe. Meanwhile, the Net team, moving together, try to encircle as many fish as possible by having the end players of your team join hands.
2. Fish, you cannot go under hands or break through, but if the net breaks you can escape.
3. Captain of the Net team, count the number of fish that are caught and record your score on the chalkboard.
4. Again, Captain, call the Fish team to swim across to the opposite line. How many fish will your team catch this time? After three crossings, have teams change roles and play the game again. Which team will catch the most number of fish?

SG–35 SQUID

FOCUS: Throwing; running and dodging

EQUIPMENT: One Nerf™ ball; four cone markers

ORGANIZATION:

- Mark out a rectangular play area. Choose one player to be the Squid and stand in the center of the play area holding the ball. The other players, the Fish, line up behind one of the endlines. Insist that Squid must hit below the waist with the ball. Emphasize that hit Fish must not move their feet from the spot where they were tagged.

DESCRIPTION OF ACTIVITY:

1. When you are ready, Squid, call out "Come, fish, come." Fish, you must then try to run to the opposite endline as the Squid tries to hit you below the waist with the ball.
2. Hit Fish, you must stay on the spot where you were hit and try to tag other Fish as they go by. These tagged Fish then try to tag other Fish until all the Fish are hit by Squid or tagged.

VARIATION: Have two Squid, each with a ball.

FOCUS: Running and dodging

EQUIPMENT: Four cone markers; three beanbags

ORGANIZATION:

- Mark out a large rectangular area with the cones. Select one player to be Darth Vader, who is IT, along with two helpers, who are called Stormtroopers. Have these players each hold a beanbag and stand across the middle of the play area, facing one endline. Divide the rest of the class into three or four groups (depending upon the size of the class) and call the groups: R2D2s, Chewbaccas, C-3POs, and Luke Skywalkers. Have groups stand side-by-side on the endline facing the IT group.
- Designate an area just outside of the play area as the Trash Compactor. (This area is controlled by the Teacher and perhaps a student who is unable to participate actively.)
- Remind Darth Vader and the Stormtroopers that they start in the middle of the play area each time, before calling another group. Emphasize that players must run inside the boundaries of the play area; otherwise, they are automatically caught.

DESCRIPTION OF ACTIVITY:

1. Darth Vader, call one group at a time to run across the play area to the safety of the opposite endline. As they move across, you and your two helpers, the Stormtroopers, try to tag these players by touching them with your beanbags.
2. Those players tagged must go to the "trash compactor," miss one turn, and perform a task such as jumping jacks, push-ups, sit-ups.
3. Darth Vader, after each group has been called to cross the play area, then call each group, in turn, to cross the play area again.
4. Then I will choose a new Darth Vader and two Stormtroopers, and we will play the game again.

VARIATIONS:

a. Use other names for the groups such as Hans Solos, Princess Leias, Wickets.
b. Have players wear flags, tucked into the waistbands at the back of their shorts or sweat pants, which are pulled by Darth Vader and the Stormtroopers to make a capture.

SG-37 INTRODUCING PLAY DAYS

FOCUS: Teaching guidelines; organization   **EQUIPMENT:** None

ORGANIZATION:

• The purpose of a primary Play Day is to provide an opportunity for everyone to participate and enjoy various fun-filled, low-skilled, and fitness-oriented activities. The emphasis is on cooperation, sportsmanship, and team spirit, rather than on winning and individual performance. Therefore, the stations could be scored but the results not recorded. At the closing, a participation certificate or ribbon could be given to every child to acknowledge their efforts.

• The number and types of stations will depend upon the overall objective or theme of the Play Day; the number of children and staff involved; the facilities available (indoor or outdoor); availability of equipment; and the availability of a senior class as officials to run the Play Day.

• A notice concerning the date, time, and location of the Play Day; appropriate dress for the event (T-shirts, shorts, running shoes, sun-hat, sunscreen, and insect repellent); and invitations for parents to watch could be sent home a week in advance.

SG-38 ORGANIZING PLAY DAYS

FOCUS: Official's duties; organization

EQUIPMENT: Equipment list for each station;
description of each event;
posterboard and marking pens;
stopwatch or digital watch;
whistle;
litter cans;
list of senior groups, leaders, and teams;
participation certificates or ribbons;
treats (optional);
music (optional)

ORGANIZATION:

• Grades 1, 2, and 3 should be combined to participate in the Play Day and placed on teams of eight to ten players. The number of stations required for the Play Day is one half of the number of teams.

• The senior class is divided into four groups of leaders: Team Leaders, Station Leaders, Rest Station Leaders, and Clean-Up Gang.

—A ***Team Leader*** is assigned to each team and is responsible for choosing a team name; making name tags for the team players and team name; and looking after the team and getting the players from one station to the next.

—***Station Leaders*** are responsible for setting up the equipment needed for each station; making the appropriate sign; explaining how the activity is performed; and effectively and safely running the station. The rules for each station should be simple and easily scored.

—***Rest Station Leaders*** are responsible for the Rest or Break Station where treats, such as frozen fruit treats or nutritious drinks, are given to the children.

—***Clean-Up Gang*** is responsible for setting up litter cans as needed, picking up any litter on the playground, and putting away the equipment at the completion of the Play Day.

SG–39 SETTING UP A PLAY DAY

FOCUS: Teaching guidelines; organization

EQUIPMENT: Equipment list for each station;
list of senior groups, leaders, and teams;
posterboard and marking pens;
list of events;
diagram of location of events and rotation;
stopwatch or digital watch;
whistle;
litter cans;
participation certificates or ribbons;
treats (optional);
music (optional)

ORGANIZATION:

- The senior class groups should be briefed of their duties. A list of events including rules, procedures, and a diagram should be prepared and distributed to all Station and Team Leaders and Teachers. A list of equipment should be prepared and checked at least three days in advance. The diagram should show the placement of the events and the rotation order. Have the Station group organize each station about two hours beforehand.

- Prior to the start of the Play Day, have all teams assemble to meet their Team Leaders and be taken to their starting stations. The activities at each station should be duplicated, if possible, as two teams will be participating at the same time at each station: Teams 1 and 2 will start at Station 1; teams 3 and 4 at Station 2; teams 5 and 6 at Station 3, and so on. Have the station activity last for about five minutes. Use a whistle signal or music signal to indicate when teams rotate to the next station.

- At the closing of the Play Day, have teams again assemble at the starting area. During this time, Leaders give participation certificates or ribbons to each of their team members, and then dismiss their team. Now the Clean-Up Gang goes quickly into action, under your supervision.

- Following the Play Day, meet with the Senior Class and teachers involved to discuss and evaluate the overall event, the planning and organization, the station activities, and children's reactions. Hopefully suggestions will be made for implementing an even better Play Day the next time!

SG–40 STATION IDEAS 1 AND 2

FOCUS: Equipment manipulation

EQUIPMENT: Cone markers;
two tablespoons and one sugar cube;
large marble or small potato;
two paddles;
one ping-pong ball

ORGANIZATION:

• For *Sugar Cube Relay,* have each team stand in single file formation behind a starting line, facing a turning cone 6 meters (20 feet) away. The first two players of each team hold a spoon. The first player has a sugar cube in his or her spoon.

• For *Paddle Ball Race,* use the same formation as above, but have the first player hold a paddle and a ping-pong ball and the second player hold a paddle.

DESCRIPTION OF ACTIVITY:

Station 1, Sugar Cube Relay: Each player, in turn, carry a sugar cube on a spoon while travelling to the turning cone, around it, and back to your team to hand the cube to the next player in line. If you drop the cube, pick it up and keep going!

Station 2, Paddle Ball Race: Each player, in turn, balance a ping-pong ball on your paddle as you travel to the cone marker and back to hand the ball to the next player in line. If the ball slides off, pick it up, put it on your paddle, and continue running.

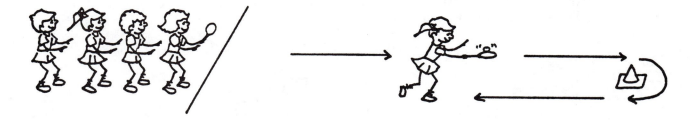

VARIATION:

Potato Spoon Relay: Have each player, in turn, balance a small potato on a spoon while travelling to a cone marker and back.

FOCUS: Equipment manipulation

EQUIPMENT: Four potato sacks;
several cone markers;
two laundry baskets;
eight hoops or deckrings;
eight beanbags

ORGANIZATION:

- For **Potato Sack Relay,** have each team in shuttle formation with each half facing the other half, 10 meters (30 feet) away. The first player stands inside a potato sack, grasping it firmly on the sides.

- For **Junk Relay,** have each team stand in file formation behind a starting line, facing a row of four hoops (or deckrings) spaced 1 meter (3 feet) apart and 2 meters (6 feet) from the line. In each hoop place a beanbag, and on the starting line place a laundry basket.

DESCRIPTION OF ACTIVITY:

Station 3, Potato Sack Relay: The first player inside the sack, hop across to the opposite file, quickly step out of the sack to let the second player step inside, and then join the file. The second player hop in the same way across to the opposite file to give the sack to the third player. Continue in this way.

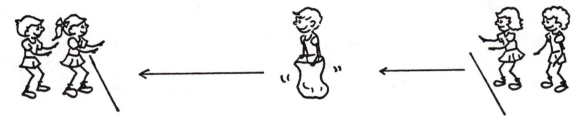

Station 4, Junk Relay: The first player, run to the first hoop, pick up the beanbag, carry it back to your team and drop it in the basket, and then run to the second hoop, pick up the beanbag, and return to drop it in the basket. Continue to the third and fourth hoop to do the same. The second player, grab one beanbag out of the basket and place it in a hoop. Return to the basket to grab a second beanbag and place it in another hoop. Repeat in this way until all the beanbags have been returned to the hoops. The third player, then collect all the beanbags, one at a time. The fourth player, return the beanbags, one at a time, to the hoops, and so on.

VARIATIONS:

a. **Garbage Relay:** Have each team stand in single file formation behind a starting line, facing a pile of "garbage" (two beanbags, two skipping ropes, two sponge balls, two scoops, two banners, two batons, etc.) 6 meters (20 feet) away. The first player must run to the "garbage pile," pick it all up, and carry it back to the starting line to dump it there. The second player then picks it all up, carries it back to its original place, and runs quickly back to tag the next player, who repeats the first player's actions. If at any time a player drops an object, it must be picked up before continuing.

b. In **Junk Relay,** use eight small buckets and eight flags on sticks.

SG–42 STATION IDEAS 5 AND 6

FOCUS: Equipment manipulation

EQUIPMENT: Two large beachballs; one two-meter (six-foot) cageball or inner tube; several cone markers

ORGANIZATION:

- For *Keep-It-Up,* have players of each team form a circle. One player gets the beach ball.
- For *Weave and Roll,* place a line of five cones about two meters (six feet) apart from a starting line. Have players pair off in each team and stand in single file formation behind the starting line, facing the cones. The first pair gets the cageball.

DESCRIPTION OF ACTIVITY:

Station 5, Keep-It-Up: The object of the activity is to keep the beachball in the air. Don't let it touch the ground! How many times in a row can your team hit the ball upward before it touches the ground?

Station 6, Weave and Roll: Each pair, in turn, roll the ball in and out of the cones, around the end cone, and directly back to pass the ball to the next pair, who does the same.

VARIATION:

Shuttle Roll: Arrange each team in pairs in a shuttle formation and have each pair roll an inner tube across to the opposite pair, who does the same.

FOCUS: Throwing and rolling; accuracy

EQUIPMENT: Six ice cream pails;
eighteen clothespins;
several cone markers;
several small utility balls;
several bowling pins or bleach bottles;
several beanbags

ORGANIZATION:

- For *Clothespin Toss,* have players stand behind a throwing line and face an ice cream pail, placed 3 meters (10 feet) away. Give each of the first players three clothespins. For each team, set up three duplicate activities to provide more participation.

- For *Three-Pin Bowling,* place three bowling pins in a triangular formation about 6 meters (20 feet) from a rolling line. Place three small utility balls near the rolling line. For more participation, set up as many of these three-pin bowling activities as you have equipment available.

DESCRIPTION OF ACTIVITY:

Station 7, Clothespin Toss: Each player, in turn, take three tries to toss the clothespins into the ice cream pail. Can you get all three in the pail? Keep track of how many good tosses you make in all.

Station 8, Three-Pin Bowling: Each player, in turn, bowl three balls at the pins, trying to knock them all down. How many pins will you knock down altogether?

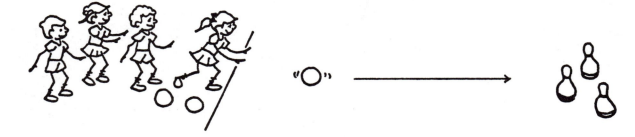

VARIATION:

Three for a Quarter: Have each team leader hold a bucket and stand in a spot about 10 meters (30 feet) from a throwing line. The other players of his or her team stand in a file just behind the throwing line. Have each player, in turn, toss three beanbags toward the bucket-holder, who tries to catch the beanbags in the bucket. After every player has had a throw, change the bucket-holder.

FOCUS: Throwing accuracy;
agility running;
kicking

EQUIPMENT: Several cone markers;
six plastic rings or small hoops;
two to four benches;
eight safety mats;
twenty beanbags and deckrings;
twenty deckrings;
eight bases;
four nets;
eight soccer balls;
eight tennis balls;
eight hockey sticks;
eight batons

ORGANIZATION:

- For *Hoop-La,* place three large cone markers in a triangle formation, equally spaced one meter (three feet) from each other, and three meters (10 feet) from a throwing line. Set up a duplicate activity if equipment is available.
- For *Log Play,* place two benches butted against each other and two long folding mats on either side of the benches.
- For *Base Run,* set up the bases in a diamond pattern. Have each team start at home plate, standing in a file in the infield. The first player holds a baton.
- For *Soccer Kick,* place four nets near a wall spaced two meters (six feet) apart. Mark out a kicking line using cones. Place two soccer balls on the kicking line for each net. Designate each team to kick into any two of the four nets. Have players stand in a file at the kicking line, facing either of the two nets.

DESCRIPTION OF ACTIVITY:

Station 9, Hoop-La: Each player, in turn, toss three plastic rings toward the cone markers. How many cones will you ring?

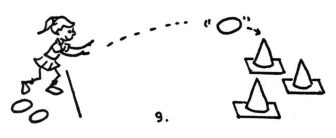

Station 10, Log Play: Each team, arrange yourself on the bench in any order. Can you—without stepping off the bench—reverse your positions so that the last player now becomes the first player?

Station 11, Base Run: Each player, in turn, hold the baton and run as fast as you can around the bases, tagging each cone in order with your foot as you go past. When you reach home plate, hand the baton to the next player, who repeats the activity.

Station 12, Soccer Kick: Each player, in turn, kick a soccer ball into the net, and then retrieve your ball before the next player goes. How many goals will you score?

VARIATIONS:

a. *Horseshoes:* Partners face a deckring that is 5 meters (15 feet) away from them. Each partner, in turn, tosses a beanbag toward the deckring. Which partner will come closest to the ring?

b. *Ring Toss:* Have players in pairs. Each partner holds a baton in one hand and a deckring in his or her throwing hand. Partners face each other about 3 meters (10 feet) away to start. Each partner, in turn, tosses his or her deckring toward the other partner's stick. The receiving partner tries to catch the deckring on his or her stick.

c. *Hockey Shoot:* Set up the same equipment as for "Soccer Kick," except use tennis balls instead of soccer balls and give each team hockey sticks. Each player, in turn, shoots the ball at the net.

SG–45 STATION IDEAS 13 AND 14

FOCUS: Agility; coordination

EQUIPMENT: Chairs; tables; ropes; hoops; benches; cones; box horse; mats; crash pad; high jump standards; poles; various balls; two sets of old clothes; 10 meters (30 feet) of thin rope; several clothespins; two laundry baskets

ORGANIZATION:

- For *Obstacle Course Relay,* have two identical courses set up. Refer to activity FA–16 in Section 2 for guidelines and suggestions. Set up obstacles that players must move under, over, around, through, across, in and out, on and off, or use equipment that they must manipulate.

- For *Obstacle Clothes Relay,* collect two sets of old clothes such as a hat, a pair of boots, baggy overalls, and coat. Place these on a starting line and have each team stand in single file behind the line. Use a rope to mark a turning line 20 meters (60 feet) away.

DESCRIPTION OF ACTIVITY:

Station 13, Obstacle Course Relay: Each player, in turn, move through the obstacle course as safely and quickly as you can, and then join the end of your file. As soon as the player in front of you has reached the halfway point, you may go.

Station 14, Obstacle Clothes Relay: Each player, in turn, quickly put on the old clothes, run to the turning line where you just as quickly remove the clothes, and then carry them back to hand to the next player in your file, who does the same.

VARIATION:

Clothesline Relay: Erect a clothesline at a height that all players can reach. Place four different clothes on it with clothespins and place a laundry basket on the starting line. Have each team stand in file formation behind the starting line, facing the clothesline 10 meters (30 feet) away. The first player runs to the clothesline, quickly removes the clothes, runs back to the starting line and puts them in the basket, and then tags the second player, who takes the clothes out of the basket, runs to the clothesline and hangs them back up; and then runs back to tag the third player, who repeats the first player's actions. The relay continues in this way.

FOCUS: Strength; cooperation

EQUIPMENT: One parachute;
one tug-o-war rope;
three flags;
two long ropes

ORGANIZATION:

- For *Parachute Play,* spread the parachute flat along the ground. Have players spread themselves evenly around the parachute and grab onto the edge with an overhand grip.
- For *Team Tug-o-War,* extend the tug-o-war rope flat along the ground. Use flags knotted around the rope to mark the center and a point 60 centimeters (2 feet) on either side of the center marker. Draw a line directly under the center marker. Have each team stand alongside one half of the rope with players evenly spaced apart. The first player of each team is at his or her marker.

DESCRIPTION OF ACTIVITY:

Station 15, Parachute Play: (Refer to activities GS–84 through GS–89 in Section 6. Choose one of the many activities using a parachute.)

Station 16, Team Tug-o-War: Each team, grip the rope on your side of center. On the signal "Tug!" try to pull the other team's marker over the center to win. All players, stay on your feet throughout the pull. Which team will do better out of three Tug-o-Wars?

VARIATION:

Long Rope Play: Each team gets one long rope. Players should take turns being jumpers and rope turners. Challenge the team to see how many players can jump at the same time in the middle of the rope! (Refer to activities GS–73 through GS–78 in Section 6 for activities using a long rope.)

Closing Activities

After a vigorous physical workout, the Closing Activity serves as a quiet, cool-down activity and leaves children ready to continue with classroom work.

The 30 Closing Activities in Section 8 include:

CA-1 FRIENDSHIP BUILDERS

FOCUS: Self-worth; positive feelings

EQUIPMENT: Quiet background music; tape or record player

ORGANIZATION:

- These promoters of self-esteem show the children that you really do care for them as persons. Used often, they will help to promote a warm and friendly atmosphere in your lessons. Choose one or two of these Friendship Builders to use at the beginning, during, or at the end of the lesson. To teach, have children stand and face you. For homework, have the children teach the Friendship Builders to at least one other person.

DESCRIPTION OF ACTIVITY:

1. *Hug Yourself:* Wrap your arms around yourself and say "I love me!"

2. *Hugging Huddle:* Put your arms around the shoulders of the players on either side of you and chant a favorite cheer such as "Awesome!"

3. *I Love You:* Say "I love you!" in sign language. With thumb and fingers extended, close your third and fourth fingers to your palm.

4. *I Really Love You:* Say "I really love you!" in sign language. With thumb and fingers extended, close your third finger to your palm and cross your first and second fingers.

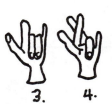

3.   4.

5. *Respectful Greeting:* Stand tall, facing the person or persons to be honored. On the signal "1, 2, 3!" form a fist, slap it into the palm of your other hand, and bow graciously from the waist. (Use to greet your class each morning and during the day.)

5.

CA-2 PLAYER OF THE DAY

FOCUS: Class recognition; self-esteem

EQUIPMENT: None

ORGANIZATION:

- Use this self-esteem activity at the end of every physical education lesson. Have class gather in a listening circle. Recognize a child (children) in your class as the "Player of the Day" and have this person stand facing the class. Tell the class why you think this "Player of the Day" is so special: perhaps for cooperating with others, playing fairly, sharing equipment, being cheerful, helping others, helping you, or trying hard to improve at a skill. When you have finished telling them, have the class give the "Player of the Day" a big "round of applause" by clapping their hands while moving CW or CCW in a large circle. Ensure that each player in the class is given recognition at some time during the school year. You may wish to give a "Player of the Day" certificate to the boy or girl you have recognized.

CA-3 THIS IS MY FRIEND

FOCUS: Getting acquainted; friendship   **EQUIPMENT:** None

ORGANIZATION:

- This activity is a good way of introducing the members of your class to each other. Have the players stand in a big circle and all join hands. Join the circle yourself.

ORGANIZATION:

1. Turn to the person on your right and on your left and tell them your name.

2. I will start off by introducing the person on my right, "This is my friend John." At the same time, I will raise and lower his hand.

3. Then John, you introduce the person on your right.

4. Let's continue in this way, around the circle, until everyone has been introduced.

VARIATIONS:

a. Next time, have each player introduce the player on his or her left.

b. Give older players a couple of minutes at the beginning to ask more questions, and ask them to provide additional information about their new friend as he or she is introduced.

CA-4 THE TRAVELLING GAME

FOCUS: Getting acquainted; friendship   **EQUIPMENT:** One hoop per player

ORGANIZATION:

- This game is excellent for the players to get to know each other's names. Have the players collect a hoop each, and then scatter to sit in the hoop at their home. Suggestions for locomotor movements: walking, hopping, running, sliding, galloping, skipping, crawling, spinning, animal walks, etc.

DESCRIPTION OF ACTIVITY:

1. When I call out the name of a player, that player becomes "The Traveller." For example, when I call "Julie, hop to Jimmy's place!" Julie, you will hop to Jimmy's hoop, shake hands with him, and take his place in his home. Jimmy, you now become the new Traveller.

2. I will then call, "Jimmy, run backwards to Peter's!" This is the signal for you to run to Peter's home, shake hands, and take his place.

3. We will continue like this until everyone has had a turn.

4. On the signal "Goodbye Travellers," each player move to the exit using a locomotor movement of your choice. Carry your hoop with you and place it over my arm as you go by.

CA–5 HEALTHY HABITS

FOCUS: Health concepts; listening skills; fair play

EQUIPMENT: Four cone markers

ORGANIZATION:

- Mark two endlines about 6 meters (20 feet) apart. Have the players stand side-by-side in a line, at one end of the play area, facing you. Explain that the object of the game is for each player to reach the other end of the play area—and to help them do so, you will ask them various questions.

DESCRIPTION OF ACTIVITY:

If you can honestly answer "Yes" to any of the questions that I am going to ask about a healthy lifestyle, you may take one step forward. If you answer "No," stay where you are:

— Did you brush your teeth before coming to school?
— Did you floss your teeth last night before going to bed?
— Do you wash your hands before you eat?
— Do you drink at least a glass of milk a day?
— Did you exercise yesterday?
— Did you eat fruit or vegetables yesterday?
— Did you make your own bed this morning?
— Did you hug your mom or dad today?
— Did you eat no junk food yesterday?
— Did you get at least eight hours' sleep last night?
— Have you done someone a good deed today?
— Have you combed your hair today?
— Did you eat a healthy breakfast this morning?
— Did you walk or bike to school this morning?

FLOSS YOUR TEETH?

CA–6 "OLE MOTHER O'LEARY"

FOCUS: Cool-down; singing; miming

EQUIPMENT: "Hot Time in the Old Town Tonight"; tape or record player

ORGANIZATION:

- This favorite action song is about how Mrs. O'Leary's cow kicked the lantern over in the barn and burned down much of Chicago in 1871. Have the children sit cross-legged inside a circle reasonably close to each other, facing you. Go over the song and the actions two or three times. Have them join in and sing along with you until learned.

DESCRIPTION OF ACTIVITY: Follow me as I sing and do the actions of the song "Ole Mother O'Leary":

"Oh! Oh!, one fine night, when we were all in bed!
(lean head on hands and pretend to go to sleep)
Ole Mother O'Leary left the lantern in the shed!
(hang out a lantern)
The cow kicked it over and winked her eye and said:
(lean back, kick one leg, and wink)
There'll be a hot time in the Old Town Tonight!
(rub both hands together)
Fire!-Fire!-Fire!"
*(stand quickly, raise one fist in the air as you yell
"Fire!" "Fire!" "Fire!" and then quickly sit down.)*

FIRE! FIRE! FIRE!

CA-7 WHAT TIME IS IT, MR. WOLF?

FOCUS: Alertness; running; fair play

EQUIPMENT: Four cone markers

ORGANIZATION:

- Mark out the play area with the cone markers. Choose one player to be "Mr. Wolf" to stand at one end of the play area. Have all other players, the "Sheep," line up along the other endline.

DESCRIPTION OF ACTIVITY:

1. The Sheep, move toward Mr. Wolf, repeatedly calling out, "What's the time, Mr. Wolf?"

2. Mr. Wolf, answer by saying: "2 o'clock, 5 o'clock, 7 o'clock, etc." Then the Sheep must take the same number of steps forward.

3. But if Mr. Wolf answers by saying "Dinner time!" Sheep, you must race to get back home without being caught by Mr. Wolf. Those sheep caught become Mr. Wolf's helpers. The last sheep to be caught becomes the new Mr. Wolf for the next game.

CA-8 POSSUM

FOCUS: Alertness; fair play

EQUIPMENT: Four cone markers

ORGANIZATION:

- Mark out the play area with a starting line and a goal line. Have all players line up along the starting line. Choose one player to be IT, who stands with her or his back to the others, in front of and facing the goal line. All other players line up on the starting line.

DESCRIPTION OF ACTIVITY:

1. IT, start counting "1, 2, 3, 4, 5, . . ." This is the signal for all the other players to move toward the goal line. At any time you may call out "Possum." When you do, the other players must stop immediately and freeze on the spot.

2. IT, if you see anyone moving, that player must return to the starting line and start all over again.

3. The first player to run over the goal line shouting "Possum" becomes the new IT.

CA-9 BUBBLE GUM FUN

FOCUS: Creative expression; cool-down   **EQUIPMENT:** None

ORGANIZATION:

- Have the class sit in their listening circle and listen as you recite the "Bubble Gum" poem. Then recite the poem together. Have them find their homes.

DESCRIPTION OF ACTIVITY:

1. Recite the "Bubble Gum" poem as you walk around the play area. Can you put your own actions to the words as you move?

   Bubble gum, bubble gum, Chew and blow,
   (*Pretend to chew and blow gum.*)
   Bubble gum, bubble gum, touch your toe.
   (*Touch toes of both feet.*)
   Bubble gum, bubble gum, tastes so sweet,
   (*Smile.*)
   Get that bubble gum off my feet!
   (*Pretend that bubble gum is stuck to your feet.*)

2. Repeat several times.
3. Finally, walk to the exit to line up, pretending that bubble gum is stuck to your feet.

CA-10 I'M SO TALL, I'M SO SMALL

FOCUS: Stretching; relaxation; fair play   **EQUIPMENT:** None

ORGANIZATION:

- Have the players form a circle and face inward, standing about an arm's length apart. Choose one player to squat in the center covering her or his eyes. Explain the activity and teach the action poem.

DESCRIPTION OF ACTIVITY:

1. Say after me:

   "I'm so tall, Oh so tall,
   I'm so small, Oh so small,
   Sometimes tall, sometimes small,
   Guess what I am NOW?"

2. This time as we say "tall," stretch up as high as you can! As we say "small," make yourselves as small as you can! When we say "NOW," I will point up for tall or down for small, and I want you all to follow my directions.

3. The center player, try to guess whether the circle players are tall or small. If you guess correctly, you choose someone else to take your place in the center and the game continues.

CA-11 RAGGEDY ANN

FOCUS: Creative play; miming

EQUIPMENT: None

ORGANIZATION:

- Have the players find a free space and stand facing you. Go over the poem and the actions slowly several times. Have them say the poem along with you, providing their own actions to the words.

DESCRIPTION OF ACTIVITY:

Repeat after me, as I say the words of the "Raggedy Ann" poem:

"Raggedy Ann is my best friend,
She's so floppy, just see her bend,
First at the waist, then at the knee,
Her arms are swinging wide and free.
Her head rolls around like a rubber ball,
She hasn't any bones at all.
Raggedy Ann is stuffed with rags,
That's why her body wigs and wags."

VARIATION: If possible, have children bring their Raggedy Ann or Raggedy Andy dolls to the class and show how they can really dance.

CA-12 I'M A LITTLE PIECE OF TIN

FOCUS: Creative play; action singing

EQUIPMENT: None

ORGANIZATION:

- Have the players stand in a free space, facing you. Teach the words of the song and the actions. Go over them several times. Have the players join in and sing along with you. Try to get the players to sing and do the actions faster each time through the song.

DESCRIPTION OF ACTIVITY:

1. Can you do these actions as we drive along singing our song?

"I'm a little piece of tin,	(*driving*)
Nobody knows where I have been,	(*shake a finger*)
Got four wheels and a running-board,	(*show four fingers and run on the spot*)
I'm a Chevy—not a Ford!	(*two foot jumps in the air*)
Honk! Honk!	(*squeeze each hand*)
Rattle! Rattle!	(*shake all over*)
Crash! Crash!	(*slap thighs*)
Beep! Beep!"	(*raise both arms in the air*)

2. Let's do it again, only this time a little faster!

VARIATION: Have the players make up their own actions.

CA-13 ZOO CHATTER

FOCUS: Cooperation; listening skills; fair play   **EQUIPMENT:** None

ORGANIZATION:

- Have the class sit around in a big circle, about an arm's length apart, with eyes closed. Remind players that to play fairly, they must keep their eyes closed.

DESCRIPTION OF ACTIVITY:

1. I am the Zookeeper. I will move around the circle whispering the name of one of four zoo animals in your ear: "Elephant," "Seal," "Lion," or "Monkey." Now remember which animal you are!
2. When you hear the signal "Chatter," stand and move about the play area, making the sound of your animal and keeping your eyes closed. Whenever you hear a sound that is the same as yours, hold on to that animal and together try to find the others.
3. When all the "Elephants" are trumpeting together; all the "Seals" are baying; all the "Lions" are roaring loudly; and all the "Monkeys" are chattering together on all fours, the game is over.

VARIATIONS:

a. For a small class, name only three animals.
b. Call different animals each time the game is played, such as: snakes, frogs, sheep, ducks, cows, chickens, cats, dogs, etc.

CA-14 POT OF GOLD

FOCUS: Observation skills; fair play   **EQUIPMENT:** One penny or other small object

ORGANIZATION:

- Have the players gather in one corner of the play area with eyes closed. Hide the "Pot of Gold" (penny) somewhere in the play area, close to the floor.

DESCRIPTION OF ACTIVITY:

1. Stand up, scatter, and try to find the Pot of Gold. When you find it, quietly come and tell me, whispering its location in my ear. I will be standing in the middle of the play area. Then sit down there. Do not tell the others where the Pot of Gold is located.
2. The first player to find the Pot of Gold will get to hide the object for the next game.

VARIATION: Challenge the children to see if all the girls can find the hidden object before the boys do.

CA–15 TAP HEADS

FOCUS: Relaxation; cool-down; listening   **EQUIPMENT:** None

ORGANIZATION:

- Have the children lie on the floor in the back-lying position, well spaced apart from each other. Lead the line, weaving in and out in a snake-like formation among the lying children. Stress that there must be no talking or touching while the line moves among the lying children. When the last child has been tapped, lead the line through the door into the change-room.

DESCRIPTION OF ACTIVITY:

1. Stretch, making yourself as long as you can. Hold the stretch until I count to ten. Relax.

2. Now slowly breathe in through your nose and out through your mouth. Good—once more!

3. Hook-sit. Rest your head on your arms, which are resting on your knees. Close your eyes. Relax.

4. I am going to walk around, and when I tap you on the head, get up, join the line, and quietly follow me. Remember, do not get up until I tap you on the head.

CA–16 PINK PANTHER

FOCUS: Concentration; self-control   **EQUIPMENT:** Music: "Pink Panther Theme" by Henry Mancini; record or tape player

ORGANIZATION:

- Choose one player to be the Pink Panther. All other players scatter in well-spaced positions around the play area, and lie on their backs with legs straight and hands folded across their chests, pretending to be asleep.

DESCRIPTION OF ACTIVITY:

1. When the music starts, Pink Panther, prowl around the play area, trying to wake the other players by making them laugh. You may speak to them to try to wake them, but do not touch them! Hold your hands behind your back and lean over as you speak to them.

2. Sleeping players, if you move in any way, such as opening your eyes, changing your expression, smiling, or giggling, you must stand up, join the Pink Panther, and try to wake the other players.

3. Sleeping players, who can stay asleep without being awakened by the Pink Panthers until the music ends?

VARIATION:

Have more than one Pink Panther at the start of the game.

CA-17 ELECTRIC SHOCK

FOCUS: Cooperation; concentration   **EQUIPMENT:** None

ORGANIZATION:

• Form a circle with players sitting cross-legged and holding hands. Choose one player to be the "Inspector" to sit in the center of the circle.

DESCRIPTION OF ACTIVITY:

1. Inspector, close your eyes while I select a player to begin passing the Electric Shock around the circle. The shock is passed by squeezing the hand of the player on the right or left.

2. Inspector, try to guess where the Electric Shock is, but remember that the Shock can be reversed at any time. If you guess where the Shock is, that player becomes the new Inspector.

3. Circle players, keep a straight face and try not to let the Inspector know where the Shock is.

VARIATION:

Have the players sit in the circle with feet wide apart and touching, and leaning back on their hands. Have them pass the Shock by tapping their neighbor's foot.

CA-18 GUESS WHO'S LEADING

FOCUS: Cooperation; concentration   **EQUIPMENT:** None

ORGANIZATION:

• Have the players form a circle and stand an arm's length apart. Choose one player to be IT to sit in the middle of the circle with eyes closed.

DESCRIPTION OF ACTIVITY:

1. Circle player, if I point to you, you become the Leader and lead everyone in a quiet exercise. All the players must do exactly as you do.

2. On the signal "Wake up," IT, open your eyes and try to guess who the Leader is.

3. The game continues until IT discovers the Leader, or IT fails to guess who the Leader is after three tries. Then the Leader replaces IT in the center and a new game begins.

CA-19 ALPHABET POPCORN

FOCUS: Listening; spelling concepts

EQUIPMENT: None

ORGANIZATION:

- To start, have the players stand in the listening circle. Move around the play area giving each player a letter of the alphabet. As each player receives the letter, he or she squats down. When everyone has a letter, begin the game. Select words that are meaningful to the players: F-r-i-e-n-d-s, etc.

DESCRIPTION OF ACTIVITY:

1. To see if you are all listening, I am going to call out different letters of the alphabet: C, R, X, O, P, D, E, Y. . . . When I call out your letter, "pop up" and then quickly squat down again.

2. Now that I see you are all listening well, let's try spelling some words:

P-o-p-c-o-r-n	R-u-n	S-c-h-o-o-l
M-o-m	J-u-m-p	B-o-y
D-a-d	S-k-i-p	G-i-r-l
T-o-m	B-e-t-h	H-o-u-s-e

CA-20 STICKY POPCORN

FOCUS: Social interaction; listening; cooperation

EQUIPMENT: Music: "Popcorn"; tape or record player

ORGANIZATION:

- Divide the class into two groups. Half the players are the "Popcorn" and crouch down in the middle of the "Frying Pan," a circle formed by the other half of the class. Choose a leader for the Frying Pan group and have them crouch down also. They show the Popcorn how the heat is turned up under the pan.

DESCRIPTION OF ACTIVITY:

1. Frying Pan, follow your leader and all together gradually rise as the heat is turned up, raise your arms overhead, and shake them hard to show how hot it is.

2. Meanwhile, Popcorn, slowly begin to "pop." Get faster and higher as the pan gets hotter. When the pan is at its hottest, pop up and down rapidly.

3. Now, I am pouring sticky marshmallow sauce all over you, which will make more and more Popcorn pieces stick together, until all pieces are in a big sticky Popcorn ball.

4. Change groups and repeat.

VARIATION:

Have the Frying Pan group raise and lower themselves and have the Popcorn group pop accordingly.

CA-21 STORYTELLER

FOCUS: Creative thinking; dramatization   **EQUIPMENT:** None

ORGANIZATION:

- Have the players sit cross-legged in a circle facing the center. Choose one player to be the "Storyteller," who stands at the edge of the circle. Help the storyteller only if necessary. Have the players put up their hands to make a guess.

DESCRIPTION OF ACTIVITY:

1. Storyteller, start your story by saying: "While I was walking down the street, I spied with my little eye . . ." Instead of telling what you say, go to the center of the circle and mime it out by using gestures. You are allowed to make the sounds of what you saw.

2. *Suggestions:* a speeding car; a running dog; a fire engine; an airplane; a lady pushing a baby carriage; a mailman delivering the mail; a boy on a skateboard.

3. Circle players, try to guess what the Storyteller saw. If you guess correctly, then you become the new Storyteller and the game starts again.

VARIATION: Have the Storyteller tell the story in whatever way he or she chooses, such as: "As I was walking . . . through the park; . . . along the beach; . . . through the zoo; . . . through the store."

CA-22 STEAM TRAIN

FOCUS: Cooperation; imaginative play   **EQUIPMENT:** None

ORGANIZATION:

- Have the players get into groups of four or five. Have them choose one player to be the Leader and stand in front. All others get in single file formation, holding on to the waist of the person in front with the left hand and holding on to the right elbow with the right hand.

DESCRIPTION OF ACTIVITY:

CHUG-CHUG-CHUG! ...

1. Leader, you are the "engine" of the train. On the signal "All aboard," Leader, start your train moving around the play area. As you move, can your train make sounds like an old choo-choo train? Show me how you can move your right arms together in a circular motion, like the piston-rod. Can you lean to one side as the train moves around corners? Can your train back up and go into reverse?

2. Now let your train slow up and "puff" as you struggle up the hills. Then speed up as you race down the mountain track. Oh-oh, duck down as you go through a tunnel! On signal "Station," each train jog on the spot making "chug-chug" sounds.

3. On the signal "Change," Leader, go to the back of the line, and the next in line becomes the new engine of the train.

VARIATION:

Have all the smaller trains hook up into two big trains. The trains return to the classroom in this way.

CA-23 WRAP UP

FOCUS: Following the leader; cooperation

EQUIPMENT: Walking music; tape or record player

ORGANIZATION:

- Have all the players join hands. Lead the activity yourself, explaining the necessity for everyone to keep their hands joined throughout this activity.

DESCRIPTION OF ACTIVITY:

1. The Leader, lead the class around the play area in a large circle, then in a "snake-like" pattern, then back into a large circle again.

2. From the circle, lead the line in ever-diminishing circles, spiraling in toward the center, until the line is coiled around you. Reverse the direction, moving back out again through the encircling line.

3. Each player in the line, gently pull the player behind you until the circle is unwrapped.

4. Leader, lead the line to the exit.

CA-24 BRIDGES

FOCUS: Working with a partner

EQUIPMENT: Lively music; tape or record player

ORGANIZATION:

- Have the players find a partner, hold hands, and scatter over the play area. Choose four pairs to be the "Bridges," who stand facing each other, holding hands and raising arms. Spread the Bridges throughout the play area. Play until each pair has been a Bridge.

DESCRIPTION OF ACTIVITY:

1. When the music starts or on the signal "Go," hold hands and walk around the play area going under all the Bridges, while keeping in time with the music.

2. Now, let's try going under the Bridges while skipping around the play area. Can you jog and go under?

3. When you hear the music stop, change partners. We will choose new Bridges and start again.

VARIATIONS:

a. Have the Bridges kneel, and have the pairs crawl through or slide through on their tummies while still holding hands.

b. Start with more Bridges.

CA-25 STORKS IN THE CIRCLE

FOCUS: Balancing; alertness   **EQUIPMENT:** None

ORGANIZATION:

- Have the players form a circle, join hands, and face the center. Choose three players to be the "Storks" and go to the center of the circle.

DESCRIPTION OF ACTIVITY:

1. On the signal "Go," the Storks in the center, stand on one leg, while the circle players walk around the circle singing:

   "Storks in the circle,
   One, two, three,
   Storks in the circle,
   You won't get Me!

2. On the word "Me!" the circle players, stop, drop your hands, and try to hold a Stork stand on one leg.

3. The center Storks, each choose a circle player who falls over to take your places in the center.

VARIATION: Have the circle players run, slide-step, or hop around the circle.

CA-26 CAT AND MICE

FOCUS: Alertness   **EQUIPMENT:** One hoop per player; one stool

ORGANIZATION:

- Choose one player to be the "Cat" to sit on the stool. Have each of the other players, the "Mice," collect a hoop, take it to their homes, and sit in their "Mouseholes" (hoops). To start, have the Cat turn his or her back on the Mice. Encourage the Mice to be daring and to get as close as possible to the stool. Caution Mice, who are being chased, to avoid colliding with Mice who are sitting in their holes.

DESCRIPTION OF ACTIVITY:

1. I will point to four Mice. When I point to you, sneak up to the Cat to scratch on his or her stool.

2. The Cat, when you hear scratching on your stool, chase the Mice, who try to get back to their Mouseholes without being caught.

3. The first Mouse caught becomes the new Cat for the next game and swaps places with the old Cat.

4. If no Mice are caught, the Cat, you keep going until you can catch one.

VARIATION: Call Mice wearing a certain color, or wearing white sneakers, or wearing stripes, and so on to sneak up to the Cat.

CA-27 WHO'S GOT THE BEANBAG?

FOCUS: Concentration; fair play   **EQUIPMENT:** One beanbag

ORGANIZATION:

- Choose one player to be IT. All other players stand in a circle shoulder to shoulder, with their hands behind their backs. IT stands in the middle with his or her eyes closed. Encourage circle players to keep the beanbag moving even while IT is watching. Remind them to look innocent and to try not to smile.

DESCRIPTION OF ACTIVITY:

1. Circle players, hold your hands out behind your backs. I will walk around the outside of the circle and place the beanbag in someone's hand. You can then pass the beanbag from one to the other around the circle, even when I give the word for IT to open his or her eyes.

2. IT, try to guess who is holding the beanbag. If you guess correctly, change places with that player. If you miss your guess two times in a row, I will choose another IT.

3. Circle players, you may pretend to pass the beanbag to confuse IT.

4. The game continues in this way.

VARIATION:

For a large number, divide the class into two circles.

CA-28 WHO'S BEHIND?

FOCUS: Social interaction; fair play   **EQUIPMENT:** None

ORGANIZATION:

- Have the players choose a partner and stand one behind the other, facing you and forming a front and a back row. Encourage players to play fairly.

DESCRIPTION OF ACTIVITY:

1. On the signal "Change!" the players in the back row, change places with each other until you are all standing behind a new partner.

2. The front players, without turning your head around, see if you can guess "who's behind" you, by bending forward and looking between your legs to see that player's feet.

3. If you guess correctly the player behind you, then you and that player exchange places. The game continues in this way.

CA-29 BALANCE FEATHERS

FOCUS: Coordination and balance

EQUIPMENT: One balancing feather per child; relaxing background music; tape or record player

ORGANIZATION:

- A "balance feather" is a peacock feather that can be purchased from physical education equipment suppliers. Have each player get a balance feather and take it to a free space. Emphasize the importance of handling the feathers with gentleness, as they are quite fragile. Ensure that players are well spaced to avoid any interference with other players. Emphasize that players need to concentrate on the feather, never letting their eyes leave it.

DESCRIPTION OF ACTIVITY:

1. Can you balance your feather in the palm of your right hand; in the palm of your left hand? Now show me how you can balance it on the back of each hand in turn.
2. Who can balance the feather on your index finger of the right hand; your left hand? Try balancing it on each of the other fingers.
3. Balance your feather on other body parts: elbow; shoulder; wrist; knee; forehead; nose; foot. On how many different body parts can you balance your feather?
4. Now try to balance your feather while slowly moving; while bending and straightening your knees; while moving around in a circle; while touching the floor or a wall or another body part.
5. Invent other balancing challenges. We will all try to perform your challenge.

VARIATIONS:

a. *Feather Challenge:* Set up a contest to see who can balance their feather the longest. Time the event, and provide opportunity for the record to be broken.
b. Wands (which are one meter [three feet] in length and six millimeters [¼ inch] dowelling) can be substituted for balance feathers.

CA-30 BEACHBALL BALANCE

FOCUS: Balance; cooperation

EQUIPMENT: One beachball or large utility ball per pair

ORGANIZATION:

- Have players find partners who are approximately the same size. Have one of the partners collect a beachball, and then find a free space. Check for good spacing.

DESCRIPTION OF ACTIVITY:

1. How many different ways can you balance the ball between you and your partner without using your hands?
2. Now, place the ball between you and try these balances: side to side; back to back; tummy to tummy; seat to seat; shoulder to shoulder; knee to knee; head to head; etc.
   — Can you do all those balances again as you move about the play area?
3. Show me how you and your partner can pick the ball up from the floor without the use of your hands and using your: elbows only; knees only; heads only; feet only; etc. Explore other ways of balancing a beachball with your partner.